Absolute Beginner's Guide to

iPod and iTunes

Third Edition

Brad Miser

800 East 96th Street,
Indianapolis, Indiana 46240

Absolute Beginner's Guide to iPod and iTunes, Third Edition

International Standard Book Number: 0-7897-3627-6

Library of Congress Catalog Card Number: 2005929931

Printed in the United States of America

Second Printing: December 2006

09 08 07 06 4 3 2 1

Trademarks

All terms mentioned in this book that are known to be trademarks or service marks have been appropriately capitalized. Que Publishing cannot attest to the accuracy of this information. Use of a term in this book should not be regarded as affecting the validity of any trademark or service mark.

Warning and Disclaimer

Every effort has been made to make this book as complete and as accurate as possible, but no warranty or fitness is implied. The information provided is on an "as is" basis. The author and the publisher shall have neither liability nor responsibility to any person or entity with respect to any loss or damages arising from the information contained in this book.

Bulk Sales

Que Publishing offers excellent discounts on this book when ordered in quantity for bulk purchases or special sales. For more information, please contact

U.S. Corporate and Government Sales
1-800-382-3419
corpsales@pearsontechgroup.com

For sales outside the United States, please contact

International Sales
1-317-428-3341
international@pearsoned.com

Safari BOOKS ONLINE ENABLED

This Book Is Safari Enabled

The Safari® Enabled icon on the cover of your favorite technology book means the book is available through Safari Bookshelf. When you buy this book, you get free access to the online edition for 45 days. Safari Bookshelf is an electronic reference library that lets you easily search thousands of technical books, find code samples, download chapters, and access technical information whenever and wherever you need it.

To gain 45-day Safari Enabled access to this book

- Go to http://www.quepublishing.com/safarienabled
- Complete the brief registration form
- Enter the coupon code FBAB-QRCC-21TY-R3BR-8GE5. If you have difficulty registering on Safari Bookshelf or accessing the online edition, please email customer-service@safaribooksonline.com.

Associate Publisher
Greg Wiegand

Acquisitions Editor
Stephanie J. McComb

Development Editor
Kevin Howard

Managing Editor
Gina Kanouse

Project Editor
George E. Nedeff

Copy Editor
Margo Catts

Indexer
Cheryl Lenser

Proofreader
Karen A. Gill

Technical Editor
Brian Hubbard

User Reviewer
Rick Ehrhardt

Publishing Coordinator
Cindy Teeters

Book Designer
Anne Jones

Page Layout
Nonie Ratcliff

Contents at a Glance

Table of Contents

About the Author

Brad Miser has written more than 25 books about computers and related technology, with his favorite topics being anything that starts with a lowercase *i*, such as the iPod and iTunes. In addition to *Absolute Beginner's Guide to iPod and iTunes, Third Edition*, Brad has written *Mac User's Guide to Living Wirelessly*; *Pimping Your Mac Mini*; *Special Edition Using Mac OS X, Tiger*; *Special Edition Using Mac OS X, v10.3 Panther*; *Absolute Beginner's Guide to Homeschooling*; *Mac OS X and iLife: Using iTunes, iPhoto, iMovie, and iDVD*; *iDVD 3 Fast & Easy*; *Special Edition Using Mac OS X v10.2*; and *Using Mac OS 8.5*. He has also been an author, a development editor, or a technical editor on more than 50 other titles. He has written numerous articles in *MacAddict* magazine and has been a featured speaker on various topics at Macworld Expo, at user group meetings, and in other venues.

Brad is a solutions consultant, meaning that he helps customers understand how to benefit from the software that the company he works for produces. Previously, he was the director of product and customer services for a software development company and the manager of education and support services for a different software company. He was also the lead proposal specialist for an aircraft engine manufacturer, a development editor for a computer book publisher, and a civilian aviation test officer/engineer for the U.S. Army. Brad holds a Bachelor of Science degree in mechanical engineering from California Polytechnic State University at San Luis Obispo and has received advanced education in maintainability engineering, business, and other topics.

In addition to his passion for technology, Brad likes to ride his motorcycle whenever and wherever possible.

A native of California, Brad now lives in Brownsburg, Indiana, with his wife, Amy; their three daughters, Jill, Emily, and Grace; and a rabbit named Bun-Bun.

Brad would love to hear about your experiences with this book (the good, the bad, and the ugly). Please visit his website at web.mac.com/bradmacosx/ to send an email to him.

Dedication

I leave you, hoping that the lamp of liberty will burn in your bosoms until there shall no longer be a doubt that all men are created free and equal.

—Abraham Lincoln

Acknowledgments

To the following people on the *ABG iPod and iTunes* project team, my sincere appreciation for your hard work on this book:

Stephanie McComb, my acquisitions editor, who made this project possible and convinced the right people that this was a good idea and that I was the right one to write it. **Marta Justak** of Justak Literary Services, my agent, for getting me signed up for this project and providing advice and encouragement along the way. **Kevin Howard**, my development editor, who helped make the contents and organization of this book much better. **Rick Ehrhardt**, my user reviewer, who made the jump to an iPod and iTunes at just the right time and provided lots of invaluable feedback that made this book much better.

Brian Hubbard, my technical editor, who did a great job ensuring that the information in this book is both accurate and useful. **Margo,** my copy editor, who corrected my many misspellings, poor grammar, and other problems. **George Nedeff**, my project editor, who skillfully managed the hundreds of files that it took to make this book into something real. **Que's production and sales team**, for printing the book and getting it into your hands.

And now for some people who weren't on the project team but who were essential to me personally. **Amy Miser**, my wonderful wife, for supporting me while I wrote this book; living with an author under tight deadlines isn't always lots of fun, but Amy does so with grace, understanding, and acceptance of my need to write. **Jill**, **Emily**, and **Grace Miser**, my delightful daughters, for helping me stay focused on what is important in life. Although an iPod can play beautiful music, these precious people are beautiful music given form! (And, a special mention to **Bun-Bun** the rabbit for his early-morning visits to cheer me up while I was working!)

We Want to Hear from You!

As the reader of this book, *you* are our most important critic and commentator. We value your opinion and want to know what we're doing right, what we could do better, what areas you'd like to see us publish in, and any other words of wisdom you're willing to pass our way.

As an associate publisher for Que Publishing, I welcome your comments. You can email or write me directly to let me know what you did or didn't like about this book—as well as what we can do to make our books better.

Please note that I cannot help you with technical problems related to the topic of this book. We do have a User Services group, however, where I will forward specific technical questions related to the book.

When you write, please be sure to include this book's title and author as well as your name, email address, and phone number. I will carefully review your comments and share them with the author and editors who worked on the book.

Email: feedback@quepublishing.com

Mail: Greg Wiegand
Associate Publisher
Que Publishing
800 East 96th Street
Indianapolis, IN 46240 USA

For more information about this book or another Que Publishing title, visit our website at www.quepublishing.com. Type the ISBN (excluding hyphens) or the title of a book in the Search field to find the page you're looking for.

INTRODUCTION

If you've seen lots of people with white wires dangling from their ears and wondered if you were missing out on something.... If you have been toying with the idea of getting into digital music.... If you have an iPod and aren't sure what to do with it.... If you wish you could stop messing around with a bunch of CDs when you want to listen to music.... If you've heard about podcasts but don't know what they are or why you should care.... If you think the idea of taking TV shows and movies with you wherever you go is a good one.... If you've heard and seen the iPod hype but wonder if all the fuss is for a good reason.... If you've heard great things about iPods, have seen the commercials for the iTunes Store, and want to know what all the excitement is all about, then welcome to the *Absolute Beginner's Guide to iPod and iTunes*!

Meet the Digital Triumvirate

In this book, you'll learn about three of the most amazing things to happen to music, photos, audiobooks, radio, and video since the first time someone decided that banging a stick on a rock had an appealing sound and that scratching a drawing of the day's hunt on the cave wall was a good idea. These three amazing things are the iPod, iTunes, and the iTunes Store.

The iPod Rocks

Apple's iPod has taken the portable digital device market by storm—and for good reason. Because most of the iPods include a hard drive with up to 80GB of space, you can take your music collection wherever you go. The iPod's tools enable you to organize, customize, and listen to your music in many ways while you are on the move—in your car, at home, or working at your computer. But wait, there's more....

In addition to music, iPods enable you to listen to audiobooks and podcasts. Some models even let you watch all kinds of video from music videos to TV shows to movies.

With its tight integration with iTunes and the iTunes Store, managing your digital content is both fun and easy. Your trusty iPod can also be used as a portable drive (for example, you can use it to carry files from your home to your office), to capture sound, and to store pictures; there are numerous peripheral devices that expand its amazing capabilities even further. And, iPods are just plain cool (see Figure I.1).

FIGURE I.1
Whatever iPod model you choose will rock your world.

If you have never used an iPod before, this book is perfect for you and will help you learn everything you need to know. If you have some experience with an iPod, this book will help you take your iPod skills to the next level. (If you are already an iPod expert, well, you aren't likely to be picking up a book called *Absolute Beginner's Guide to iPod and iTunes,* now, are you?)

iTunes Jams

With iTunes, you can create, organize, listen to, and watch your entire digital Library from your computer (see Figure I.2). iTunes enables you to build as large a Library as you have space on your computer's hard drive to store it. Then you can customize music, audiobook, podcast, and video playback through playlists and smart playlists, as well as create custom CDs and DVDs in a variety of formats. It also provides other useful features, such as custom labeling and information tools, the capability to share your audio and video on a local network, and more. Because Apple's iTunes Store is tightly integrated into iTunes, you can easily purchase and add audio and video to your Library from within the application. Moreover, iTunes is by far the best software tool available to manage music and other content on your iPod.

Just as with the iPod, if you have never used iTunes before, this book is perfect for you and will help you learn everything you need to know. If you have some experience, my hope is that you will learn how to get even more out of this outstanding program. Even if you have used iTunes quite a bit, you might manage to find some tidbits that will help your iTunes expertise grow.

FIGURE I.2
iTunes will change the way you listen to audio and watch video.

iTunes Store

Using the iTunes Store, you can find, preview, and purchase music from a collection of hundreds of thousands of songs and download that music into your iTunes Library. Songs can be purchased individually or in albums, for $.99 per song (less when purchasing an entire album). Music you buy can be listened to, placed on a CD, and moved onto your iPod. Since its inception, the iTunes Store has rapidly become the most popular source of legal digital music on the Internet. After you have used it a time or two, you'll understand why.

The iTunes Store has a lot more than just music on its digital shelves. You'll also find thousands of podcasts to which you can subscribe and then download. (Most of them are free.) You'll find many audiobooks that you can buy. And, you can access the Store's large and rapidly growing collection of video content, such as movies and TV shows. Even with this variety of content, you use the same set of tools to find and get the content you want when you want it.

Quick Guide to *Absolute Beginner's Guide to iPod and iTunes*

Absolute Beginner's Guide to iPod and iTunes provides all the information you need to get the most out of these amazing digital content tools. From the basics of listening to audio CDs with iTunes to the advanced customizing of music on an iPod and purchasing video online, this book equips you with the information you need.

The book is organized into the following three major parts, each focusing on one of the three components of the iPod/iTunes/iTunes Store triumvirate:

- Part I, "The iPod"
- Part II, "iTunes"
- Part III, "The iTunes Store"

Within each part, the chapters generally start with the basics of the topic and get more advanced as you continue. Within the chapters, the information is presented in roughly the order in which you will typically perform the tasks being described.

Speaking of tasks, this book contains many step-by-step instructions—I hope your motto will be "learn by doing." You should be able to learn how to do a task fairly quickly and relatively painlessly by following the steps while using your own content and your own tools. Although my writing is so utterly fascinating that you will likely want to read this book like a good novel, try to resist that urge because you will probably get better results if you actually work with the tools while you read this book.

Of course, you can read this book from start to finish in the order in which the chapters are presented. This will work fine if you have some experience with iTunes and have some music in your iTunes Library. However, because these tools are so well integrated, you can't really use the iPod or the iTunes Store effectively without knowing the basics of using iTunes first.

If you are totally new to these topics, I recommend that you get a jumpstart on iTunes by reading the core iTunes chapters first, which include Chapters 14–19. Then, you should read the core iPod chapters, which are Chapters 1–6. From there, read Chapters 25–28 to get the scoop on working with the iTunes Store.

After you have finished these core "courses," read the rest of the chapters as they interest you. For example, when you are ready to burn your own CDs or DVDs, check out Chapter 22, "Burning Your Own CDs or DVDs." Or, when you want to learn how you can use an iPod for digital photos, read Chapter 9, "Using an iPod to Store and View Photos," to learn how to view photos and slideshows.

Going Both Ways

Because the iPod, iTunes, and the iTunes Store all work equally well on both Windows and Macintosh computers, this book covers these topics from both perspectives. So you'll notice that some of the figures are screenshots taken on a Windows computer, whereas others are taken on a Macintosh. Although the screens on these two computers look slightly different, they work very similarly, so seeing a screen on the Mac shouldn't cause a problem for you if you use a Windows computer, and vice versa. When there are significant differences between the two platforms, I explain them in the text.

Special Elements

As you read, you will see three special elements: notes, tips, and (only rarely) cautions. Also, each chapter ends with a section titled "The Absolute Minimum." Explanations of each of these are provided for you here.

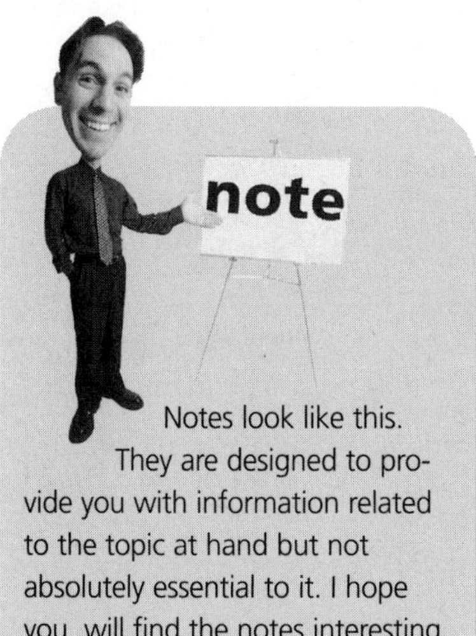

Notes look like this. They are designed to provide you with information related to the topic at hand but not absolutely essential to it. I hope you will find the notes interesting, even if you don't find them useful immediately.

tip

Tips help you get something done more quickly and easily, or they tell you how to do a task related to what's being described at the moment. You might also find an explanation of an alternative way to get something done.

caution

If something you can do (and probably shouldn't) might end in a bad result, I warn you in a caution. Fortunately, you won't find many of these throughout the book, but when you do see one, you might want to take a close look at it.

THE ABSOLUTE MINIMUM

Finally, each chapter ends with "The Absolute Minimum" section. The contents of this section vary a bit from chapter to chapter. Examples of this content include the following:

- A summary of the key points of the chapter
- Additional tips related to the chapter's topic
- References to sources of additional information

So, now that you know all you need to about this book, it's time to strike up the band....

PART i

The iPod

IN THIS CHAPTER

- Understand why the iPod is more hip than hype.
- Get an overview of what makes an iPod an iPod.
- Meet the iPods.
- You've got an iPod...now what?

1

TOURING THE iPOD

Apple's iPod has become one of the most popular personal digital devices ever created; maybe even the most popular digital device ever. When initially released, the iPod's critics said it was too expensive when compared to other digital music players and that people would never spend the additional money to get the iPod's much superior functionality and style. (Even the critics couldn't deny the iPod's amazing attributes.) As they often are, the critics were very much mistaken. People who love music love the iPod. People who love podcasts also love the iPod. People who love to have their photos with them wherever they go dig it, too. And those folks who like to enjoy their favorite TV shows or movies while on the move think iPods are the greatest. Because of the iPods' combination of features and style, and because they are simply very, very cool, iPods quickly dominated sales of portable digital video content players and have an overwhelming share of the market. In fact, iPods are so popular that they have become part of the culture too, with terms like *pod* and *podcast* being part of the everyday lingo many people use. And with continuous improvements in features and a variety of models from which to choose, the iPod won't be slowing down any time soon.

The Apple iPod: A Lot of Hype or Really Hip?

So, what's the iPod all about?

It's about being able to take your entire music collection with you and listen to anything you want when you want to listen to it. And, using iPod's companion iTunes software, you can create and carry customized collections of your music to make getting to the specific music you want to hear even easier and more fun.

The way your music sounds on an iPod is just amazing, too. You definitely don't have to compromise music quality for portability. With the iPod, you get the best of both. If you have never heard music on an iPod before, prepare to be amazed.

You can also take podcasts with you when you want to hear their radio-like or watch their TV-like content.

Want to listen to audiobooks? No problem. Store them on your iPod and listen anytime, anywhere.

You can store your photos on an iPod and view them on its screen or connect it to a TV to view them there.

If an iPod is video capable, you can store and watch TV shows, movies, and other video on it, too.

Finally, if you want to pass some time playing games, you can do that on an iPod too.

That's the bottom line, but it isn't the whole story. With the iPod, you can do much more, as you will learn through the rest of this part of this book. And because of the iPod's stylish design and ease of use, you will likely want to take it with you wherever you go.

So What Is an iPod, Anyway?

The iPod is a small digital device that includes memory (most models include a hard drive just like the one in a computer, only smaller), an operating system, a processor and other computer components, as well as an LCD screen (all models except the iPod shuffle), controls, and other system elements needed to deliver its amazing functionality. It also includes a rechargeable lithium battery to give you plenty of listening and viewing time, a Headphones port to which you attach audio devices (including earbuds, headphones, powered speakers, and so on), and a Dock connector to enable you to move music and video from a computer onto the iPod and recharge its battery.

The iPod's software enables you to manage and play digital audio files. Some models also can play video. You can also use the iPod's software to set a variety of preferences, as well as to use the iPod's other built-in tools.

Even with all this, iPods are quite small. The largest iPod is only 2.4 inches wide, is 4.1 inches tall, is .55 inches thick, and weighs a mere 5.5 ounces. This is roughly the size of a deck of playing cards. The smallest model, the iPod shuffle, comes in at a svelte 1.07 inches wide, 1.62 inches tall, 0.41 inches thick, and a mere 0.55 ounces, which is about the size of a book of matches.

All iPod Models Aren't Equal, but They Are All Cool

iPods come in three basic models: iPod, iPod nano, and iPod shuffle. All these models are definitely cool, and all perform similar functions, which are to enable you to listen to music and other audio whenever and wherever; the iPod also enables you to watch video. Each iPod model offers specific features and options, as you will see in the following sections.

Before we get into the details of each model, let me warn you that just like the times, the iPod is a changin'. The models listed and described in this chapter are the ones available at press time. Apple regularly makes changes to existing models and introduces new models. The good news is that even if you use a model that isn't specifically described in this chapter, the information in this book will still help you because in many ways, to know one iPod is to know them all. The controls and options might vary a bit, but most functionality is quite similar, regardless of model.

note

To get the scoop on the iPod models available right now, go to www.apple.com/ipod/ipod.html.

The iPod (AKA iPod Video)

You could call the iPod Video the "standard" iPod, although that word seems to imply that it is less than it really is (see Figure 1.1). The iPod offers the most features of all the models in a cool package that you will be proud to carry with you anywhere you go. In addition to your music, you can use an iPod to store your digital images and then display them on its screen or on a TV through its AV port. Even better, you can store and watch video on it, including TV shows, movies, music videos, and video you create. Because it's designed to hold more data, this model offers the largest hard drives.

FIGURE 1.1
The iPod will definitely rock your world.

At press time, the iPod's specifications were the following:

- A 30GB hard drive rated for 7,500 songs, or a 80GB drive rated for 20,000 songs. (Although its drive is rated in songs, you can also store a heap of photos and video on it, too.)
- A black or white finish. (I like the black myself, but they are both very nice.) There's currently an iPod U2 special edition that has the black finish with a red Click Wheel.
- A battery rated for up to 14 hours of music playing time, up to 4 hours of slideshows with music, and up to 3.5 hours of video on the 30GB model. The same ratings for the 80GB model are 20 hours, 6 hours, and 6.5 hours, respectively.
- A 2.5-inch color LCD screen with LED backlight.
- Dock connector and Headphone/Composite AV jack.
- Dimensions of 4.1 inches by 2.4 inches by 0.43 inches and a weight of 4.8 ounces for the 30GB model, or 4.1 inches by 2.4 inches by 0.55 inches and a weight of 5.5 ounces for the 80GB model.

With the optional iPod Camera Connector, you can connect a digital camera to your iPod and download images from the camera to the iPod.

- Accessories including earbud headphones, a USB cable, Dock adapter, and case.
- A price of $249 for the 30GB model, $279 for the U2 Special Edition, or $349 for the 80GB model.

The iPod nano

The iPod nano is smaller than an iPod (which you might be able to guess from its name). It has a smaller hard drive than the iPod and can't play video. But it packs an amazing feature set into such a small and really cool package (see Figure 1.2).

FIGURE 1.2
With an iPod nano, a world of music comes in a package thinner than a pencil.

At press time, the iPod nano offered the following:

- A 2GB hard drive rated for 500 songs, a 4GB drive rated for 1,000 songs, or an 8GB drive rated for 2,000 songs
- A variety of colors including silver, green, blue, pink, black, and red
- A battery rated for up to 24 hours of music playing time or up to 5 hours of slideshows with music
- A 1.5-inch color LCD screen with LED backlight
- Dock connector and Headphone jack
- Dimensions of 3.5 inches by 1.6 inches by 0.26 inches and a weight of 1.4 ounces

- Accessories including earbud headphones, USB cable, and Dock adapter
- Prices of $149 for the 2GB model, $199 for the 4GB model, or $249 for the 8GB model; via the online store only, a special edition 4GB red model for $199

The iPod shuffle

Of all the iPod models and variants, the iPod shuffle is the "most" in many ways (see Figure 1.3). It is the most different from the technical point of view because it does not have a hard drive but instead uses a flash drive to store your music. The benefit to this is that it has no moving parts and will never skip, along with being even more resistant to damage. This also means it uses much less power and so can play for the same amount of time with a smaller battery. The downside is that it can store much less music than any of the other models. The shuffle is the smallest model and is much less than half the size of even the iPod nano. The flipside to this is that the shuffle has no screen, so you can't see information about the music you are playing or select what you want to hear. The shuffle also uses the most different interface with your computer in that you always use its Dock to connect it to your computer. Finally, the shuffle is the most cost-efficient model (meaning it is the least expensive model).

FIGURE 1.3
The iPod shuffle looks quite different from the other iPod models because it *is* very different from them.

The following is the skinny on this skinniest of iPod models:

- 1GB of memory rated for 240 songs
- A battery rated for up to 12 hours of music playing time
- Headphone port
- Dimensions of 1.62 inches by 1.07 inches by 0.414 inches and a weight of 0.55 ounces
- Accessories including earbud headphones and a dock
- A price of $79

note

Throughout this book, when I use the term *iPod*, I usually am referring to the iPod (AKA iPod Video) and iPod nano because these are pretty similar except for the iPod Video's video capability. Because the shuffle is an iPod of a different feather altogether, you'll often see it excepted in generic iPod references (as in, *except the shuffle*). Confused? I hope you won't be as you get further into this book.

iPod: The Previous Generations

Rome wasn't built in a night, and neither did the iPod evolve into the elegant family of products that you will learn about in this book (and there might be even better iPods available when you read this). There have been many generations of iPods, with each adding new features, different disk sizes, more or fewer controls, different screens, colors, and so on. If you don't have one of the models described in this chapter, don't despair (especially if you have an even newer and better model). Most of the information in this book will still be useful for you. You might just have to use slightly different steps to get the same results; for example, some previous iPod models used buttons separate from the Click Wheel to Play, Fast Forward, and so on. And, believe it or not, there was a time when iPods could handle only audio content, so the photo and video content in this book won't help you if you have one of these more limited ancestors. (You just might be inspired to buy a new one if you aren't careful, though.)

Which iPod Is Right for You?

If you already have an iPod and don't envision buying another one, you can skip to the next section. Otherwise, read on for some general guidance on choosing an iPod model.

One of the most frequent questions I get asked is, "Which iPod should I buy?" Unfortunately for me, this is also one of the hardest questions I get asked. That's because each model offers features and benefits that the others don't. And, of course, each costs a different price. There is never a clear-cut answer to this question, unless you can afford to spend only $79, in which case your only choice is the iPod shuffle (which isn't a bad choice, by the way).

Like all electronic devices, choosing an iPod is a matter of balancing features and options against cost. I can't address your individual choice, but I can provide some general guidance because each model does offer some distinct benefits.

If you want to be able to watch video on it, your options get limited immediately. You'll need either the 30GB or 80GB iPod. Which size you get really depends on how much you can afford to spend. If you can afford the 80GB model, that's the one you should get, because it offers more than twice as much storage space than the 30GB model, yet costs only $100 more. It also offers longer battery life, which is a good thing.

If you don't want to use it for vide but do want an iPod with a screen so you can see information about what you play and want to be able to see photos, the iPod nano becomes a contender for your iPod dollars. The nano is roughly half the size of the iPod, so if size is important to you, you might consider one of the iPod nano models. Also, the iPod nano models are less expensive than the iPods, so if you are on a tight budget, the nano might be a better fit financially speaking.

However, the disk space available on even the "largest" nano is 8GB. If your music collection is large, you probably won't have enough room to store all of it on the nano, not to mention the room that photos you might want to store on it will require. This means you will have to choose a subset of your music and photos to take with you. If you are like me and want to hear what you want when you want, this is a problem.

If you can afford one of the iPod (video) models, I think they are a better value than the nanos because of their disk size and the capability to play video, which is really cool.

If you can't afford an iPod or if a smaller iPod is better for you, the nano is an excellent option.

If you are going to be using an iPod under "extreme" conditions, such as during heavy exercise, sporting activities, or work situations, an iPod shuffle is a good choice because this model is much more resistant to damage than the other models and, with its lower cost, you are risking less by using it in these situations. Plus, it is very small and extremely light, so carrying it is definitely the easiest.

So, what is the bottom line? There isn't one. All iPods are a good choice. Some will fit your needs and budget better than others, but you really can't go wrong with any of them. Pick the most you can afford to spend, and then get the model that fits your budget and specific needs.

What You Can Do with an iPod

The iPod is definitely a great music player, but it is much more than that, as you will learn throughout this part of the book. For now, here are just some of the great things you can do with an iPod:

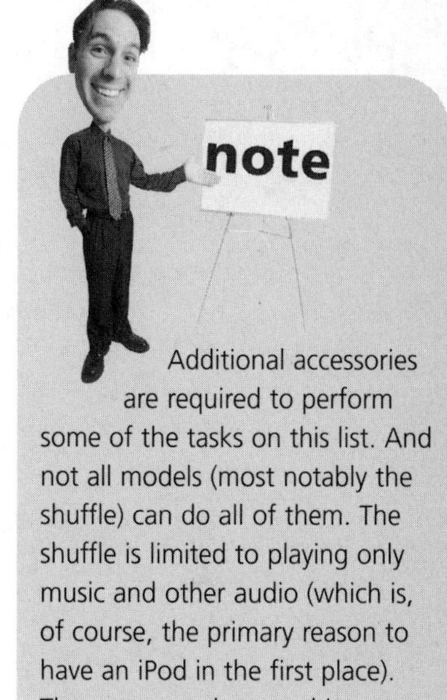

Additional accessories are required to perform some of the tasks on this list. And not all models (most notably the shuffle) can do all of them. The shuffle is limited to playing only music and other audio (which is, of course, the primary reason to have an iPod in the first place). The nano can do everything except video.

- Take your entire music collection, or at least a large part of it, with you wherever you go.
- Watch a TV show or movie of your choice while you are out and about.
- Enjoy podcasts of all kinds.
- Play music in many different ways, such as by album, artist, genre, song, playlist, and so on.
- Eliminate the need to carry CDs with you anywhere; using an adapter or an FM transmitter, your iPod can provide music in your home, car, or any other place you happen to be.
- View your calendar on the move.
- Access contact information for your favorite people and companies for quick and easy reference.
- Keep track of the time and date and have a portable alarm clock.
- Listen to your favorite audiobook.
- Transfer information between computers or back up your important files.
- Store pictures from a digital camera.
- Play games.
- View pictures and slideshows and play the same on a TV.

The Absolute Minimum

The iPod just might be the neatest gadget ever. After you have tried one, you will likely find it to be indispensable, and you might wonder how you ever got along without it. Before we jump into configuring and using an iPod, consider the following points:

- An iPod enables you to take your music and other audio with you and listen to it anytime, anywhere. You can also take video and photos with you. A nano can handle audio or photos. A shuffle can play music and other audio just as well as its larger siblings.
- The iPod is actually a mini computer and includes a hard drive or flash memory, an operating system, and other computer components.
- There were three types of iPods in production at press time: iPod, iPod nano, and iPod shuffle. There are also variants of some models, such as the 30GB iPod or the 4GB iPod nano.
- The iPod has evolved over time. If you have an older model, it might not be able to do all that the current models can. The good news is that most of the information in this book is just as applicable to any of the older models you might have as it is to the latest and greatest versions.
- No matter which iPod you have, you'll be amazed at all the cool things it can do, from playing music to being your own personal portable hard drive (all models except shuffle) or flash drive (shuffle).
- Current iPod models work just as well for Windows and Macintosh computers. Whether you use a Windows computer, a Mac, or both, your iPod will work great.
- Like potato chips, I'll bet you can't get by with just one iPod. After you use one model, you'll probably want to get at least one more for yourself. For example, if you have an iPod, you might want to get a shuffle for those times when the device's size and weight is important, or when you don't want to risk damaging the iPod's screen. And if you have a family, expect to also need a family of iPods!

In This Chapter

- Find out what good stuff came with your iPod.
- Install iTunes on your computer.
- Connect an iPod to your computer and transfer good stuff from your computer onto it.
- Use a Dock to make connecting an iPod to your computer even easier.

2

Getting Started with an iPod

Getting started with an iPod involves the following general steps:

1. Understand what is included with your iPod.
2. Install the iPod's software (iTunes) on your computer.
3. Connect the iPod to your computer, and transfer music and other content from your iTunes Library to the iPod.
4. Disconnect the iPod from your computer.

After you have performed these steps, you will be ready to learn how to use the iPod in detail, which you'll start doing in the next chapter.

As you learned in the previous chapter, there are three basic models of iPod. Considering that iPods work with both Windows and Macintosh computers and how many models and variations of those there are, covering all possible combinations of iPod and computer just isn't possible.

So, what I have done instead is to provide general guidelines to help you accomplish the basic tasks you need to do to get your iPod rolling (and rocking). You probably won't need to read every section in this chapter unless you use several kinds of iPods on both types of computers. Use the headings to determine which circumstances apply to you, and skip those sections that don't apply.

Exploring the iPod's Box

The iPod is so cool that even its box is stylish! In this section, you'll learn about the items included in that stylish box. Exactly what's included in the box depends on the model you purchase and even when you purchase it. (Apple tends to change the accessories included with each model over time even when the model remains the same.) The following list gives you a general idea of what comes with each type of iPod:

- **The iPod**—You probably didn't need this item listed, but I like to be thorough!
- **Earbud headphones**—You can use these to listen to your iPod's music. The sound quality of the earbuds included with your iPod is remarkably good.
- **USB cable**—The iPod and iPod nano include a USB cable you use to connect the iPod to a computer.
- **Dock**—The shuffle includes a Dock that you use to connect it to a computer.
- **Dock adapter**—The iPod and iPod nano come with the adaptor you need to mount them in the universal Dock.
- **Information pamphlets**—These provide basic information you can use to get started with your iPod. (Because you have this book already, you might not find these to be very useful.)
- **Accessories**—Different iPod models purchased at different times include different accessories. (Did I use *different* in this sentence enough?) For example, the iPod includes a basic case.

Notice that the previous list does not include a CD containing software. You get the software you need for an iPod, namely iTunes, from the Internet.

Installing the iPod's Software (iTunes)

Your computer needs software to be able to communicate with your iPod, along with the iTunes application you will use to manage the content you place on it. (You'll learn all about iTunes in Part II, "iTunes.") Install iTunes by using the steps in the section that is appropriate for the type of computer you are using (a Windows PC or a Mac).

Installing iTunes on a Windows PC

The first step into the iPod and iTunes world is to download and install the software you need from the Internet. To do this, perform the following steps:

1. Open your favorite web browser, such as Internet Explorer.
2. Move to http://www.apple.com/ipod/start. You will see the Download iTunes tool (see Figure 2.1).

tip

As you are handling an iPod, it turns on if you press any control. For now, turn it off again by pressing and then holding down the **Play/Pause** button until the iPod shuts off again. If you have a shuffle, ignore this because it doesn't apply.

FIGURE 2.1
Downloading iTunes is easy and free; what could be better?

3. Click the **Windows 2000 or XP** radio button.
4. Uncheck the boxes for the Apple newsletters you don't want to receive. (They are both checked by default.) For example, the *New Music Tuesday* newsletter lets you know about music that has been added to the iTunes Store. If you want that information, leave its check box checked.
5. Enter your email address if you left either of the check boxes checked; if you unchecked both of them, you can leave this blank.
6. Click **Download iTunes—Free**. In most cases, you then see the Security Warning dialog box. If you don't have your web browser configured to

present this, you move directly to the Save As dialog box, in which case you can skip the next two steps.

7. In the Security Warning dialog box, click **Run** to indicate that you want to download and run the iTunes Installer. The software downloads to your computer. How long this process takes depends on the speed of your Internet connection and your hardware. When the download is done, you see yet another Security Warning dialog.
8. Click **Run**. The installation process starts.
9. If you are prompted to choose a language, do so and click **OK**. After a moment or two, you see the first iTunes Installer window (see Figure 2.2).

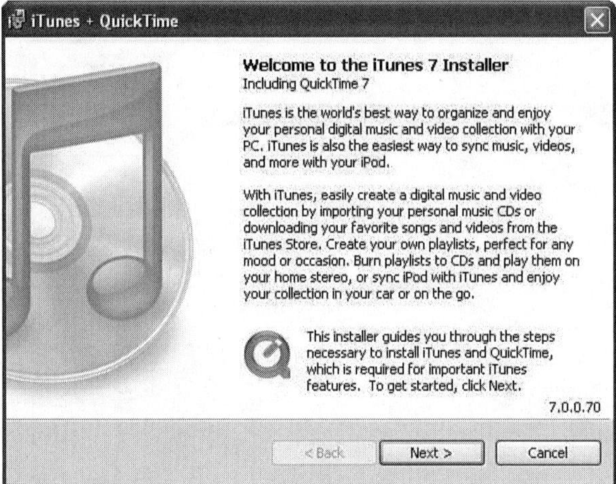

FIGURE 2.2
Working through the iTunes Installer is mostly a matter of reading and clicking **Next**.

10. Read the information in the installer window and click **Next**.
11. If you have a lot of time and patience, read the license agreement; when you are finished (if you are like me, you will realize it is incomprehensible and will just assume you aren't giving away your firstborn), click **I accept the terms in the license agreement** and then click **Next**. You then see the iTunes Installer Options window (see Figure 2.3).
12. If you don't want an iTunes icon installed on your desktop, uncheck the **Install desktop shortcuts** check box.
13. If you don't want to use iTunes as the default application, uncheck the **Use iTunes as the default player for audio files** check box.
14. If you don't want to install the Apple Software Update application, which keeps your iTunes and iPod software current, uncheck the **Install Apple Software Update to easily update iTunes and other Apple software** check box. I recommend that you leave this check box checked so your iTunes and iPod software can be kept current easily.

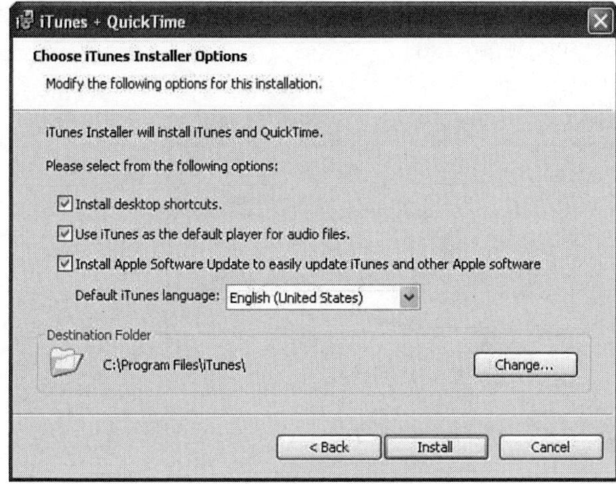

FIGURE 2.3
Use this window to set basic iTunes installation options.

15. Choose the language you want iTunes to use on the **Default iTunes language** drop-down list.
16. If you want to accept the default installation location (which is `C:\Program Files\iPod\`), skip to the next step. If you don't want to accept the default installation location, click the **Change** button and choose the location in which you want iTunes to be installed.
17. Click **Install**. The status window appears to display the progress of the process. When the installation is complete, you see the Congratulations window (see Figure 2.4).

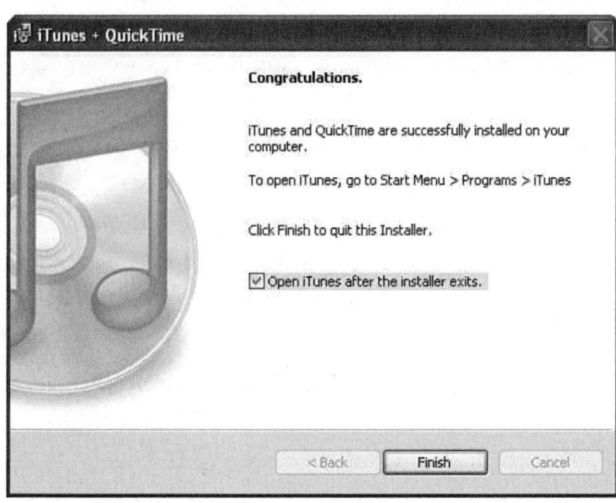

FIGURE 2.4
Ah, sweet success, at last I've found you.

18. Click **Finish**. iTunes launches, and you see the iTunes Software License Agreement screen.

19. Read the license (right!) and click **Agree**. You move into the iTunes Setup Assistant (see Figure 2.5).

FIGURE 2.5
Use the iTunes Setup Assistant to perform the initial configuration of iTunes. (You can undo anything you set later using iTunes Preferences.)

20. Click **Next**. You'll see the Find Music Files dialog box.
21. If you already have music and other audio files that you want to add to your iTunes Library now, leave both check boxes checked; if you don't want to add those files now, uncheck both check boxes. Click **Next**. You'll see the Keep iTunes Music Folder Organized dialog box.
22. Check the **Yes, keep my iTunes Music Folder organized** radio button. This setting causes iTunes to consistently name and organize your music files. Unless you have a specific reason not to allow this, I recommend you let iTunes do this for you. Click **Next**. You'll see the Download Album Artwork dialog box.
23. Click **Next**. (This dialog box is purely informational.) You'll see the iTunes Store dialog box.
24. Check the **No, take me to my iTunes Library** radio button and click **Finish**. iTunes opens and converts and imports any music files it finds on your computer into the iTunes Library. When that process is done, you'll see the iTunes window (see Figure 2.6). This means you're finished installing the software you need to use an iPod.

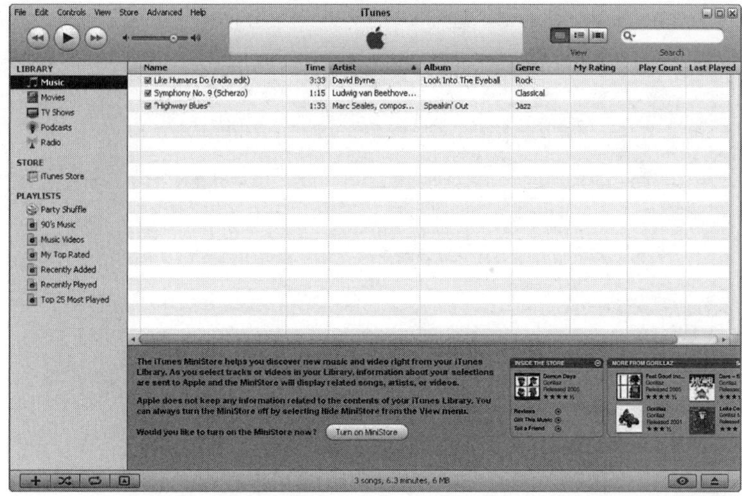

FIGURE 2.6
When you see the iTunes window, you're ready to get started with an iPod.

Installing iTunes on a Macintosh

To work with an iPod, you need to have iTunes installed on your Macintosh computer. Because you are using a Mac, it is extremely likely that iTunes is already installed on your computer because iTunes is installed on new Macs and as part of the Mac OS X installation. You should update the version you have installed to ensure you are using the most current version of iTunes. To make sure your version of iTunes is up-to-date, perform the following steps:

1. Choose **Apple menu**, **Software Update**. The Software Update application opens, connects to the Internet, and looks for updates to the Apple software installed on your Mac, including iTunes (see Figure 2.7).

   If the application finds a newer version of iTunes than the one you have installed on your Mac, you'll see it in the Software Update window and you should move into step 2. If a newer version of iTunes is not found, your version is current and you can skip to the next section.

2. Leave iTunes selected for installation and click **Install**.
3. Follow the onscreen instructions to download and install the newer version of iTunes. Typically, all you have to do is agree to the license, and the Software Update application takes care of the rest.

If you've removed iTunes from your Mac for some reason, you can download a copy from the Internet. Use steps similar to those in the section called "Installing iTunes on a Windows PC" on page **21** to do so; of course, you should select the Mac version of iTunes rather than the Windows version. Follow the onscreen instructions to download and install iTunes on your Mac.

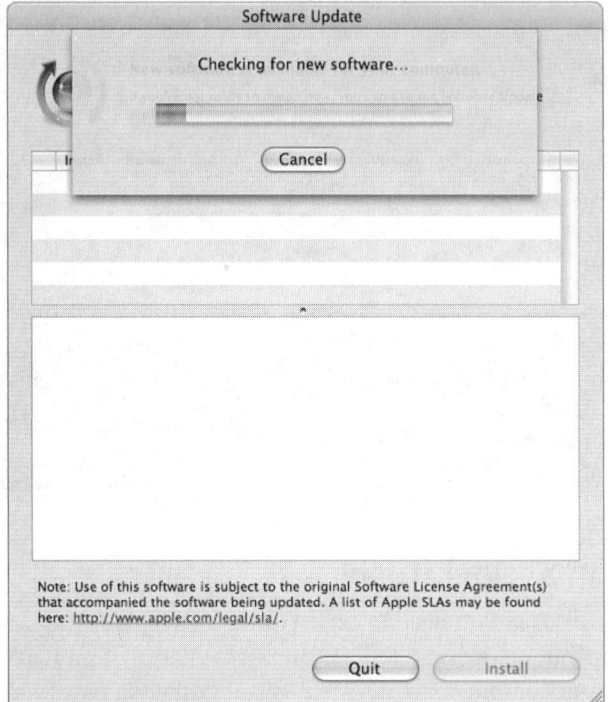

FIGURE 2.7
Use the Software Update application to ensure that your version of iTunes is the latest and greatest.

Connecting and Configuring an iPod on Your Computer

To load music, other audio, or video onto an iPod, you must connect the iPod to your computer so the files can be moved from your iTunes Library onto the iPod. The first time you connect your iPod to your computer, you'll need to configure it.

Preparing an iPod to Connect to a Computer

To connect all iPods (except the shuffle) to a computer, you use the USB cable supplied with your iPod. All iPod cables have the Dock connector plug on one end; the Dock connector is wide and thin. Connect this end to the iPod's Dock connector port located on the bottom of the iPod (see Figure 2.8). The icon on the connector should face you when you are looking at the face of the iPod.

The iPod shuffle includes a Dock into which you place the shuffle; the plug on the Dock is inserted into the Headphones jack on the shuffle.

FIGURE 2.8
You use the Dock connector port on the bottom of the iPod to connect it to a computer.

Connecting an iPod to a Computer

You connect the other end of the iPod's cable to a USB 2 port on your computer.

A USB 2 port is a rectangular port that is fairly thin (see Figure 2.9). USB is also marked with a trident-like icon. You should use a USB 2 port that is located on your computer's case so the port will provide enough power to charge your iPod when it is connected.

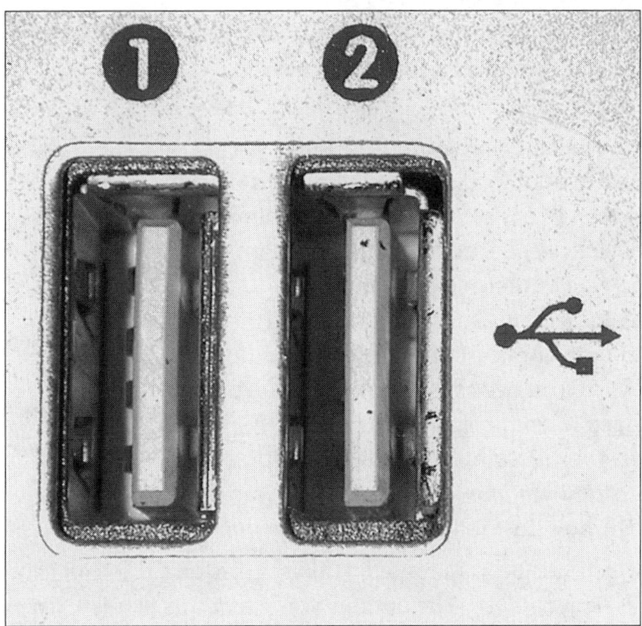

FIGURE 2.9
You use a USB 2 port to connect your iPod to your computer.

The slightly confusing thing about USB is that there are two basic kinds of USB ports: USB 1 and USB 2. And some computers have both kinds.

Locate the USB ports on your computer's case.

Unfortunately, you can't tell by observation whether a USB port supports USB 2 or USB 1 because the ports are identical in appearance. Check the documentation that came with your computer to determine which ports support USB 2. If you can't find that information, contact your computer's manufacturer.

If you still can't determine which ports support USB 2, try one of the USB ports on your computer's case. If the iPod's battery charges when it is connected, you have a USB 2 port. If not, you probably are using an USB 1 port. Try a different one until you locate a USB 2 port.

Plug the USB end of the USB 2 cable into the USB port on your computer. The connector will fit only one way, so if it isn't going in easily, turn the connector over. After it is connected, you'll be ready to configure your iPod.

tip

Diagnostic applications are available that will tell you whether your computer supports USB 2. However, these are beyond the scope of this book. You can do a web search to find one.

Configuring an iPod on Your Computer

The first time you connect an iPod to your computer, the iPod turns on and immediately is mounted on your computer. Its battery also starts charging.

If your iPod needs to be reformatted or there is new software available for it, you see a warning explaining that this is so. Click **OK** in the dialog and then click the **Restore** button in iTunes. Then click **Restore and Update**. Follow the onscreen instructions in the iPod Software Update application to restore your iPod's software. The newest software for the iPod is downloaded to your computer and then installed on your iPod. After that is complete, the iPod restarts and you move into the iPod Setup Assistant. (You'll learn more about this later. For now, just follow the on-screen instructions to complete the process.)

caution

If you use an older computer, it might not have USB 2 ports on it. While an iPod might work with a USB 1 port, you won't have a good experience because its battery might not charge and the speed at which content transfers from the computer to the iPod will be slow. Make sure you use a USB 2 port when working with an iPod.

After your iPod has been mounted, iTunes opens and the iPod Setup Assistant appears (see Figure 2.10). The options you see in this window depend on the kind of iPod you are using. For all iPods, type a name for your iPod in the text box. You can use any name you'd like; this will be the name of your iPod when it is shown in the iTunes Source List and on your computer's desktop. For an iPod video, leave the **Automatically sync songs and videos to my iPod** check box checked. For an iPod nano, leave the **Automatically sync songs to my iPod** check box checked. If you want to also load photos on the iPod, check the **photos** check boxes and then choose the source of the photos you want to move onto the iPod. (I recommend that you leave the **photos** check boxes unchecked for now.) Then click **Done**. You move to the Registration screen. If you want to register your iPod, click the **Register My iPod** button and follow the onscreen instructions to complete the registration process. iTunes updates the iPod and transfers all the music in your iTunes Library onto the iPod—if it can.

FIGURE 2.10
The trusty iPod Setup Assistant is ready to do its work.

While content is being transferred, the iPod screen fills the iTunes window, and the update icon appears next to the iPod on the Source list (see Figure 2.11). You can also see information about the transfer in the iTunes Information area at the top of the iTunes window.

If all the content in your iTunes Library will fit on the iPod, the process will complete without further action from you. When this process is complete, you will hear a "whoosh" sound, and you'll see the `iPod update is complete` message in the Information window at the top of the iTunes window. Click the **Eject** button next to the iPod's icon on the Source List. The iPod will be removed from the Source List, and after a moment or two, the `OK to disconnect` message will also be displayed on the iPod's screen (except the shuffle, which doesn't have a screen). When you see this message, you can disconnect your iPod from your computer. Squeeze the sides of the Dock connector end of the cable and remove the cable from the iPod or remove the shuffle from its Dock; the iPod will be ready to use. You can leave the cable plugged in to your computer if you want.

If there is more content in your iTunes Library than can fit on the iPod, you will see a message telling you that the iPod doesn't have enough room for all your content. You'll be prompted to have iTunes select songs that will fit onto the iPod. Click **Yes** to allow this. In this case, iTunes will create a playlist of music that will fit on the iPod and then transfer this music to your iPod. This is fine for now; in later chapters, you'll learn how to choose which content is transferred onto your iPod.

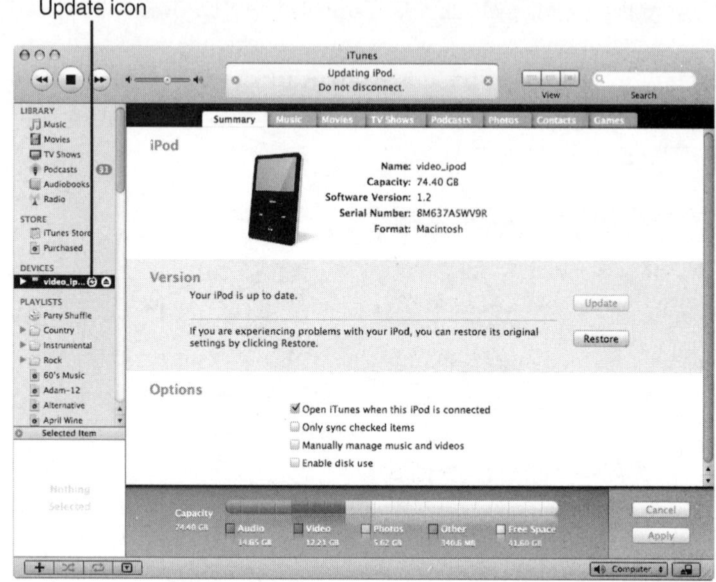

FIGURE 2.11
When an iPod is selected as the source in iTunes, the iPod screen fills the iTunes window.

iTunes will move the playlist it created (whose name will be the name of your iPod plus the word "Selection") onto your iPod. When this process is complete, you'll hear a "whoosh" sound, and you'll see the `iPod update is complete` message in the Information window at the top of the iTunes window. Click the **Eject** button next to the iPod's icon on the Source list. The iPod will be removed from the Source list, and after a moment or two, the `OK to disconnect` message will also be displayed on the iPod's screen (except the shuffle, which doesn't have a screen). When you see this message, you can disconnect your iPod from your computer. Squeeze the sides of the Dock connector end of the cable and remove the cable from the iPod or remove the shuffle from its Dock; the iPod will be ready to use. You can leave the cable plugged in to your computer if you want to.

If you haven't charged your iPod's battery previously, you should leave your iPod connected to your computer until its battery is fully charged, which will take about 3–4 hours, depending on the model you have.

Connecting an iPod to a Computer with a Dock

Dealing with a cable each time you connect your iPod to your computer is a bit of a pain. An iPod Dock provides a cradle for your iPod so you don't need to use the cable itself. When you want to transfer content to the iPod or charge its battery, you simply set it in the Dock (see Figure 2.12). The connection is made instantly, and your iPod is updated while its battery charges.

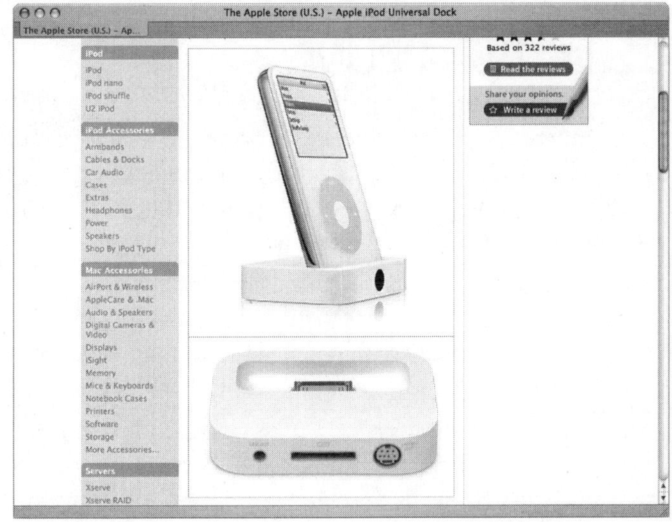

FIGURE 2.12
An iPod Dock eliminates the need to mess around with cables every time you connect your iPod to your computer.

You can purchase a Universal Dock for any iPod (including older models) from any retailer that carries iPod accessories or from the online Apple Store located at www.apple.com/store.

The iPod shuffle includes its own Dock, so you don't need to buy one for that model.

In addition to making it easier to connect your iPod to a computer, the Docks for various models include other ports you might find useful. For example, Docks include the Line Out port, with which you can connect the iPod's audio output to a receiver or other audio device, and its video output to a TV to display slideshows and video on the TV. A Dock is the only way to use the better-quality S-video connection to display an iPod's slideshows and video on a TV.

To use a Dock, connect the Dock connector end of the cable you use to connect the iPod to your computer into the Dock connector port on the Dock (instead of the port on the iPod). To connect the iPod to the computer, simply set it into the Dock; iPods include a plastic adapter that you place into the Dock first; you then place the iPod in the adapter to fit it securely into the cradle. (The Universal Dock includes adapters for just about any iPod model.) When the Dock can communicate with the iPod, you'll hear a tone, and your iPod will be mounted on your computer.

When you want to disconnect your iPod from the computer, lift it out of the Dock. (You might have to place one hand on the Dock to keep it from lifting up when you lift the iPod out.)

THE ABSOLUTE MINIMUM

Fortunately, a lot of the material in this chapter is useful only the first time you use your iPod. (And besides, the installation software guides you through most of the steps anyway.) After all, installing software and connecting cables isn't all that thrilling. But it *is* necessary to do the thrilling stuff that starts in the next chapter. Before we leave this topic, consider the following points:

- You need to install iTunes on your computer to use an iPod. On Windows PCs, you download and install iTunes from the Internet. Most Macs have iTunes installed already; you just need to use the Mac's Software Update feature to make sure you are using the current version.
- To transfer contents (music, podcasts, video, and so on) from your iTunes Library onto your iPod and to charge its battery, you connect the iPod to your computer. For iPods and iPod nanos, use a USB 2 cable to do this. If you have a shuffle, use its Dock.
- The first time you connect your iPod to your computer, you need to do some basic setup. Fortunately, iTunes will guide you all the way.
- You can install more than one iPod on the same computer. For example, you might be fortunate enough to have an iPod and an iPod shuffle. If you have more than one iPod, use a different name for each so you can keep them straight. You can even connect them to your computer at the same time if you have enough ports and cables available to do so.
- A Dock makes it easier to connect your iPod to your computer. It also includes Line Out and other ports. You can use these to connect the Dock to speakers or another audio device to play the iPod's music on that device. You can use the Line Out or S-Video port to connect an iPod's video output to a TV so you can view your iPod's contents on a big screen.

IN THIS CHAPTER

- Connect an iPod to headphones or speakers so you can hear its sound.
- Turn on an iPod and learn how to control it.
- Tour the iPod's menus and screens.
- Light up your iPod's world with the Backlight.
- Put an iPod on hold.
- Turn off an iPod.

3

CONTROLLING AN IPOD OR IPOD NANO

The iPod is a well-designed device that is easy to control—as soon as you understand its controls and how they work, that is. Because the iPod is likely quite different from other devices you have used, it can take a little time to get totally comfortable controlling one. That's where this chapter comes in. You'll learn about the iPod's controls and how to use them. You'll also come to know (and love) the iPod's menu structure and the major screens that you'll use. You'll get into the details of using all these controls and screens in subsequent chapters.

In this chapter, you'll learn how to use specific controls on the current generation of iPods (current to when I was writing this book, that is). Previous generations used different kinds of controls. For example, before the Click Wheel was standard on all iPod models, some models had separate buttons for Play and other actions. Because the iPod and iPod nano were the current models when I wrote this chapter, it focuses on their controls. If you have an older (or newer) model, the controls might be located in slightly different places, but their functions will be the same.

Getting Ready to Play

To hear the audio stored on your iPod, you must attach a sound output device to it. The most common is the set of earbud headphones that were included in the iPod's package.

To use these, you connect the mini-jack on the earbud cable to the Headphones jack located on the top of the iPod video (see Figure 3.1). On iPod nanos, this jack is located on the bottom. When you do so, you'll hear any sound coming from the iPod through the earbuds.

The iPod shuffle works differently from the other iPods. If you only use an iPod shuffle, you don't need to read this chapter or the next, so move ahead to Chapter 5, "Listening to Music on an iPod shuffle."

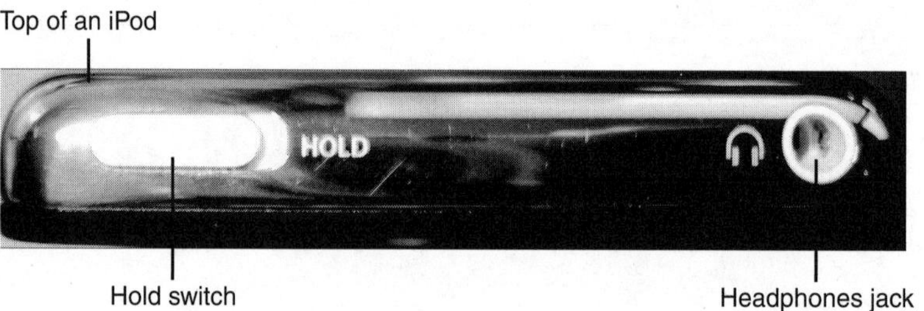

FIGURE 3.1
The Headphones jack is where you plug in headphones, speakers, or other audio output devices.

Although you are most likely to use earbuds or other headphones with an iPod, those are certainly not the only audio or video output devices through which you can play an iPod's content. Following are some other devices you might want to use to play your iPod's output:

- **Powered speakers**—You can connect a set of powered speakers to the Dock connector or Headphones jack to play your iPod's music on those speakers. For example, you can use any set of computer speakers to create a mini stereo system. (There won't be anything mini about the sound quality, though.)
- **FM transmitter**—You can connect an FM transmitter to the Dock connector on the bottom of the iPod or the Headphones jack to broadcast your iPod's output over FM. You can then tune into your iPod's music on an FM tuner, such as the one in your car or home stereo system.
- **Home or car stereo**—You can use various cables and connectors to connect the Dock connector or Headphones jack to an input port on a home stereo receiver, car stereo, or boom box to play your iPod's music over one of these devices.

- **AV cable**—If you purchase an optional AV cable, you can view the video output of an iPod on a TV by connecting one end of that cable to the Headphones jack. You can connect the other end to a TV and home theater receiver to view and hear the iPod's output on those devices.

Some audio devices connect to the iPod's Dock connector. Examples of these are iPod speakers, certain FM transmitters, and so on. Others plug into the Headphones jack. Whenever you connect it, the point is that your iPod needs something connected to it for you to hear its output. However, you can view the video output of the iPod directly on its screen (or use the optional cable to view that output on a TV).

Controlling an iPod

The primary controls for an iPod are located on its Click Wheel (see Figure 3.2).

Turning On an iPod

To turn on an iPod, press the **Click Wheel** in any location or press the **Select** button. During the startup process, you'll see the Apple logo on the iPod's screen, and after it starts up, you'll see its Main menu.

FIGURE 3.2
Most of the controls on an iPod are on its Click Wheel.

Choosing an iPod's Language

The first time you turn on an iPod, you'll immediately move to the Language selection screen that you use to choose the language in which your iPod will display information. To choose a language, slide a finger or thumb clockwise on the **Click Wheel** to move down the language list or counterclockwise to move up the list. When the language you want to use is highlighted, press the **Select** button to choose it. You will then move to the Main menu. You'll have to do this the first time you turn on an iPod and each time you restore it.

Making Selections on an iPod

The previous paragraph about selecting a language gives you the general idea of how you control an iPod. Now, let's give you a very specific idea of how you move around your iPod to make it follow your commands.

The iPod is based on menus from which you make choices. To make a choice on a menu, you slide a finger or thumb clockwise on the **Click Wheel** to move down the current menu or counterclockwise to move up the current menu. As you move up or down, a different command or option on the current menu will be highlighted. When the command or option you want to use is highlighted, press the **Select** button to choose it. If an option is highlighted when you press the **Select** button, the option's state will change, such as from `Off` to `On`. If a highlighted command is for a menu, that menu will appear. You can then move up and down that menu to choose another command. If the menu provides a list of songs, albums, or other categories, you can use the same process to select and play an item, such as a song.

To move back (or up if you want to think about moving up or down an iPod's menu structure) to a previous menu, you press the **Menu** button. You move "up" one level of the menu structure each time you press the **Menu** button. When you reach the Main menu, pressing the **Menu** button will have no effect because that is the "top" menu on the iPod's menu structure.

You'll learn the specific menus and screens you will use later in this chapter. For now, just understand how to move up and down the iPod's menu structure.

Using the iPod's Click Wheel

The iPod's Click Wheel is kind of cool because it contains both the wheel you use to move up and down the menus and the various buttons you use to control the iPod. These buttons are located at each 90° point around the Click Wheel and at its center (the Select button). To use a button around the edge of the Click Wheel, you simply press down on its icon on the wheel. The button will click and the action it represents will happen.

Because there isn't a clear delineation between locations on the wheel, you don't have to be precise when you press a button. Press down close to the button's icon on the wheel, and you will likely get the expected action.

When a song is playing and the Now Playing screen is displayed, you control the iPod's volume by sliding a finger or thumb on the **Click Wheel** clockwise to increase the volume or counterclockwise to decrease it. There are other options that work similarly to the volume, such as when you want to rate something to which you are listening.

When content is playing, you can also fast-forward, rewind, and rate music using the Click Wheel after you press the **Select** button one time to change to fast-forward or rewind mode or two times to get to the rating mode. The detailed steps to access and use these modes are covered later in this part of the book.

Looking at the iPod's Menus and Screens

Now that you have an idea of how to move around your iPod, let's get a good understanding of its menus and screens.

The steps you use to move around the iPod's menus are the following:

1. Slide your finger or thumb clockwise on the **Click Wheel** to move down a menu or counterclockwise to move up a menu. As you move your digit, different menu options will be highlighted on the screen to show that they are selected.
2. When you want to use a menu command, highlight it and press the **Select** button. That command will be active and the screen will change to reflect what you have done. For example, if you selected another menu, that menu will appear on the screen. If you selected a song, the Now Playing screen will appear and that song will start to play. If you selected an application, that application will run.
3. To move back to a previous screen, press the **Menu** button. You'll move back to the screen you were on before the current one. Each time you press the **Menu** button, you'll move back one screen until you get back (or up) to the Main menu.

The Main Menu

The iPod's Main menu provides the major (dare I say *main*?) commands available to you. The specific commands you see on the Main menu by default will depend on the model of iPod you are using. For example, if you use an iPod video, as shown in Figure 3.3, you'll see the Videos command, which won't appear on the iPod nano because it isn't applicable to that model.

FIGURE 3.3
The Main menu is a good place to start using an iPod, which is why you will move there when you first turn it on.

When no music is playing, the default Main menu commands are the following:

- Music
- Photos
- Videos (iPod only)
- Extras
- Settings
- Shuffle Songs

> **tip**
>
> You can change the contents of various menus, as you will learn later in this part of the book. The menus I describe here are the default menus.

All these commands take you to their respective menus, except for Shuffle Songs. The Shuffle Songs command puts the iPod in Shuffle mode, where it plays songs in a random fashion. (You'll learn more about this later.)

When you are playing audio or video, the Now Playing command appears. This command takes you to the Now Playing screen. If you aren't viewing the Now Playing screen, the Play icon will be in the upper-left corner of whatever screen you are seeing if the iPod is currently playing or the Pause icon if whatever is currently playing has been paused.

When a menu choice leads to another menu, a right-facing arrow will appear along the right edge of the screen for that choice. If you don't see an arrow for a command, that command will cause an action to happen instead.

When there are more options on a menu than can be listed on the screen, you will see the scrollbar along the right edge of the screen; the dark part of the bar represents how much of the menu you are seeing on the screen out of the total menu, which is represented by the full bar. (Remember that to scroll up and down a menu, you use the Click Wheel.)

The Music Menu and Screens

The Music command takes you to the Music menu, which provides access to a number of other menus relating to the selection of music and other audio to which you want to listen (see Figure 3.4).

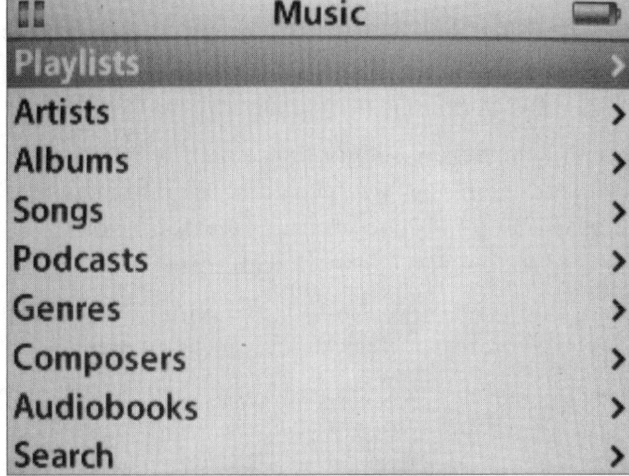

FIGURE 3.4
The Music menu enables you to access your content in a number of ways.

The menu options you have on the Music menu are the following:

- **Playlists**—The Playlists command takes you to the Playlists menu, which lists the playlists stored on your iPod. (If you haven't read Part II, "iTunes," *playlists* are collections of music that you create in iTunes.) On the Playlists menu, you will see each playlist you have created in iTunes and have moved to the iPod. Because each playlist represents a "menu" of the songs in that playlist, when you select it, you will see the Songs menu, which lists each song in the playlist. You'll learn how to work with the Playlists menu and screens in detail in Chapter 6, "Building an iPod's Music Library."
- **Artists**—Similar to the Playlists menu, this command takes you to a menu on which your music is organized by artist. You can choose an artist and then browse all the music by that artist that is stored on your iPod.

note

There is one playlist on the iPod that you won't initially find in iTunes because it wasn't created there: the On-the-Go playlist. You can create this playlist from music that is stored on the iPod. You'll learn how to use this in Chapter 4, "Listening to Music on an iPod or iPod nano."

- **Albums**—This command and menu enables you to browse and select your music by album.
- **Compilations**—This command, which is not displayed by default, and related menu enable you to browse and select your music by compilations, which means those collections of music that contain songs produced by various artists. This command is controlled by a setting that you'll learn about in Chapter 12, "Configuring an iPod to Suit Your Preferences."
- **Songs**—This command takes you to a menu containing all the songs on your iPod, listed in alphabetical order.
- **Podcasts**—Podcasts are similar to radio or TV broadcasts except that you can download them onto your iPod and listen to them at a time of your choosing. Selecting the Podcasts command takes you to the podcasts stored on your iPod so that you can work with them.
- **Genres**—I'll bet you can guess that this command takes you to a menu that enables you to browse and select your music by genre.
- **Composers**—Are you detecting a pattern here? I'll leave this one for you to figure out.
- **Audiobooks**—This takes you to a menu showing all the audiobooks available on your iPod.
- **Search**—This command takes you to a search tool that you can use to find specific content stored on the iPod.

You'll learn all about using the Music menu and screens to listen to music in Chapter 4. You'll learn about the menus and screens for other functions in later chapters, such as podcasts in Chapter 7, "Using an iPod to Listen to and Watch Podcasts," and audiobooks in Chapter 8, "Using an iPod to Listen to Aubiobooks."

The Photos Menu and Screens

As you can tell from its title, you use the Photos menu to access the photos stored on an iPod (see Figure 3.5). On this menu, you'll see the Slideshow Settings command that enables you to configure how slideshows are played on the iPod. Below that command is the list of all the photos on your iPod, grouped into collections. To view the photos in a collection, you highlight the collection whose photos you want to view and click the **Select** button.

Chapter 9, "Using an iPod to Store and View Photos," is devoted to explaining everything you need to know to work with your iPod's photos.

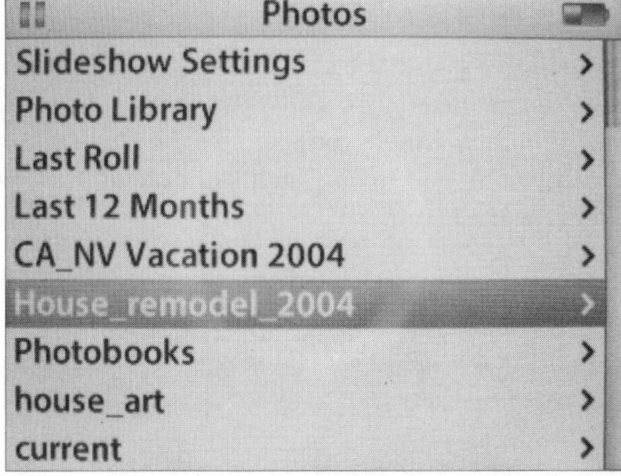

FIGURE 3.5 On the Photos menu, you can access Slideshow Settings or choose a collection of photos to view.

The Videos Menu and Screens (iPod Only)

The Videos menu and screens (iPod only) enable you to enjoy the video content stored on your iPod (see Figure 3.6). (Because the nano is not designed to display video, this menu option doesn't appear on nano models.) On the menu, you see video organized into various categories including Video Playlists, Movies, Music Videos, TV Shows, and Video Podcasts. You'll also see the Video Settings command, which provides access to several controls you can use to configure an iPod's video playback.

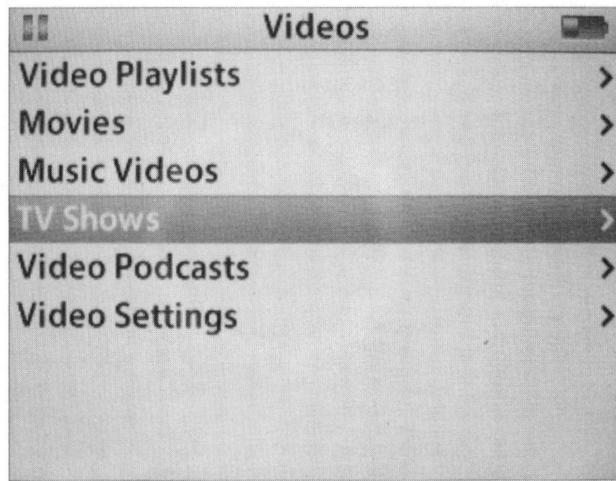

FIGURE 3.6 Using the Videos menu, you can get to the video content on an iPod, including movies, TV shows, and video podcasts.

You'll get the scoop on using an iPod for video in Chapter 10, "Using an iPod to Watch Video."

The Extras Menu and Screens

The Extras command takes you to the Extras menu. On this menu, you will find various options that are related only because they are on the same menu (see Figure 3.7). These commands enable you to access the iPod's non-music features, such as the Clock, Calendar, and so on. You'll learn about these extras in Chapter 11, "Taking the iPod Further."

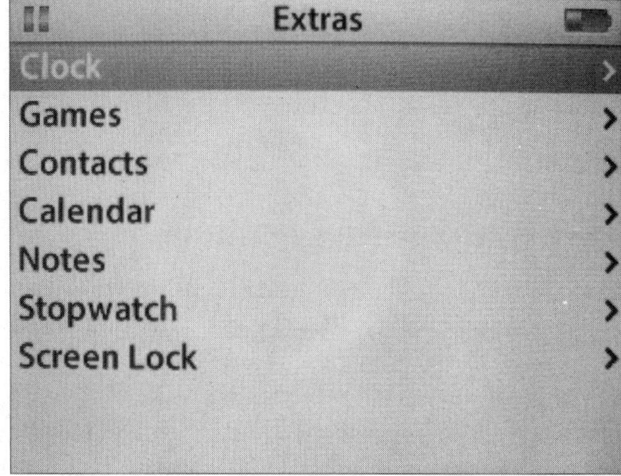

FIGURE 3.7
The Extras menu is aptly named.

The Settings Menu and Screens

The Settings command is like the Preferences command in most computer programs (see Figure 3.8). It enables you to configure various aspects of your iPod, such as the commands on the Main menu, the Clicker settings, and so on. You'll use this command to configure the Backlight later in this chapter, and we'll get into it in detail in Chapter 12.

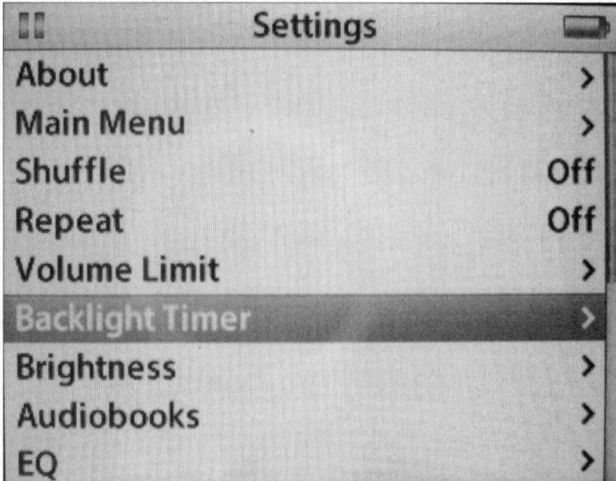

FIGURE 3.8
If you want to make the iPod work according to your preferences, use the Settings menu.

The Shuffle Songs Command

Unlike the other items on the Main menu described so far, this is a command that doesn't take you to a menu. Instead, it puts your iPod in Shuffle mode. You'll learn how to configure and use this command in Chapters 4 and 12.

The Now Playing Command and Screen

The Now Playing command appears on the Main menu only when you have selected and are playing audio or other content. When you choose this command when you are playing audio, you'll move to the Now Playing screen, which will show you the audio that is currently playing (see Figure 3.9). This is an important screen because you can control various aspects of how music is playing, such as the volume level, from this screen. You'll explore the Now Playing screen in detail in Chapter 4. When you are viewing video, this command will take you back to the Now Playing screen, but instead of information about what you are viewing, you'll see the content of the video.

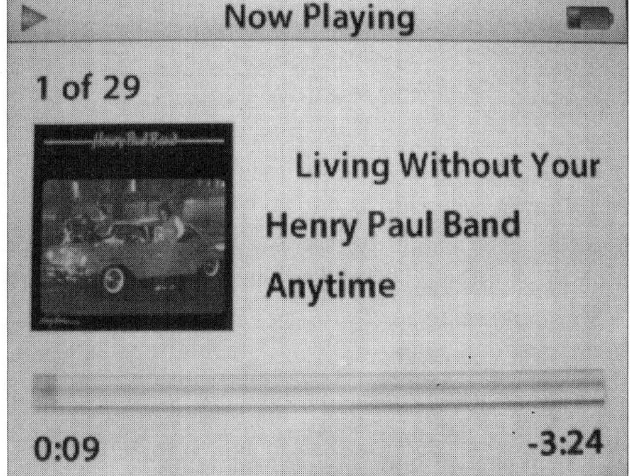

FIGURE 3.9
The Now Playing screen shows you the music currently playing on an iPod.

Using the iPod's Backlight

The Backlight lights up the iPod's screen so you can see it in dark conditions or at other times when you might have trouble reading it. You can configure it to turn off automatically after a specific period of time, and you can turn the Backlight on or off manually.

Configuring the Backlight

You can configure the iPod to turn its Backlight on briefly each time you press a button. This is useful because you can always see what you are doing no matter what the lighting conditions may be. You can also have the Backlight on at all times, but I don't recommend that option because of the drain on the iPod's battery.

You can configure your iPod's Backlight settings by performing the following steps:

1. Select **Main** menu, **Settings**. You'll see the Settings screen.
2. Select **Backlight Timer**. You'll see the Backlight menu (see Figure 3.10).

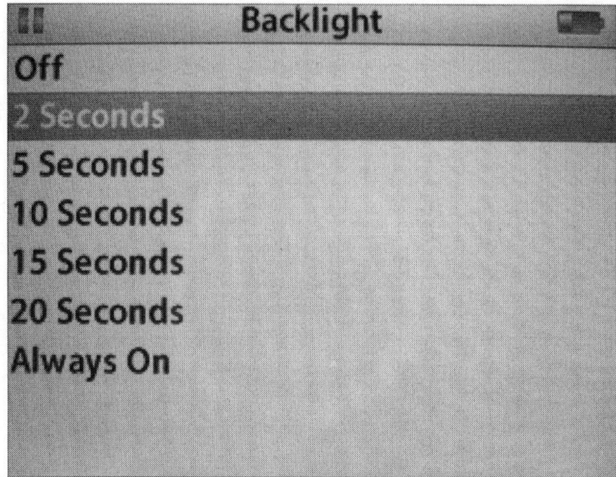

FIGURE 3.10
You use the Backlight menu to configure your iPod's Backlight.

3. If you want the Backlight to come on each time you press a control, choose the amount of time you want it to remain on after you stop touching a control. Your options are 2, 5, 10, 15, or 20 seconds.
4. If you want the Backlight to come on only when you manually activate it, select **Off**.
5. If you want the Backlight on all the time, select **Always On**. Again, I don't recommend this option because it will drain your battery more quickly.
6. Press **Menu** twice to move back to the Main menu.

tip

For battery conservation, I don't recommend the 10-, 15-, or 20-second setting. Try the 2- or 5-second settings because they provide a decent length of illumination time but won't be quite so hard on your battery.

Turning On the Backlight

The iPod has a Backlight command that you can use to turn it on or off manually. This command is not displayed on the Main menu by default. If you want to use it, add it to the Main menu by doing the following:

1. Select **Main** menu, **Settings**. You'll see the Settings screen.
2. Select **Main** menu. You'll see the Main Menu screen on which you can configure the options on the Main menu. (You'll learn about this in more detail in Chapter 12.)
3. Scroll down to and highlight **Backlight** and press the **Select** button. You'll see On listed next to that option. This indicates that the command is now on the Main menu.
4. Press **Menu** twice to move back to the Main menu.

When you move back to the Main menu, you'll see it now has the Backlight command. (Remember that you can tell it is a command because it doesn't have an arrow along the right edge of the screen.)

To turn on the Backlight, move to the **Main** menu, select **Backlight**, and click the **Select** button. The Backlight will come on, and your iPod's world will be a lot brighter.

After the current Backlight time passes, the Backlight will turn off automatically. Or, choose the command again to manually turn the Backlight off.

Putting an iPod on Hold

If you refer back to Figure 3.1, you can see the iPod's Hold switch. This switch disables all the controls on an iPod so that you don't inadvertently press a button, such as if you carry your iPod in your pocket.

To disable the iPod's controls, slide the **Hold** switch to the right (assuming you are looking at the iPod's face with its top pointing up). When you do so, the area underneath the switch that will be exposed when you slide it will be orange to indicate that the iPod is in the Hold mode. If the iPod is currently turned on, you'll also see the Lock icon on the iPod's screen (see Figure 3.11).

To reenable the iPod's controls, slide the **Hold switch** to the left. The orange area under the Hold switch and the Lock icon on the iPod screen will disappear, and you can again control your iPod.

tip

If your iPod isn't responding to your attempts to control it, check the Hold switch to make sure it isn't active. It is amazing how easy it is to forget that you put your iPod in Hold mode and then start troubleshooting to figure why the iPod isn't working. (Not that this has happened to me, of course.)

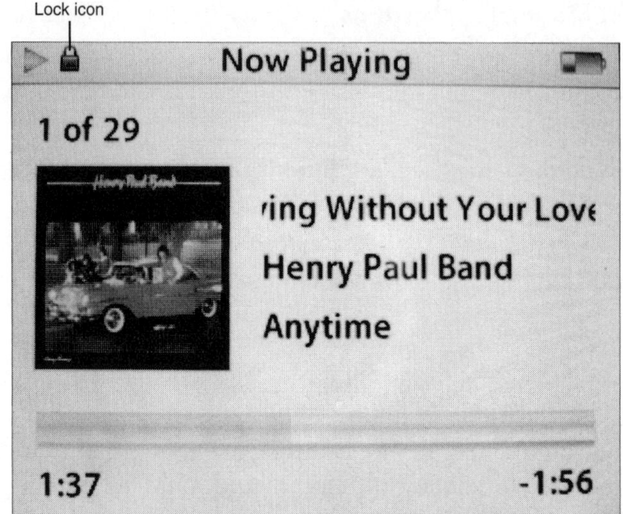

FIGURE 3.11
When you see the Lock icon, the Hold switch is active, and you can't use any of the iPod's controls.

Turning Off an iPod

To turn off an iPod, press and hold down the **Play/Pause** button for a second or two. The iPod screen will turn off. You can turn off the iPod from any screen, regardless of whether anything is playing or not.

iPods really have two Off modes. When you use the Play/Pause button to turn an iPod off, you are really putting it to sleep. In the Sleep mode, the iPod's screen is dark, and it will pause any content that is currently playing. In Sleep mode, the iPod uses less battery power than when it is awake or playing audio, photos, or video. You should put your iPod to sleep whenever you aren't actively using it.

After it's been in Sleep mode for a time, the iPod will power itself down. This shuts down all the tasks currently running and stops the iPod's disk. This is the lowest energy state.

You'll be able to tell in which mode an iPod has been by the amount of time it takes to respond to your pressing one of its controls. If it responds immediately and picks up right where you left off, the iPod was asleep. If you see the Apple logo instead, the iPod was powered all the way down and needs to restart. The Apple logo will be displayed on its screen during this process. After a few moments, you'll see the Main menu, and your iPod will be ready for action.

THE ABSOLUTE MINIMUM

iPods are great devices that do all sorts of cool things. Like any other piece of technology, iPod controls can require a bit of getting used to before you feel as if using one has become second nature. (This won't take long.) Fortunately, as you have seen in this chapter, the iPod's design does make sense, and after you gain an understanding of how the menus and screens are laid out, you won't have any trouble learning to use them in detail, which is where we are headed next. For now, review the following list to see where you've been:

- To hear your iPod's music, you need to attach an output device to it, such as its earbud headphones or powered speakers.
- You control an iPod with its Click Wheel. To select an option on a menu, you slide your finger or thumb (and why isn't the thumb included in the term *finger* anyway?) around the **Click Wheel** to move up or down the menu. When the option you want is highlighted, press the **Select** button. You can control music playback by pressing the **Click Wheel** on or near the icons on its face; for example, to play or pause music, you press the **Click Wheel** at the bottom of the wheel (the 6 o'clock position on the Click Wheel dial) where the Play/Pause icon is located.
- iPods have a menu structure that enables you to access its various screens and commands; in this chapter, you saw an overview of these, such as the Main menu, Music menu, and so on.
- You won't always be using an iPod in bright conditions; its Backlight helps you see the screen better.
- You turn on the Hold switch to prevent unintentionally activating commands.
- To put an iPod to sleep, press and hold the **Play** button until its screen turns off. The iPod will shut itself down after it's been in Sleep mode for a while.

IN THIS CHAPTER

- Pick some music, any music.
- Control your music like a pro.
- Shuffle your tunes to keep them fresh.
- Create and listen to an On-The-Go playlist.
- Check your battery.

4

LISTENING TO MUSIC ON AN IPOD OR IPOD NANO

In this chapter, you'll learn how to listen to and control your iPod tunes. Like any other device on which you listen to music, listening to music on an iPod is a two-step process. You first select the music you want to listen to. Then you play and control that music.

As you rock on, jazz up, classical out, and so on, you'll also find some other tasks useful, such as shuffling your tunes, creating and using an On-The-Go playlist, rating your tunes, and monitoring your battery.

Selecting Music You Want to Listen To

The iPod is cool, but it isn't psychic. You need to tell it what music you want to listen to. There are three primary ways you do this: You can use playlists, you can browse the music stored on the iPod in various ways, or you can search for specific music to which you want to listen.

Selecting Music with Playlists

When you transfer music from your iTunes Library to an iPod, the playlists you have created and that are shown in the iTunes Source List come over, too. You can select music to listen to by using the following steps to choose a playlist:

1. Select **Main** menu, **Music**, **Playlists**. You'll move to the Playlists screen (see Figure 4.1).
2. Highlight the playlist you want to listen to and press the **Select** button. The songs in that playlist will be shown (see Figure 4.2).

tip

If you want to play the entire playlist and don't need to see the songs it includes first, you can just select the playlist and press the **Play/Pause** button. (In other words, step 3 is optional.) The Now Playing screen will appear, and the first song in the playlist will begin to play.

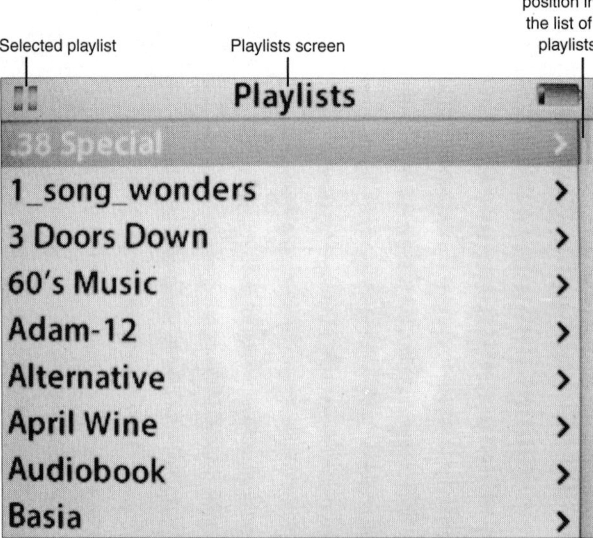

FIGURE 4.1
Almost all the playlists you see on an iPod's Playlists menu should look familiar because they are the same playlists that appear in your iTunes Library.

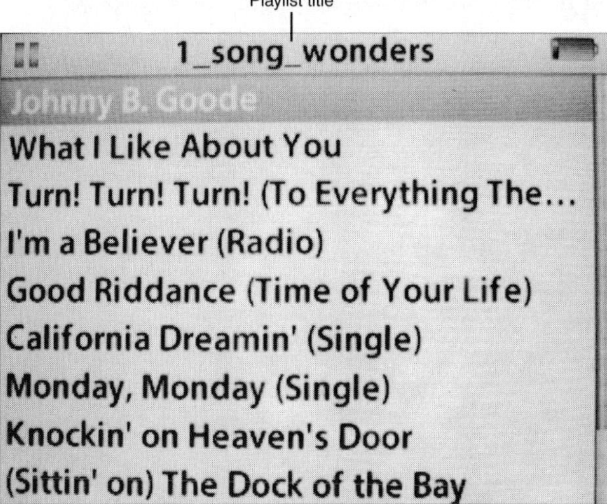

FIGURE 4.2
This playlist contains songs from artists of whose music I have only one song. Here, you see the list of songs in the playlist.

3. If you want to play the entire playlist, press the **Play/Pause** button. If you want to start with a specific song, highlight it and press the **Select** button. The Now Playing screen will appear, and the first song in the playlist or the one you highlighted will begin playing (see Figure 4.3).

FIGURE 4.3
One of the songs from the selected playlist is now playing.

4. Use the techniques you'll learn throughout this chapter to control the tunes as they play.

Browsing Your iPod's Music

Choosing music with playlists is great, and you might find that method to be the one you end up using most because it gets you to the specific music you want quickly and easily. However, some music stored on your iPod might not be in a playlist or you might want to listen to all the music by a specific artist, and so on. In such cases, you can browse the music stored on your iPod to choose the music to which you want to listen. In addition to playlists, you can browse your iPod's music by the following categories:

- Artists
- Albums
- Compilations
- Songs
- Podcasts
- Genres
- Composers
- Audiobooks

If you are wondering how this information gets associated with your music, don't wonder any longer. It all comes from your iTunes Library. See Chapter 18, "Labeling, Categorizing, and Configuring Your Music," to learn how data is associated with your music.

To browse your iPod's music, do the following:

1. Select **Main** menu, **Music**. You'll see the Music menu, which contains the categories listed previously (see Figure 4.4).

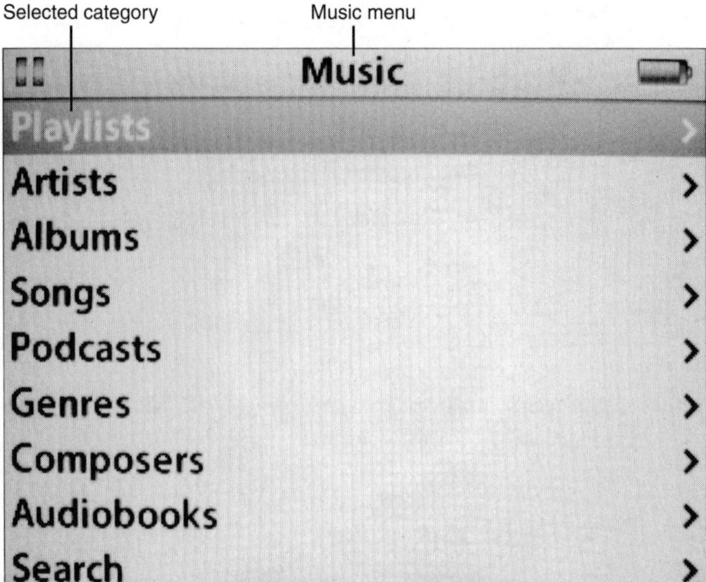

FIGURE 4.4 The Music menu enables you to browse your music by various categories.

2. Highlight the category by which you want to browse your music, such as **Artists** to browse by artist, and press the **Select** button. You will see the menu that shows you all the music that is associated with the category you selected. For example, if you select Artists, you will see all the artists whose music is stored on your iPod (see Figure 4.5).

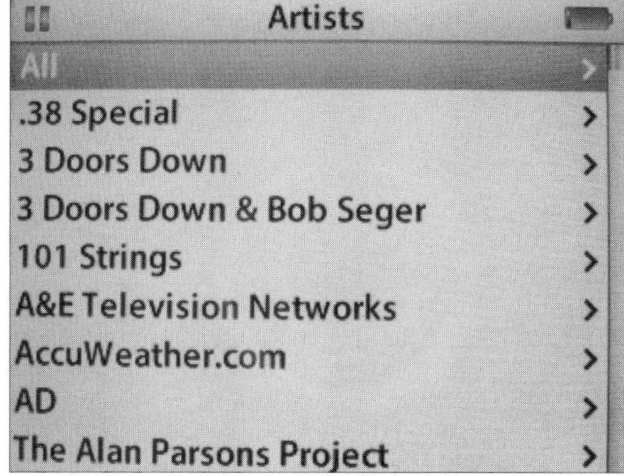

FIGURE 4.5
When you browse by a category, such as Artists, you will see all the music on your iPod in that category.

3. Browse the resulting list of music that appears until you find the specific subcategory in which you are interested.
4. Highlight that subcategory and press the **Select** button. You will see the list of contents of the subcategory you selected. For example, when I was browsing by artist and selected B.B. King, the list of my B.B. King music was displayed (see Figure 4.6).

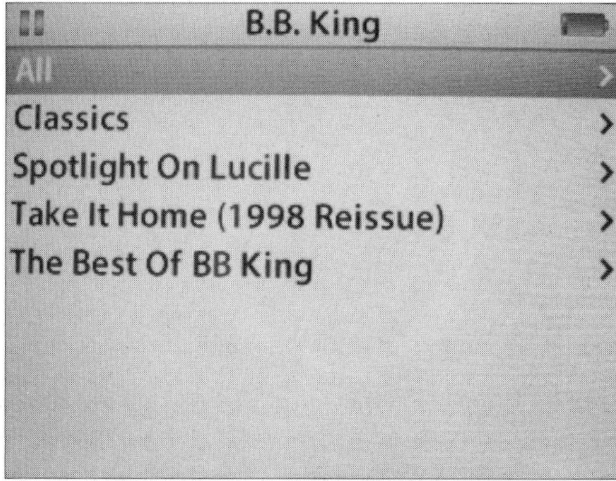

FIGURE 4.6
This artist screen shows all the music on this iPod by B.B. King.

5. To move down to the next level of detail, select an item on the current list and click the **Select** button. The resulting screen will show you the contents of what you selected. For example, I selected the B.B. King album called *Spotlight on Lucille* and saw that album's contents (see Figure 4.7).

FIGURE 4.7
Here, I am looking at the contents of a specific album by B.B. King.

6. To play everything shown on the screen, starting at the top, press the **Play/Pause** button. To start with a specific song, highlight it and press the **Play/Pause** button. The Now Playing screen will appear, and the first song or the song you selected will start to play (see Figure 4.8).

FIGURE 4.8
I drilled down to a specific album and pressed the **Play/Pause** button to hear it.

Although the previous steps used the Artists category as an example, you can browse and select music in any of the other categories in just the same way. Each time you select a category on a menu and press the **Select** button, you'll drill down into a more detailed screen for that category until you get down to (literally and figuratively) listening to the tunes you are browsing.

Searching for Music in All the Right Places

Browsing for tunes is great, but there might be situations in which you want to jump to specific tunes. Perhaps you've just got to hear all the versions of the classic song "Ghost Riders in the Sky," and you've got to hear them right now. You could browse by categories to find the song, which would work but could take a while. A better way would be to use the iPod's Search function to move directly to the tunes you want to hear. Here's how:

1. Select **Main** menu, **Music**. You'll see the now very familiar Music menu.
2. Select **Search**. You'll see the iPod's Search screen (see Figure 4.9). At the bottom of the screen, you'll see the characters you can use to create a search term, which are all the letters of the alphabet plus the numbers 0–9, the Delete character (the left-facing arrow), and the Done option. The *a* will be highlighted by default.

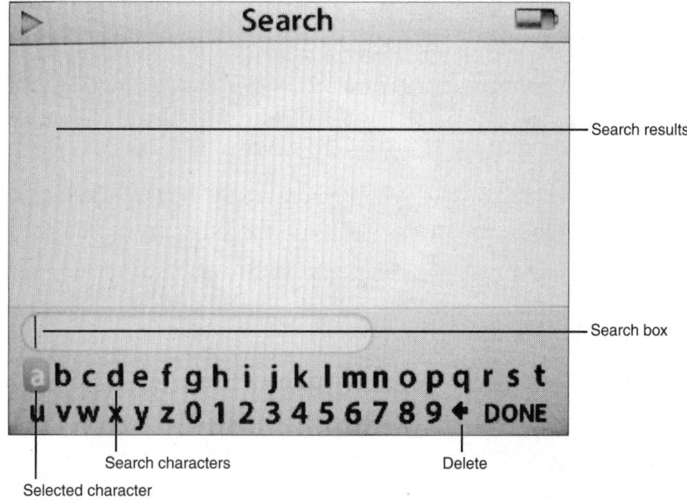

FIGURE 4.9 Using the iPod's Search screen, you can search for music that you want to hear.

To create a search term, you highlight each character in the term you want to use and press the **Select** button to add it to the Search box.

3. Slide a digit around the Click Wheel until the first character you want to enter is highlighted, and press the **Select** button. That character will move into the Search box, and the songs and albums that contain that character in their titles will be shown in the Search results area of the screen (see Figure 4.10). To the right of the Search box, you'll see the number of songs that meet your search.

FIGURE 4.10
As you enter each character of your search term, your iPod searches for songs with which that character is associated.

4. Use the Click Wheel to highlight the second character in your search, and press the **Select** button. That character will be added to the search term, and the songs shown in the Results section will be reduced to include only those containing both characters.

   To remove a character you just entered, select the **Delete** character and press the **Select** button.

5. Repeat step 4 until you've found the songs or albums you are searching for (see Figure 4.11). Albums will be marked with the Album icon, which looks sort of like a CD.
6. When the results shown contain the music you want to listen to, choose **Done**. You'll move to the Search Results screen, which will contain only those songs and albums that met your search criteria (see Figure 4.12).
7. To play something shown on the Search Results screen, highlight it and press the **Play/Pause** button. If you select a song, you move to the Now Playing screen, and the song begins to play. If you select an album, you move to a screen showing the contents of the album; you can select a specific song to play and then press the Play/Pause button to play it or just press that button to play all the album's songs.

FIGURE 4.11
As you create a more detailed search term, the results of the search will become more focused.

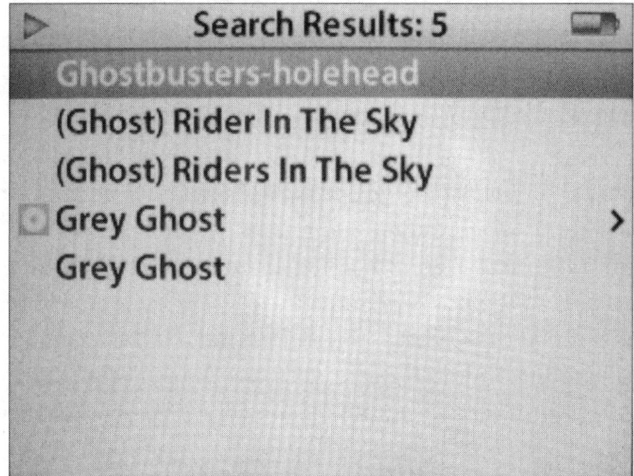

FIGURE 4.12
Got ghosts in your tunes?

After you've performed a search, your iPod will remember it so that you can move back to it at any time to explore or refine its results. You can clear the search by selecting the **Delete** option and pressing the **Select** button until all the characters are removed from the Search term.

Controlling Your Music

Okay, so now you have selected music (by browsing or searching) and started to play it. What's next? Learn to control it, of course.

Playing the Basic Way

Here are the basic controls you can use to play music:

- **Play/Pause button**—When music is not playing or is paused, pressing this button will cause it to play again. When music is playing, pressing this button will cause the music to pause.
- **Previous/Rewind button**—If you press this button once quickly, you will jump back to the start of the current song. If you press this button twice quickly, you will jump back to the start of the previous song. If you press and hold this button a while, the current song will rewind; release the button when you get to the point at which you want it to start playing again.
- **Next/Fast-forward button**—Press this button once, and you will jump to the start of the next song. Press this button and hold it, and you will fast-forward in the current song; release the button when you get to the point in the song where you want to be.
- **Click Wheel**—When the Now Playing screen is shown, drag a digit clockwise over the Click Wheel to increase the volume or counterclockwise to decrease the volume. When you touch the Click Wheel, the Volume bar will appear on the screen to indicate the current volume level visually; the shaded part of the bar represents the current volume level (see Figure 4.13). As you change the volume, the shaded area will expand or contract, depending on whether you increase or decrease the volume. A second or so after you take your finger or thumb off the Click Wheel, the Volume bar will disappear.

  You can change the volume with the Click Wheel only when the Now Playing screen is shown. That is why the Now Playing option is listed on the Main menu. You can quickly jump to this screen to change the volume when you need to.

tip

As you control your music, you can use the information at the bottom of the Now Playing screen to see where you are. You'll learn all about this screen shortly.

FIGURE 4.13
When you touch the Click Wheel, the Volume bar appears, and you can drag on the Wheel to change the volume level.

Playing the iPod Way

The basics of listening to music are cool. Now let's take a look at some of the cool iPod playback features that aren't so obvious.

tip

Remember that you move "up" the menu structure by pressing the **Menu** button.

You can move around menus while music is playing just like you can when it isn't. As you choose other menus, the music to which you are currently listening will continue to play until you pause it or choose different music and play that instead.

If music is playing and you move away from the Now Playing screen, such as to change a setting on a menu, you'll automatically move back to the Now Playing screen a couple of seconds after you release the Click Wheel. So, as long as music is playing, you'll always wind up back at this screen.

note

The Play/Pause indicator (refer to Figure 4.10) appears on every iPod screen while music (or other content, for that matter) is playing or is paused.

The Now Playing screen provides lots of information about the music that is currently playing or paused (see Figure 4.14).

At the top of the screen, you'll see the number of the current song out of the total you selected. For example, if you are playing the first song in a playlist containing 50 songs, this will be 1 of 50. This information helps you know where you are in the selected source.

FIGURE 4.14
The Now Playing screen is packed with features, some of which might not be obvious.

In the center of the screen, you will see information about the song currently selected, including the song title, artist, and album. If any of this information is too long to be shown on one line, it will begin scrolling across the screen a second or two after a song starts playing. If you have artwork associated with music in iTunes, the album art will appear next to the song's information.

At the bottom of the screen, you will see the Timeline bar. In the normal mode, this gives you a visual indication of the song's length and how much of the song you have played so far (represented by the shaded part of the bar). Under the left edge of the bar, you will see the amount of time the current song has been playing. Under the right end of the bar, you will see the time remaining to play. (This is a negative number and counts up to zero as the song plays.)

If you click the **Select** button one time, the Timeline bar changes to indicate that you can now use the Click Wheel to rewind or fast-forward (see Figure 4.15). When the Timeline bar is in this mode, you can drag the **Click Wheel** clockwise to fast-forward or counterclockwise to rewind the music. As you drag, the Playhead moves to its new location and the time information is updated. When you release the Click Wheel, the Timeline bar will return to its normal mode in a second or so.

If a song with artwork is playing on an iPod and you click the **Select** button twice, the artwork will expand so it fills most of the screen (see Figure 4.16). After the Artwork screen has appeared for more than a second or two, press the **Select** button once to return to the normal Now Playing screen. (If you press the button again quickly, you'll move to the Rating screen instead.)

FIGURE 4.15
When the Timeline bar looks like this, you can rewind or fast-forward using the Click Wheel.

FIGURE 4.16
If you like a song's album art, you can show it "full screen."

If you press the **Select** button three times, the Timeline bar will be replaced by the Rating screen. If the song currently playing has been rated, you will see the number of stars for that song (see Figure 4.17). If the song hasn't been rated, you see five dots instead (see Figure 4.18). You can rate the current song by dragging the Click Wheel clockwise to give the song more stars or counterclockwise to reduce the number of stars. A second or so after you stop touching the Click Wheel, the Timeline bar will return to its normal mode.

note

You can also rate your music in iTunes. For more information on why and how you do this, see Chapter 17, "Building, Browsing, Searching, and Playing Your iTunes Music Library."

FIGURE 4.17
You can rate your music in iTunes and display the rating on your iPod.

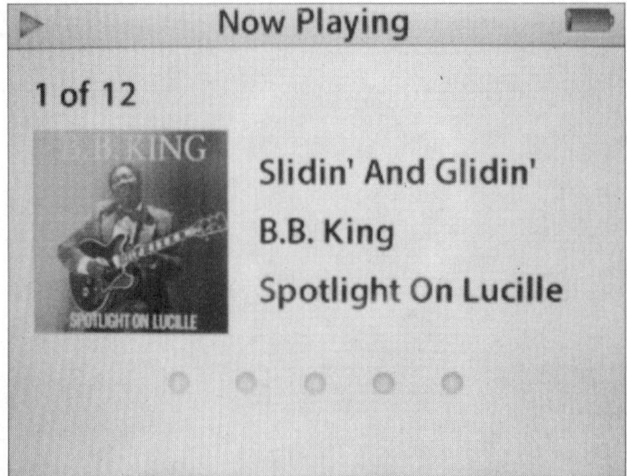

FIGURE 4.18
You can rate music on your iPod by sliding your finger around the Click Wheel until stars replace the dots shown here.

The neat thing about rating music on the iPod is that the next time you connect your iPod to your computer, the rating information you set on the iPod is carried over to that music in your iTunes Library. So you need to rate a song in only one place.

Shuffling Music

When you select and listen to a category of music, such as a specific album, the iPod will play that music in the order it appears on the related screen from top to bottom. After one song finishes, the next one will start until all the songs in the selected subcategory have played. At the point, the music will stop playing and you'll move back to the Main menu. However, there may be times when you don't want your music to play in such a linear fashion. The iPod's Shuffle Songs command was made for times like this.

By default, the Shuffle Songs command appears on the iPod's Main menu. To shuffle among all the songs on your iPod, select **Main** menu, **Shuffle Songs**. The iPod will select a song at random and play it; the Now Playing screen will appear to show what your trusty iPod has selected. In the upper-right corner of the screen, you'll see the Shuffle icon (see Figure 4.19). When that song is done, the iPod will select another and play it. This process will continue until all the songs on the iPod have played.

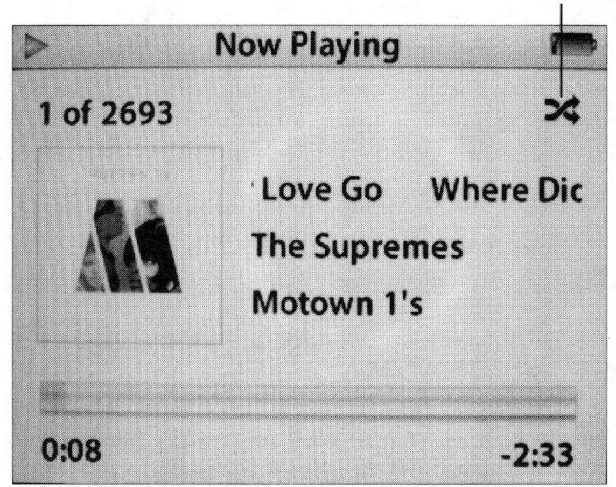

FIGURE 4.19
Using the Shuffle Songs command plays all the songs on your iPod randomly.

To move out of shuffle mode, select music in one of the categories and play it. The iPod will return to its linear ways.

The Shuffle Songs command only works on all your iPod's music; you can't choose to shuffle within a specific category (such as a playlist or album). However, you can choose whether the iPod shuffles by song or album. You'll learn how to configure this setting in Chapter 12, "Configuring an iPod to Suit Your Preferences."

note In addition to the Shuffle Songs command, there are several settings that control how music plays back, such as the Repeat setting. You'll learn about these playback settings in Chapter 12.

Creating and Using an iPod On-The-Go Playlist

Working with playlists that you create in iTunes is what you'll do most of the time, but you can also create a single playlist (called the On-The-Go playlist) on the iPod and listen to that playlist as much as you'd like. This enables you to create a playlist when you are away from your computer to listen to a specific collection of songs.

To add a song to your On-The-Go playlist, view a list—such as the list of songs on an album—on which the song is listed. Highlight the song you want to add and hold down the **Select** button until the highlighting on the song flashes. Continue adding songs using the same process until you have added a group of songs to the playlist.

tip

When you are viewing a playlist—including the On-The-Go playlist—that contains the song that is currently playing, it is marked with a speaker icon.

To see the contents of your On-The-Go playlist, select **Main** menu, **Music**, **Playlists**, **On-The-Go**; the current On-The-Go playlist will always be at the bottom of the Playlists menu. You will see the contents of the On-The-Go playlist you have created. You can play this playlist just like any other playlist on your iPod.

When you connect your iPod to your computer, the On-The-Go playlist will be transferred into iTunes and will be available on the iTunes Source List.

If you want to clear the On-The-Go playlist, select **Main** menu, **Music**, **Playlists**, **On-The-Go**, **Clear Playlist**, **Clear Playlist**. (No, that isn't a mistake; you select this command twice, but each is on a different screen.) All the songs that were in the playlist will be removed, and it will become empty again. (The songs that were in that playlist are not removed from your iPod; the playlist is just cleared of those songs.)

After you have transferred the On-The-Go playlist to your iTunes Library, you can create a new On-The-Go playlist on your iPod by using the steps you learned in this section. When you connect your iPod to your computer again, this version of the playlist will also be added to your iTunes Source List, but a sequential number will be added to its name to keep the versions straight (as in On-The-Go 14).

Each time you synch your iPod with your iTunes Library and these playlists are part of the synch options, each On-The-Go playlist will be added to your iPod. You can listen to them just as you can other playlists.

No matter how many of these playlists you accumulate, the current On-The-Go playlist will always be the last entry on the Playlists menu.

Monitoring an iPod's Battery

Even though an iPod's battery lasts a long time, it will eventually run out of juice, and your music or other content will stop playing if you happen to be listening to something at the time. (If the iPod was in sleep mode when its battery ran dry, it won't come to life when you touch a control, but will instead display the empty battery icon on its screen.) To prevent an iPod's battery from running out of juice, keep an eye on your iPod's Battery icon (see Figure 4.20). As your battery drains, the shaded part of the battery will decrease to indicate how much power you have left. When 1/4 or less is shaded, you should think about recharging your iPod. (For more information about the iPod's battery, see Chapter 13, "Maintaining an iPod and Solving Problems.")

FIGURE 4.20
This iPod's battery is running low.

THE ABSOLUTE MINIMUM

Now you know just about everything you need to listen to music on your iPod. It isn't that difficult because the iPod's controls are well designed. Not to get controlling on you, but here are a few more control points for your consideration:

- The first step in listening to music is to choose the music you want to listen to. You do this by choosing playlists or browsing your iPod's music by various categories, such as by artist, album, and so on. You can also search for specific tunes.
- After you've selected music, you can use the pretty-obvious playback controls to control it. You also learned some useful but not so obvious ways to control it.
- After you have used it for a bit, you'll find that you can easily control an iPod with a single thumb. Often, the best way to hold an iPod is to set it in your palm and use your thumb to control it. It doesn't take long until you can navigate like a pro.

continues

- When you use the Click Wheel to move around the iPod's screens or to control music, don't think you have to drag on it slowly or in small increments. You can move quite rapidly by dragging your finger or thumb quickly. The faster you move your finger, the faster things will happen on your iPod. You can move even faster by moving your digit in complete circles.
- If you want to have a nonlinear musical experience, check out the iPod's Shuffle Songs command.
- You can use the On-The-Go playlist to create a playlist on the iPod.
- As you play your tunes, keep an eye on your iPod's battery so you don't run out of power at an inopportune (pun intended) time.

IN THIS CHAPTER

- Get your shuffle's groove on.
- Turn on your shuffle, control it, and then turn it off.
- Put your shuffle on Hold if you need to.
- Keep an eye on your battery status so your shuffle doesn't run out of gas...whoops, I mean, electricity.

LISTENING TO MUSIC ON AN IPOD SHUFFLE

The iPod shuffle is the most different member of the iPod family. Although sometimes having someone so different in a human family can be not such a good thing (you know, like that Uncle Fred of yours who no one ever talks about), the shuffle is very different in a good way. One of the "good" things about the shuffle is that it is simple to use. The previous two chapters were required to go into all the details of playing audio and video on the other iPods, but this short chapter will tell you all you need to know about playing audio on a shuffle.

Getting Ready to Play

To hear the good stuff stored on your iPod shuffle, you must attach a sound output device to it. The most common one you might think of is the earbud headphones that were included in its package.

To use these, you connect the mini-jack connector on the earbud cable to the Headphone jack located on the top of the iPod shuffle (see Figure 5.1). When you do so, you'll hear any sound coming from the iPod through the earbuds.

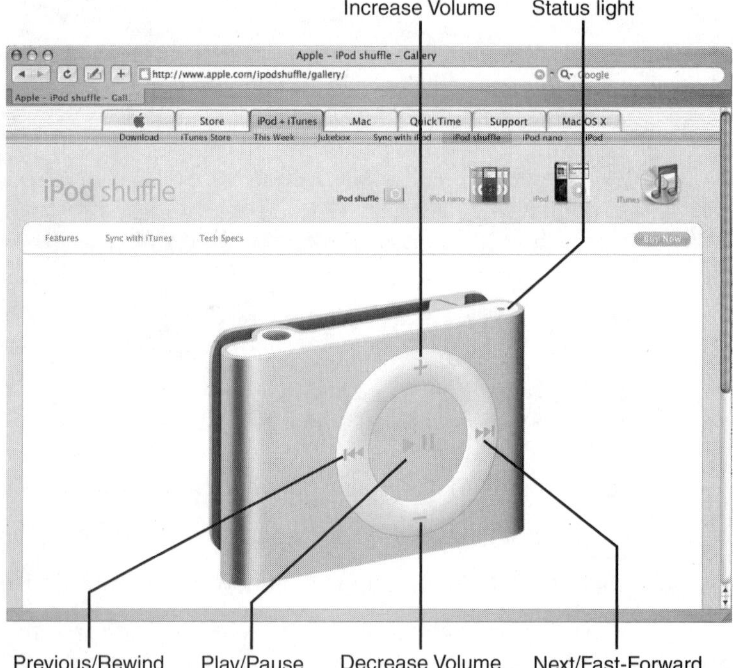

FIGURE 5.1
It's easy to figure out where to plug headphones into a shuffle because there is only one option.

Although you are likely to use earbuds or other headphones with an iPod shuffle, those are certainly not the only audio output devices through which you can play a shuffle's music. For example, you can also connect this jack to powered speakers to hear the shuffle's tunes on those speakers. Using an adapter, you can also connect the shuffle to a home stereo receiver or other audio device.

Turning On, Controlling, and Turning Off an iPod shuffle

Playing music on a shuffle couldn't be much easier. First, you choose how you want the music to play. Then you use the shuffle's simple controls to control that music. When you are finished, you turn off the shuffle.

Turning On a shuffle and Choosing How Music Will Play

One limitation of a shuffle is that you can't select the music that plays on it. You can, however, choose whether the music plays in the order you loaded it from the first song to the last or choose to have the music play at random, with the iPod shuffle choosing the order in which the music plays.

To get the shuffle going, slide the Power slider on the bottom side of the shuffle's case; the Power slider is marked with the word "Off." To turn it on, move the slider away from Off. The green area under the slider will be exposed, and the green power light will illuminate to show you that the shuffle is ready to play.

Use the other slider to determine whether the shuffle will play its music in order or by shuffling it. With the slider on the "circular arrow" side, the music will play straight through. With the slider in the shuffle position (the icon is the same as in iTunes, which is the criss-crossed arrows), the shuffle will shuffle its content while it plays.

tip

Although I mostly refer to playing music on the shuffle, it will play any audio content in your iTunes Library just as well, including audiobooks and podcasts. If you can load it in your iTunes Library, the shuffle can play it—except for video, of course.

Using the iPod shuffle's Playback Controls

After the shuffle is powered up and ready to go, controlling it is a snap. You use the controls on the Control pad to play, pause, change the volume, and so on (refer to Figure 5.1).

The following controls are available on the Control pad:

- **Play/Pause**—When the music is stopped, pressing this makes it play. When music is playing, pressing this pauses it. (If you keep this button pressed down for a couple of seconds, it also puts the shuffle on hold; more on that in a bit.)
- **Increase Volume**—Press and hold this one to increase the volume.
- **Next/Fast-Forward**—Press this once to move to the next song. Press it and hold it down to fast-forward in a song.

Using the Next or Previous button is affected by whether you have the shuffle set to shuffle or to play in order. For example, if you have the shuffle shuffling and press the **Next** button, you'll move to the next song at random, not in the order in which songs are loaded onto the shuffle.

- **Decrease Volume**—Press and hold this one down to decrease the volume.
- **Previous/Rewind**—Press this once to move to the previous song. Press it and hold it down to rewind within a song.

Each time you press a button, the green status light on the top of the shuffle will light up to indicate that your input was received. It will go out as soon as you stop using the control.

Turning Off an iPod shuffle

When you are finished playing music, you should turn off the shuffle to conserve battery power. To do so, slide the slider on the bottom to the Off position; if you don't see green in the slider, you know the shuffle is powered down.

Putting an iPod shuffle on Hold

Because the shuffle is so small and light, you are likely to stuff it in a pocket or clip it in some other place where it might get jostled. If it gets jostled in just the right place, one of the buttons might get pushed accidentally and disrupt your musical experience. And we can't have that!

To inactivate the buttons on the shuffle, press the **Play/Pause** button and hold it for about three seconds; the status light will remain green while you are holding the button down. When it blinks orange, the shuffle is in Hold mode, and its controls will have no effect. If you press a button while your shuffle is on hold, the status light will blink orange so you know the shuffle is still in Hold mode, but the control itself will have no effect.

To make the controls active again, press and hold the **Play/Pause** button for about three seconds. When the status light blinks green, release the button. The shuffle's controls will be active again.

Monitoring an iPod shuffle's Battery

Just like all iPods, the shuffle has an internal battery. You should monitor its charge level periodically so you don't run out of music.

When you turn the shuffle on, the Power light on the bottom of the shuffle will illuminate for a second or two. If it is green, your shuffle has plenty of charge; if it is yellow, you should think about recharging your shuffle soon. If it is red, your world is about to become a lot quieter, so get thee to your shuffle's Dock immediately. (Don't worry too much. If your shuffle does run out of juice, no damage will be done. You just won't be able to use it again until you recharge it.)

Remember that every time you plug your shuffle into its Dock that is connected to your computer, its battery will be charged. And, as you'll learn in Chapter 13, "Maintaining an iPod and Solving Problems," it is actually good for an iPod's battery to be charged frequently. So, it's a good idea to plug your shuffle into its Dock regularly, whether you have been listening to it a lot or not.

tip

If you use your iPod to listen to audiobooks or podcasts, you probably don't want to use the shuffle setting because you might hear things out of order. Also, if you've set an item's option in the iTunes Info window so that it is skipped when shuffling (you'll learn about that in Part II, "iTunes"), it might not play on the shuffle at all when you use the Shuffle mode.

The Absolute Minimum

This is a short chapter because there just isn't that much to controlling a shuffle. But, in case your mind wandered, here are the highlights:

- You can listen to a shuffle's music with the included earbuds, but you can also connect it to a set of powered speakers.
- Turn on a shuffle and choose how its music will play (straight through or shuffling), using the sliders on the bottom of its case.
- Use the Control pad to control music playback and volume.
- Use the Power slider to turn off the shuffle when you are finished with it.
- Use the Hold mode to prevent unintentional control presses.
- Check on the shuffle's battery every so often by looking at the light next to the Power slider when you turn it on.
- If you've read this chapter and don't have a shuffle yet, what are you waiting for? Shuffles make great companions to your other iPods. (Don't worry, they won't get jealous.)

In This Chapter

- Get an overview of how to build your iTunes music Library.
- Determine how much iPod space you need and how much you have available.
- Understand and configure your iPod music synchronization options.
- Synchronize specific playlists on your iPod automatically.
- Manage your iPod's music manually.
- Manage the music on an iPod shuffle.
- Use the same iPod with more than one computer.
- Use more than one iPod with the same computer.

6

Building an iPod's Music Library

The first time you connect your iPod to your computer, all the music in your iTunes Library will be transferred to your iPod automatically—that is, all the music that *fits* within the iPod's disk or memory space limitations. If your iPod has enough storage space to hold all your iTunes music, then everything is just fine. However, as you build your iTunes Library, there may come a day when this isn't true anymore and you can't just let everything run on automatic to keep your iPod's music Library current. That's where this chapter comes in. Here, you'll learn how to take control over the music stored on your iPod, especially if your iPod's storage space isn't large enough to hold all your iTunes music.

FOR IPOD SHUFFLE READERS

If you use an iPod shuffle, and only an iPod shuffle, most of this chapter doesn't apply to you. Like just about everything else you do with an iPod, you manage the music on a shuffle quite differently from how you manage music with the other iPod models. So, if you are an iPod shuffle-only user, you can skip to the section "Adding Music to an iPod Shuffle" on **page 91**.

Creating an iTunes Music Library

As you learned in Chapter 2, "Getting Started with an iPod," and read in each of the subsequent chapters, you manage the music and other content you store on your iPod with iTunes. The iTunes Library and the playlists you create within iTunes are the sources of music you listen to with an iPod (along with all the other content on your iPod, such as audiobooks and video). The two general steps to creating these music sources are building your iTunes Library and creating iTunes playlists.

Building an iTunes Music Library

You can get music for your iTunes Library from three main sources: audio CDs, the iTunes Store, and the Internet. Although the specific steps you use to add music from these various sources to your Library are a bit different, the end result is the same. Your iTunes Library will contain all the music in your collection.

I don't provide the details of building and managing an iTunes Library here because Part II is dedicated to iTunes and provides all the information you need to use this excellent application. The chapters that specifically focus on building your Library are Chapter 17, "Building, Browsing, Searching, and Playing Your iTunes Music Library," and Chapter 18, "Labeling, Categorizing, and Configuring Your Music," but you'll also want to read Chapters 14–16 to install and learn how to use iTunes.

Creating iTunes Playlists

From the earlier chapters in this part of the book, you learned that the playlists stored within iTunes are transferred to your iPod so you can listen to them. You create and manage these playlists within iTunes. Chapter 19, "Creating, Configuring, and Using Playlists," provides an in-depth look at playlists and gives you all the information you need to create and manage your playlists in iTunes.

Remember that there is one special playlist, called the *On-The-Go playlist*, that you can create on the iPod (except the shuffle).

Assessing the Size of Your iTunes Library and How Much Space Your iPod Has

To determine how you are going to have to manage the music on your iPod, you need to understand how large your iTunes Library is and how much storage space is available on your iPod. This information will determine the way in which you build and maintain your iPod's contents, including the music you store on it.

Determining the Size of Your iTunes Library

You can determine how much storage space you need to move your entire iTunes Library in just a few steps. Open iTunes. Select **Music** in the Source list. In List view with the Browser open, select **All** in the Genre, Artist, and Album columns. The iTunes Content pane will show all the music you have placed in your Library. Look at the Source Information area at the bottom of the iTunes window (see Figure 6.1). Here, you will see the number of items, the total playing time, and the disk space required to store all the music content in your iTunes Library. The number you should be most interested in is the disk space required, because that is what you use to determine whether all the Library's content can fit in your iPod's available memory space. Make a note of this number.

FIGURE 6.1
At this point in time, the music content in my iTunes Library required 14.33GB of disk space.

If you have other kinds of content in your iTunes Library, which you probably will, you'll need to determine the total space required to store each kind of content. The total of the space you'll need for each type of content will determine how much memory your iPod has to have to be able to contain your entire collection. For example, to find out how much disk space your TV shows require, select the **TV Shows** source. The Source information will be updated to reflect that source (see Figure 6.2). Make a note of how much space that source requires.

> **tip**
>
> You can use the information in this section to be precise about managing your iPod's storage. However, you can also just try to move content onto it to see whether you have enough room or not. If you run out of room, you'll know you need to be more careful about how much you try to store on the iPod. You won't cause any problems by using this trial-and-error method.

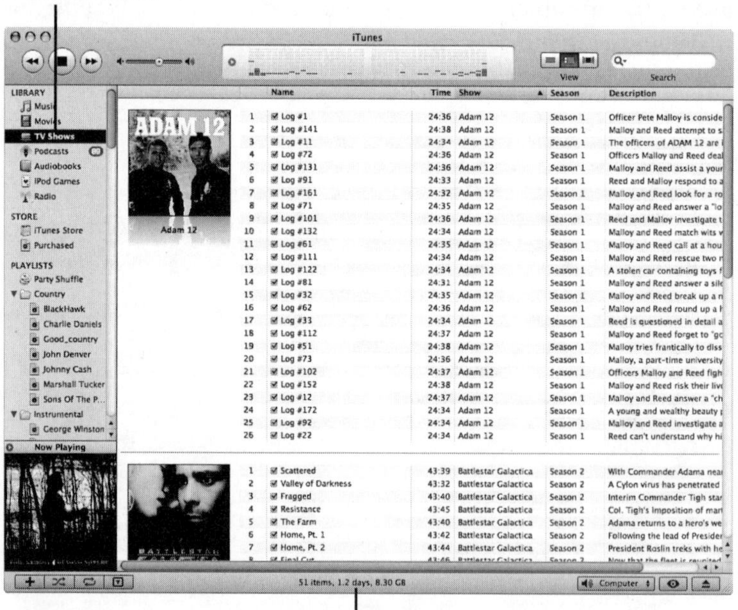

FIGURE 6.2
Because the TV Shows source is selected, you can see that this iTunes Library has 8.3GB of TV shows stored in it.

Repeat the process of selecting sources until you've determined how much space each source takes. (Ignore any sources whose content you aren't going to move onto the iPod.) Add the amount for each source together. This will tell you how much space you need to store your entire Library.

However, this doesn't quite tell the whole story. One type of content that can be stored on an iPod but that doesn't come from your iTunes Library is photos.

Because photos aren't actually stored in your iTunes Library but instead are moved from where they are stored onto the iPod through iTunes, you can't figure out how much storage space you'll need to add photos to your iPod, too. If you do store photos on an iPod, you'll just have to experiment to see whether all of your photos will fit on the iPod or you'll be able only to store selected photos there.

You can select the content you want iTunes to move from its Library onto an iPod, so if your iPod isn't large enough to hold all your iTunes content plus photos, you can determine exactly which content is moved onto the iPod.

note

You can also store contact and calendar information on an iPod. However, these items are not likely to take up much room, so you usually don't have to worry about figuring out how much space they'll require.

Determining How Much Storage Space You Have on an iPod

There are three ways to determine how much storage space you have on your iPod.

One is to refer to the documentation that came with your iPod, or perhaps you can simply remember the size of iPod you purchased. At press time, the possibilities were about 2GB, 4GB, or 8GB for an iPod nano; 30GB or 80GB for an iPod; or 1GB for an iPod shuffle. This method is easy and provides a pretty good estimate of the storage capability of your iPod.

If you want to determine the disk space on an iPod or iPod nano more accurately, you can get this information directly from the iPod. To do this, select **Main** menu, **Settings**, **About**. On the resulting About menu, you'll see the capacity of your iPod's memory, along with information about the items currently stored on it, such as the number of videos and photos (see Figure 6.3).

The capacity shown on the About menu is the amount of storage space available for all the content you can place on the iPod. Some space is required to store the files needed for the iPod to function; this is the reason the capacity you see will always be slightly less than the rated size of the iPod's disk.

You can also get information about the status of the iPod's disk by connecting it to your computer and selecting it on the Source list. The Content pane will be filled with the Summary tab of the iPod screen, which you'll learn a lot more about in this and subsequent chapters (see Figure 6.4). At the bottom of the pane, you'll see the Capacity information for the iPod. This bar shows the total space available for the iPod. Within the bar, you'll see a representation of how much space is being used by each type of content, including audio, video, photos, and other (such as contacts and games). Each type of content is color-coded in the bar, and you also see exactly how much space is being used next to the type in the legend. The farthest right section of the bar represents the free space on the iPod, which is the additional room available for more content.

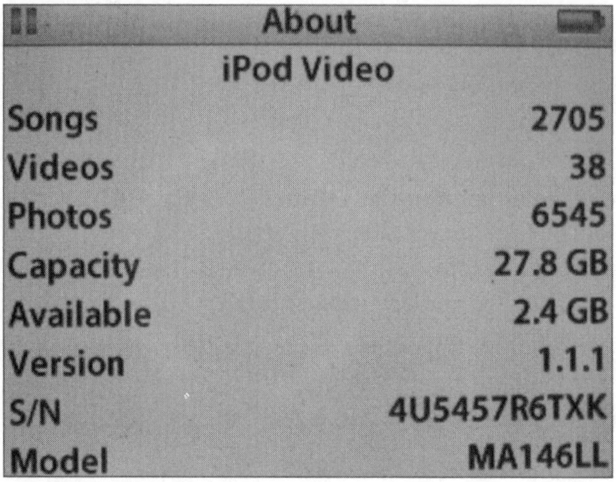

FIGURE 6.3
This iPod has a disk capacity of 27.8GB (it's a 30GB model) and currently has 2.4GB of space available.

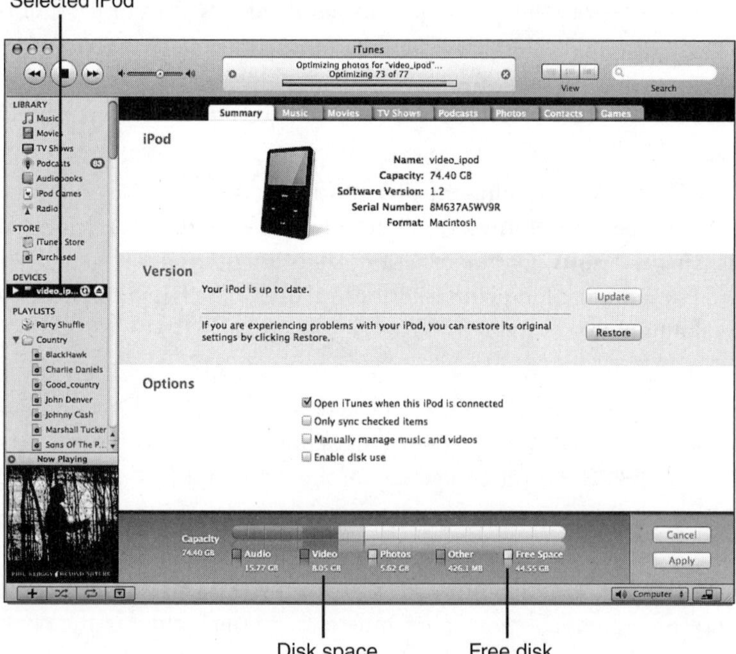

FIGURE 6.4
This 80GB iPod has lots of room to spare.

Understanding and Configuring iPod Music Synchronization Options

After you know how much space you need to store your iTunes content (the size of your iTunes Library, if you want to store all kinds of content on the iPod) and how much space is available on your iPod (its disk capacity), you can choose how you want to build and manage your iPod's music Library.

note Each kind of content you store on an iPod has its own synchronization options. For example, if you use an iPod that can play video, you set its Movies and TV Shows options to determine how video content gets placed on it. You'll learn about the other synchronization options in the related chapters, such as in Chapter 10, "Using an iPod to Watch Video," where you'll learn about setting those very video options.

Understanding Your Music Synchronization Options

Three basic options are available for managing the library of music on your iPod:

- **Automatically sync all songs and playlists**—When you use this method, the entire process is automatic; iTunes ensures your iPod's music Library is an exact copy of the music in your iTunes Library each time you connect your iPod to your computer. This is the ideal method because you don't have to do any additional work, and you always have all your music on your iPod.
- **Automatically sync selected playlists only**—When you use this method, iTunes still manages the synchronization process for you, but it synchronizes only specific playlists that you select. This option is useful when you have more music in your iTunes Library than will fit on your iPod and don't want to have to manage your iPod's music manually. Each time the playlists you select change, the music on your iPod is synchronized automatically.
- **Manually manage music**—When you use this method, you manually move songs and playlists onto your iPod. This option is mostly useful in special situations, such as when you want to use the same iPod with more than one computer. It can also be useful if you have a large music library and use an iPod with a relatively small amount of storage space, because you can be very specific about how you fill that space.

The first time you connected your iPod to your computer, an automatic method was used to move songs onto your iPod. However, if there were more songs in your iTunes Library than could be stored on your iPod, some slight of hand was done by iTunes so you wouldn't have to get into the details of this process before listening to music on your iPod. In that case, iTunes created a playlist containing a selection of your music that would fit on your iPod, and iTunes moved that music to your iPod so you could listen to it.

After the first time you connect an iPod to your computer, you should choose the synchronization method you want to use. Finding the right method for you is a matter of your iPod's memory and your preference, but I can provide some general guidelines for you.

If all the music and other content in your iTunes Library will fit onto your iPod (the space required for your iTunes Library is less than your iPod's disk capacity), I recommend you use the All songs and playlists option. This option is the easiest because it requires literally no work on your part. Each time you connect your iPod to your computer, the synchronization process is performed automatically, and you will have your complete music collection available on your iPod. With this option, all the music in your iTunes Library is moved to your iPod, along with the playlists you have created. So, even if some music is not contained in at least one playlist, it still gets moved onto the iPod.

> **note**
>
> Even if you have enough space on your iPod for all your iTunes music, you can still choose one of the other synchronization options if it suits your preferences better. Or, you might not have enough disk space to store all your iTunes Library and other content (such as photos or video) on the iPod, and you want to make sure you have enough room for the other content you want to store. Use the **Selected playlists** or **Manually manage** option to limit the music moved onto the iPod to make more room for other kinds of content.

If your iPod isn't large enough to store your entire Library and you take full advantage of iTunes playlists to create collections of music to which you listen, using the option **Selected playlists only** is a good choice. After you choose the playlists you want to be synchronized, iTunes handles the process of keeping them up-to-date for you so you don't have to think about it each time you connect your iPod to your computer. Of course, you need to make sure you create and can select playlists that contain the music you want to be able to listen to on your iPod. This can require some effort, but because playlists are so useful, you will likely do that work anyway so you can listen to them on your computer. And, be aware that if you use this option, *only* the music in the selected playlists is moved onto your iPod. (If you have music in your Library that isn't in a playlist you select, it won't be moved onto the iPod, even if it is from the same albums as music that is included in a playlist that gets synchronized.)

Finally, if you don't use a lot of playlists or you simply want to choose the specific music you want to place on your iPod, you can use the manual method to do so.

After you determine how you want to manage your iPod's music library, you need to configure iTunes to implement your decision.

Understanding How iTunes Synchronizes Playlists on the iPod

When iTunes moves a playlist onto your iPod, it first takes a "snapshot" of that playlist and places that snapshot on the iPod. If you change the playlist in some way, the next time you synchronize your iPod, the previous "snapshot" is replaced by the new version of the playlist. For example, suppose you have a smart playlist that is dynamic and plays the 50 songs you have played most frequently. As you listen to songs in iTunes, the contents of that playlist change to reflect the songs you have listened to most often. When that playlist is moved to the iPod, it contains the songs as they were in the playlist when you performed the synchronization. The playlist on the iPod will remain unchanged until you perform the next synchronization, even though the playlist in iTunes continues to change as you listen to music. The next time you perform a synchronization and the contents of the playlist have changed, the revised playlist will replace the one currently stored on the iPod.

caution

If you use the same iPod with more than one computer, you need to be careful before selecting one of the automatic methods. When you use an automatic method, iTunes will copy the selected contents of its Library onto the iPod. When it does this, it will also remove any content on the iPod that isn't in its Library, so that the music on the iPod is an exact copy of the music selected in the iTunes Library. If you share the iPod on more than one computer, you should not use either automatic option for both computers if you have different music in the iTunes Library on each computer. Fortunately, you can leave one computer set to automatic and the others set to manual. You'll learn how to use the same iPod with more than one computer at the end of this chapter.

The same principle applies when you make changes to a playlist manually. For example, if you sort a playlist to change the order in which songs play, that order will be reflected in the playlist when you move it onto your iPod. If you change the order of the songs in the playlist again in iTunes, the next time you sync the iPod, the songs will play in the new order on the iPod.

If you use the **Selected playlists** option, when iTunes moves a playlist from its Library onto an iPod, it moves *only* the songs in that playlist onto the iPod. This can be confusing sometimes. For example, suppose you purchase an album by a specific artist and include only some of its songs in a playlist. If you move that playlist onto an iPod, only those songs by that artist that are in the playlist get moved onto the iPod. This can be confusing if you forget you've done this, and when you browse your iPod by artist, you might not be able to figure out why a song you know you have by that artist is not on your iPod. (It's because it wasn't included in a playlist that was moved onto the iPod.)

Configuring iTunes to Automatically Synchronize All Songs and Playlists

Choosing the "fully automatic" method is automatic in itself, in that this is the default option. However, should you ever need to choose this option, you can do so with the following steps:

1. Connect your iPod to your computer. (Remember Chapter 2!) iTunes will open automatically if it isn't open already, the iPod will be selected as the source, and the iPod screen will appear.
2. Click the **Music** tab of the iPod screen (see Figure 6.5).
3. Check the **Sync music** check box. You'll see a warning dialog box that explains you're about to replace all the content on your iPod (see Figure 6.6).
4. Click **Sync Music**.
5. Click the **All songs and playlists** radio button.
6. If you don't want album artwork to be displayed on your iPod for some reason (I can't think of a reason you wouldn't want this, but that doesn't mean you won't think of one), you can disable this feature by unchecking the **Display album artwork on your iPod** check box.
7. Click **Apply**. The synchronization process will start. If your iPod can store all the music in your Library, the process will continue until the sync is complete. The next time you connect your iPod to your computer, iTunes will attempt to synchronize its Library again. As long as there is enough space on your iPod, you won't need to do anything else.

tip

By default, when iTunes performs a synchronization, it moves all the songs from each affected source onto the iPod. If you don't want specific songs to be moved onto an iPod, uncheck the check box next to the songs that you don't want moved onto an iPod, and then open the Summary tab of the iPod screen and check the **Only sync checked items** check box. If a song's check box is not checked, it won't be included in the music moved onto the iPod during a synchronization.

Whichever synchronization method you choose, make sure the `OK to disconnect` message is showing on your iPod's screen before you disconnect it from your computer. It is also safe to disconnect your iPod when the large battery charging icon or battery charged icon appears on the iPod's screen.

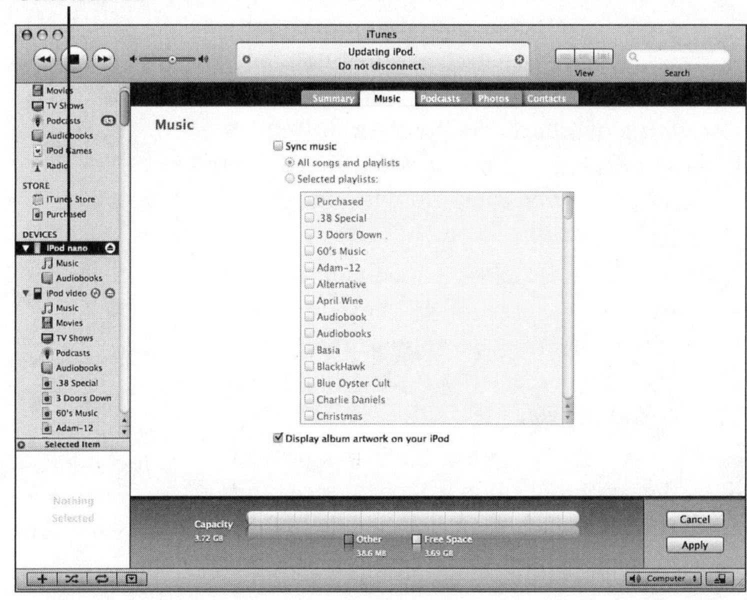

FIGURE 6.5
To choose an automatic synchronization method, start by selecting the Music tab of the iPod screen.

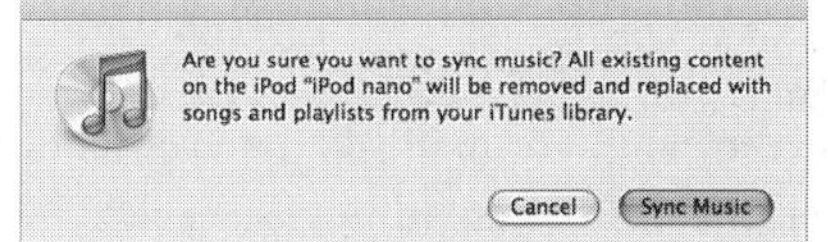

FIGURE 6.6
When you choose an automatic sync option, you'll be warned that it will replace all the contents on your iPod.

If your iPod doesn't have enough room to store all your music, you'll see a warning prompt telling you so. iTunes will offer to choose a selection of songs to put on the iPod.

If you click **Yes** in this dialog box, iTunes will create a special playlist called *nameofyouripod* Selection, where *nameofyouripod* is the name you gave your iPod when you configured it. This playlist contains a selection of music from your iTunes Library that will fit on your iPod. iTunes will move the music it selects into this playlist and then move it onto the iPod to complete the sync.

If you don't change the synchronization option, iTunes will synchronize this playlist (and only this playlist) each time you connect your iPod to your computer.

(iTunes actually changes the synchronization mode to **Selected playlists** and chooses the *nameofyouripod* Selection playlist on the playlists list on the Music tab.) You can use this playlist just like the others in your iTunes Source List, such as by adding songs to it, removing songs from it, changing their order, and so on.

If your iTunes Library is too large for your iPod's disk space, you will have to use one of the other methods to synchronize it or live with the "Selection" playlist that iTunes creates for you.

If you click **No** in the dialog box instead, the synchronization will be aborted, and you'll have to use one of the other synchronization options to put music on the iPod.

note

The tabs you see on the iPod screen will depend on the kind of iPod you connect to your computer. For example, if you don't see the Videos tab, the iPod you are using is not capable of working with video. In other words, iTunes figures out the kind of iPod you are using and presents only the appropriate tabs for that kind of iPod.

Every time you connect your iPod to your computer, the synchronization will be performed. You will see the update information in the iTunes Information window, and the update icon (it's a set of spinning curved arrows) will appear next to the iPod icon on the Source list. When the process is complete, you will see the `iPod update is complete` message in the Information window and the `OK to disconnect` or `charging` message will be displayed on the iPod's screen. Then it is safe to disconnect your iPod from your computer. Of course, you should leave the iPod connected until its battery is fully charged.

You can also activate a synchronization manually, such as when you add or change your Library while the iPod is still connected to your computer (such as creating a new playlist) after the automatic sync is done. You can do this by opening the iPod's contextual menu (right-click on its icon with a two-button mouse or Ctrl-click on its icon with a one-button mouse) and selecting **Sync**. Or, you can select **File**, **Sync *nameofyouripod***, where *nameofyouripod* is the name of your iPod. This will perform the same synchronization that is done when you connect your iPod to your computer.

caution

If you disconnect your iPod during the synchronization process, you can damage its data, such as the music it contains. This won't actually damage the iPod, but it can mess it up so much that you'll have to restore it to make it work again.

Configuring iTunes to Automatically Synchronize Selected Playlists Only

To have iTunes automatically synchronize selected playlists only, use the following steps:

1. In iTunes, create the playlists you want to place on your iPod. (See Chapter 19 for the lowdown on playlists.)
2. Connect your iPod to your computer. (Remember Chapter 2!) iTunes will open automatically if it isn't open already, the iPod will be selected as the source, and the iPod screen will appear.
3. Click the **Music** tab of the iPod screen.
4. Check the **Sync music** check box. You'll see a warning dialog box that explains you're about replace all the content on your iPod.
5. Click **Sync Music**.
6. Click the **Selected playlists** radio button. Just below this button you will see a list of all the playlists configured in your iTunes Library. Next to each is a check box. If that box is checked, that playlist will be synchronized automatically; if that box is not checked, that playlist will be ignored.
7. Check the check box next to each playlist that you want to be moved onto the iPod (see Figure 6.7).
8. If you don't want album artwork to be displayed on your iPod for some reason, you can disable this feature by unchecking the **Display album artwork on your iPod** check box.
9. Click **Apply**. The synchronization process will start. If your iPod can store all the music in the playlists that you selected, the process will continue until the synchronization is complete. The next time you connect your iPod to your computer, iTunes will attempt to synchronize the selected playlists again. As long as there is enough space on your iPod, the synchronization of these playlists will happen without any help from you, and you can skip the rest of these steps.

   If your iPod doesn't have enough room to store all the music contents of the playlists you selected, you'll see a warning prompt telling you so.
10. Click **OK** to close the warning dialog box.
11. Uncheck the check boxes for playlists to remove them from the synchronization.
12. Click **Apply**. If the music in the selected playlists will fit on the iPod, the process will start, and you're finished. If you see the warning dialog box again, that means there is still too much in the selected playlists to fit on the iPod.

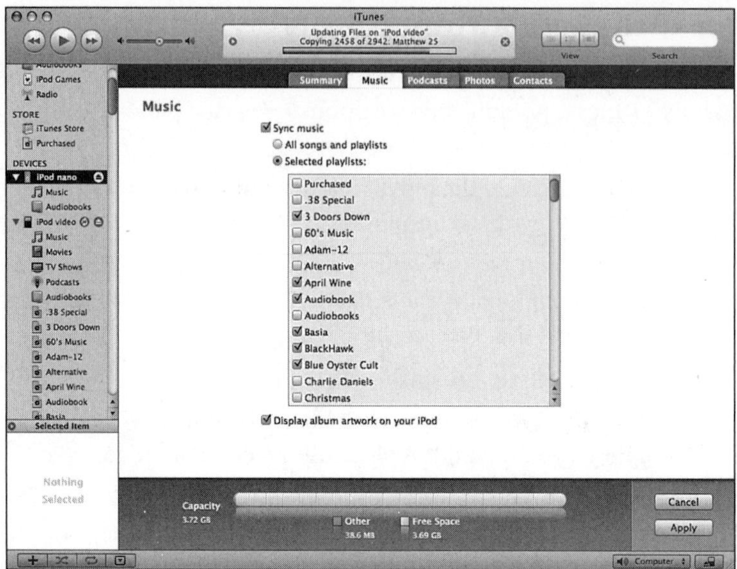

FIGURE 6.7

You can choose the playlists that are synchronized automatically by checking their check boxes.

13. Repeat steps 11 and 12 until you don't see the warning dialog box after you click **Apply**. The synchronization process will start, and the playlists you selected will be moved onto the iPod.

Over time, the contents of the playlists you selected can change. For example, if a playlist is a smart playlist and you've enabled live updating, its size can grow as you add more music to your Library. Eventually, it might grow so large that the iPod will no longer have room for the playlists you've selected. In this situation, you have two choices. You can deselect some of the playlists until the selected ones fit on your iPod, or you can remove songs from the selected playlists until they fit. (If you read Chapter 19, you'll discover that the only way to remove songs from smart playlists is to change their criteria.)

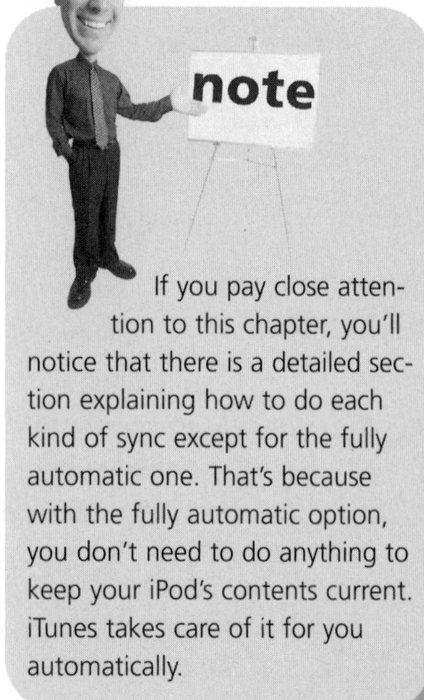

If you pay close attention to this chapter, you'll notice that there is a detailed section explaining how to do each kind of sync except for the fully automatic one. That's because with the fully automatic option, you don't need to do anything to keep your iPod's contents current. iTunes takes care of it for you automatically.

Configuring iTunes So You Can Manage Songs and Playlists Manually

When you choose this option, you manually place songs and playlists on your iPod. To choose this option, follow these steps:

1. Connect your iPod to your computer. It will appear on the Source list and will be selected. The iPod screen will appear, and synchronization will be performed according to the current settings.
2. Select the iPod for which you want to set the manual sync option.
3. Click the **Summary** tab if it isn't selected already.
4. Click the **Manually manage music and videos** (iPod) or the **Manually manage music** (iPod nano) radio button. You will see a prompt explaining that with this option, you must eject the iPod manually before disconnecting it safely. (I'll explain what this means in a later section.)
5. Click **OK** to close the prompt.
6. Click **Apply**. Nothing will appear to happen, but you'll be able to manually add or remove songs or playlists to or from the iPod. (The steps to manually move music onto an iPod appear in a later section of this chapter.)

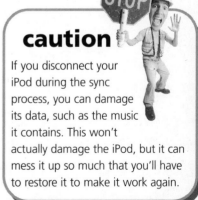

note

Smart playlists can change over time automatically. These playlists will also automatically change on your iPod each time you connect it to your computer. This is a great way to keep the music on your iPod fresh.

Synchronizing Specific Songs and Playlists Automatically

If you chose the **Selected playlists** option, the playlists you selected are updated on your iPod each time you connect it to your computer. To change the contents of your iPod's music Library, change the contents of the playlistsyou have selected to synchronize or choose a different set of playlists that you want iTunes to synchronize. When you connect the iPod to your computer, the playlists currently selected will be synchronized. For example, you can add songs to the selected playlists, remove songs from them, change a smart playlist's criteria, and so on. The next time you connect your iPod to your computer or activate the Sync command manually, the changes you made will be reflected in the iPod's version of those playlists.

caution

If you disconnect your iPod during the sync process, you can damage its data, such as the music it contains. This won't actually damage the iPod, but it can mess it up so much that you'll have to restore it to make it work again.

Every time you connect your iPod to your computer, the sync will be performed. You will see update information in the iTunes Information window, and the Sync icon will appear next to the iPod's icon on the Source list. When the process is complete, you will see the `iPod update is complete` message in the Information area, and the `OK to disconnect` or `Charging` message will be displayed on the iPod's screen. Then it is safe to disconnect your iPod from your computer.

Manually Managing the Music on an iPod

If you choose the manual option, you manually move songs and playlists onto the iPod. To do this, use the following steps:

> **tip**
>
> If you double-click a source, such as a playlist, it will open in a separate window. This can make it much easier to drag songs and playlists from the playlist to the iPod. You can also collapse the iPod on the Source list so you see more of the iTunes Source list.

1. Connect your iPod to your computer.
2. Select the iPod you want to manage. If it isn't expanded already, click the expansion triangle next to the iPod on the Source list and select the iPod's **Music** source. Under the iPod's icon on the Source list, you will see the playlists it contains. In the iTunes Content pane, you will see all the songs in the iPod's music Library (see Figure 6.8).
3. To add a playlist to the iPod, drag it from its location on the iTunes Source list and drop it on the iPod's icon (see Figure 6.9). When you are over the iPod, the plus sign will appear next to the pointer to show that you can release the mouse button. When you do so, the playlist and the songs it contains will be moved onto the iPod. During the process, the iPod sync icon will appear next to the iPod's icon on the Source list.

note
As songs are moved onto the iPod, you will see information about the process in the iTunes Information area at the top of the iTunes window.

4. To remove a playlist from the iPod, select it by clicking it in the list of playlists under the iPod and press the **Delete** key. Unless you have disabled it, you will see a prompt asking you to confirm that you want to delete the playlist. If you have disabled the warning prompt, the playlist and its songs will be removed from the iPod, and you can skip step 5.

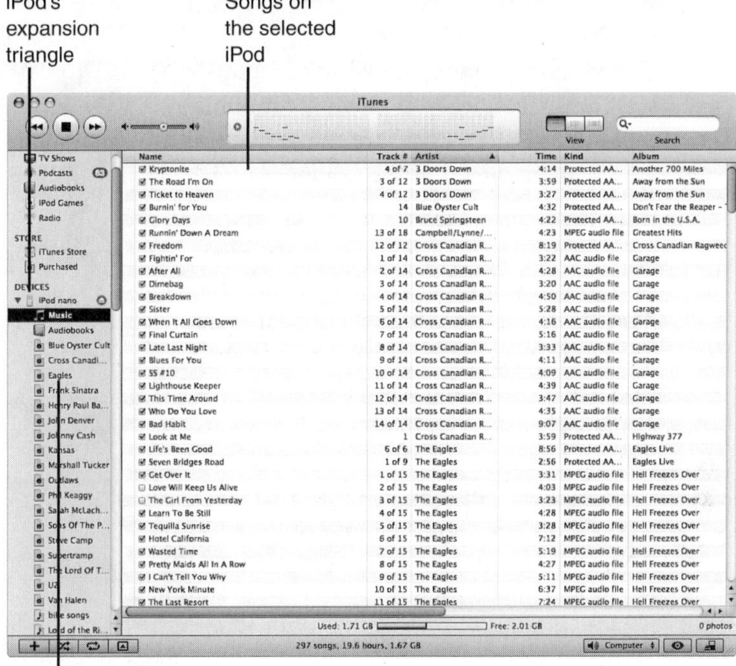

FIGURE 6.8

When you configure an iPod for manual updating, you can move songs onto it by dragging them onto its icon.

FIGURE 6.9

When you drag a playlist into an iPod, it and the songs it contains will be moved into the iPod's music Library.

5. If you see the prompt, click **OK**. The playlist will be deleted from the iPod.
6. To add songs to the iPod, select the source, such as the Library or a playlist, containing those songs. The contents of the source you select will be shown in the Content pane.
7. Drag the songs you want to add from the Content pane and drop them on the iPod's icon. When you move the pointer over the iPod's icon, the plus sign will appear to let you know you can release the mouse button to move the songs. You'll also see a number representing the number of songs you are moving onto the iPod. The songs you drop on the iPod will then be copied from the iTunes Library onto the iPod. During this process, information about it will be shown in the Information area.
8. To remove songs from the iPod, select the iPod, and then select the songs you want to remove in the Content pane and press the **Delete** key. These songs will be deleted from the iPod and will also be deleted from any playlists on the iPod containing them.
9. When you are finished updating the iPod, unmount it by selecting its icon and clicking the **Eject** button that appears next to the iPod or in the lower-right corner of the iTunes window (see Figure 6.10). After the iPod has been successfully unmounted, it will disappear from the Source list, and you will see the `OK to disconnect` message on its screen.
10. Disconnect your iPod from your computer.

When you remove a playlist from an iPod, you remove only the playlist, not the songs it contains. You can still play those songs by browsing for them.

tip

You can drag multiple songs from the Content pane onto the iPod at the same time. To select songs next to one another, hold the **Shift** key down while you select the first and last song in the group you want to move. Those songs and all the songs between them will be selected. To select multiple songs individually, hold the **Ctrl** key (Windows) or ⌘ key (Mac) while you click on each song you want to select.

tip

If you don't want to be bothered by the confirmation prompts, check the **Do not ask me again** check box.

FIGURE 6.10
Before you disconnect an iPod that you manage manually, you must eject it.

You must eject an iPod that you manually manage before disconnecting it because iTunes doesn't know when it should shut down any processes it is using that are related to the iPod. Because it is, in effect, a hard disk, the iPod must not be in use when you disconnect it; otherwise, its data can be damaged. When you do the sync manually, you need to tell iTunes that you are finished (by "ejecting" the iPod) so that it can prepare the iPod to be disconnected safely.

Adding Music to an iPod shuffle

As in all other areas, managing the music on an iPod shuffle is different. There are different sync options, and one of those is a special tool that is not available for other iPod models.

The reason for this is that unless your music library is very small, it won't fit on a shuffle because the largest memory in the current shuffle model is 1GB. So the shuffle does things a bit differently.

There are two ways to get music onto an iPod shuffle: You can use the Autofill tool to have

> **caution**
>
> Don't disconnect your iPod from your computer unless the `OK to disconnect` message is displayed on its screen. If you do so, you can damage its data. It is also safe to disconnect your iPod when the large battery charging icon or battery charged icon appears on the iPod's screen.

iTunes move music onto the shuffle for you. Or you can manually configure the songs and other audio that the shuffle contains.

Prior to updating its music, configure your shuffle's preferences.

Configuring an iPod shuffle

The shuffle also has a different set of options you can configure using the following steps:

1. Plug your shuffle into its Dock (which should be connected to your computer). iTunes will open if it isn't already, and the shuffle will appear on the Source list. The iPod screen will appear.
2. Click the **Settings** tab (see Figure 6.11).

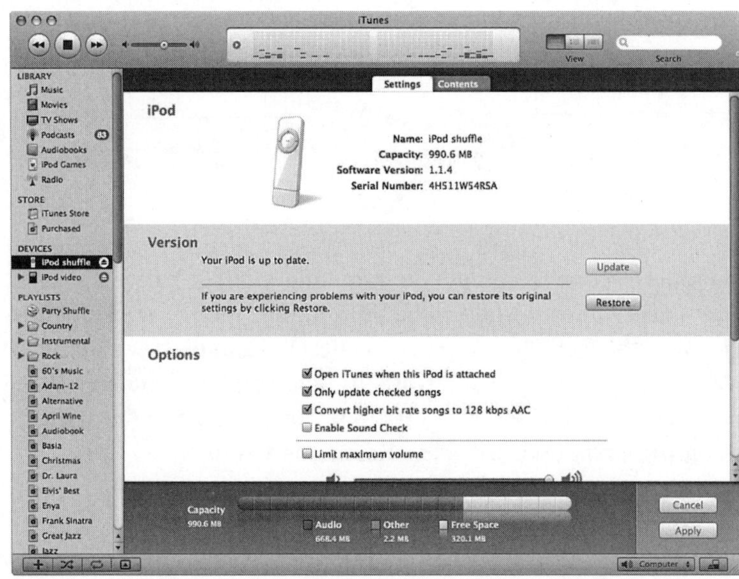

FIGURE 6.11
The iPod shuffle offers settings that are much different from those of other iPod models.

3. Configure the settings for the shuffle. The options are explained in the following list:
   - **Open iTunes when this iPod is attached**—When this is checked, which it is by default, iTunes will open whenever you plug your shuffle into its Dock (assuming the Dock is connected to your computer).
   - **Only update checked songs**—If you check this, only songs with their check boxes checked will be moved onto the shuffle.
   - **Convert higher bit rate songs to 128 kbps AAC**—This option is useful if you have a lot of music that uses a higher-quality encoder, such as Apple Lossless. With this option checked, when you put music

like this on the shuffle, it is converted into the 128Kbps AAC format so that it takes up less of the shuffle's memory. You should leave this option checked so you can get the maximum amount of content on your shuffle.

- **Enable Sound Check**—Sound Check is an iTunes function that attempts to level the volume of the audio you play so that quiet songs play more loudly and loud songs play more quietly, keeping everything at an "average" level. If you want audio on the shuffle to play with Sound Check, check the **Enable Sound Check** check box.
- **Limit maximum volume**—If you want to limit the maximum volume of the shuffle, check the **Limit maximum volume** check box and use the slider to set the relative maximum volume on the shuffle. For example, if you want to limit its volume to half its normal, place the slider at the center point of the slider's range. Use the lock icon to prevent changes to this setting, such as to prevent other people from resetting the maximum volume to a higher limit.
- **Enable disk use**—You use this check box and slider to configure a shuffle so you can use it as a flash drive. You'll learn about this in Chapter 11, "Taking the iPod Further."

4. Click **Apply**. The changes you made will take effect.

Using Autofill to Put Music on an iPod shuffle

Using the iTunes' Autofill tool, you provide the parameters for a sync, and iTunes takes care of moving music to or from the shuffle as needed, based on your criteria.

To perform an Autofill sync, perform the following steps:

1. Connect your shuffle to your computer. iTunes will open (assuming you left this preference on), the shuffle will be selected, it will appear on the Source list, and the iPod screen will open.
2. Click the **Contents** tab if it isn't selected already (see Figure 6.12).
3. Choose the source of music you want to place on the shuffle on the **Autofill from** pop-up menu. You can choose your Music source or any of your playlists. When it autofills your shuffle, iTunes will choose only music from the selected source.

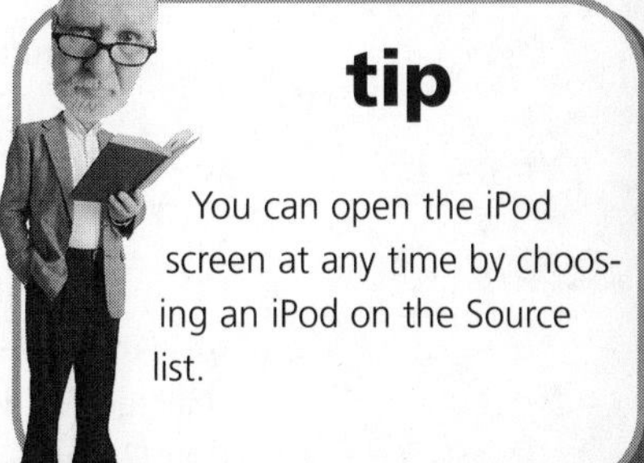

tip
You can open the iPod screen at any time by choosing an iPod on the Source list.

FIGURE 6.12
You can use the Autofill tool to place music onto an iPod shuffle.

4. If you don't want all the songs currently on the shuffle to be replaced by the Autofill, uncheck the **Replace all songs when Autofilling** check box. If this check box is checked, the entire contents of the shuffle are replaced. If it isn't checked, iTunes will try to add more songs from the Autofill until the shuffle's memory is full.
5. If you want to Autofill with songs selected at random from the source you selected in step 3, check the **Choose songs randomly** check box. If you uncheck this check box, Autofill will select songs in the order in which they are listed in the source you selected in step 3 and add them to the shuffle until its memory is full.
6. If you rate songs and want Autofill to choose higher-rated songs more frequently, check the **Choose higher rated songs more often** check box. This option is available only when you use the random option described in step 5. If you uncheck this box, Autofill will select songs truly at random and ignore your ratings.
7. Click **Autofill**. The Content pane will fill with the songs that Autofill has selected, and the sync process will start (see Figure 6.13). It will continue until the shuffle's memory is full or until all the music from the source you selected

tip

If you have elected the random option, each time you click **Autofill**, a new set of songs will be placed on your shuffle.

has been moved onto the shuffle, whichever comes first. The amount of your shuffle's memory that is being consumed will be shown on the bar just above the Source Information area at the bottom of the iTunes window.

FIGURE 6.13
This shuffle is getting filled up with the good stuff.

8. When the sync process is complete, click the **Eject** button next to the shuffle's icon on the Source list or the one located in the bottom-right corner of the iTunes window.
9. Unplug the shuffle from its Dock, and enjoy some tunes! (Of course, you should leave the shuffle plugged in to charge its battery.)

Although the focus of this section is on moving music onto a shuffle, you can move other kinds of audio, such as audiobooks or podcasts, onto it by following the same steps. To use the AutoFill tool, put whatever you want on the shuffle into a playlist. Or use the manual method to drag content onto the shuffle.

Manually Adding Songs to an iPod shuffle

You can also add songs to a shuffle manually by performing the following steps:

1. Connect your shuffle to your computer. iTunes will open (assuming you left this preference on), and the shuffle will appear on the Source list.

2. Select the source containing music that you want to place on the shuffle. You can choose music from many different sources, including the Library, Podcasts, Party Shuffle, or any playlist.
3. Drag the songs you want to place on the shuffle from the **Content** pane onto the shuffle's icon. When you are dragging songs or other content and the pointer is over the shuffle, the shuffle icon will be highlighted. You'll also see the number of songs or other items that you are currently dragging. Release the mouse button, and the songs you are dragging will be copied onto the shuffle (see Figure 6.14).

FIGURE 6.14
You can drag songs from any source onto the shuffle's icon to add those songs to it.

4. Select the next source from which you want to get music.
5. Repeat step 3 to move that source's music onto the shuffle.
6. Continue dragging songs from your sources until you have added all you want or until the shuffle's memory is full.

You can combine methods. For example, you can use Autofill and then manually add more songs. However, if you have the **Replace all**

tip

You can use the usual methods to select and drag multiple songs at the same time. Hold the **Shift** key down to select a set of songs. Or, hold the **Ctrl** key (Windows) or ⌘ key (Mac) to select multiple songs individually.

songs when Autofilling check box checked, all the songs currently on the shuffle will be replaced each time you Autofill.

Removing Songs from an iPod shuffle

You can manually remove songs from the shuffle, whether you put them there manually or they were added by Autofill.

1. Select the shuffle on the Source list and click the **Contents** tab if it isn't open already.
2. Select the songs you want to delete.
3. Press the **Delete** key.
4. If you are prompted, click **Remove**. The songs you selected will be removed from the shuffle. If you have previously checked the **Do not ask me again** check box, you won't see any prompt, and the songs will be removed immediately.

Using an iPod with More Than One Computer

You can use the same iPod with more than one computer (which I'm sure you could have guessed from this section's title). However, when you use one of the automatic sync options, an iPod is linked to the iTunes Library from which you set that option. An iPod can be linked with only one computer at a time. If you set an automatic sync option on one computer, the iPod is linked to the iTunes Library on that computer. To use it with another computer, you'll either need to replace its contents with that from the second computer (to change the computer with which it is linked) or manually manage the content of the iPod from both computers.

Use the following points to help you use the same iPod with more than one computer:

- If the iPod you are using is linked to one computer (because it has an automatic sync option set on that computer) and you plug it into a different one, iTunes will prompt you to see whether you want to replace the songs on the iPod with the selected contents on the current computer (see Figure 6.15).

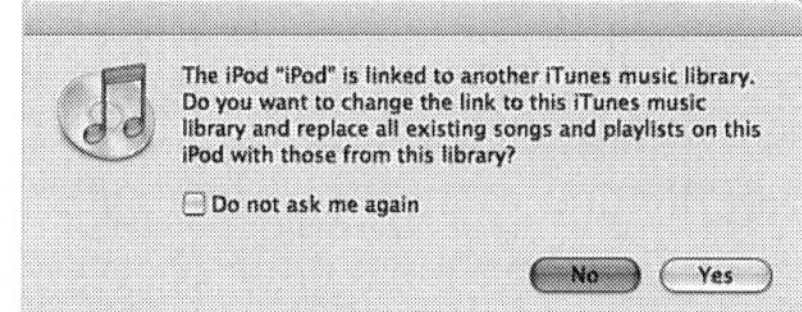

The iPod "iPod" is linked to another iTunes music library. Do you want to change the link to this iTunes music library and replace all existing songs and playlists on this iPod with those from this library?
Do not ask me again
No
Yes

FIGURE 6.15
When you've linked an iPod to one computer and then connect it to a different one, you'll see this prompt.

- When you see the prompt in Figure 6.15 and click **Yes**, the iPod will be shown on the Source list, and its current contents will be replaced by the contents of the iTunes Library on the current computer.
- If you click **No** in the prompt, the iPod will be shown on the Source List, but nothing will be done to its contents.
- To change the contents of the iPod, you'll need to set it to use the Manual option. (See the sections earlier in this chapter if you don't recall how to do this.) You can then drag content onto the iPod's icon to move it onto the iPod.
- When you plug the iPod back into the computer with which it was previously linked, nothing will happen. That's because its sync option will be set to Manual because you changed it on the second computer. You can move content manually from the current computer onto the iPod.
- If you change the sync option back to one of the automatic settings, the iPod will be linked to the iTunes Library again, and all its contents will be replaced according to the automatic option currently set. Any content from other computers will be replaced.
- So you don't accidentally replace content on the iPod, leave it set to use the Manual sync option. Each time you connect it to a computer, you'll be able to manually add or remove content from the iPod.
- You can share the same iPod with Windows and Mac computers. However, if you've used an iPod with a Mac first, you'll need to reformat it on the Windows computer. If you used it on a Windows computer first, you don't need to reformat it to use it on a Mac. You'll learn how to format an iPod later in this part of the book.

Using More Than One iPod with the Same Computer

iPods are so cool that you are likely to have more than one. That's no problem for iTunes because it recognizes each iPod uniquely. You can work with each iPod as if it is the only one you use. For example, you can set each iPod to use different sync options. Each time you connect an iPod to your computer, it will be synchronized according to the preferences you set for it.

You can also have more than one iPod connected to your computer at the same time. (If you look closely at some of the figures in this chapter, you'll see more than one iPod on the Source list.) Each iPod will be shown on the Source list, and you can work with one by selecting it. Multiple iPods can also be synced at the same time. When you select an iPod on the Source list, information about its sync process will be shown in the Information window. When you select another one, its sync information will be shown instead.

THE ABSOLUTE MINIMUM

Managing the music on your iPod is essential if you are going to be able to listen to the music you want to when the mood strikes you. Fortunately, maintaining your iPod's music Library isn't all that hard. As you build and maintain your iPod's music Library, keep the following points in mind:

- You use the iTunes application to manage the contents on your iPod.
- You can determine the amount of used and free space on an iPod in a number of ways, including by using the iPod's About command (except the shuffle). Or, you can select an iPod and use the memory information that appears just above the Source information area at the bottom of the iTunes window. This is important information so you know whether you can fit all your iTunes content on your iPod or not.
- There are three ways to synchronize the music in your iTunes Library and on your iPod.
- When you use the "fully automatic" option, this is done for you automatically, and your iPod will be synced with your current iTunes Library each time you connect the iPod to your computer.
- You can also choose to have only specific playlists synced automatically.
- You can manage the music on your iPod by manually moving content onto it as well.
- Although I've mostly focused on music in this chapter, you can use the same techniques to manage the video, audiobooks, podcasts, and other content on an iPod. In fact, if your iPod has enough room for you to use the fully automatic method, all the content in your iTunes Library will be moved onto the iPod no matter what kind of content it is. (Of course, if your iPod isn't capable of video, the Library's video content won't be moved onto it.)
- Most of this list doesn't apply to the shuffle. You sync its music by using the Autofill tool or by manually configuring its contents.
- You can share the same iPod with more than one computer, but you'll want to use the manual option so you don't accidentally replace all its contents.
- If you're lucky enough to have more than one iPod, you can use all you have with the same computer.
- If you have more than one iPod, such as an iPod and an iPod nano, you can choose different sync options for each. For example, you might want to use the Automatically sync selected playlists only option for the iPod nano and the fully automatic option for the iPod.

IN THIS CHAPTER

- Understand how to add podcasts to your iTunes Library.
- Move podcasts from your iTunes Library onto an iPod.
- Listen to or watch podcasts on an iPod.
- Remove podcasts from an iPod.

7

USING AN iPOD TO LISTEN TO AND WATCH PODCASTS

Podcasts are radio-like broadcasts (iPod plus broadcast equals *podcast*) that you can download to your iPod so you can listen to them. Podcasts are provided in segments, which are called *episodes*. When you listen to a podcast, you listen to one or more episodes. A bewildering number of podcasts are available on just about every topic you can imagine (and some that you probably can't imagine). You add podcasts to which you want to listen to your iTunes Library and then move those podcasts onto your iPod. After you have your iPod fully stocked with podcasts, you can listen to them just like music and other content you have added to it.

If you have an iPod that is capable of video, you can also watch video podcasts, which aren't really that different from audio podcasts except, of course, they also include video, making them more like TV than radio.

Building Your iTunes Podcast Library

Just as you can with music, video, and other content, you build your podcast library in iTunes and then move the podcasts you want to enjoy on an iPod from your iTunes Library onto your iPod.

Subscribing to Podcasts

To add podcasts to your iTunes Library, you subscribe to them. There are two sources of podcasts to which you can subscribe:

- **iTunes Store**—You can find thousands of audio and video podcasts in the iTunes Store. Almost all of them are free, and subscribing to a podcast is as easy as clicking its **Subscribe** button.
- **Web**—There are lots of podcasts available on the web. You can subscribe to these almost as easily as you can those in the iTunes Store.

After you've subscribed to a podcast, iTunes downloads its episodes according to the preferences you've set.

To learn how to use iTunes to subscribe to and manage podcasts, see Chapter 20, "Subscribing, and Listening to Podcasts" on page **329**.

Using the Podcasts Source

After you've subscribed to podcasts, they'll be downloaded to your iTunes Library based on the preferences you set. The podcasts in your iTunes Library are collected and managed in the Podcasts source (see Figure 7.1). Of course, you can listen to and watch them within iTunes, just as you can with content from other sources. See Chapter 20 for all the information you need to set your podcast preferences and to work with the Podcasts source.

tip

The good news is that if you subscribe to a podcast via the iTunes Store, you don't need to manually configure these settings because they are preconfigured automatically. That's true for most, but not necessarily all, podcasts that you subscribe to via websites, too.

Configuring Podcasts for Playback

In most cases, you'll want podcasts to remember where you were when you last listened to or watched them so you don't have to search for that point when you listen to or watch them again. And, you probably don't want podcasts included when you use the Shuffle feature to hear content in a random order (else you might hear an episode of a news podcast sandwiched between Elvis' *Hound Dog* and The Rolling Stones' *Satisfaction*).

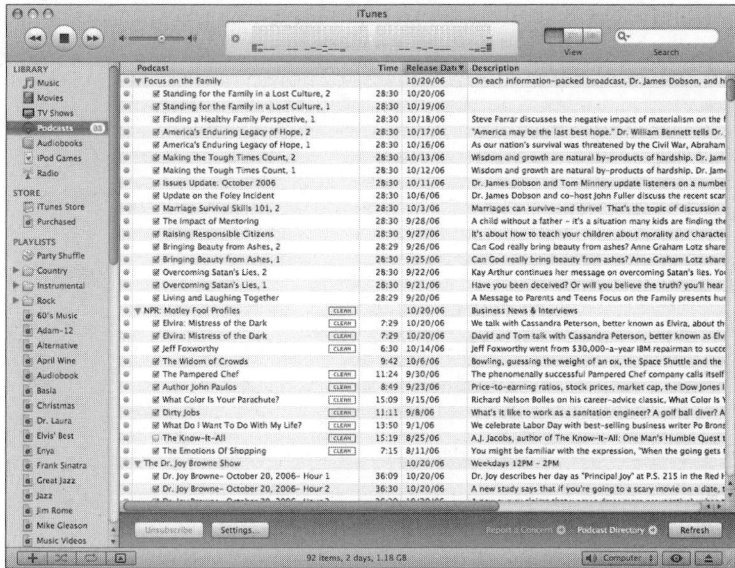

FIGURE 7.1
Want Podcasts? You got 'em!

To configure these properties, you can use the iTunes Info window, which you'll learn about in great detail in Part II, "iTunes." For now, read the following steps to learn how to configure a podcast for playback:

1. Select the episodes of the podcast you want to configure.
2. Choose **File**, **Get Info**. The Info window will appear.
3. Click the **Options** tab (see Figure 7.2).
4. Check the **Remember playback position** check box. This will cause iTunes and your iPod to remember the point at which you last listened to or watched a podcast. The next time you listen to or watch it, you'll start at this point.
5. Check the **Skip when shuffling** check box. If you listen to a source containing the podcast in the Shuffle mode, the podcast will be skipped.
6. Click **OK**.

If you stop listening to or watching a podcast before it's done and then come back to it later, such as after you've listened to music for a while, you'll pick up right where you left off.

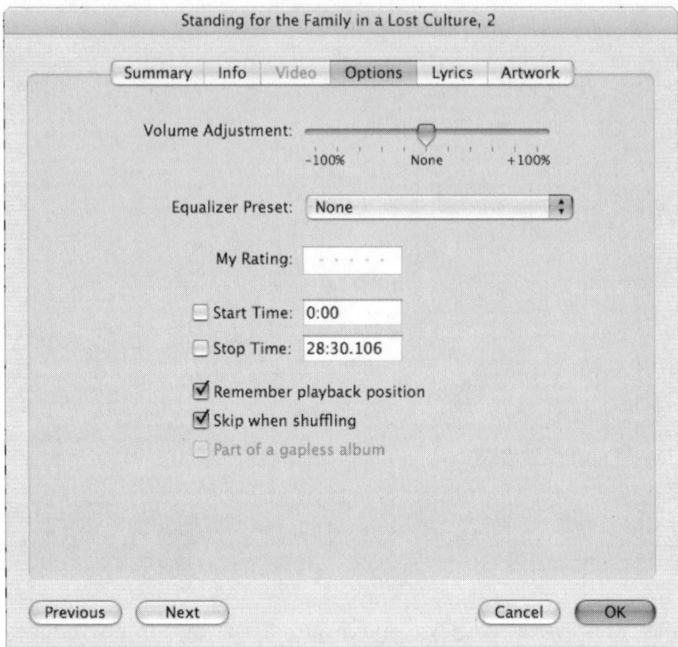

FIGURE 7.2
Use the Options tab of the Info window to configure a podcast for playback.

Moving Podcasts onto an iPod

After you have subscribed to podcasts in iTunes, you have three ways to move those podcasts onto an iPod. These are analogous to how you move music onto an iPod, so if you already know how to do that, you're more than halfway home. The three ways are the following:

- Move all your podcasts onto an iPod automatically.
- Move only selected podcasts onto your iPod automatically.
- Move podcasts onto an iPod manually.

Automatically Moving All Your Podcasts onto an iPod

To have all your podcasts moved onto an iPod automatically, perform the following steps:

1. Connect your iPod to your computer. iTunes will open, the iPod will be selected on the Source list, and the iPod screen will appear. (If your iPod is already connected to the computer, select it on the Source list.)
2. Click the **Podcasts** tab (see Figure 7.3).

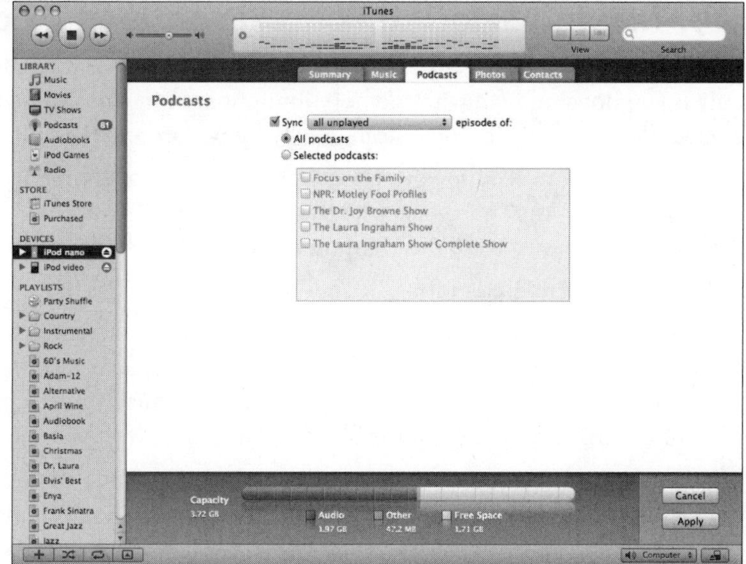

FIGURE 7.3
Use the Podcasts tab to determine how podcasts will be moved onto your iPod.

3. Check the **Sync** check box. Depending on your preferences, you might see a warning explaining that if you do this, you'll replace all the podcasts currently on your iPod with those in your iTunes music library; click **OK** to clear the warning if you see it (assuming that is okay with you, of course).
4. On the pop-up menu at the top of the screen, choose which episodes you want synced. The basic choice is between all episodes or unplayed episodes (meaning episodes to which you haven't listened using iTunes). Within each of those choices, you can choose how many of the most recent episodes you want to download to the iPod, including all of them, 1, 3, 5, or 10. For example, to have the most recent 5 episodes that you haven't played in iTunes moved to the iPod automatically, choose **5 most recent unplayed episodes**. To have all episodes downloaded to the iPod regardless of whether you've listened to them in iTunes or not, choose **all**. To have all episodes to which you haven't listened downloaded to the iPod, choose **all unplayed**.
5. Click the **All podcasts** radio button.
6. Click **Apply**. The podcasts will be moved onto the iPod according to the preferences you set. Each time you connect the iPod to your computer, its podcasts will be synched. For example, if you selected the 5 most recent unplayed option, you'll get the 5 most recent episodes that you haven't listened to of each podcast to which you've subscribed on your iPod.

Automatically Moving Selected Podcasts onto an iPod

You might not want all your podcasts to be moved onto your iPod all the time, especially if you have an iPod with memory limitations. You can choose to move only selected podcasts to your iPod automatically by performing the following steps:

1. Connect your iPod to your computer. iTunes will open, the iPod will be selected on the Source list, and the iPod screen will appear. (If your iPod is already connected to the computer, select it on the Source list.)
2. Click the **Podcasts** tab.
3. Check the **Sync** check box. Depending on your preferences, you might see a warning explaining that if you do this, you'll replace all the podcasts currently on your iPod with those in your iTunes music library; click **OK** to clear the warning if you see it (assuming that is okay with you, of course).
4. On the pop-up menu at the top of the screen, choose which episodes you want synced. The basic choice is between all episodes or unplayed episodes (meaning episodes to which you haven't listened using iTunes). Within each of those choices, you can choose how many of the most recent episodes you want to download to the iPod, including all of them, 1, 3, 5, or 10. For example, to have the most recent 5 episodes that you haven't played in iTunes moved to the iPod automatically, choose **5 most recent unplayed episodes**. To have all episodes downloaded to the iPod regardless of whether you've listened to them in iTunes or not, choose **all**. To have all episodes to which you haven't listened downloaded to the iPod, choose **all unplayed**.
5. Click the **Selected podcasts** radio button.

   In the box below the radio button, you'll see the podcasts to which you've subscribed (see Figure 7.4).
6. Check the check box next to each podcast you want to be moved onto the iPod automatically.
7. Click **Apply**. The selected podcasts will be moved onto the iPod and will be synced automatically each time you connect the iPod to the computer or when you perform a manual sync. The number of and types of episodes that will be moved onto the iPod are determined by the selection you made on the pop-up menu. For example, if you choose all unplayed, all the episodes of the selected podcasts to which you haven't listened will be moved onto the iPod.

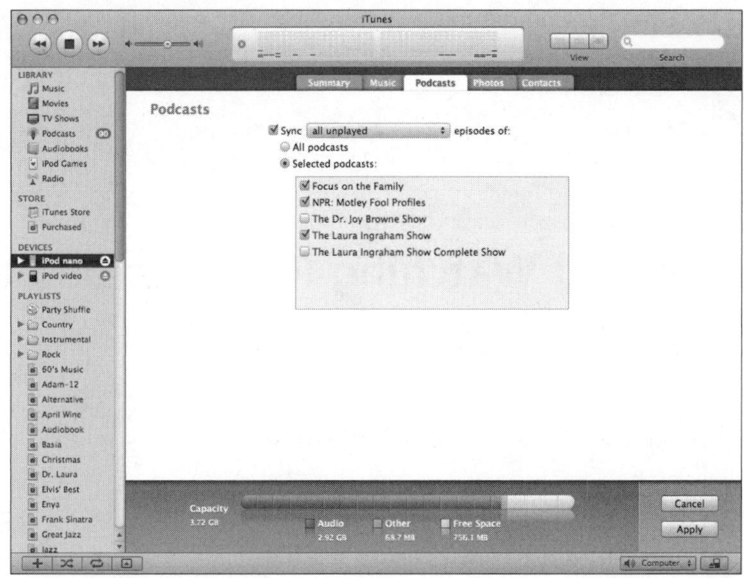

FIGURE 7.4
You can select specific podcasts to be moved onto an iPod automatically by checking their check boxes.

Manually Moving Podcasts onto an iPod

You can also move episodes of podcasts manually from iTunes onto an iPod if you don't want to use one of the automatic options for some reason. To set your preferences for manually moving podcasts, perform the following steps:

1. Connect your iPod to your computer. iTunes will open, the iPod will be selected on the Source list, and the iPod screen will appear. (If your iPod is already connected to the computer, select it on the Source list.)
2. Click the **Summary** tab.
3. Check the **Manually manage music and videos** (iPod) or **Manually manage music** (iPod nano) check box.
4. Click **Apply**.

Interestingly (well, it's interesting to me, anyway), the **Manually manage music and videos** setting controls whether you can move all types of content, including podcasts, onto an iPod. And, this setting doesn't impact the automatic settings. So you can have some podcasts moved onto the iPod automatically if you follow the steps you learned earlier, and you can move others manually by using the following steps:

1. Connect your iPod to your computer.
2. In iTunes, select **Podcasts** on the source list. You'll see all of the podcasts to which you are subscribed.

3. Drag the episodes that you want to move onto an iPod from the Content pane onto the iPod's icon on the Source list. Those episodes will be copied onto the iPod.
4. Continue moving episodes onto the iPod manually until you have added all that you want to be able to listen to on the iPod.

Listening to and Watching Podcasts on an iPod

The point of putting podcasts on an iPod is to listen to or watch them, right? That's where this section comes in.

Listening to Audio Podcasts on an iPod

After you have moved podcasts onto an iPod, perform the following steps to listen to them:

1. Choose **Main Menu**, **Music**, **Podcasts**. You'll see the Podcasts menu that lists all the podcasts stored on your iPod (see Figure 7.5).
2. Highlight the podcast to which you want to listen and press the **Select** button. You'll move to the episode menu for the podcast you selected; the menu name will be the name of the podcast. Here, you'll see all the episodes of the podcast that are stored on the iPod (see Figure 7.6).

Many podcast titles are too long to be displayed on a single line on the iPod screen. When you highlight a podcast, its name will scroll across the screen so you can read the entire name.

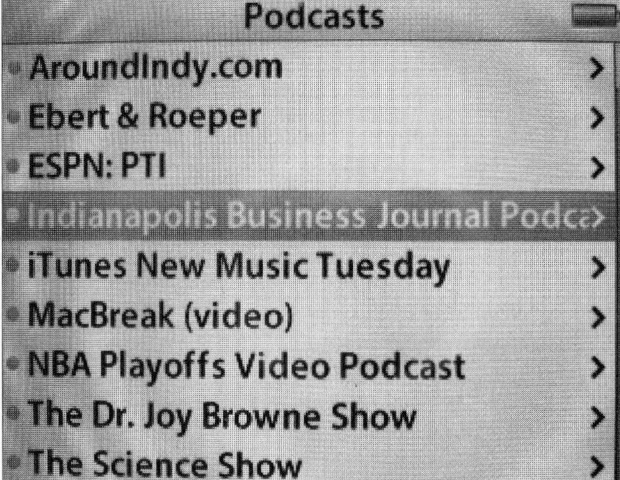

FIGURE 7.5 The Podcasts menu contains all the podcasts you have downloaded to your iPod.

FIGURE 7.6
This menu shows all of the episodes of a podcast that have been downloaded to this iPod.

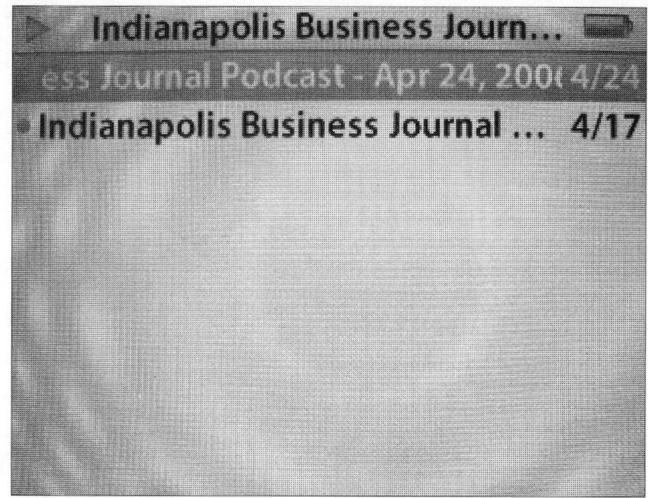

3. Highlight the episode to which you want to listen and press the **Select** button. The podcast will begin to play and you'll move to the Now Playing screen (see Figure 7.7).

FIGURE 7.7
Listening to an audio podcast isn't much different from listening to music.

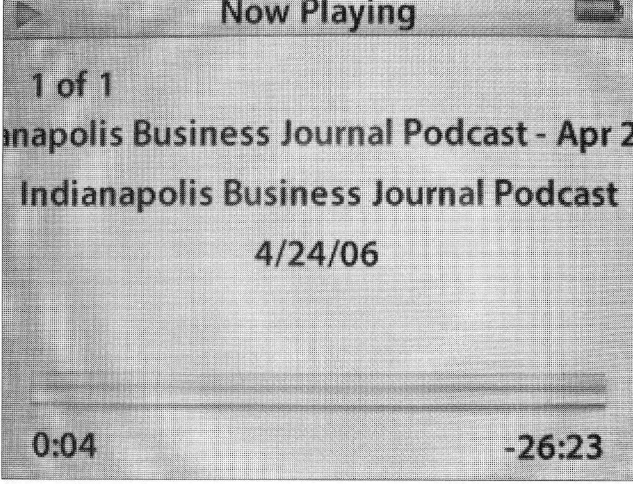

4. Control the podcast's playback using the same controls you use to listen to music. You can fast forward, rewind, and use the other controls just as you can with music. For example, press the **Select** button once to move into fast forward/rewind mode.
5. Press the **Select** button two times to see a text summary of the episode to which you are listening (see Figure 7.8).

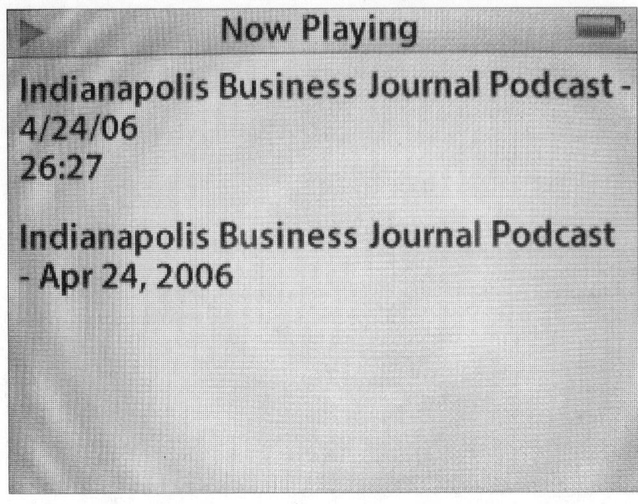

FIGURE 7.8
You can view a text summary of a podcast by clicking the **Select** button two times when the Now Playing screen is visible.

When the episode ends, you'll move back to the Main menu. Of course, you can stop the podcast at any time by clicking the **Pause** button or moving to another source and listening to it.

Watching Video Podcasts on an iPod

Watching a video podcast isn't much different from listening to an audio podcast, as the following steps demonstrate:

1. Choose **Main Menu**, **Videos**, **Video Podcasts**. You'll see the Video Podcasts menu that lists all of the video podcasts stored on your iPod (see Figure 7.9).
2. Highlight the video podcast you want to watch and press the **Select** button. You'll move to the episode menu for the podcast you selected; the menu name will be the name of the podcast. Here, you'll see all the episodes of the video podcast that are stored on the iPod (see Figure 7.10).

> **tip**
>
> If the **Remember playback position** preference is enabled for a podcast (it is by default for podcasts to which you are subscribed) and you stop a podcast to listen to or watch something else, when you come back to the podcast, it will resume playing right where you left off.

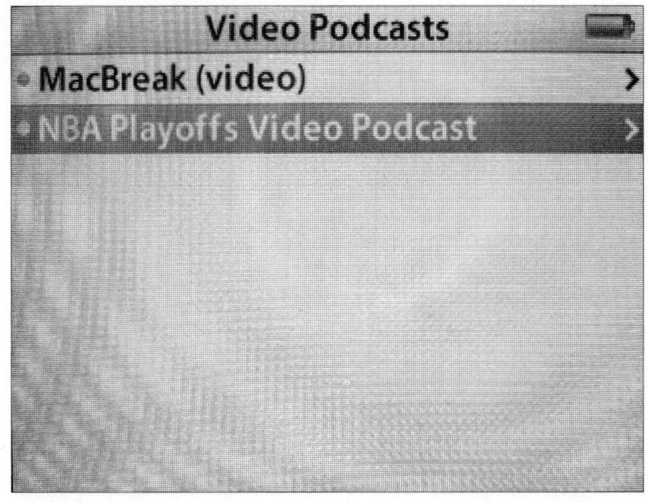

FIGURE 7.9
The Video Podcasts menu lists, amazingly enough, the video podcasts stored on your iPod.

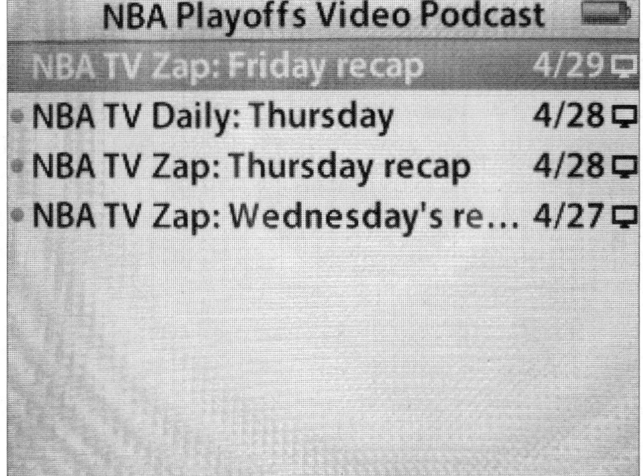

FIGURE 7.10
This menu shows the episodes of the NBA Playoffs video podcast that have been downloaded to this iPod.

3. Highlight the **episode** you want to watch and press the **Select** button. The podcast will begin to play and will fill the iPod's screen (see Figure 7.11).
4. Use the playback controls to fast forward, rewind, and so on. These work as they do for music except that if you press the **Next** or **Previous** buttons, you'll move back to the podcast's menu.

   When the episode is done playing, you'll move back to the podcast's menu. Of course, you can pause playback, or you can move to and select something else to listen to or watch at any time.

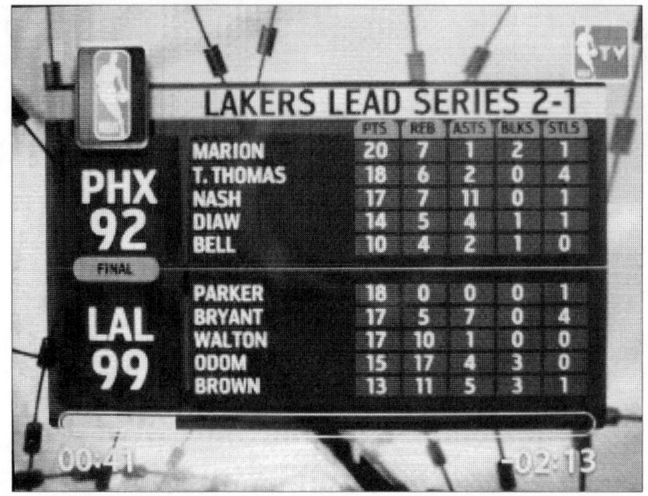

FIGURE 7.11
Video podcasts look marvelous in color. (Of course, this a black-and-white book.)

Removing Podcasts from an iPod

How you remove podcasts from an iPod depends on the sync options you have selected.

If you use the fully automatic option, the podcasts on your iPod will be replaced each time you sync the iPod according to the sync options you've selected and the podcast preferences set in iTunes. For example, if you selected one of the unplayed options, any podcasts to which you've listened on the iPod or in iTunes will be deleted from the iPod when it is synced.

When you use the **Selected podcasts** option, episodes of the podcasts you chose to sync will be replaced each time you sync the iPod.

If you configured the **Manually manage** option, you can remove episodes from an iPod with the following steps:

1. On all iPods except the shuffle, click the **Podcasts** icon listed underneath the iPod's icon on the iTunes Source list. On an iPod shuffle, select **its icon** on the Source list and then scroll in the content pane until you see the episodes that you want to remove.
2. Select the episodes that you want to delete from the iPod.
3. Press the **Delete** key. The episodes you selected will be deleted from the iPod.

THE ABSOLUTE MINIMUM

Podcasts open up a world of audio and video content for your iPod. You can find podcasts of many different types in the iTunes Store and on the Internet. After you've subscribed to podcasts, you can move them from iTunes onto your iPod in a number of ways. To get the most from podcasts on your iPod, cast your pod upon the following:

- Podcasts are episodic, just like radio or TV shows.
- Like radio, podcasts can be audio only. Video podcasts are more like TV broadcasts; of course, you need an iPod that is video capable to view a video podcast on it.
- As you can with other types of content, you place podcasts in your iTunes Library and move them from there onto an iPod for your listening and viewing pleasure.
- You can subscribe to podcasts to add them to your Library from the iTunes Store or the web.
- You can also manually download podcast files from the web and add them to your iTunes Library, but those podcasts behave like music you add rather than podcasts to which you subscribe.
- There are three ways to get podcasts onto an iPod: All podcasts are synced automatically, only selected podcasts are synced automatically, or podcasts are managed manually. You can choose to manually manage podcasts on an iPod even if you also choose one of the automatic options.
- After podcasts are on your iPod, you can enjoy them easily, whether they are of the audio-only or video type.
- Removing podcasts from an iPod is related to your selected sync option; if you choose one of the automatic sync options, iTunes manages this for you. If you choose the manual option, you'll need to delete podcasts from the iPod manually.

IN THIS CHAPTER

- Add some audiobooks to your iTunes Library's shelves.
- Configure your audiobooks with a digital bookmark.
- Move audiobooks onto your iPod.
- Hear your audiobooks on an iPod.
- Speed your audiobooks up or slow them down.

8

USING AN iPOD TO LISTEN TO AUDIOBOOKS

Audiobooks make it possible to enjoy books on your iPod. You can purchase audiobooks from the iTunes Store or Audible.com and easily add them to your iTunes Library. From there, you can even more easily move them to an iPod so you can listen to them anywhere, anytime.

Adding Audiobooks to Your iTunes Library

If you read the previous chapters, I bet you can guess that you put audiobooks in your iTunes Library before you move them onto an iPod. You can add audiobooks to your iTunes Library from several sources:

- **iTunes Store**—You can purchase audiobooks from the iTunes Store. You buy and download them from the iTunes Store just as you do music and video; after you do so, the books you buy will be added to your iTunes Library automatically. You'll learn how to do this in Part III, "The iTunes Store." The process is very fast and easy. My only complaint is the cost. Unlike music and video content, which are both relatively inexpensive, audiobooks are often quite expensive when compared to what a physical book costs.

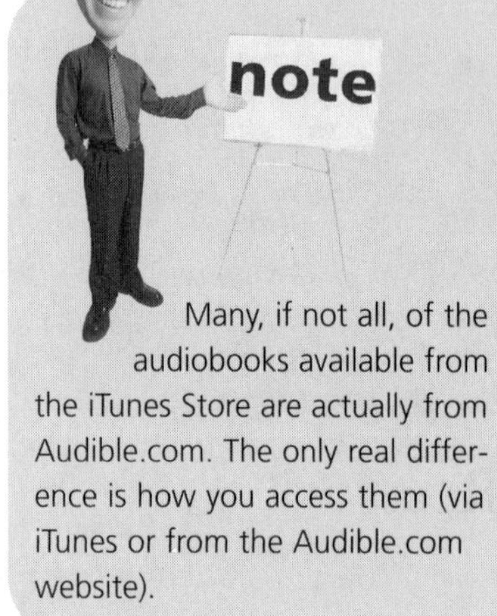

Many, if not all, of the audiobooks available from the iTunes Store are actually from Audible.com. The only real difference is how you access them (via iTunes or from the Audible.com website).

- **Audible.com**—This website offers audiobooks that are designed to work with iTunes and iPods. Just visit the site, create an account, and purchase the books you want. After they are downloaded to your computer, they will be added automatically to your iTunes Library.
- **Web**—The web contains many sites that offer audiobooks for a fee and for free. You can download these books in different formats, but most of them are offered in the MP3 format, which you can easily import into your iTunes Library. (See Part II, "iTunes," for the details of adding content to your iTunes Library, labeling it, and so on.) The audiobooks you get this way aren't quite as integrated with iTunes and iPods as those from the iTunes Store or Audible.com, but they work about as well and are often much less expensive.

tip

A good site for free audiobooks is www.gutenberg.org/audio/, which is the home page for Project Gutenberg's audiobooks. You can find many audiobooks available here for free, especially older books and classics.

- **Audio CD**—A fourth source of audiobooks are those on an audio CD that you can import into iTunes just like music CDs. Audiobooks on CD might behave like an audiobook from one of the sources described in this chapter, or they might behave like an audio CD; the behavior depends on how the audiobook CD is produced.

When you download an audiobook from the web and its filename doesn't end in `.m4b`, change its extension to that before you add it to your iTunes Library. If you do so, it will be placed in the Audiobooks source, just like audiobooks you purchase from the iTunes Store.

From whichever source you choose, you'll end up with audiobooks in your iTunes Library, whether they are placed there automatically (iTunes Store or Audible.com) or added manually (other websites). If you purchase audiobooks from the first two sources, they will be stored in the Audiobooks source in the Library section of the iTunes Source list. If you add them from the web, you might have to place them in playlists you create because they won't be added to the Audiobooks source automatically unless the filename ends in `.m4b`.

Remembering Playback Position

Unless you listen to short books or are spending a lot of time with your iPod, it's unlikely that you'll listen to an entire audiobook in one "sitting." And when you do come back to listen to an audiobook again, you'll likely want to start at the same place you stopped at the end of your previous listening session. There's an optional setting that can be applied to any content in your Library so that iTunes (and an iPod) will remember the last playback position for audio and video so that the next time that item is played, it will start playing where it was last paused.

If you obtain an audiobook from the iTunes Store or from Audible.com, this setting is preconfigured, and iTunes or an iPod will always start playing these books from where you last played them. If you obtain audiobooks from other sources, you should make sure this option is set; if not, you'll have to fast forward or rewind to find the point at which you stopped listening to a book.

To configure this setting, perform the following steps:

1. Select the audiobook you want to configure by selecting it in your iTunes Library.
2. Choose **File**, **Get Info**. The Info window will appear.
3. Click the **Options** tab (see Figure 8.1).
4. Check the **Remember playback position** check box. This will cause iTunes and your iPod to remember the point at which you last listened to the audiobook. The next time you listen to it, you'll start at this point.

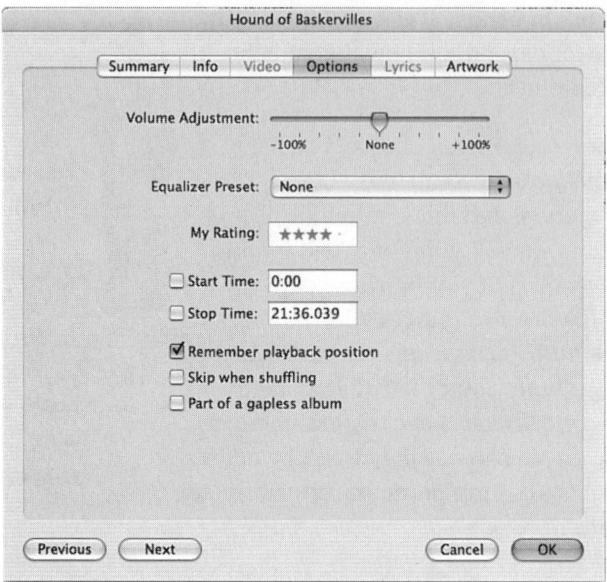

FIGURE 8.1
Use the Options tab of the Info window to have iTunes and an iPod remember where you stopped listening to an audiobook.

5. Check the **Skip when shuffling** check box. If you listen to a source containing the audiobook in the Shuffle mode, the book will be skipped. This will prevent audiobooks from getting mixed into music you are listening to in the Shuffle mode.
6. Click **OK**.

Moving Audiobooks onto an iPod

When it comes to moving content from your iTunes Library onto an iPod, audiobooks are treated just like music. The details of moving music from your iTunes Library onto an iPod are provided in Chapter 6, "Building an iPod's Music Library." As you should recall (assuming you've read that chapter), there are three ways to do this. You can choose the fully automatic option so that everything in your iTunes Library is automatically placed on your iPod. Or, you can choose specific playlists to keep updated automatically; if you choose this method, your audiobooks will need to be included in the playlists you select to have updated. The Audiobooks source on the iTunes Source list will appear as a playlist automatically,

note

There's only one option to move audiobooks onto an iPod shuffle, which is the manual way. Drag the audiobook from the iTunes Library onto the iPod shuffle's icon on the Source list.

so it's easy to select it for automatic syncing. The third, but not least, option is to use the manual option, in which case you simply drag audiobooks from the iTunes Library onto an iPod's icon on the Source list.

Listening to Audiobooks on an iPod

To listen to an audiobook on an iPod, you first have to select it. How you do this depends on the source of the audiobook to which you are listening.

Listening to Audiobooks from the iTunes Store or Audible.com on an iPod

If you purchased an audiobook from the iTunes Store or Audible.com, it will be placed into the Audiobooks category, which you can access on the iPod through the Audiobooks menu options. Listen to this kind of audiobook by using the following steps:

1. Choose **Main** Menu, **Music**, **Audiobooks**. You'll see the Audiobooks menu that lists all the audiobooks stored on your iPod (see Figure 8.2).

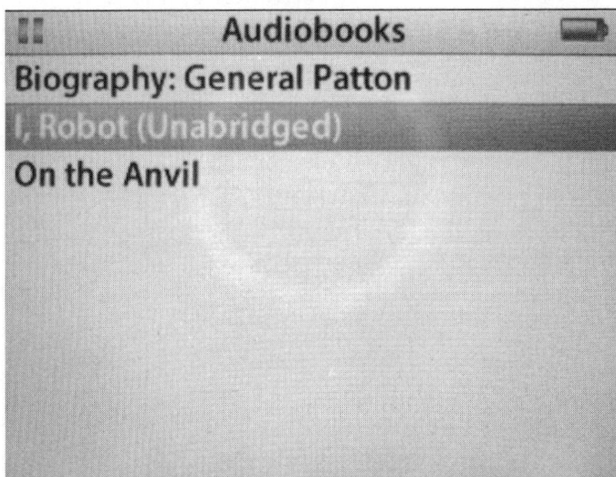

FIGURE 8.2
The Audiobooks menu lists all the audiobooks on your iPod.

2. Select the audiobook to which you want to listen and press the **Select** button. The book will start to play, and you'll see the Now Playing screen (see Figure 8.3). Some audiobooks will include chapter markers that appear on the Timeline bar; chapters are indicated by the vertical lines in the Timeline bar.
3. To move to the next chapter in the book, press the **Next** button. The playback will jump to the next chapter marker.
4. To move to an earlier chapter, press the **Previous** button.

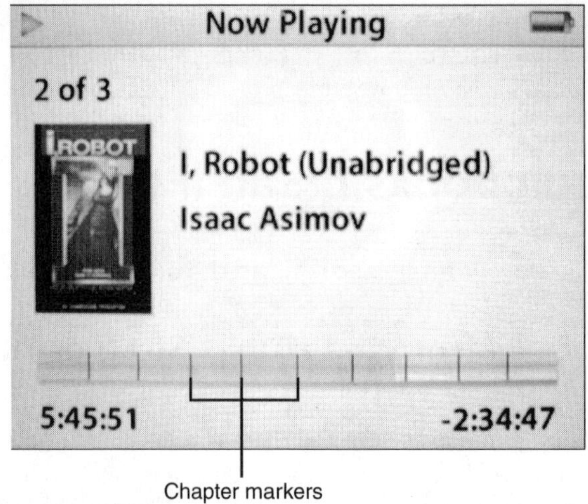

FIGURE 8.3
Here you can see that the book, *I, Robot* is playing.

5. To move within chapters, press the **Select** button once. The Timeline bar will be updated, and you'll see the blue diamond that indicates the current position in the book (see Figure 8.4). Slide your thumb around the Click Wheel to move ahead or behind in the book. When you take your thumb off the Click Wheel, the audiobook will resume playing at the current position.

FIGURE 8.4
When this version of the Timeline bar appears, you can move ahead or back in an audiobook by sliding your thumb around the iPod's Click Wheel.

6. If the audiobook includes cover artwork, click the **Select** button twice to view it (see Figure 8.5).

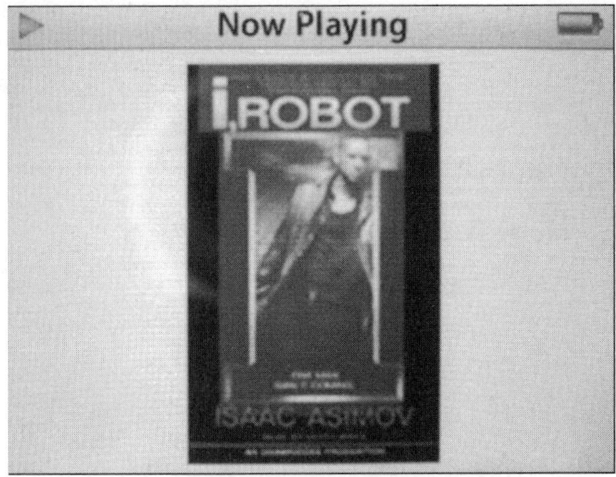

FIGURE 8.5
Why miss out on a book's cover just because it's an audiobook?

7. To rate an audiobook, click the **Select** button three times while you are viewing the Now Playing screen. The Timeline bar will be replaced by rating dots. Slide your thumb around the Click Wheel until the number of stars you want to apply to the book is shown (see Figure 8.6).

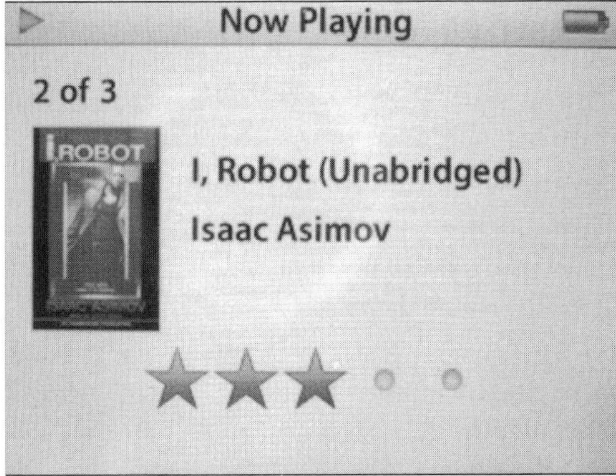

FIGURE 8.6
Like a book? Give it some stars.

8. To change the speed at which the book plays, press the **Select** button four times. The Timeline bar will be replaced by the Speed setting (see Figure 8.7). Slide your thumb clockwise to set the speed to **Faster** or counterclockwise to set the speed to **Slower**. The book will begin to play at the selected speed.
9. Stop the book by pressing the **Pause** button. You can then resume the audiobook; it will start playing at the point you last heard it.

FIGURE 8.7
Save time by making a book play faster.

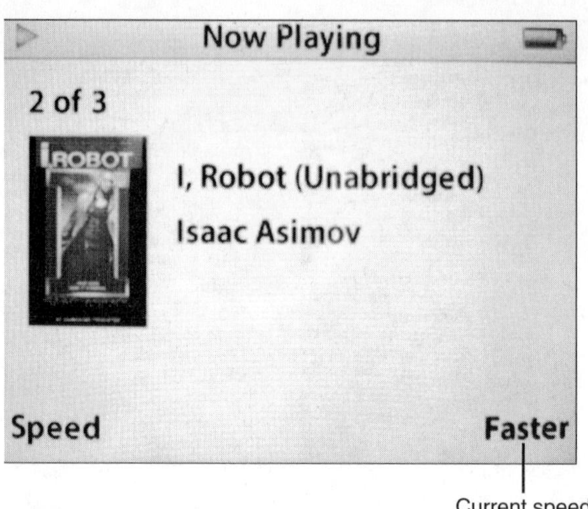

Listening to Audiobooks from Other Sources on an iPod

If you obtained the audiobook from another source, it won't be part of the Audiobooks structure on the iPod because it isn't recognized as being an audiobook. Although not all the iPod's audiobook functionality will work with these kinds of audiobooks, you can still listen to them, which is really the point anyway. To listen to this kind of audiobook, use the following steps:

1. Choose **Main** menu, **Music**, **Songs**. The Songs menu will appear.
2. Scroll on the menu until you see the title of the audiobook you want to hear.
3. Select the audiobook. It will begin to play, and you'll see the Now Playing screen (see Figure 8.8).
4. Use the music controls to listen to and work with the audiobook, such as by clicking the **Select** button twice to rate it (see Figure 8.9).

If you change the filename extension of an audiobook's file to be `.m4b` as you learned earlier, it will be in the Audiobooks source and will behave on the iPod just like audiobooks you purchase.

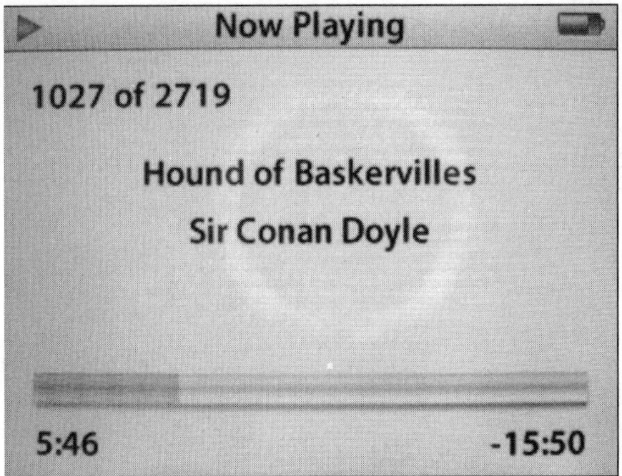

FIGURE 8.8
Although it might not look as special as a "real" audiobook, it sounds just as good. (And besides, it was free!)

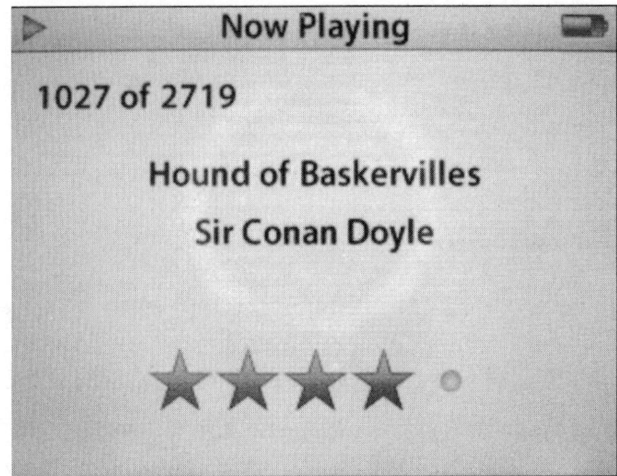

FIGURE 8.9
It's hard to beat a classic like this one.

Setting an iPod's Audiobook Default Speed Setting

As you saw in the earlier steps, you can change the speed at which an audiobook plays. For example, if the narration is somewhat slow, you can speed it up to hear more of the book in less time. There is also a default speed setting for all the audiobooks on your iPod. You can change this so that the default speed is what you prefer; you can always override it for specific audiobooks by using the information earlier in the chapter. To set your iPod's default audiobook speed, perform the following steps:

1. Choose **Main** menu, **Settings, Audiobooks**. You'll see the Audiobooks settings menu (see Figure 8.10).

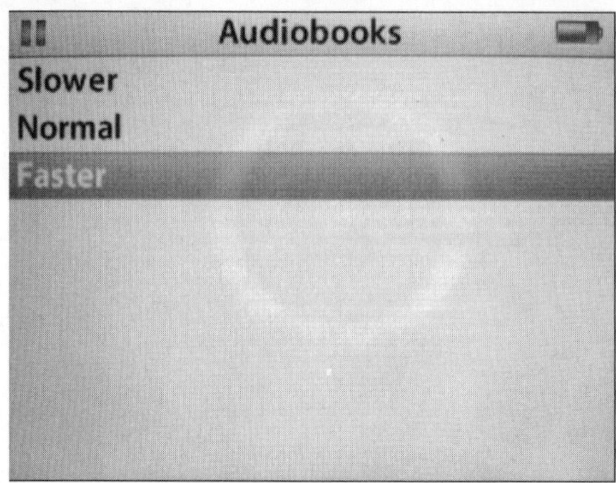

FIGURE 8.10
If you like to move audiobooks along, choose the Faster default speed.

2. Select the default speed you want to use; the options are **Slower**, **Normal**, or **Faster**. You'll return to the Settings menu.

When you play an audiobook, it will play at the default speed you've selected.

THE ABSOLUTE MINIMUM

Listening to audiobooks on an iPod is a great way to enjoy books while you are on the move. iPod "reading" can be done quite easily, as you have learned in this chapter. As you read (or listen) on, remember the following:

- To put audiobooks on an iPod, you first move them to your iTunes Library.
- To get audiobooks into your Library, you can purchase them from the iTunes Store or Audible.com. When you do so, the audiobooks will be added to your iTunes Library automatically.
- You can also find audiobooks on many websites; some offer audiobooks for free. You download these audiobooks and then manually add them to your iTunes Library.
- If you purchase audiobooks on CD, you can import them into iTunes just like music on CD.
- Make sure the **Remember playback position** setting is enabled for any audiobooks you get outside of the iTunes Store or Audible.com so that you'll always start where you left off. (This setting is enabled automatically for audiobooks you get from the iTunes Store or Audible.com.)

- After audiobooks are in your iTunes Library, you move them onto an iPod in the same ways you do music (fully automatically, selected playlists automatically, or manually).
- After audiobooks are on an iPod, listening to them is as easy as listening to other kinds of content, such as music.
- You can set the speed at which an iPod plays audiobooks, such as making them play faster so you can hear more of a book in less time.

IN THIS CHAPTER

- Learn how an iPod is a perfect companion to a digital camera.
- Move photos onto an iPod.
- View pictures on an iPod.
- Add some flair by viewing your pictures in slideshows.
- Connect your iPod to a TV to show your photos and slideshows on a bigger screen.
- Turn things around and move photos from the iPod to your computer.

9

USING AN iPOD TO STORE AND VIEW PHOTOS

If you have a digital camera (it seems as if everyone does these days) your iPod is a great companion to it. You can store digital images on the iPod, where you can view them and perform other cool image tricks, such as watching slideshows accompanied by the great tunes your iPod contains. Check out the following list of photographic tricks your iPod can perform:

- Use iTunes to move photos from your computer onto an iPod.
- View photos on the iPod individually or in slideshows.
- Use an iPod to display photos and slideshows on a TV.
- Connect a digital camera (with an optional iPod Camera Connector) to an iPod and move photos from the camera to the iPod, where you can view them.
- Move photos from an iPod onto a computer.

Moving Pictures onto an iPod

To view photos on an iPod, you first have to move them there. There are three ways to do this:

- Use a supported application to move images onto an iPod via iTunes.
- Manually move photo files from a computer onto an iPod.
- Transfer photos from a digital camera onto an iPod.

Card readers for iPods enable you to transfer photos from the memory cards in digital cameras onto your iPod. You can use these devices with an iPod to store photo files on the iPod. However, you can't view photos on the iPod if you load them in this way. You can use the iPod only to transport those files, in which case this is like using the iPod as a disk with any other kind of computer file. Although this is useful in some cases, this isn't covered in this chapter. The focus here is on using the iPod to view photos along with transporting them. Besides, it's better and less expensive to use the optional adapter to connect a camera directly to the iPod so that you can download photos directly from the camera to the iPod.

Using an Application to Move Pictures from a Computer onto an iPod

With a supported application, you can transfer photos from photo albums stored on your computer onto an iPod via iTunes. To use this technique, you must store your digital photos in one of the following applications:

- Adobe Photoshop Album, version 2.0 or later (Windows)
- Adobe Photoshop Elements, version 3.0 or later (Windows)
- iPhoto, version 4.0.3 or later (Macintosh)

If you use an application other than one of these to manage your digital photos, you can still move those photos onto an iPod; you just have to manage them outside the application, which you'll learn how to do in the next section.

If you do have one of these applications, use the following steps to move images from the application onto an iPod:

1. Connect the iPod to your computer.
2. Select the iPod on the **Source** list if it isn't selected already.
3. Click the **Photos** tab. You'll see the Photos synchronization tools (see Figure 9.1).
4. Check the **Sync photos from** check box.

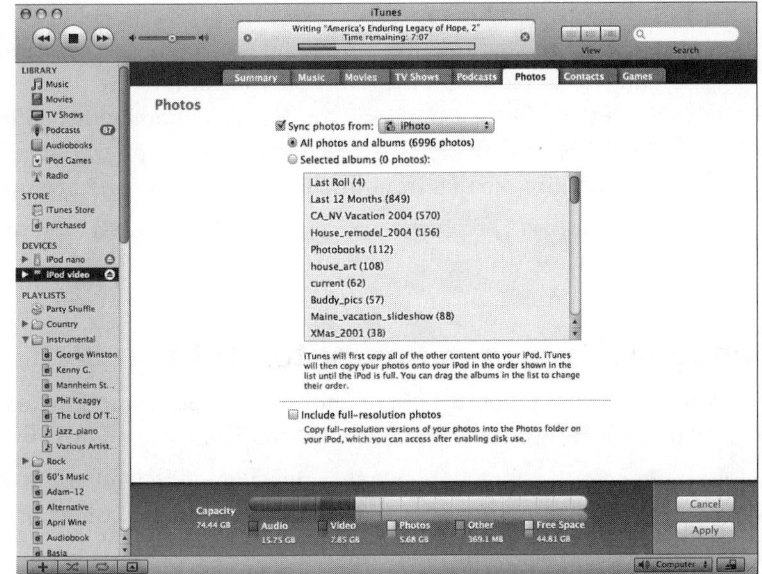

FIGURE 9.1
Use the Photos tab of the iPod screen to move photos from a supported application onto an iPod.

5. On the pop-up menu, choose the application you want to use. If you use a Mac, select **iPhoto**. If you use a Windows PC, select either **Photoshop Album** or **Photoshop Elements**.
6. If you want to move all the photos and photo albums stored in the selected application onto your iPod, click the **All photos and albums** radio button (the number of photos you'll move will be shown next to the text) and skip the next step.
7. If you want to move only selected photo albums onto the iPod, click **Selected albums** and then click the check box next to each album you want to move onto the iPod.

   Photos are the last kind of content that gets moved onto an iPod. If you've configured other kinds of content to get synced and your iPod doesn't have enough memory to hold all the photos you've selected, drag the albums containing the photos you want most to the top of the list of checked albums. This will give you the best chance of fitting those albums into your iPod's memory.

You can use an iPod to back up your photo files by checking **Include full-resolution photos**. Each time you synch your iPod, copies of your photo files will be placed on your iPod. If you ever need to recover them on your computer, you can use the iPod as a disk to do so.

8. If you also want to move full-resolution photo files onto the iPod, check **Include full-resolution photos**. An iPod uses an optimized version of the photo to display it on the screen. If you want to use the iPod to move full-resolution files, say from one computer to another, this option will copy those files onto the Photos folder on the iPod. You can then use the iPod as a disk to move the files from that folder onto a different computer.
9. Click **Apply**. The photos you selected will be moved onto the iPod, ready for you to view.

Moving Image Files from a Computer onto an iPod

If you don't use a supported photo application, you can still transfer images onto an iPod for viewing. This requires slightly different steps, as you will see here:

1. Prepare the photos you want to move onto the iPod, using the application you use to transfer photos from a digital camera onto your computer.
2. Create a folder on your computer.
3. Copy or move the photo files you want to place on the iPod into the folder you created in the previous step.
4. Connect the iPod to your computer.
5. Select the iPod on the Source list.
6. Click the **Photos** tab. You'll see the Photos synchronization tools.
7. Check the **Sync photos from** check box.
8. On the pop-up menu, select the folder in which you placed the photos you want to move onto the iPod. The menu will show the folder you selected (see Figure 9.2). In the box, you'll see the folders contained within the folder you selected.
9. If you want to copy all the photos in the selected folder onto the iPod, click **All photos**. Next to this text, you'll see how many photos that folder contains.
10. If you want to copy only photos within specific subfolders of the folder you selected in step 8, click **Selected folders** and then check the check box next to each folder containing the photos you want to move into the iPod.
11. If you also want to move full-resolution photo files onto the iPod, check **Include full-resolution photos**. An iPod uses an optimized version of the photo to display it on the screen. If you want to use the iPod to move full-resolution files, say from one computer to another, this option will copy those files onto the Photos folder on the iPod. You can then use the iPod as a disk to move the files from that folder onto a different computer.

12. Click **Apply**. The photos you selected will be moved onto the iPod, ready for you to view.

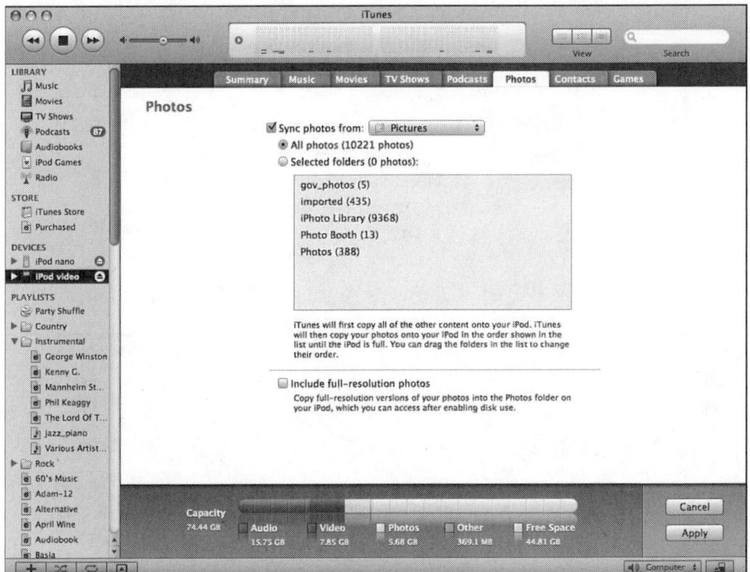

FIGURE 9.2
The menu next to the Sync photos from check box shows the name of the folder containing images I want to move onto an iPod (in this case, the folder called Pictures).

Moving Photos Directly from a Digital Camera onto an iPod

Using the iPod Camera Connector accessory (available at the online Apple Store), you can connect the USB cable you use to transfer images from your digital camera to your computer to also transfer them onto an iPod (see Figure 9.3). In addition to viewing those images on the iPod, you can also transfer them from the iPod to your computer.

To transfer photos from a digital camera to an iPod, use the following steps:

1. Connect the **iPod Camera Connector** to the **Dock connector port** on the iPod.
2. Connect the **USB cable** for your camera to the camera and to the iPod Camera Connector, and put your camera in transfer mode. On the iPod, you'll see the Import screen. On this screen, you'll see

tip

This is a great way to expand the number of images you can capture without a computer. If you fill up your camera's memory card, you can move the images on that card to the iPod, erase the card, and then shoot more photos. Later, you can move the photos you stored on the iPod onto your computer.

the number of photos that are ready to transfer and how much disk space they will consume.

FIGURE 9.3
Using the iPod Camera Connector, you can transfer images directly from a digital camera onto an iPod.

3. Highlight the **Import** command and press the **Select** button. The photos will be imported onto the iPod. On the Photo Import screen, you'll see a thumbnail of each image as it is moved from the camera onto the iPod. The progress bar will show you a graphical representation of the process and you'll see a counter, such as *x* of *y*, where *x* is the number of the current photo and *y* is the total number of photos on the camera's card.

   When the process is complete, you'll see the Import Done screen.

4. To exit the Import mode, select **Done**. You'll move to the Photo Import screen that shows each import session identified by Roll (see Figure 9.4). For each roll, you'll see the number of photos imported.

To erase the camera's memory card, select **Erase Card**. Then select **Erase Card** again on the Erase Card screen. Obviously, you shouldn't do this unless you're sure you don't want to keep the images on the camera's memory card.

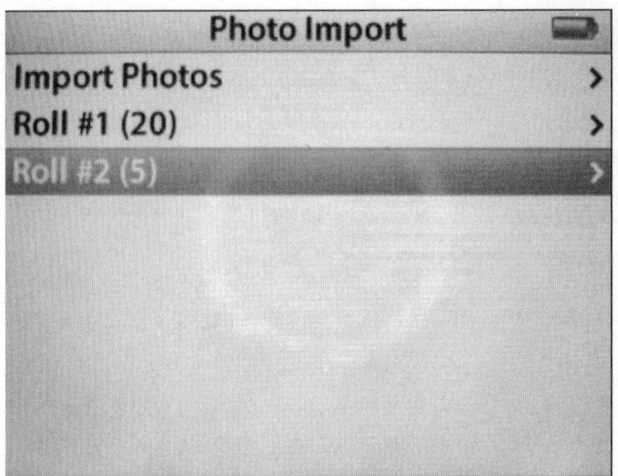

FIGURE 9.4
I've used the iPod Camera Connector to import two "rolls" of photos from my camera onto this iPod.

When you've imported at least one session of photos from a camera onto an iPod, the Photo Import command will appear on the Photos menu. Choose this command to move back to the Photo Import menu to work with photos you've imported. When you select an imported roll, you'll see information about it and can choose to browse or delete its images. Rolls behave just like photo albums that you've imported from a photo application.

After you have imported images from a camera onto the iPod, you can work with them on the iPod (to view them or move them to a computer), just like photos you move onto the iPod with one of the other methods, which brings us to the next section.

Viewing Photos on an iPod

After you have stored photos on an iPod, using any of the methods you learned earlier in this chapter, you can view them by following these steps:

1. Select **Main** menu, **Photos**. You'll see the Photos menu (see Figure 9.5). On this menu, you'll see the photos you have imported to the iPod organized in photo albums if you used a compatible application to import them. If you've imported photos using an iPod Camera Connector, you'll also see the Photo Import option, which leads you to images you have imported from a camera.
2. Select the source of the photos you want to view. For example, to view the images in a photo album, select that album on the menu. To see all the images on the iPod, select **Photo Library**. To see images you have imported from a camera, select **Photo Import** and then select the roll you want to view.
3. Press the **Select** button. You'll see thumbnails of all the images in the selected source (see Figure 9.6). The current image will be indicated by a yellow box around it.

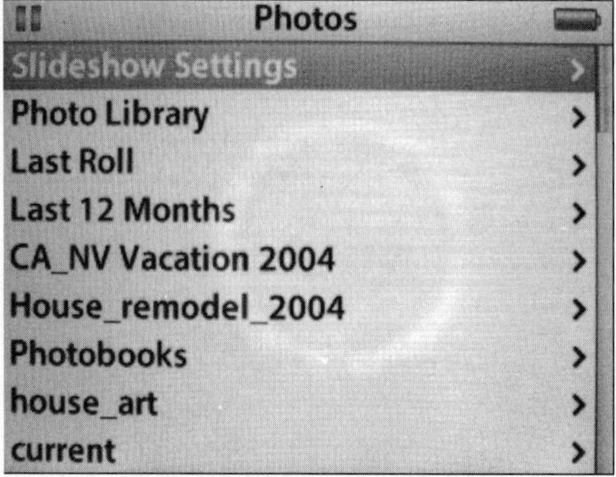

FIGURE 9.5
When I imported photos onto this iPod, I used the iPhoto application, so I see my photo albums on the iPod.

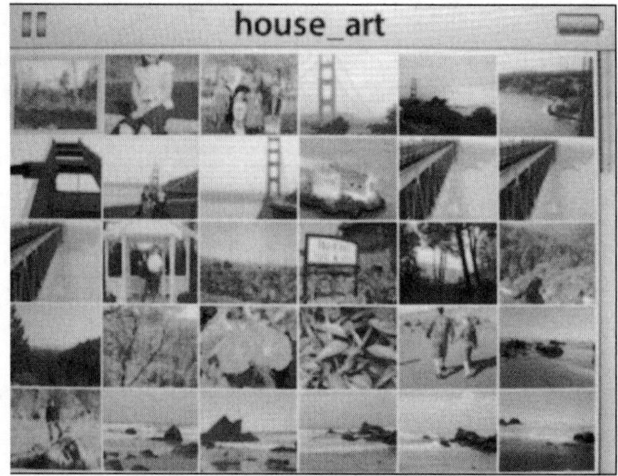

FIGURE 9.6
Here, I've selected a photo album and can see thumbnails of the images it contains.

4. Use the **Click Wheel** to move to the image you want to view. As you do, the yellow box will move around to show you which photo is currently selected.
5. Press the **Select** button. The image you selected will fill the iPod's screen (see Figure 9.7).
6. Press the **Fast Forward** button to view the next image in the source or the **Rewind** button to view the previous image. You can also move among the photos by dragging your thumb around the Click Wheel.
7. When you have finished viewing images in the selected source, press the **Menu** button to move back to the source's thumbnail menu, and then press **Menu** again to move back to the Photos menu.

FIGURE 9.7
I've selected a photo's thumbnail to view it full screen.

Viewing Slideshows on an iPod

You can view the images on your iPod in a slideshow. There are two general steps to do this. First, configure the slideshow options. Then, watch the show.

Setting Up an iPod Slideshow

To configure a slideshow, perform the following steps:

1. Select **Main** menu, **Photos**, **Slideshow Settings**. You'll see the Slideshow Settings menu (see Figure 9.8).

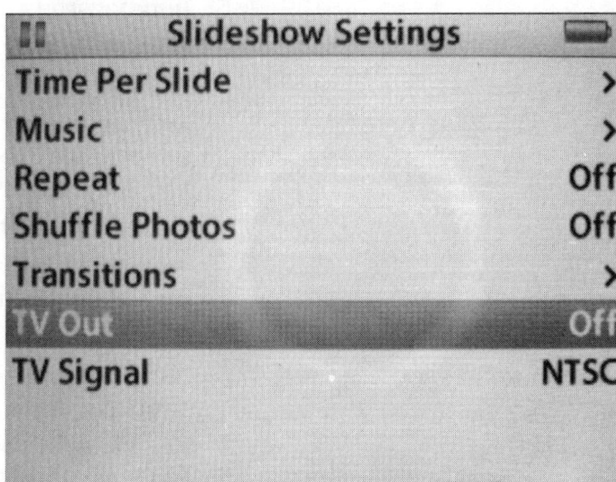

FIGURE 9.8
Your iPod offers a number of options for its slideshows that you can configure on the Slideshow Settings menu.

2. Select the option you want to configure, and press the **Select** button.
3. Use the resulting menu to choose the specific options you want to configure. See Table 9.1 for a description of the available settings.
4. Press the **Menu** button to move back to the Photos menu.

Table 9.1 Slideshow Settings Options

Setting	What It Does	Options
Time Per Slide	Controls the amount of time each image is displayed	`Manual`: means you must press the Fast Forward button to advance the slideshow `2, 3, 5, 10,` or `20 Seconds`: plays the image for the selected amount of time
Music	Chooses the music that should be played when the slideshow is playing	`From iPhoto` (Mac only): plays the music associated with the source in iPhoto `Now Playing`: uses the music currently playing `Off`: no music `Playlist name`: plays the selected playlist
Repeat	Repeats the slideshow	`Off`: the slideshow plays once and then stops `On`: repeats the slideshow until you stop it
Shuffle Photos	Displays photos in random order	`Off`: plays the photos in order `On`: displays the images randomly
Transitions	Controls the transition effect used between photos	`Off`: no transition is used `Random`: uses a random transition between each image `Transition name`: uses the selected transition between all images
TV Out	Sets the iPod to play to a TV	`Ask`: displays a prompt for you to select to play to a TV each time you play a slideshow `On`: sets the iPod to always display on a TV `Off`: sets to always play on the iPod only
TV Signal	Chooses a format for the signal sent to a TV	NTSC: uses the NTSC format (standard for various regions, including the United States) PAL: uses the PAL format (standard for Europe and other regions)

Playing an iPod Slideshow

To view a slideshow, perform the following steps:

1. Select **Main** menu, **Photos**. You'll see the Photos menu.
2. Highlight the source of the images you want to view in a slideshow. The options are the same as when you are viewing images individually. For example, if you moved photo albums onto the iPod, you could select one of them to view its images in a slideshow.
3. Press the **Play** button. The slideshow will play, using the current slideshow settings (see Figure 9.9). Sit back and enjoy the show!

If you configure slideshows with the Manual setting, you'll need to press the **Fast Forward** button to advance the images in the show.

FIGURE 9.9
Although you can't tell it from the figure, this slideshow includes a nice soundtrack and transition effects.

4. When the last image in the slideshow appears, press the **Menu** button to return to the Photos menu.

Using an iPod to Display Slideshows on a TV

Using the optional iPod AV Cable, you can connect your iPod (you can't do this with an iPod nano) to a TV and display slideshows on the TV (see Figure 9.10). Connect the cable to your iPod and to the RCA input jacks on your television. Then play a slideshow by setting the TV Out option to **Yes**, or select the **Ask** option and then select the **TV On** option. The slideshow will be played on the TV.

FIGURE 9.10
Using this cable, you can display images and slideshows on a TV.

You can use the iPod Dock for this as well. The benefit is that you can use an S-video cable to connect the Dock to your television, which will improve the quality of the images on the TV. Then you connect the Audio Out port on the Dock to the Audio In ports on the TV. Drop your iPod in the Dock and play a slideshow.

> **tip**
>
> You can stop the slideshow by pressing the **Menu** button. You can pause it by pressing the **Pause** button.

While a slideshow plays, you'll see full-screen images on the TV. On the iPod, you'll see thumbnails of the previous, current, and next images. You'll also see how many images are in the slideshow and the amount of time remaining for each image being displayed (see Figure 9.11).

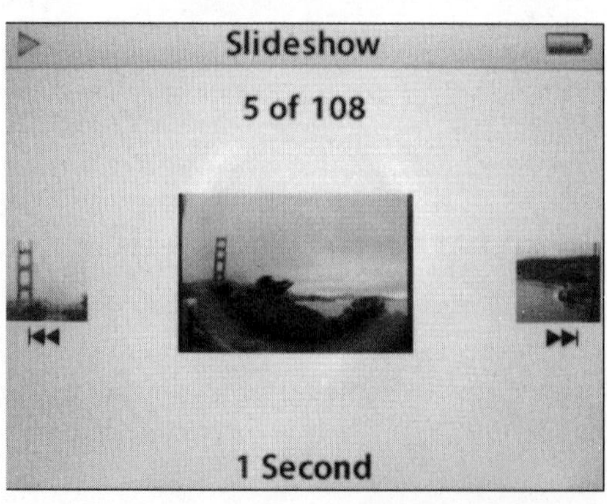

FIGURE 9.11
While you're watching a slideshow on a TV, you'll see the Slideshow screen on the iPod.

Moving Photos from an iPod onto a Computer

You can move photos from an iPod to a computer. For example, you might want to transfer images you have moved from a digital camera onto the iPod to your photo collection on your computer. Or, you might want to move images from one computer to another.

Using an Application to Move Photos from an iPod onto a Computer

You can transfer photos from the iPod to a computer using the same application you use to transfer images from a digital camera onto a computer. The steps to do this are as follows:

1. Connect the iPod to your computer, just as you do when you want to update it.
2. Open the application you use to import images from your digital camera. It should recognize the iPod as a source of photos, just as it does when you connect a camera to your computer.
3. Import the images from the iPod (see Figure 9.12).

If your iPod is not recognized by your photo application, you'll have to use the method described in the next section to move images from the iPod to your computer.

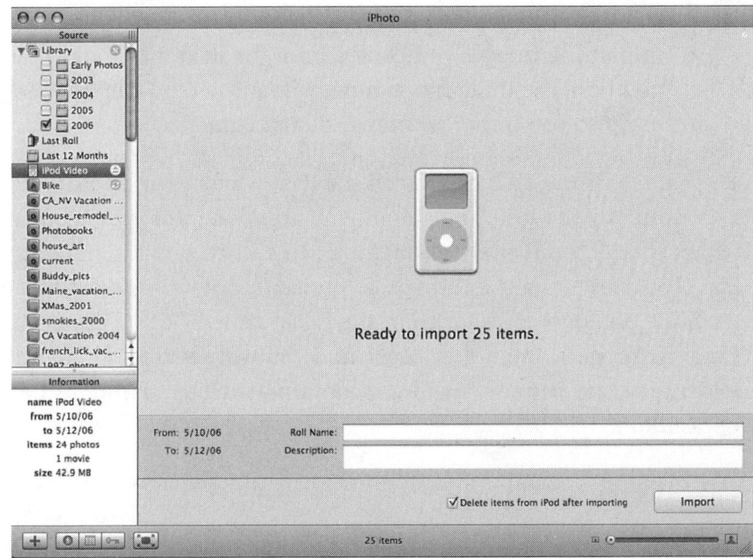

FIGURE 9.12
Here I am importing images from an iPod into my iPhoto Library on a Mac.

Manually Moving Files from an iPod to a Computer

You can store image files on an iPod and move them onto a computer similarly to how you store and move any other files. To do so, perform the following steps:

1. Enable your iPod for disk use. (See "Using an iPod As a Portable Hard Drive" on page **169** for the steps to do this.)
2. Connect your iPod to your computer.
3. Open a window on the desktop that shows the contents of your iPod (see Figure 9.13).

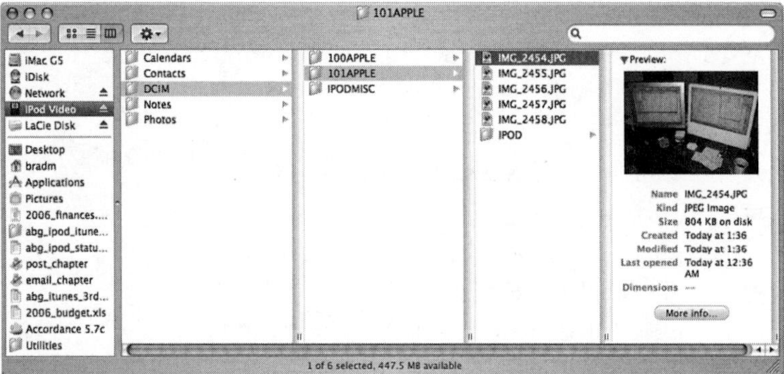

FIGURE 9.13
On this Mac, I've selected the iPod and can see the folders and files it contains.

4. Drag the image files from the iPod to a location on your computer to copy them there.
5. Open the application you use to manage your images.
6. Import the images you copied from the iPod into that application. From this point on, the images you moved from the iPod can be used in the same way as those you imported from a digital camera.

There are a couple of locations on the iPod where your photos might be stored. If you manually moved photos from your computer onto the iPod, look in the folder in which you placed them. (You might do this when you are moving image files from one computer to another.) If you imported images from a digital camera onto the iPod, the photos will be stored in the folder called DCIM (which stands for Digital Camera Images). Open this folder, and you will see a folder for each import. Open a folder to access and use the files it contains, such as to import them into your photo application.

The Absolute Minimum

An iPod is a useful partner for you if you're into digital photography. In addition to carrying your photos around with you on the iPod for easy viewing, you can store images from a camera on the iPod and later move them onto your computer. As you use an iPod to work with digital photos, keep the following points in focus:

- An iPod enables you to store images on it and view those images individually or in slideshows (shuffle excluded, of course).
- There are three ways to move images onto an iPod so you can view them. You can use iTunes to synchronize your photos stored in a supported photo application (Photoshop Elements, Photoshop Album, or iPhoto) on your iPod. You can also use iTunes to move photos stored in specific folders on your computer onto your iPod. Or, with an iPod Camera Connector, you can download images directly from a digital camera onto an iPod.
- If you often run low on card memory on your camera, using an iPod Camera Connector is a great way to make sure you don't run out of room. After you fill up your camera's memory card, connect the camera to an iPod and download its images onto the iPod. Then erase the camera's memory card and keep shooting. When you get back to your computer, move the photos from the iPod to your image application or a desktop folder.
- You can select and view images on your iPod individually.
- You can also view photos on an iPod in slideshows that can include music and transition effects.
- With an optional cable or Dock, you can connect an iPod to a TV and show your photos and slideshows on a TV.
- You can also move photos from an iPod onto your computer. You can do this by importing its images into your photo application or into a folder on your computer's desktop.

IN THIS CHAPTER

- Move video from your computer onto an iPod.
- Watch video on an iPod. (Prepare to be impressed.)
- View iPod video on a TV. (You'll be impressed with this, too.)

10

USING AN iPOD TO WATCH VIDEO

They say confession is good for the soul. So, here it goes. When the first iPod video was released, even though I am a huge iPod fan (obviously), I thought that it wasn't such a good idea and that Apple might have gone a bit too far this time. After all, in this age of 50-inch plus HDTVs, who would want to watch video on an 2.5-inch iPod screen? Sure, it had a kind of geeky, gadget appeal, but practically speaking, why bother? I couldn't have been more wrong.

After seeing video on an iPod for the first time, I was totally hooked. Sure, the screen wasn't huge. But, the quality was and is huge, so much so that it was very compelling to watch. And being able to carry around a full-featured video player with plenty of content on it (now you can leave your DVDs at home along with your CDs) as easily as a cell phone immediately won me over. Since that time, I've used an iPod for watching video regularly and often. I suspect that if you have any interest in a mobile video device, you'll become hooked as quickly as I was.

Moving Video onto an iPod

Like all other content, the first step to enjoying video on an iPod is to move that content onto it. Also like other kinds of content, you first put video content into your iTunes Library and then move it onto the iPod.

To learn how to add video to iTunes, see Chapter 21, "Working with iTunes Video."

Within iTunes, there are three basic kinds of video: movies, TV shows, and music videos. You can move each of these types onto an iPod separately by performing the following steps:

1. Connect the iPod to your computer.
2. Select the iPod on the **Source** list if it isn't selected already. The iPod screen will appear.
3. Click the **Music** tab. You'll see the Music synchronization tools that you learned how to use in Chapter 6, "Building an iPod's Music Library" (see Figure 10.1).

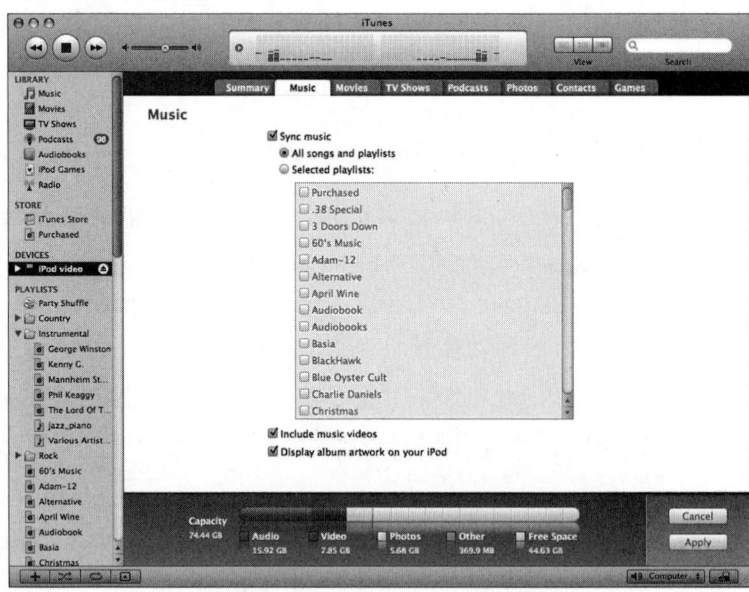

FIGURE 10.1
If you have music videos in your Library, move them onto an iPod by checking the Include music videos check box.

4. If you have music video content in your Library that you want moved onto your iPod, check the **Include music videos** check box.
5. Click the **Movies** tab (see Figure 10.2). Use this tab to configure how your movie content is moved onto the iPod.

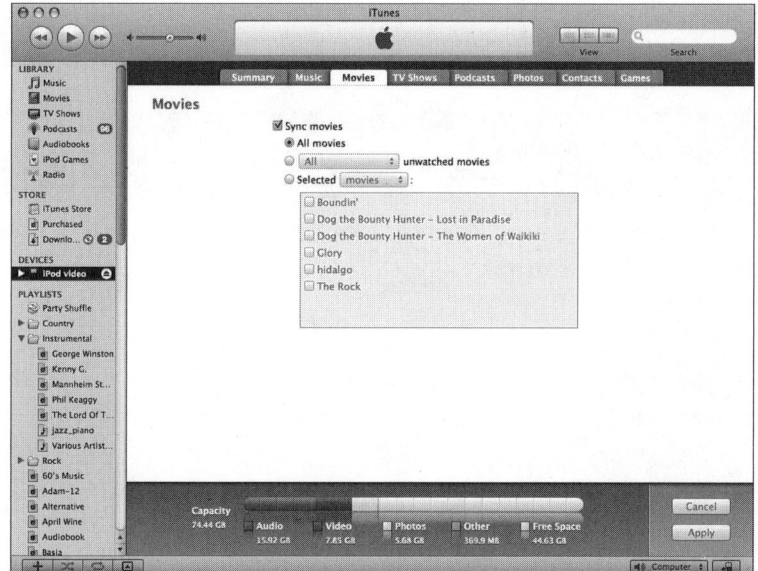

FIGURE 10.2
If you've added movies to your Library, select their sync options on the Movies tab.

6. Check the **Sync movies** check box if you want movie content to be available on the iPod. (If not, leave it unchecked and skip to step 10.)
7. To have all your movie content moved onto the iPod, click **All movies**.
8. To sync only movies that you haven't watched yet, click the **unwatched movies** radio button, and choose the number of unwatched movies that you want to sync on the menu; the choices are **All**, **1 most recent**, **3 most recent**, **5 most recent**, and **10 most recent**.
9. To select specific movies to move onto the iPod, click the **Selected** radio button. On the Selected menu, choose **movies** to select individual movies to sync or **playlists** to select playlists that contain the movies you want to move onto the iPod. Then check the check boxes next to the movies or playlists you want to sync in the box located under the Selected menu. (What you see listed there depends on the selection you make on the menu.)

note

Depending on your current video synchronization settings, you might or might not see warning dialog boxes when you choose an automatic sync option. These inform you that all the current content of the related type (such as TV Shows) will be replaced when you use an automatic option. If that's okay with you, click the **Sync** button in the warning dialog box to proceed.

10. Click the **TV Shows** tab (see Figure 10.3).
11. Check the **Sync** check box.

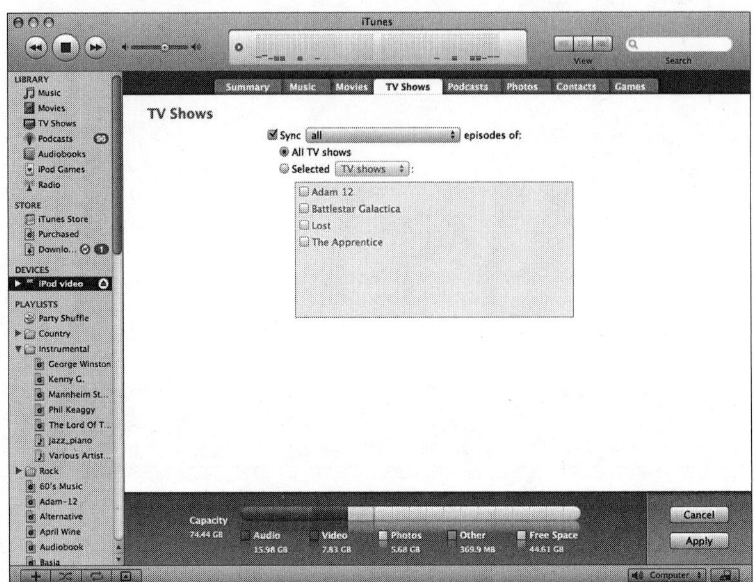

FIGURE 10.3

As you can probably guess by now, you use the TV Shows tab to configure the TV content you want to move onto an iPod.

12. On the **Sync** menu, choose the category and number of episodes that you want to move onto the iPod. The basic categories are watched or unwatched. Within each of those, you can choose **all** to move all the episodes in that category or a number of episodes that you want to move onto the iPod. For example, to move all the episodes onto the iPod regardless of whether you've watched them, choose **all**. To move only the most recent 3 episodes that you haven't watched, choose **3 most recent unwatched** instead.
13. To synchronize all the series you have added to your Library, click the **All TV Shows** radio button.
14. To select specific TV content to sync, click the **Selected** radio button. On the Selected menu, choose **TV shows** to choose content by series or **playlists** to select playlists containing the TV content you want to move onto the iPod. Then check the check box next to each series or playlist that you want to move onto the iPod. (What you see on the list depends upon the selection you make on the Selected menu.)
15. Click **Apply**. The video content that matches your synchronization options will be moved onto the iPod. If the video content you selected exceeds the available space on your iPod, you'll have to reconfigure the synchronization options to make it fit, such as by choosing selected content or limiting the number of series that you include in synchronizations.

Depending on how much video content you have and how different the synchronization options are from the last time you synced video, the update process can be pretty fast, or it might take several minutes if you are moving lots of video onto the iPod. (Video files are very large.)

16. When the update process is complete, click the **Eject** button and disconnect the iPod from your computer.

tip

If you want to move video content onto the iPod manually, open the **Summary** tab of the iPod screen and check the **Manually manage music and videos** check box. (This will cause all the automatic synchronization options to be deselected.) Then drag the **video content** you want to place on the iPod from the Library onto the iPod's icon.

Selecting and Playing Video on an iPod

After you've moved video onto an iPod, you can watch it by doing the following:

1. Select **Main** menu, **Videos**. You'll see the Videos menu (see Figure 10.4). The menu contains sources of video on your iPod, including Video Playlists, Movies, Music Videos, TV Shows, Video Podcasts, and Video Settings.

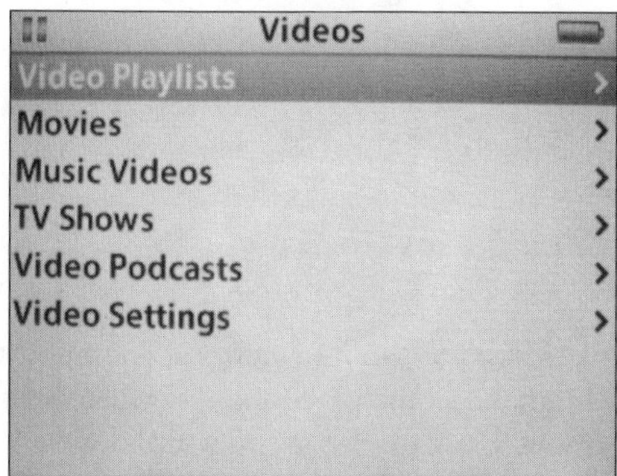

FIGURE 10.4 First, select the source of the video you want to watch.

2. Select the source of video you want to watch. For example, if you want to watch video you've stored in a playlist that is updated on the iPod, select the **Video Playlists** option; you'll see the Video Playlists menu on which you can see the playlists containing video that you've stored on the iPod (see Figure 10.5). To watch a movie, select Movies, and you'll see the movies stored on the iPod. If you want to watch video that is classified as being

TV shows, select **TV Shows** and you'll see the TV Shows menu, which shows the content organized by series (see Figure 10.6). (You can probably guess what happens if you select the Music Videos source.)

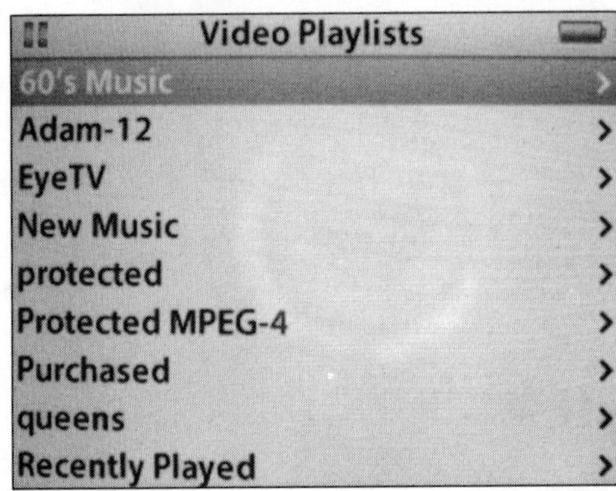

FIGURE 10.5
This iPod has a number of playlists that contain video content.

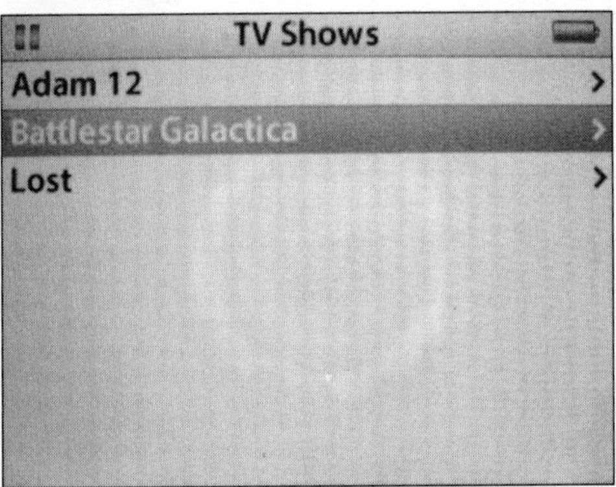

FIGURE 10.6
On the TV Shows menu, you'll see all the video categorized as being a TV show, organized by series title.

3. Select the category of video you want to view. For example, if you selected the **Video Playlists** option, select the playlist whose video you want to watch. If you selected **TV Shows**, select the series you want to view. You'll see a screen showing the content of the item you select, such as the episodes of a series (see Figure 10.7).
4. Select the specific content you want to view, such as an episode of a TV series, a movie, a video podcast, and so on. The video will start to play and will fill the iPod's screen (see Figure 10.8).

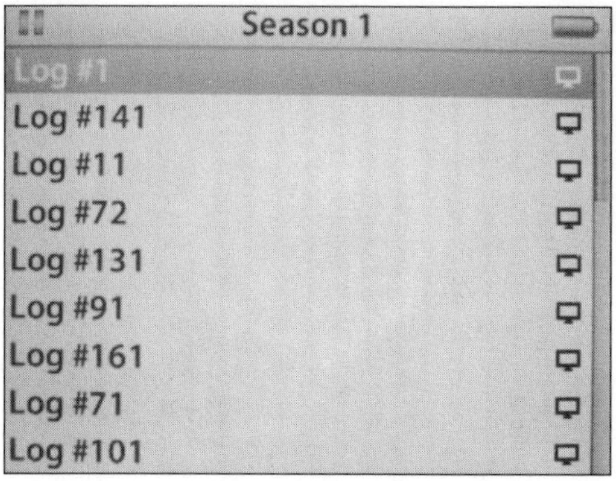

Season 1
Log #1
Log #141
Log #11
Log #72
Log #131
Log #91
Log #161
Log #71
Log #101

FIGURE 10.7
This menu shows episodes of the TV series *Adam-12*.

FIGURE 10.8
Okay, so seeing video in a book isn't so exciting; seeing it on an iPod is.

5. Use the **iPod's Click Wheel** to control the video. This works mostly as it does for music and other audio content. An exception is the Fast Forward/Next button; if you click this once, you'll move to the previous menu rather than to the next video content on that menu. Otherwise, Play/Pause and the other buttons on the Click Wheel work as you expect. As with audio content, you can drag a digit around the Click Wheel to change the volume.

   Also as with audio content, you can fast forward or rewind by pressing the **Select** button once so that the Timeline appears and then use the **Click Wheel** to move ahead or back.

   Note that the battery icon isn't displayed when video is playing. You can cause it to appear dragging on the **Click Wheel** (which also changes the volume) or by pressing the **Select** button (which doesn't cause any change to what is playing unless you do something else, too).

You can change the brightness by pressing the **Select** button twice, which will cause the brightness bar to appear; the default brightness level is indicated by the vertical line on this bar. (You can't see this until you change the brightness from the default.) You can change the brightness by dragging a digit on the **Click Wheel** clockwise to make the display brighter and counterclockwise to make it less bright.

Unlike audio content, video can't be rated, and you can't view its artwork on the iPod.

When the video is done playing, you'll return to the previous menu. Of course, you can stop it at any time by pressing the Play/Pause button. Video will also pause automatically if you press the Menu button to move back to the previous menu (unlike audio, which continues to play as you maneuver through menus). This makes sense because when you view a menu, you can't see the video screen.

tip

If video contains commercials or other undesirable content, you can fast forward through them by holding the Fast Forward button down or by pressing the Select button once and dragging a digit clockwise around the Click Wheel. (The Click Wheel method works better for me because it is more precise.) In either case, the Timeline bar will appear on the screen so that you can use the times shown to move ahead (or back for that matter). Most commercials are in 30-second increments, so you can use the Elapsed Time information to easily jump ahead to get past the commercials without missing the good stuff.

Watching an iPod's Video on a TV

You can display an iPod's video content on a TV to see it at a larger size. You'll likely be impressed by the quality of the video you see, too.

First, you need to connect the iPod to a TV, using the optional iPod AV cable available at the Apple Store or other retailers (see Figure 10.9). Plug the mini-jack end into the iPod's Headphones jack. Connect the RCA connectors to the video and audio inputs of a TV or other device.

Second, configure the iPod to play its output on a TV by doing the following:

1. Select **Main** menu, **Videos**. You'll see the Videos menu.
2. Select **Video Settings**. You'll see the Settings menu (see Figure 10.10).
3. Highlight **TV Out**.

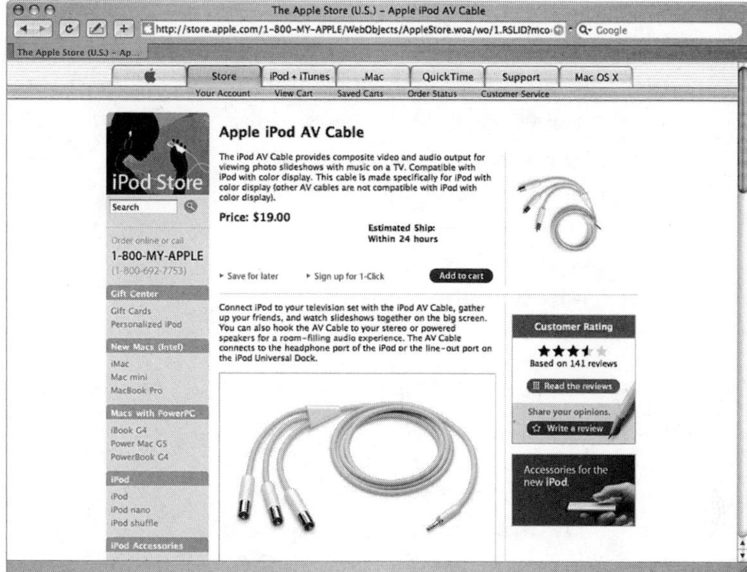

FIGURE 10.9
An iPod AV cable enables you to view iPod video content on a TV.

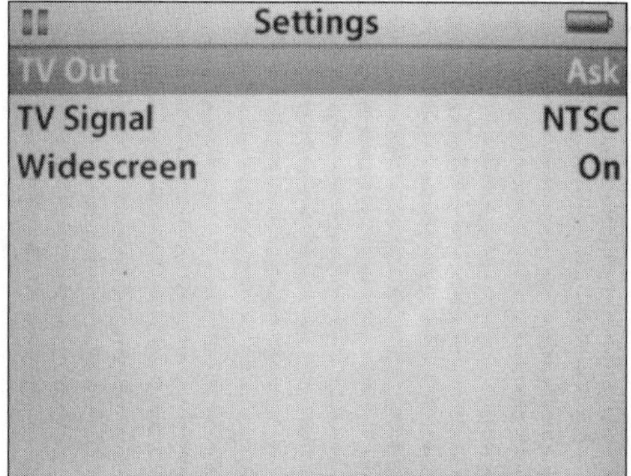

FIGURE 10.10
Use these settings to prepare your iPod to show off its video talents.

4. Press the **Select** button once. The TV Out setting will become `Ask`. When this is shown, you'll be prompted to select the output source each time you play video. This is useful if you regularly watch video on a TV and on the iPod. If you press the **Select** button again, the TV Out setting changes to `On`. This means that the iPod is in TV mode all the time; when it is in this mode, video does not appear on the iPod's screen. Press the **Select** button again, and the setting changes to `Off`, which means video plays only on the iPod's screen.

5. Highlight the **TV Signal** option and press the **Select** button to choose the format appropriate to the kind of TV you will be using. The options are NTSC or PAL.
6. Highlight the **Widescreen** option and press the **Select** button to set it to `On` if you will be displaying the iPod's video on a widescreen TV or `Off` if you'll be using a TV that doesn't have the widescreen format.

note

The TV Signal option you use depends on the area of the world in which you live. It's not possible to list the options for every part of the world, but in general, NTSC is used in North America and Japan while PAL is used in Europe and most other locations.

After you've configured the iPod to play on a TV, select and play video just as you do when you watch it on the iPod's screen. If you selected the Ask option, you'll first see the Play Video screen (see Figure 10.11) when you play video. Select **TV Off** to view video on the iPod's screen or **TV On** to see it on the big screen.

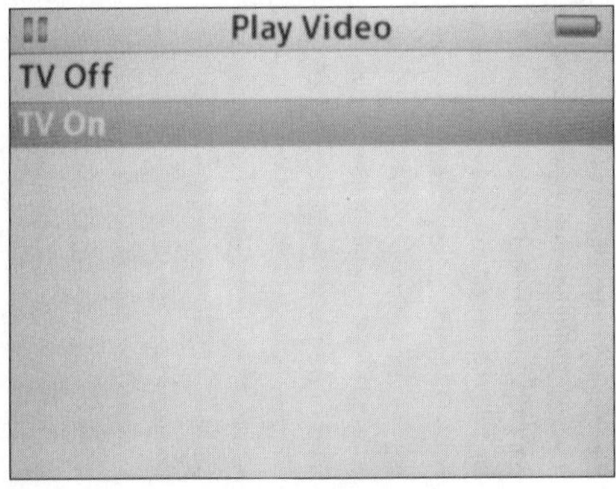

FIGURE 10.11
Use this screen to send the iPod's video to its screen (TV Off) or to a TV (TV On).

If you choose **TV On**, the video will start to play, and you'll see it on the TV. On the iPod's screen, you'll see the Now Playing screen, which will provide information about what you are seeing on the TV; the TV icon indicates that the iPod's output is going to a TV (see Figure 10.12).

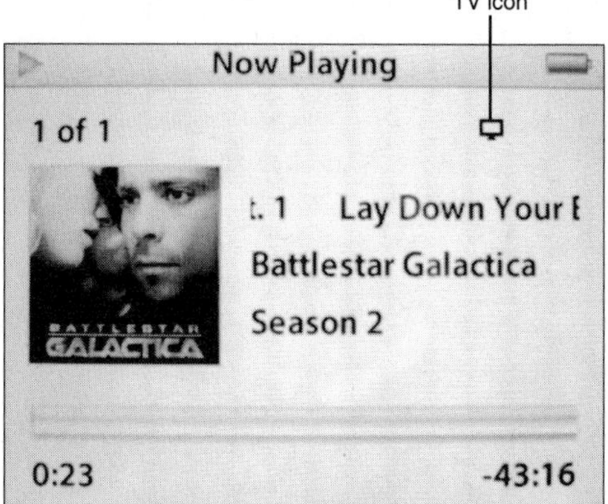

FIGURE 10.12
I'm seeing this episode of *Battlestar Galactica* on a TV while it plays on the iPod.

THE ABSOLUTE MINIMUM

Watching video on an iPod is really fun, and it's a handy way to take and enjoy video content with you wherever you go. This is a short chapter because watching iPod video just isn't a hard thing to do. As you enjoy your iPod theater, consider the following video tidbits:

- Like other content, video for your iPod is stored in your iTunes Library. You can move all the video in your Library onto an iPod, or you can choose specific content to move there.
- After you've added video to an iPod, you can watch it using steps that are very similar to those you use to listen to audio content.
- You can play an iPod's video on a TV or other video device by connecting it to the video device using an AV cable. Although the resolution of video on an iPod is relatively small, it will look pretty good on all but the largest TV screens.
- Playing video on an iPod consumes battery power much faster than listening to audio does. With the current models, you'll get about 3.5 hours of video on the 30GB model or 6.5 hours on the 80GB model. You can use a power adapter to enable the iPod to play video longer when you are near a power outlet or an optional battery pack to extend playing time when you are on the move.
- If you regularly display an iPod's video on a TV, consider purchasing Apple's iPod AV Connection Kit. This includes the AV cable, a Dock, a power adapter, a USB cable, and a remote. You connect the Dock to the TV and to the power adapter. After you place the iPod in the Dock, you'll see its output on the TV. You can use the included remote to control the iPod from afar. (You can also buy each component separately if you don't want to use all of them.)

IN THIS CHAPTER

- Use your iPod like it's a $2 watch, only a lot better.
- Play some iPod games.
- Keep your appointments by placing calendar events on your iPod's calendar.
- Take your contact information with you wherever you go.
- Store text gems on your iPod so you can read them at your leisure.
- Use your iPod as a portable hard drive.
- Use an iPod shuffle as a flash drive.
- Move music from your iPod onto a computer.

11

TAKING THE iPOD FURTHER

The iPod is one amazing device, isn't it? It excels as a music, podcast, and even video player, but it does so much more. This chapter provides your education in iPod utility and includes lots more uses for your trusty iPod, including managing your time, calendar, and contact information. If you don't want to be efficient, you can kill some time by playing iPod games. You'll also learn how you can use an iPod to read text files. You'll see that using an iPod as a hard drive and an iPod shuffle as a flash drive are both simple to do and really useful. Lastly, you'll learn how to use an iPod to move your music collection from an iPod onto a computer for backup or other purposes.

Using an iPod to Tell Time

You can use your iPod to tell what time it is and as a basic, but perfectly functional, alarm clock. This is handy when you travel because you don't need to carry a separate clock with you. Or, if you are like me and don't wear a watch, an iPod can help you keep track of time no matter where you are. Even better, you can configure multiple clocks at the same time to help you deal with multiple time zones.

Configuring an iPod's Date and Time

Before you use the iPod as a clock, you need to configure its primary time and date. Use the following steps to do this:

1. Select **Main** menu, **Settings**, **Date & Time**. You'll see the Date & Time menu.
2. Select **Set Time Zone**. You'll see the Time Zone menu.
3. Highlight your time zone and press the **Select** button. The iPod's time zone will be set to the one you selected, and you will return to the Date & Time menu.
4. Select **Set Date & Time**. You'll see the Date & Time menu again, except that this time it will be in the set date and time mode (see Figure 11.1). The hour will be highlighted.

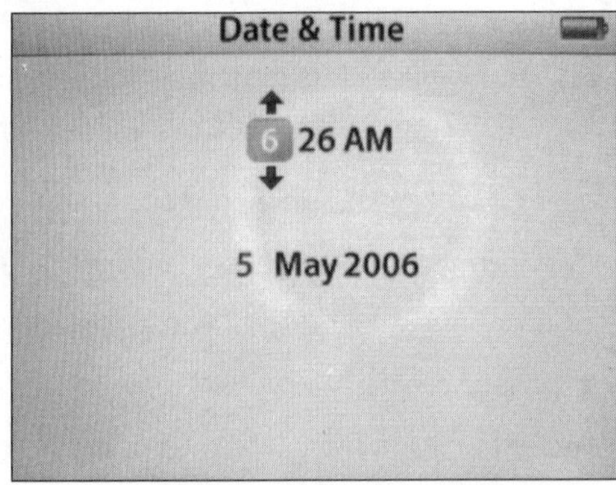

FIGURE 11.1
You use this screen to set the time and date on your iPod.

5. Use the **Click Wheel** to increase or decrease the hour until the correct hour is displayed.
6. Press the **Fast-forward** button so that the minute display is highlighted.
7. Use the **Click Wheel** to increase or decrease the minute until the correct minute is displayed.
8. Press the **Fast-forward** button so that the AM/PM indicator display is highlighted.

9. Use the **Click Wheel** to change the AM/PM to the correct value.
10. Continue using the **Fast-forward** button and **Click Wheel** to set the correct date, month, and year.
11. Press the **Select** button. The date and time you selected will be set, and you will return to the Date & Time menu.
12. Highlight the **Time** setting. The default value is to use a 12-hour clock.
13. To use a 24-hour clock, press the **Select** button. The Time setting will become `24-hour`, and a 24-hour clock will be used.
14. To display the time in the menu title area, highlight **Time in Title** and press the **Select** button. The Time in Title setting will become `On`, and the time will be displayed in the title bar instead of the menu title after the menu has been on the screen for a few seconds (see Figure 11.2).

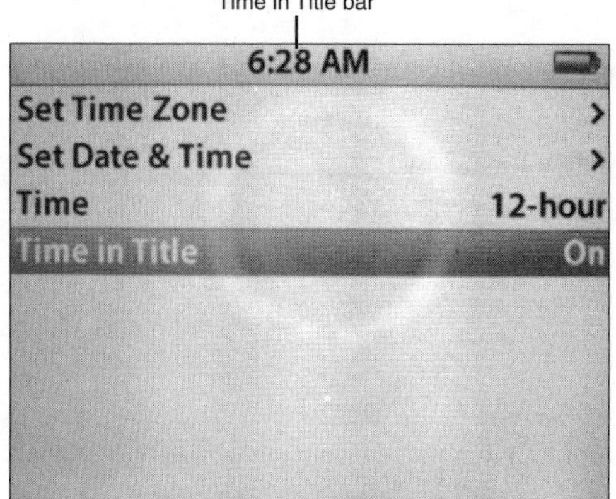

FIGURE 11.2
Placing the time in the title bar makes using an iPod as a clock much more convenient.

Configuring One or More Clocks on an iPod

You can configure multiple clocks on an iPod based on various cities and time zones. This can be useful if you need to track time in multiple time zones or if you're just curious about the time in some city in another part of the world. To set up a new clock, perform the following steps:

1. Select **Main** menu, **Extras**, **Clock**. You'll see the Clock menu. One clock exists by default.
2. Select **New Clock**. You'll see the Region menu.
3. Select the region for the clock you are creating, such as **North America** or **Europe**. You'll see the City menu.
4. Select the city for the clock. The clock will be created, and you'll move back to the Clock menu. On the menu, you'll see the clocks you have created; they'll

be named with the city you selected (see Figure 11.3). You'll see the current time, day, and date for each clock.

FIGURE 11.3
This iPod has three clocks configured on it.

5. To control daylight savings time for a clock, select the clock you want to configure. You'll see that clock's menu.
6. Highlight **Daylight Saving Time** and press the **Select** button until `On` or `Off` is displayed, indicating whether you want to use Daylight Savings Time or not.

You can repeat the previous steps to configure as many clocks as you'd like.

To delete a clock, select it on the Clock menu. You'll see that clock's menu; its title will be the city you selected for the clock. Select **Delete This Clock**. Select **Delete**. The clock will be deleted, and you'll return to the Clock menu sans one clock.

If you don't see the specific city you want to use for a clock, choose one that is in the same time zone as the city in whose time you are interested.

Displaying the Time on an iPod

There are a couple of ways to display the time and date on an iPod:

- Select **Main** menu, **Extras**, **Clock**. You'll see the Clock screen, showing all the clocks you've configured (see Figure 11.4). You'll see the current time indicated by the clock icon, along with the time shown in digital format.

FIGURE 11.4
Pick a time, any time.

- If you turn the **Time in Title** setting to On (you learned how earlier in this chapter), the time will be displayed in the title area of every screen (except the video playback screen) a second or two after you move to a new screen. When you first move to a screen, you will see the title, but after that small amount of time passes, the title will be replaced by the current time. The time displayed in the title is based on the Date & Time settings.

tip

For faster access to the Clock display, add the Clock command to the Main menu. See "Setting Up Your Main Menu Preferences" on page **186**.

Setting and Controlling an Alarm

You can also use the iPod's alarm to wake you up or remind you of an important time. You can set one alarm for each clock you've created, so you can also have as many alarms as you need by creating a clock for each alarm you want to set. To set an alarm, perform the following steps:

1. Select **Main** menu, **Extras**, **Clock**. You'll see the Clock screen with all the clocks you've created.
2. Select the clock for which you want to set an alarm. You'll see its menu.
3. Select **Alarm Clock**. You'll see the Alarm Clock menu (see Figure 11.5).
4. Highlight **Alarm** and press the **Select** button. The Alarm setting will become On, and the alarm will be active.
5. Highlight **Time** and press the **Select** button. You'll see the Alarm Time screen.

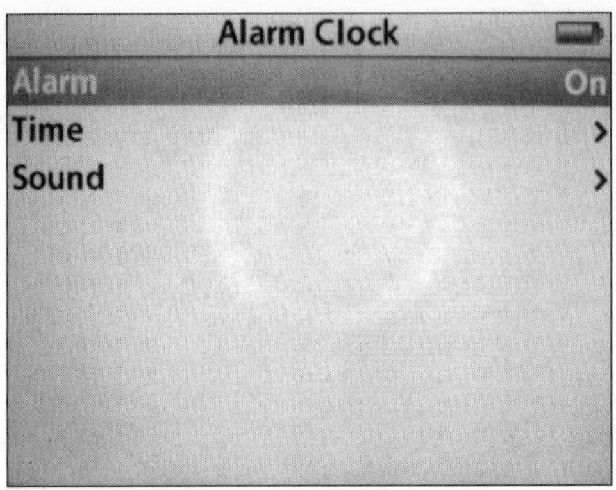

FIGURE 11.5
You use this screen to set a clock's alarm.

6. Use the **Click Wheel** to select the hour you want the alarm to sound. Drag clockwise to increase the time or counterclockwise to decrease it.
7. Press the **Select** button to set the hour.
8. Use the **Click Wheel** to set the minute, and press the **Select** button.
9. Use the **Click Wheel** to set AM or PM, and press the **Select** button. You'll go back to the Alarm Clock menu.
10. Select **Sound**. On the resulting menu, you can choose the sound that is played for the alarm. By default, the alarm sound setting will be Beep, which you can hear even if you don't have earphones or speakers connected to the iPod. If you choose a different sound, you have to have speakers or headphones attached to the iPod to hear the alarm.
11. If you want to have a playlist start playing instead of the beep, highlight the playlist you want to use as the alarm sound and press the **Select** button. You'll return to the Alarm Clock menu.

tip

Even though you set the alarm by the minute, you can get to any time quickly by rapidly dragging your finger around the Click Wheel in full circles.

When an alarm has been set for a clock, a bell icon will appear by the clock's time on the Clock menu. This lets you see that you have an alarm set for a specific clock.

When an alarm is set for a clock and the appointed time comes along, your iPod will turn on (if it's asleep) and play the beep sound or the selected playlist.

caution

Unless you are a light sleeper, don't expect the beep sound to wake you up. It isn't very loud and doesn't play very long. You'll have better luck if you connect your iPod to speakers and use a playlist instead.

If you combine an iPod with a set of speakers, it becomes a very nice bedside alarm clock. This is especially useful when you frequently stay in hotel rooms in which you can find a bewildering variety of alarm clocks, each of which requires different steps to set. With your iPod, you don't need to bother with those. Just set its alarm to use a playlist and connect it to the speakers. You can then wake up to your favorite tunes.

Using an iPod as a Stopwatch

You can also use your iPod as a stopwatch. Here's how:

1. Select **Main** menu, **Extras**, **Stopwatch**. You'll see the Stopwatch screen.
2. Select **Timer**. You'll see the Timer mode of the Stopwatch screen (see Figure 11.6).

FIGURE 11.6 If you need to time yourself, the iPod's Stopwatch can help.

3. When you're ready to start the time, highlight the **Start** button (it's selected by default) and press the **Select** button. The stopwatch will start.
4. To set a lap time, highlight the **Lap** button and press the **Select** button. That lap's time will be recorded as Lap 1. The stopwatch will create lap 2, and the time will continue.
5. To pause the stopwatch, highlight **Pause** and press the **Select** button.
6. To restart the stopwatch, highlight **Resume** and press the **Select** button.
7. To stop the stopwatch, highlight **Pause** and press the **Select** button.
8. Highlight **Done** and press the **Select** button. You'll return to the Stopwatch menu and will see the stopwatch session you just created, along with any others that were created previously.

To see the details of a stopwatch session, highlight the session on the Stopwatch menu and press the **Select** button. You'll see the information recorded during that session, including its date, time, total time, and information about the lap times.

To delete a stopwatch session, select the session, and press the **Select** button when its information is displayed. On the Delete Session menu, select **Delete**. That session will be deleted from the iPod.

Using an iPod to Play Games

Games are available for your iPod. In fact, it includes a few games by default. Although these are not the most exciting games in the world, they can be a good way to make time pass more quickly.

If you have an iPod, you can also purchase iPod games in the iTunes Store and download them onto the iPod. (nanos are currently incompatible.)

As with other types of content, after you've added iPod games to your iTunes Library, you need to move them to the iPod. Use the Games tab of the iPod screen to do this. Click the **Sync games** check box to move games onto the iPod. Then click **All games** to move all your games, or click **Selected games** and choose the games you want to sync by checking their check boxes. After you click **Apply**, the games will be synced according to these settings.

You can play the iPod's default games or any that you've purchased from the iTunes Store by selecting **Main** menu, **Extras**, **Games**. You'll see the Games menu. Select the game you want to play, and press the **Select** button. The game will start, and you use various iPod controls to play the game.

note

Even though iPod games you purchase from the iTunes Store are stored in your iTunes Library, you can't play them with iTunes. However, if you select the iPod Games source, you'll see the games you've added. Select a game to view information about it, such as an explanation of the controls you use to play it.

note

The iPod's calendar isn't designed as a replacement for a PDA or other full-featured calendar. Its purpose is only to enable you to view your calendar. For example, you can't add or delete events from the iPod; you have to make changes to the calendar on a computer.

Planning Your Days with the iPod Calendar

You can use an iPod to display a calendar, and you can add events on a calendar application, such as Outlook or iCal, to the iPod's calendar so you can view those events on the iPod.

Adding Calendar Information to an iPod

Like music, podcasts, video, and other content, you add calendar information to an iPod by updating it from iTunes. iTunes can update information from Outlook on Windows computers or from iCal on Macs.

If you don't use one of the supported applications, you can use a third-party application to transfer calendar information automatically, or you can do it yourself manually. Both of these are out of the scope of this chapter. However, because iTunes supports the most popular calendar application for each type of computer, you probably won't need to use the other options anyway.

To update your iPod's calendar, perform the following steps:

1. Connect your iPod to your computer and open **iTunes** if it isn't open already.
2. Select the iPod. You'll see the iPod screen.
3. Click the **Contacts** tab.
4. If you are using a Windows computer, check the **Sync calendars from Microsoft Outlook** check box (see Figure 11.7). Skip to step 6.

FIGURE 11.7
Keeping your iPod in sync with Outlook is as easy as checking this check box.

5. If you are using a Mac, check the **Sync iCal calendars** check box.
6. Then click **All calendars** if you want all your Outlook or iCal calendars moved onto the iPod. If you want to move only selected calendars, click **Selected calendars,** and then check the check box for each calendar whose information you want to move onto your iPod.

7. Click **Apply**. The calendar information you selected will be moved onto the iPod.

After you configure your calendar synchronization options, the iPod's calendar will be updated each time you connect it to your computer.

Viewing Your iPod Calendar

To view your iPod calendar, take the following steps:

1. Select **Main** menu, **Extras**, **Calendar**. You'll see the Calendars menu (see Figure 11.8). If you have moved multiple calendars onto the iPod, you'll see each of them listed on the screen.

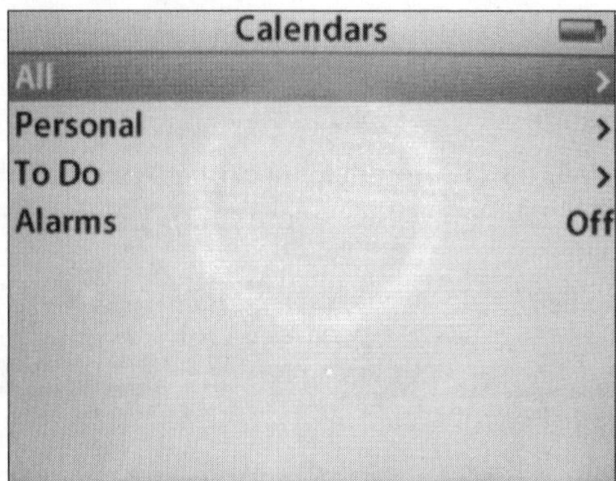

FIGURE 11.8
Choose a calendar to view it.

2. Highlight the calendar you want to view and press the **Select** button. If you want to see all calendar events, select **All** and press the **Select** button. You'll see the Calendar display (see Figure 11.9). The current date is highlighted in dark blue. Dates with one or more events scheduled are marked with a red flag.

Date with event

May 2006

Sun	Mon	Tue	Wed	Thu	Fri	Sat
30	1	2	3	4	5	6
7	8	9	10	11	12	13
14	15	16	17	18	19	20
21	22	23	24	25	26	27
28	29	30	31	1	2	3
4	5	6	7	8	9	10

FIGURE 11.9
Dates with an event are marked with a black box or a flag in the lower-right corner of the date box.

3. To get details for an event, use the **Click Wheel** to move to the date in which you are interested. As you move away from the current date, its box will take on a lighter shade, and the currently selected date will be highlighted in the darker shade.
4. When the date in which you are interested is highlighted, press the **Select** button. The events for that date will be listed.
5. To see the detailed information for an event, highlight it and press the **Select** button. You'll see the detailed information for that event.
6. Use the **Menu** button to move back to the list of events (one press) or back to the calendar (two presses).

tip

If you are looking at an event several months prior to or after the current date, the easiest way to get back to the current date is to use the Menu button to move up to the Calendars menu again and then select the calendar. When you return to it, you'll be in the current month.

The iPod calendar also picks up event alarms for the events you place on it. To configure the event alarm, open the **Calendars** menu and highlight the **Alarms** option. Set this to **Beep** to hear the beep sound for an event alarm, **Silent** to see a silent alarm, or **Off** to turn off the event alarm.

To see your To Do information, highlight **To Do** and press the **Select** button. Your list of tasks will be displayed.

To change events on or delete them from your iPod, change or delete them in the calendar application you use (Outlook or iCal) and sync your iPod. (The iPod enables you to view your calendar information, but you can't change it on the iPod itself.)

Using an iPod to Keep an Address Book

The iPod's Contacts tool is analogous to its Calendar. Storing contacts on an iPod makes accessing phone numbers, email addresses, and other information as fast and easy as grabbing your iPod.

Adding Contact Information to an iPod

As with the calendar, the first step you need to take is to move contact information from your computer to the iPod. You do this by setting the appropriate update options. On Windows computers, you can update contact information stored in Outlook or the Windows Address Book. On a Mac, you can sync information stored in the Address Book.

To set up your contact information update options, complete the following steps:

1. Connect your iPod to your computer and open iTunes if it isn't open already.
2. Select the iPod if it isn't selected already. You'll see the iPod screen.
3. Click the **Contacts** tab.
4. If you are using a Windows computer, check the **Sync contacts from** check box and choose the application you want to use, **Outlook** or **Windows Address Book**, on the drop-down menu.
5. If you are using a Mac, check the **Sync Address Book contacts** check box (see Figure 11.10).

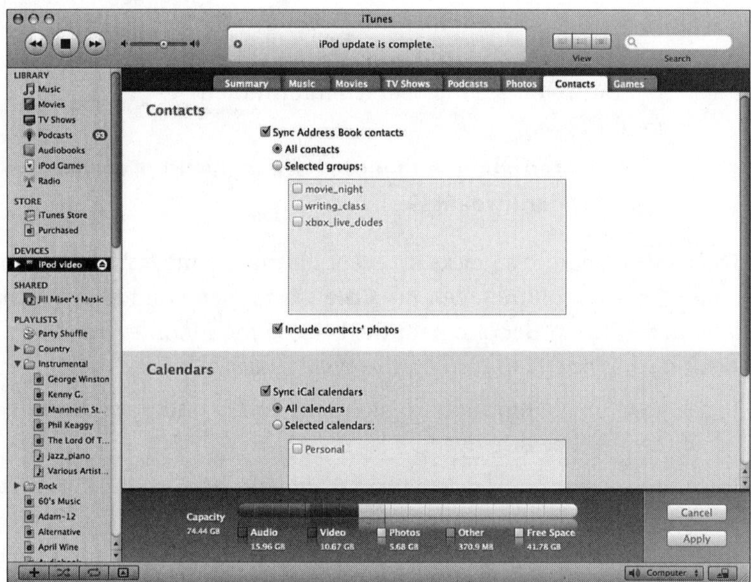

FIGURE 11.10
Keeping your iPod in sync with Address Book on a Mac is as easy as checking the Sync check box.

6. Click **All contacts** if you want all your contact information moved onto the iPod.
7. If you want to move only selected contacts onto the iPod, click **Selected groups** and then check the check box for each contact group whose information you want to move onto your iPod.
8. If you use a Mac and have photos associated with contacts in Address Book, check the **Include contacts' photos** check box if you want those photos to be imported with the contact information.
9. Click **Apply**. The contact information you selected will be moved onto the iPod.

Configuring How Contacts Appear on an iPod

When it comes to displaying contact information on an iPod, you have two options. To select an option, select **Main** menu, **Settings**, **Contacts**. You'll see the Contacts screen. This screen has two options. Use the **Sort** option to choose how contacts are sorted on the screen. Use the **Display** option to determine how contacts are displayed on the screen. In both cases, your choices are `First Last`, which lists the first name followed by the last name, or `Last First`, which places the last name fist and the first name last.

To select an option, choose the setting you want to set and press the **Select** button to toggle the option.

Viewing Contact Information on an iPod

To view your contacts, perform the following steps:

1. Select **Main** menu, **Extras**, **Contacts**. You'll see the list of contacts sorted by your sort preference (see Figure 11.11).
2. To view a contact's detailed information, highlight the contact in which you are interested and press the **Select** button. You'll see a screen showing all the information for that contact (see Figure 11.12).
3. Press the **Menu** button to return to the list of contacts.

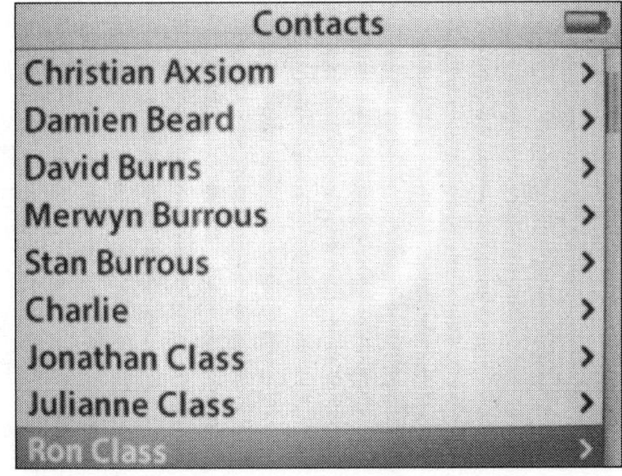

FIGURE 11.11 The Contacts screen displays a list of contacts stored on your iPod.

FIGURE 11.12 Here's contact information for Apple Computer.

Using an iPod to Store and Display Text

You can also store and display text files on your iPod. For example, you might want to store instructions to perform a task that you have trouble remembering how to do or the directions to a location on your iPod for easy reference.

Creating Notes for an iPod

To create a note on an iPod, use any word processor or other application that can create a text file. (The filename extension should be `.txt`.) Create the text you want to store on the iPod, and save it as a TXT file.

Moving Notes to an iPod

Connect your iPod to your computer, and place the text file you created in the Notes folder on the iPod's hard drive. (To do this, you need to configure your iPod so it can be used as a hard drive; see the next section to learn how to do this.)

Reading Notes on an iPod

After you have placed text files in the Notes folder, you can read them by selecting **Main** menu, **Extras**, **Notes**. You'll see the Notes screen, which contains a list of all the text files in the Notes folder on your iPod. To read a note, highlight it and press the **Select** button. You'll see the note's text on the screen (see Figure 11.13). Scroll down the screen to read all the text if you need to.

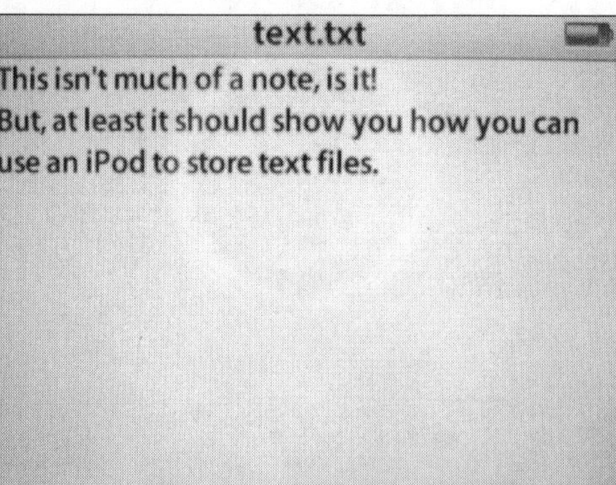

FIGURE 11.13
I hope you put your iPod's Notes feature to better use than I did.

Using an iPod as a Portable Hard Drive

Here's something that might or might not be news to you: iPods and iPod nanos are fully functional, portable hard drives. In addition to using the iPod's hard drive to store music, audio, video, and other content, you can also it just like any other hard drive you connect to your computer. Because you use USB 2 to connect it to a computer, an iPod hard drive has speedy performance, too.

> **note** Just as with any other drive you might use, you can work on files while they are stored on an iPod. So you could work on a file stored on your iPod while it is attached to your computer at work; when you connect the iPod to your home computer, the same file would be available on that computer.

The uses for an iPod as a hard drive are almost endless; following are a few examples:

- **A transport drive**—Have files you want to move from one computer to another? No problem. Connect your iPod to one computer, copy files to it, connect it to the second computer, and copy files from the iPod onto that computer.
- **Extra storage space**—Need a few extra GB of disk space? Connect your iPod, and you have it.
- **Temporary backup drive**—Have some important files you want to back up? Place them on an iPod, and there you go.

Enabling an iPod to Be Used as a Hard Drive

To be able to use an iPod as a hard drive, you need to configure it within iTunes by taking the following steps:

1. Connect your iPod to your computer. iTunes will open, and your iPod will be shown in the Source list.
2. Select the iPod if it isn't selected already. You'll see the iPod screen.
3. Click the **Summary** tab (see Figure 11.14).

> **note** If you previously selected the **Manually manage songs and playlists** option, you don't need to perform these steps, because that option automatically enables your iPod to be used as a hard disk.

FIGURE 11.14
Use the Summary tab to enable your iPod to act as a hard drive.

4. Check the **Enable disk use** check box. You'll see a warning prompt that explains that, if you enable disk use, you'll have to manually unmount the iPod before disconnecting it.
5. Click **OK** to close the warning prompt.
6. Click **Apply**. The iPod will be available to your computer as a hard drive.

If you don't enable an iPod to be used as a disk, you won't be able to see it from your computer's desktop. Only within iTunes will you be able to see the iPod when it is connected to your computer.

Using an iPod as a Hard Drive

After you have enabled this functionality, you can use an iPod as a disk by performing the following steps:

1. Connect your iPod to your computer. iTunes will open, and if you have configured automatic syncing, the iPod will be updated.
2. On your computer's desktop, open a new window that shows your computer's hard drives and other devices with which it can communicate. Select the iPod, which will be listed just like other hard drives in your system (see Figures 11.15 and 11.16).

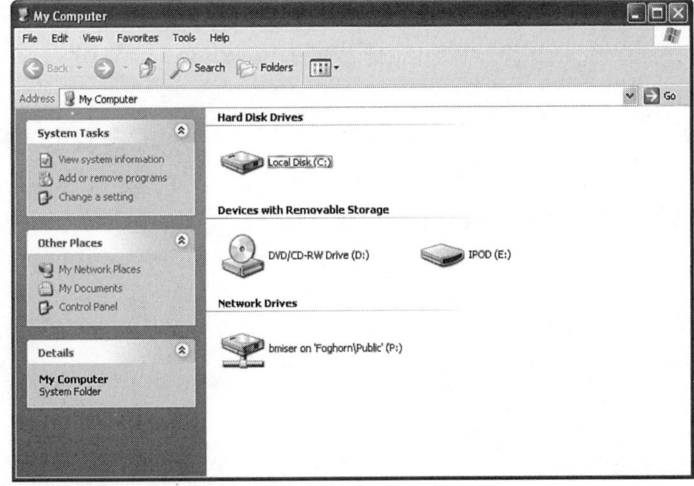

FIGURE 11.15
In the Windows' My Computer folder, you will see your iPod, which is listed in the Devices with Removable Storage section.

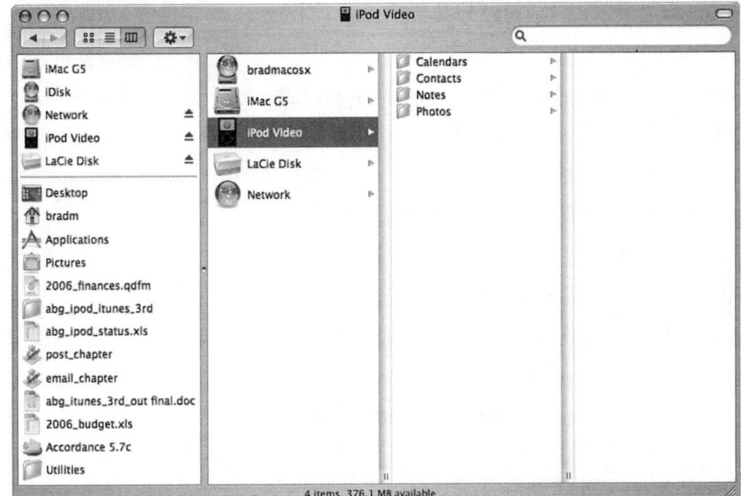

FIGURE 11.16
In the Mac's Finder, an iPod looks and works like other drives.

3. To copy files onto the iPod, drag them from other locations on your computer and drop them onto the iPod.
4. When you are finished moving files to or from the iPod, eject it. You can do this from the computer's desktop by selecting the iPod and selecting the **Eject** command or from within iTunes by selecting

tip

The iPod includes four folders by default: Calendars, Contacts, Notes, and Photos. You can create other folders on the iPod just as you can on other disks with which you work.

the iPod from the **Source** list and clicking one of the **Eject** buttons. The iPod will be unmounted, and you can safely disconnect it from your computer.

caution

When you have enabled an iPod to be used as a disk, you must manually eject it before disconnecting it from your computer. If you don't, you can damage the data stored on it. To let you know this, the `Do not disconnect` message will appear on the iPod's screen when it is mounted on your computer. Don't disconnect your iPod until you have ejected it and the `OK to Disconnect` message or its Main menu appears on its screen.

Using an iPod shuffle as a Flash Drive

Even though it doesn't have a hard drive, you can use the shuffle to store files as a USB flash drive. This works similarly to the other iPod models. First, set up the shuffle to be used as a drive. Then, use it.

Configuring an iPod shuffle as a Flash Drive

To prepare an iPod shuffle to be a flash drive, perform the following steps:

1. Plug the shuffle into your computer. iTunes will open, and the shuffle will appear on the Source list.
2. Select the shuffle if it isn't selected already.
3. Click the **Settings** tab.
4. Scroll down until you see the Enable Disk Use check box and slider (see Figure 11.17).
5. Check the **Enable disk use** check box and click **OK** in the resulting dialog box (which warns you that you must manually eject the shuffle before unplugging it when you use it as a drive). This enables your shuffle to become a USB flash drive.
6. Use the slider to set the amount of memory that should be reserved for songs. A portion of the shuffle's memory must be dedicated to the flash drive function to serve this purpose. Any memory you allocate for data won't be available for music and other audio content. As you move the slider, the information at each end of the slider will show you how much memory you have allocated for each purpose.
7. Click **Apply**. The shuffle will be ready for file storage.

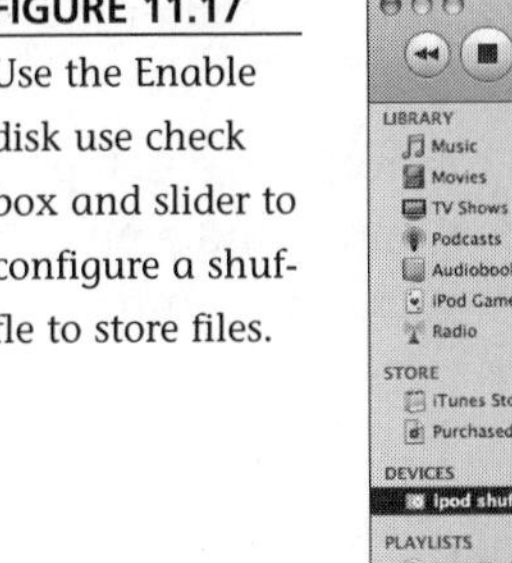

FIGURE 11.17
Use the Enable disk use check box and slider to configure a shuffle to store files.

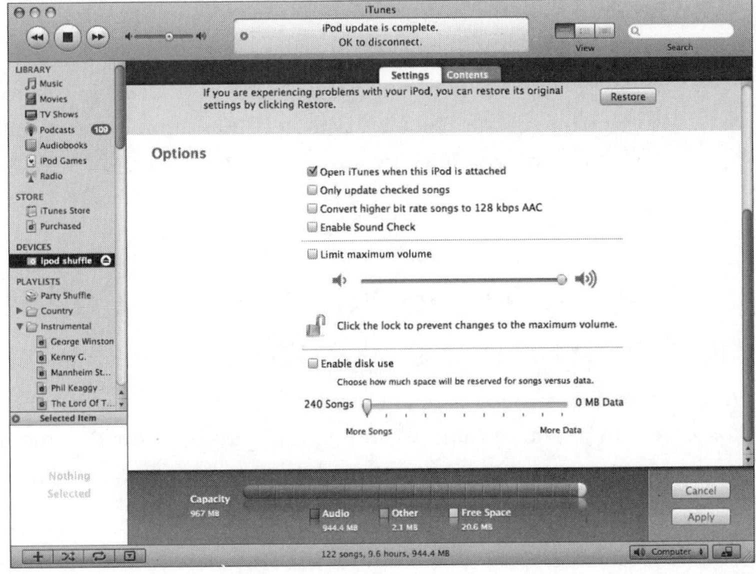

Using an iPod shuffle as a Flash Drive

After you have configured it for disk use, using a shuffle as a disk is simple:

1. Place the shuffle into the Dock connected to your computer. iTunes will open, and the shuffle will appear on the Source list. The shuffle will also be mounted on your desktop just like hard drives and other storage devices you use.
2. Move to your computer's desktop and locate the shuffle; it will have the name you gave it during the initial configuration process (or as close as your computer can come to it to create a valid disk name).
3. Open the shuffle just as you would any other storage device (see Figure 11.18).

FIGURE 11.18
The shuffle appears on the list of removable storage devices and can be used just like one of them. (This shuffle has several files stored on it.)

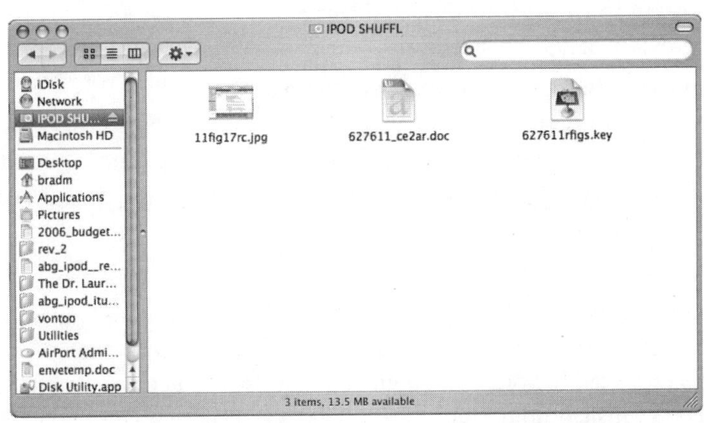

4. To add files to the shuffle, drag them from your desktop onto its icon or the folders it contains.
5. When you are finished using the shuffle as a disk, eject it from the desktop or click one of the **Eject** buttons in iTunes. (One is next to the shuffle on the Source list, whereas the other is in the lower-right corner of the iTunes window.)

Using an iPod to Move Your Music Collection from One Computer to Another

In this book, I encourage people to write to me, which they do. There is one question I am asked much more than any other, and that is, "How do I move my music from an iPod to my computer?" My answer is that using iTunes, you can't. iTunes is designed for one-way transfer, from the computer to an iPod. I suspect this is to help protect the copyright of purchased and other music.

If your iPod has enough disk space to store the music you have imported onto it within iTunes *and* all the music files in your iTunes Library on your computer's desktop, you can move the music files from the iPod onto a computer. Mount your iPod as a hard disk, copy the iTunes folder from the first computer onto the iPod, connect the iPod to another computer, copy the iTunes folder onto that computer, and import the music files into the iTunes Library on the second computer.

There are two issues with this approach, though. One is that you have to have enough room on your iPod for two versions of all your songs. The other is that it is a pain to import all that music into another iTunes Library.

> **caution**
>
> Don't use these applications to copy your music for people who aren't entitled to it. Just because an application can do this doesn't mean it is something you should do.

Applications are available that will enable you to move music from your iPod to a computer and provide lots of other features.

If you use a Windows computer, several applications can recover the music on your iPod and copy it to a computer. One example is iGadget, available at www.ipodsoft.com.

After you've downloaded and installed iGadget, launch it, get into the main interface, and you will see the iPods connected to your computer. You can then move the music on an iPod onto a computer.

If you use a Macintosh computer, you can download iPodRip from www.thelittleappfactory.com. When you install and open the application, you can work with the iPods connected to your computer. You can use the Recover iPod feature to restore an iPod's music onto a Mac.

Providing detailed steps for these applications is beyond the scope of this book, but both are relatively simple to use and include help systems if you have questions about how they work.

One of the nice things about these applications is that they, in effect, turn your iPod into a backup system for your iTunes Library (assuming your entire iTunes Library fits on your iPod, of course). Should anything happen to your iTunes Library, you can move the music from the iPod back onto your computer to restore it. Even if you can store all your iTunes files on your iPod, I still recommend that you back up on disc, through iTunes' Back-up feature.

THE ABSOLUTE MINIMUM

As you can see, the iPod is much more than just the world's best portable music and video player. As you live with your iPod, you'll likely come to appreciate its other uses, which include the following:

- You can use your iPod as a clock and even as an alarm clock. This is probably one of the most useful extra features, at least in my book (which you happen to be reading right now). You can also create and use multiple clocks for different time zones.
- You can purchase iPod games in the iTunes Store and download them onto an iPod. (Currently, the iPod nano does not support games.) The iPod also comes with a few games on its Games menu. Sure, none of these iPod games will challenge *Halo 2* on Xbox Live for the title of Best Game Ever, but they might help you kill a few minutes of time.
- You can store calendar events on your iPod's calendar to make it a handy way to keep track of where you are supposed to be and when you are supposed to be there.
- Forget carrying around a paper list of contact information; store the names, addresses, email addresses, and phone numbers of people you need to contact on your iPod, and that information will be available to you whenever your iPod is.
- You can store text files on your iPod and read them with the Notes function.
- Using your iPod as a portable hard drive or a shuffle as a flash drive just might be one of the best reasons to have an iPod. The ability to carry gigabytes of data on a device the size of a deck of playing cards is very useful indeed.
- You can move music from an iPod onto a computer, but without an additional application, it isn't the easiest task in the world. Fortunately, there are applications designed to do just this for both Windows and Macintosh computers.

IN THIS CHAPTER

- Learn where you can get information you need about your iPod's settings.
- Use some cool music playback settings, such as Shuffle and Repeat.
- Find out all you need to know about the mysterious Compilations setting.
- Set the brightness of an iPod's screen
- Customize your iPod's Main menu.
- Let your iPod get some well-earned rest by using its Sleep Timer.
- Get rid of the clicker—or not.
- Change your iPod's language.
- Secure your iPod like it is Fort Knox.
- Restore your iPod's settings to their default states.

12

CONFIGURING AN iPOD TO SUIT YOUR PREFERENCES

iPods are personal devices; because they are, you can customize them to work the way you want them to. You can control many aspects of how your iPod works by using the Settings menu. (Way back in Chapter 3, "Controlling an iPod or iPod nano," you learned how to use this menu to configure your iPod's backlight—but that was only the beginning!) In this chapter, you'll learn about many of the settings that you can use to customize an iPod to suit your personal preferences.

Learning About iPod Settings

Some iPod settings are applicable to specific tasks and are explained in the context of those tasks. Others are more general and are covered in this chapter. Table 12.1 provides an overview of all iPod settings and shows you where they are covered. If you need a quick explanation of a specific setting, you can refer to this table to see where to look for it.

If you only use an iPod shuffle, skip this chapter, because none of its information is applicable to you.

TABLE 12.1 Where to Look for iPod Setting Information

Setting	Overview	Where It's Explained
About	Provides information about the iPod	Chapter 6
Main Menu	Configures the commands on the Main menu	This chapter
Shuffle	Shuffles the music on the iPod	This chapter
Repeat	Repeats music on the iPod	This chapter
Volume Limit	Limits the iPod's maximum volume	This chapter
Backlight Timer	Controls whether or how long the backlight remains on	Chapter 3
Brightness (iPod only)	Changes the brightness of the screen	This chapter
Audiobooks	Sets the default speed for audiobook playback	Chapter 8
EQ	Configures the Equalizer	This chapter
Compilations	Determines whether compilations are grouped together	This chapter
Sound Check	Equalizes the volume of songs played	This chapter
Clicker	Determines whether you hear audio feedback when you use the Click Wheel	This chapter
Date & Time	Configures the date and time display	Chapter 11
Contacts	Sets the formats for contact information display	Chapter 11
Language	Sets the iPod's language	This chapter
Legal	Presents legal information for the iPod	This chapter
Reset All Settings	Returns iPod menus and settings to default settings	This chapter
Sleep Timer	Puts the iPod to sleep after a set period of time	This chapter

Configuring Music Playback Settings

Several of the iPod's settings relate to the way in which music and other audio plays. These include Shuffle, Repeat, Sound Check, EQ, Volume Limiter, and Compilations.

Shuffling Music

There are two ways to shuffle music on your iPod. You can configure music to shuffle by using the Shuffle setting. You can also use the Shuffle Songs command that is on the Main menu by default.

Shuffling Music with the Shuffle Setting

You can use the iPod's Shuffle feature to have songs play in a random order. To shuffle music, use the following steps:

1. Select **Main** menu, **Settings**. You'll see the Settings menu.
2. Highlight the **Shuffle** command (see Figure 12.1).

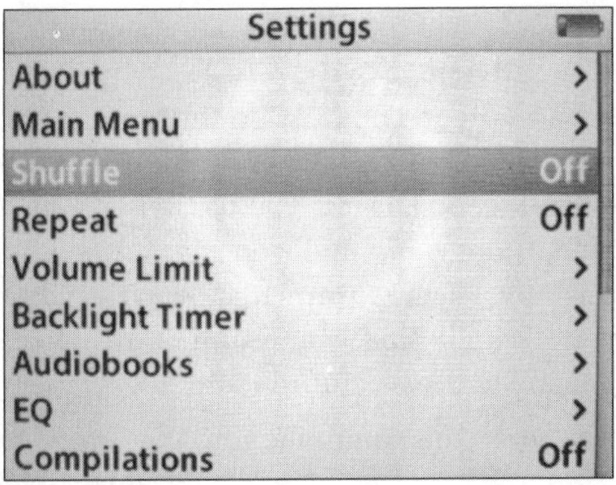

FIGURE 12.1
You can use the Shuffle setting to have an iPod play your music in random order.

3. If you want the songs within a selected Browse category or playlist to play in random order, press the **Select** button once. The Shuffle setting will become `Songs`. This causes the iPod to shuffle the songs within a music source when you play it.
4. If you want the iPod to select random albums when you select a Browse category or playlist, press the **Select** button again (two times total). The Shuffle setting will become `Albums`. This causes the iPod to select an album randomly, play all the songs on the album that are stored on the iPod, select another album randomly, and repeat this pattern until you turn off Shuffle again.
5. Select the music you want to play in a randomized fashion and play it. On the Now Playing screen, you'll see the Shuffle indicator to remind you that you are in Shuffle mode (see Figure 12.2).

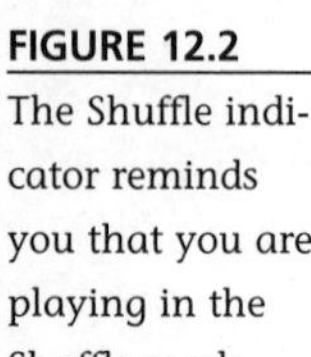

FIGURE 12.2
The Shuffle indicator reminds you that you are playing in the Shuffle mode.

6. To disable the Shuffle feature, move back to the Settings menu and press the **Select** button until you see `Off` next to the Shuffle setting. Your music will again play linearly.

Shuffling Music with Shuffle Songs

By default, the Shuffle Songs command appears on the Main menu. This command shuffles all the music on your iPod. This is different from the Shuffle setting you learned about in the previous section because you can select a specific source with that option. With the Shuffle Songs command, you can only shuffle through all your iPod's music. To shuffle this way, select **Main** menu, **Shuffle Songs**. When you play your iPod's music, you'll see the Shuffle indicator on the Now Playing screen. Music will move from one song to the next at random.

There is some interaction between this command and the Shuffle setting. If you have `Off` as the Shuffle setting, this command does what I described in the previous two paragraphs. If the Shuffle setting is Songs, both are doing the same thing and work as expected. If the Shuffle setting is Albums, using the Shuffle Songs command randomly selects an album, plays all the songs on that album in order, randomly chooses another album, plays all its songs in order, and so on.

When you want to stop shuffling music after you have selected the **Shuffle Songs** command on the Main menu, you have to select and play a music source, such as a playlist, an artist's music, and so on.

Repeating Music

The Repeat setting enables you to repeat an individual song as many times as you'd like or to repeat all the songs in a selected music source as many times as you can stand.

To repeat the same song ad infinitum, select **Main** menu, **Settings**. Highlight **Repeat** and press the **Select** button once so that `One` is displayed next to the Repeat setting. Select the song you want to hear and play it. It will play and then play again until you pause the iPod or choose a different song. While the song plays, the Repeat One indicator will appear on the Now Playing screen (see Figure 12.3).

FIGURE 12.3
You can make the same song play over and over until you just can't take it anymore.

To repeat all the songs within a selected music source, select **Main** menu, **Settings**. Highlight **Repeat** and press the **Select** button twice so that `All` is displayed next to the Repeat setting. Select the music source (such as a playlist) you want to hear and play it. It will play and then repeat until you pause the iPod or select a different music source. While the music source plays, the Repeat All indicator will appear on the Now Playing screen (see Figure 12.4).

When you have Repeat set to `One`, don't be fooled by the 1 of X indicator on the Now Playing screen. "X" will continue to be the number of songs in the selected source, but the number of the current song (such as 1 of) won't change because that song gets repeated.

To turn off Repeat, select **Main** menu, **Settings**. Highlight **Repeat** and press the **Select** button until `Off` is displayed next to the Repeat setting. Music will again play one time through and then stop.

The Repeat feature also interacts with the Shuffle Songs command. If Repeat is `Off`, Shuffle Songs plays all the songs on your iPod once (randomly, of course). If Repeat is set to `One` and you use the Shuffle Songs command, one song will be selected and played until you stop it or the iPod runs out of battery. If Repeat is set to `All` and you select Shuffle Songs, all the songs are played at random and then start over again and play in the same order until you stop playing or the iPod runs out of power.

FIGURE 12.4 You can use the Repeat All mode to repeat all the songs in a selected music source, such as a playlist.

Using Sound Check

iTunes' Sound Check feature causes songs to play back at the same relative volume level—if you have ever been jolted out of your chair because of one song's volume level being much higher than the next one, you know why this is a good thing. Using the iPod's Sound Check setting, you can cause the iPod to use the volume levels set by iTunes when Sound Check is on.

To use Sound Check, make sure it is active on the Playback pane of the iTunes Preferences dialog box. Then connect your iPod to your computer so the iPod's music will be updated, or you can perform a manual update if that is how you have configured iTunes for your iPod. After the update is complete, on the iPod select **Main** menu, **Settings**. On the Settings menu, highlight **Sound Check** and press the **Select** button. The Sound Check setting will become `On` to show you that it is in use. When you play music back, it will play at the same relative volume level.

To return the volume level to the "normal" state, select **Main** menu, **Settings**. Highlight **Sound Check** and press the **Select** button so that `Off` appears as the Sound Check setting.

Using the iPod's Equalizer

The iPod also has a built-in Equalizer you can use to improve (*improve* being a relative term, of course) the music to which you listen. The iPod includes a number of presets designed to enhance specific kinds of music and other audio sources. To use the iPod Equalizer, do the following steps:

1. Select **Main** menu, **Settings**.
2. Highlight the **EQ** setting and press the **Select** button. You'll see the EQ menu (see Figure 12.5). On this menu, you will see all the available presets. The list

is pretty long, so you will need to scroll down to see all your options. The presets include those designed for specific styles of music, such as Acoustic, Classical, Jazz, and so on, as well as for situations in which you might be using your iPod to play music, such as Small Speakers.

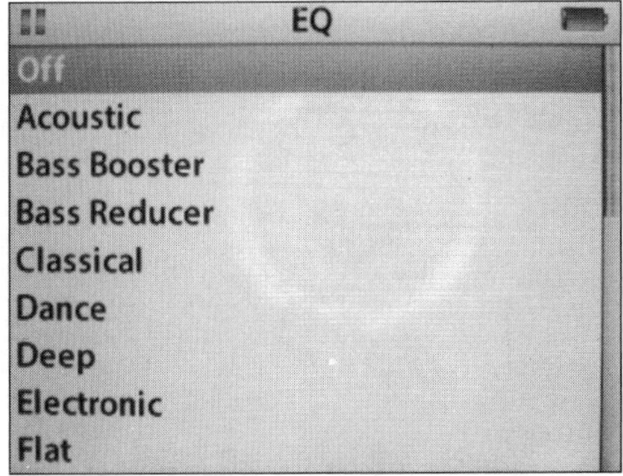

FIGURE 12.5
Choose an Equalizer preset on the EQ menu to activate it.

3. Highlight the preset you want to use and press the **Select** button. You'll return to the Settings menu. When you play music, the Equalizer will adjust the volume levels of various frequencies to enhance certain frequencies and to reduce the levels of others, according to the preset you selected.

If you have created your own presets on the iTunes Equalizer, they won't be available on your iPod. The iPod includes a set of presets, and those are all you can use. Fortunately, the list of presets is quite large, so this isn't much of a limitation.

Limiting Volume

Listening to loud sound over time can damage your hearing. The louder the sound, the more damage to your hearing you can do. Although iPods are small, the sound they can product isn't. You can set a maximum volume output limit on an iPod so that you don't exceed this limit when you are adjusting the iPod's volume from the Now Playing screen. You can also lock this limit so that it can only be changed by someone who knows a code you set.

To limit your iPod's volume output, perform the following steps:

1. Select **Main** menu, **Settings**.
2. Select **Volume Limit**. You'll see the Volume Limit screen (see Figure 12.6). At the bottom of the screen, you'll see the Volume bar. The current volume limit

is indicated by the blue triangle on this bar. The current volume range is indicated by the area of the bar that is filled in blue.

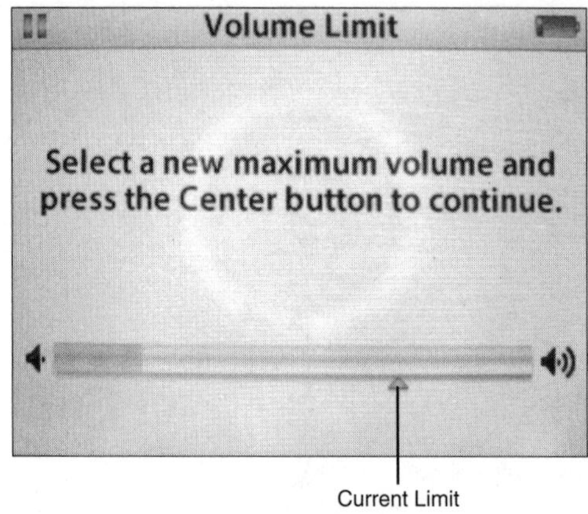

FIGURE 12.6
You can use the Volume Limit to set an iPod's maximum volume level.

3. Set the volume level at which you want to place the limit by sliding your thumb around the **Click Wheel** just as you do to change the volume while listening to music.
4. When the volume is set at what you want the limit to be, press the **Select** button. The limit indicator will move to that volume level. After a moment or two, the screen will update to enable you to choose to set a combination to lock the setting you entered or leave it available to change.
5. If you don't want to set a combination on the limiter so that it can be changed by anyone who uses the iPod, select **Done**. The volume limit will be set, and you'll move back to the Settings menu.
6. If you do want to protect the limit setting with a code, select **Set Combination**. The Enter New Code screen will appear (see Figure 12.7).
7. Slide your thumb around the **Click Wheel** until the number you want to set as the first digit in the code appears in the first box; then press the **Select** button. The second digit's box will be highlighted.
8. Repeat step 8 to set the second, third, and fourth digit in the code. After you've selected the fourth digit, the code you entered will be set, and you'll move back to the Settings menu.

When a volume limit is set and the volume is turned up to the limit, a padlock icon will appear at the right end of the Volume bar on the Now Playing screen to indicate the limit has been reached (see Figure 12.8).

FIGURE 12.7
Setting a code will prevent anyone who doesn't know the code you set from changing the volume limit.

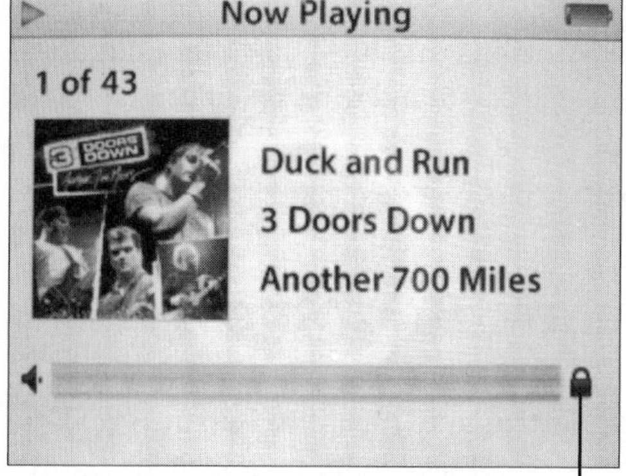

FIGURE 12.8
You can turn the iPod's volume up to here, but no further.

If you entered a code for the volume limit, you'll be prompted to enter that code the next time you select the Volume Limit setting. You enter the code in the same way you set it. If you enter it correctly, you'll be able to use the previous steps to set a new limit. If you don't, you won't be able to change the limit.

To clear the code, change the volume limit and select **Done** (instead of **Set Combination**). (You have to know the current code to be able to do this.)

Configuring Compilations

In iTunes' and iPod lingo, a compilation is a collection of songs by different artists—you know, something like *The Greatest Lounge Lizard Songs of All Time*. You can use the Compilations setting to add the Compilations command to the Music menu. When you choose this command, you'll see the compilation albums on your iPod (see Figure 12.9).

FIGURE 12.9
You won't find *The Greatest Lounge Lizard Songs of All Time* among my compilation albums.

tip

If you don't have the Compilation setting on, you can still select compilation albums by their title, using the Albums option on the Music menu.

To add the Compilations command to your Music menu, select **Main** menu, **Settings**. Highlight **Compilations** and press the **Select** button. The Compilations setting will become `On`, and the command will appear on the Music menu.

To remove the Compilations command from the menu, repeat the previous steps so that the Compilations setting shows `Off` as its status.

Setting an iPod Screen's Brightness

You can set the brightness level of the screen on an iPod (not on an iPod nano). To do so, select **Main** menu, **Settings**. Highlight **Brightness** and press the **Select** button. On the resulting screen, you'll see the Brightness slider. Use the **Click Wheel** to increase or decrease brightness to suit your preference. The relative brightness level is indicated by the part of the slider filled with blue; the default brightness level is indicated by the vertical line in the slider. When you're finished, press the **Menu** button. (If music or other audio is playing, you don't need to do that because you'll move back to the Now Playing screen automatically.)

Setting Up Your Main Menu Preferences

You can configure the commands on the iPod's Main menu to customize it to suit your preferences. For example, suppose you frequently browse your music by artist. You can add the Artists command to the Main menu so you don't have to drill down through the Music menu to get to this category that you use frequently. To configure your Main menu, do the following steps:

1. Select Main menu, **Settings**. The Settings menu will appear.
2. Highlight **Main** menu and press the **Select** button. You'll see the Main menu screen (see Figure 12.10). On this menu, each command is listed along with its current Main menu state. If `On` is listed next to a command, it

appears on the Main menu. If `Off` is listed next to a command, it doesn't appear on the Main menu. The commands are grouped into categories, including Music, Photos, Videos, Extras, and so on. (Of course, the list includes only those commands that an iPod supports.)

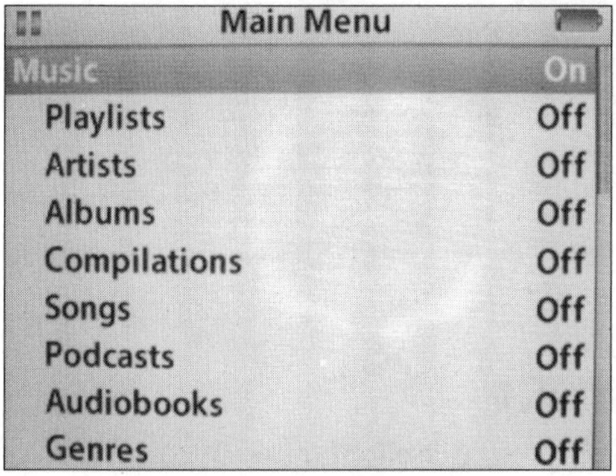

FIGURE 12.10
You can add items to the Main menu by turning them on or remove them by turning them off.

3. To add a command to the Main menu, highlight it and press the **Select** button so that `On` is listed next to that command (see Figure 12.11). That command will then appear on the Main menu.

FIGURE 12.11
When `On` appears next to a command, such as the Artists command, it will be on the Main menu.

4. To remove a command from the Main menu, highlight it and press the **Select** button so that `Off` is listed next to that command. That command will not appear on the Main menu.
5. Repeats step 3 or 4 for each command until you have set all the commands you want on the Main menu to `On` and all those you don't want to appear on the Main menu to `Off`. When you view the Main menu, your command preferences will be in effect (see Figure 12.12).

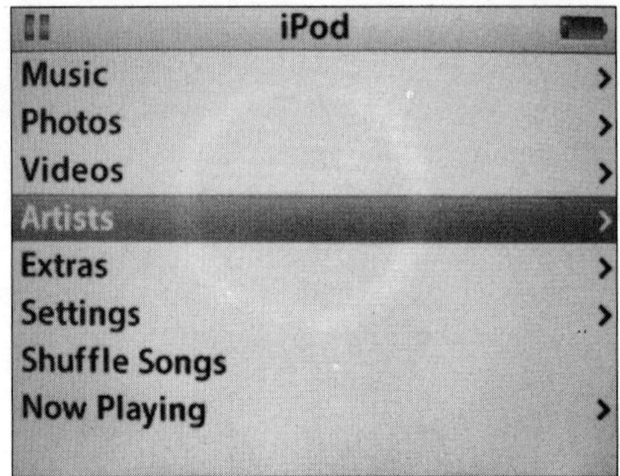

FIGURE 12.12
Using the Main menu settings, I customized the Main menu on this iPod. (Notice that I can use the Artists command on the Main menu to more quickly browse this iPod's music by artist.)

Setting the Sleep Timer

You can configure your iPod to turn itself off automatically after a specific period of time passes. Because this setting doesn't appear on the Settings menu, it isn't technically a setting. But it behaves like one, so it made sense to me to cover it here. To configure an iPod's sleep timer, take the following steps:

1. Select **Main** menu, **Extras**, **Clock**.
2. Select one of the **clocks** shown on the Clock menu. (You learned how to use the iPod's clocks in Chapter 11, "Taking the iPod Further.") You'll see that clock's menu.
3. Select **Sleep Timer**. You'll see the Sleep menu, which consists of a list of sleep time periods, from `Off` (meaning that the Sleep Timer is turned off) to `120 Minutes` (meaning that the iPod will sleep in 2 hours).
4. Select the **Sleep Timer** setting you want by highlighting it and pressing the **Select** button. The sleep timer will be set, and you'll return to the clock's menu.

When you have the Sleep Timer on and view the Now Playing screen, the current amount of time until the iPod sleeps is shown at the top of the screen (see Figure 12.13). When the counter reaches zero, the iPod will go to sleep. This happens regardless of whether you happen to be listening to music at the time. So, if your iPod suddenly shuts off and you don't first see a low battery warning, this is likely the reason.

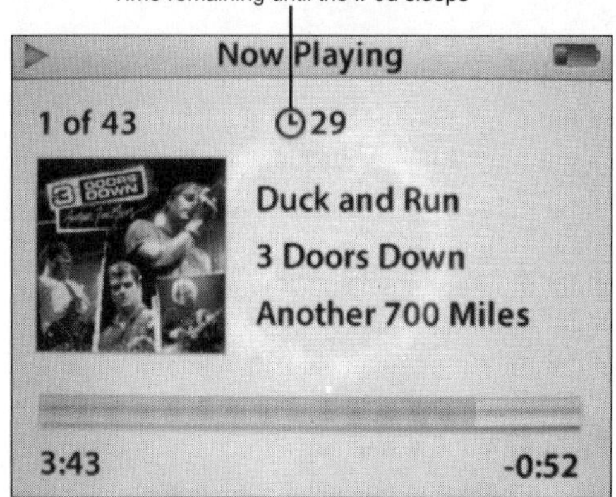

FIGURE 12.13
This iPod will turn itself off in 29 minutes.

Configuring the Clicker

As you select various menu options, your iPod "clicks" to give you audible feedback. You can turn off the Clicker if you don't want to hear it. To configure the Clicker, select **Main** menu, **Settings**. Then highlight the **Clicker** option and press the **Select** button until the setting you want is selected. If On is displayed, the Clicker will sound. If Off is displayed, it won't.

At press time, the nano had a different set of options for the Clicker. In addition to turning the Clicker off, you can select **Headphones** to have the Clicker play via the Headphones jack only, **Speaker** to have it play via the iPod's speaker (this is the same as the On setting on an iPod), or **Both** to have it play both ways.

Working with the iPod's Language

When you first turned on your iPod, you selected the language in which you wanted it to communicate with you. In most cases, you will never need to change that initial setting. However, you can change your iPod's language if you need to for some reason.

To choose a different language, select **Main** menu, **Settings**, **Language**. You'll see the Language menu (see Figure 12.14). Highlight the language you want your iPod to use, and press the **Select** button. The menus will change and use the language you selected.

tip

If you accidentally select a language you can't read, you can use the information later in this chapter to reset the language even if you currently can't read the iPod's menus.

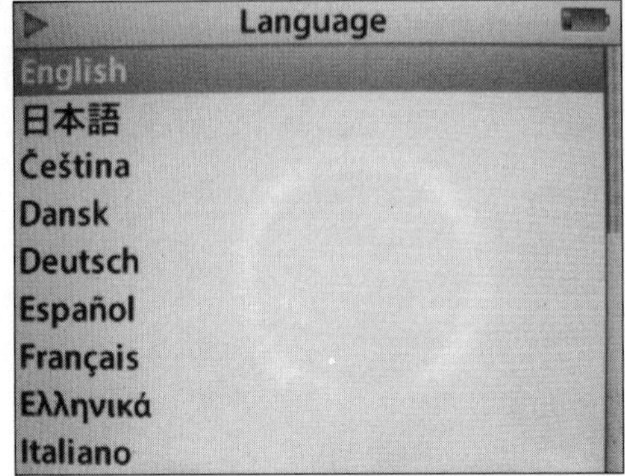

FIGURE 12.14
If I were multilingual, more of these settings might be useful, but because I am language limited, only one is applicable to me.

Locking an iPod's Screen

You can lock your iPod's screens so that commands can't be entered without first entering a code you set. To lock your iPod's screen, do the following:

1. Select **Main** menu, **Extras**, **Screen Lock**, **Set Combination**. You'll see the Enter New Code screen.
2. Slide your thumb around the **Click Wheel** until the number you want to set as the first digit in the code appears in the first box; then press the **Select** button. The second digit's box will be highlighted.
3. Repeat step 2 to set the second, third, and fourth digit in the code. After you've selected the fourth digit, the code you entered will be set, and you'll move back to the Screen Lock menu. You'll see a different set of commands on the screen now, which are Change Combination and Turn Screen Lock On.
4. To lock your iPod, select **Turn Screen Lock On**.
5. Select **Lock**. Your iPod will be locked up tight. (If you don't really want to lock it, choose **Cancel** instead.)

tip

If you find the ability to lock your iPod useful, add the Screen Lock command to the Main menu so you don't have to drill down to use it.

When your iPod is locked, the Enter Code to Unlock screen will appear (see Figure 12.15). To unlock the iPod so that you can control it, you must enter its code. You do this just like setting it; use the **Click Wheel** to enter the first digit and press the **Select** button. Do this for each digit. If you enter the code correctly, the iPod will be unlocked again and you can use it. If you don't enter the code correctly, the code boxes will flash red, and the Enter Code to Unlock screen will remain visible until you enter the correct code.

To change your iPod's code, select **Main** menu, **Extras**, **Screen Lock**, **Change Combination**. Then use the Enter Old Code screen to enter the current code. You'll see the Enter New Code screen that you can use to create a new code.

FIGURE 12.15
When you see this screen, you must enter the iPod's code to be able to use it.

Returning an iPod to That Factory-Fresh Feeling

On occasion, all your work configuring your iPod might not be what you intended. Fortunately, you can return the iPod settings to their default values with a single menu command.

To do this, select **Main** menu, **Settings**, **Reset All Settings**. You'll see the Reset All menu. Highlight **Reset** and press the **Select** button. Your iPod's menus and all other settings will be returned to their default condition. You'll see the Language menu you use to select the language you want your iPod to use. Do so, and you'll move to the Main menu.

THE ABSOLUTE MINIMUM

In this chapter, you've explored many of the options on the Settings menu and learned a number of ways to make your iPod suit your personal preferences. Check out the following list to review what you have learned and to pick up a few more pointers:

- Most of the Setting commands are explained in this chapter, but a few are covered in the context of what they control. A few settings that aren't actually on the Settings menu were also explained in this chapter.
- Use the Shuffle, Repeat, Sound Check, EQ, and Volume Limit settings to configure how music plays on your iPod.
- If your music library includes compilation albums, you might want to add the Compilations command to the Music menu so you can access your compilations quickly and easily.
- If you have an iPod, you can use the Brightness setting to make the screen brighter or dimmer.
- You can configure your iPod's Main menu by using the Main menu settings. You can put the commands you use most frequently on the Main menu so that they are easy to find and use.
- Use the Sleep Timer to have your iPod go to sleep automatically.
- If you don't like the clicking sound the iPod makes when you press a button, you can turn it off.
- Your iPod is multilingual; use the Language settings to determine which language your iPod uses.
- If you want to require that a code be entered before your iPod can be used, use the Screen Lock feature.
- You can restore your iPod to its factory settings with the Reset All Settings command.
- The About command on the Settings menu provides important information about your iPod, including its name, its disk capacity, its available space, the software version installed on it, its model, and its serial number.
- The Date & Time settings enable you to configure and work with your iPod's clock. You learned about these settings in Chapter 11, "Taking the iPod Further."
- The Legal command setting takes you to the oh-so-useful Legal screen, which contains lots of legalese you can read should you have absolutely nothing else to do.

IN THIS CHAPTER

- Maximize your iPod's battery life and durability.
- Update or restore your iPod's software.
- Identify and solve iPod problems.

13

MAINTAINING AN IPOD AND SOLVING PROBLEMS

The iPod is a well-designed device, and it is more likely than not that you will never have trouble with it, especially if you practice good battery management and keep its software up-to-date. In this chapter, you'll learn how to do those two tasks, plus you'll also learn how to handle problems in the unlikely event they do occur.

Maintaining Your iPod's Power

Like any other portable electronic device, your iPod literally lives or dies by its battery. When not connected to a power source, your iPod's battery is the only thing standing between you and an iPod-less life. Fortunately, working with your iPod's battery isn't very difficult, but it is something you need to keep in mind.

There has been a lot of controversy regarding the iPod's battery, including several lawsuits and some awards from those lawsuits. Getting into the details of the iPod battery's legal and other history isn't the point of this section. Unless you have an older iPod, you'll probably not encounter battery problems anyway. But be aware that just like all rechargeable batteries, the iPod's battery will wear out eventually. Depending on how you use it, this likely won't happen for several years, so it won't be something you need to deal with in the near term.

Monitoring and Maximizing Battery Life

The batteries on different iPod models and different generations of the same models are rated for different amounts of playing time. At press time, the 30GB iPod's battery is rated for up to 14 hours of music only, 4 hours of slideshows with music, and 3.5 hours of video. The 80GB's ratings are 20, 6, and 6.5 hours respectively. The iPod nano's battery is good for 24 hours of music or 5 of slideshows with music. The shuffle will last for up to 12 hours. Of course, these ratings are based on ideal conditions, which means the iPod plays straight through for these periods with no controls being used, no backlighting, and so on. Should you expect to get that much time under actual conditions? Probably not. Later in this section, you'll learn how to test your iPod's battery to ensure it is in good condition.

The Battery icon in the upper-right corner of the screen always tells you what your battery's status is at any point in time for all iPods (except the shuffle).

When your iPod is running on battery power, the amount of color shading within the battery icon provides a relative—and I do mean *relative*—indication of your battery's current state (see Figure 13.1). As you use battery power, the shaded part of the battery will decrease and change color as your iPod runs out of gas. When you reach the critically low point, the color will become red, and the bar will be empty. When the iPod's battery runs totally out of juice, you'll see an icon of a battery with an exclamation point that indicates your iPod is out of power and that the battery will have to be charged before you can use the iPod again.

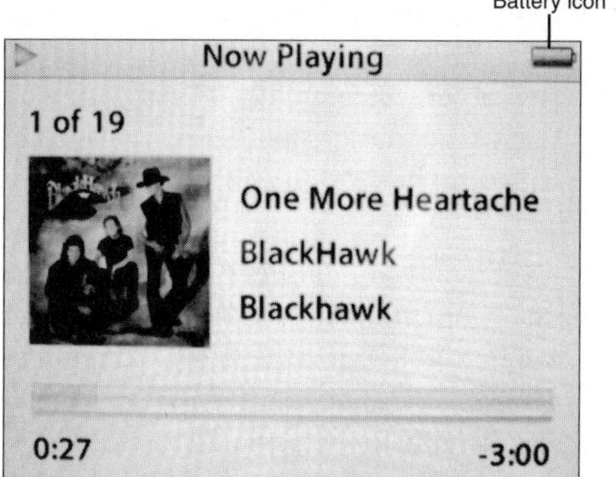

FIGURE 13.1
Keep an eye on the battery icon to make sure you don't run out of juice while you're on the move.

Determining the state of the iPod shuffle's battery is much harder (not really). The Power Status light is next to the Power slider on the bottom side of the shuffle. When you turn on a shuffle, this light will illuminate momentarily. If the light is green, you are good to go. If it's orange (Apple calls this *amber*), you are running somewhat low and should recharge when you can. If it is red, you are close to being empty and need to recharge ASAP. If the light doesn't appear at all, your shuffle is out of power and you are out of luck if you want to listen to music.

iPods and iPod nanos have two "off" modes. In the Sleep mode, the iPod's screen is dark and it isn't doing anything. This mode uses less power than the active mode. iPods can also be shut down, which is the lowest power mode. iPods put themselves into shut down mode; you can only put them to sleep. After an iPod has been in the Sleep mode for a while, it will shut itself down. You can tell the difference when you start using an iPod. If it comes back to life immediately, it was in Sleep mode. If it has to restart (during which you see the Apple logo on its screen), it was shut all the way down.

To maximize your iPod's playing time per battery charge, you can do the following:

- Keep the iPod's software up-to-date. (You'll learn how later in this chapter.)
- Use the Hold feature (the Hold switch on the iPod and iPod nano, or press and hold the **Play** button for three seconds on the shuffle) to prevent your iPod's controls from being unintentionally activated when you carry it around. You'd be amazed how easy it is for the iPod to be turned on and start playing without your knowing it, especially if you carry it in your pocket, backpack, or computer bag without a case. (It's no fun trying to listen to some tunes only to find

out your iPod's battery has been accidentally drained—not that this has ever happened to me, of course.)

- When you aren't listening or watching, don't keep your iPod playing; press the **Pause** button to stop the music, slideshow, or video. Playing content uses power at a greater rate than not playing. (You could have probably guessed that).
- Put your iPod to sleep (iPod, iPod nano) or turn it off (iPod shuffle) when you aren't using it. The Sleep or Off modes use less power. (You can press and hold the **Play/Pause** button to put an iPod or iPod nano to sleep. You can also add the Sleep command to the Main menu if you prefer to use that instead. You can turn a shuffle off by using the slider.)
- Keep backlighting at a minimum level. Backlighting is very helpful to be able to see the iPod's screen, especially in low-light conditions. However, it does use additional power, so you should use it only as necessary to maximize battery life. When you don't need it, such as in daylight conditions, turn it off. When you do need it, set it so that it remains on only a few seconds when you press a control.
- Minimize track changes. Each time you change tracks, the iPod uses more power than it would just playing tracks straight through. Likewise, using the Shuffle mode consumes power at a faster rate because the iPod's disk has to be accessed more frequently.
- Turn off the Equalizer. Using the Equalizer consumes more power than playing music without it.
- Every 30 recharges or so, fully drain the battery by playing the iPod until it runs out of power, and then recharge its battery.
- Keep the iPod at a comfortable temperature. Using the iPod in very cold or very hot conditions lowers its battery life.

If your iPod does run all the way out of battery power, even if there isn't enough power to turn it on, don't worry. Nothing will happen to the data stored on it. It will be maintained.

Charging an iPod's Battery

Fortunately, there are a number of ways to charge your iPod's battery, including the following:

- Connect the iPod to a USB 2 port on your computer either directly with a cable or via a Dock. This has the benefit of syncing your iPod at the same time you charge its battery.

- Purchase an optional AC adapter and use it to charge the iPod's battery.
- Purchase and use a power adapter designed for 12-volt sources, such as the power outlets in your vehicle, to charge the iPod on the move.

The iPod lets you know it is charging in two different ways.

When your iPod's battery is charging via a connection to a computer, the Battery icon will include a lightning bolt symbol and display a filling motion from the left to the right of the icon. When the battery is fully charged, the icon will be completely filled, and the motion will stop (see Figure 13.2).

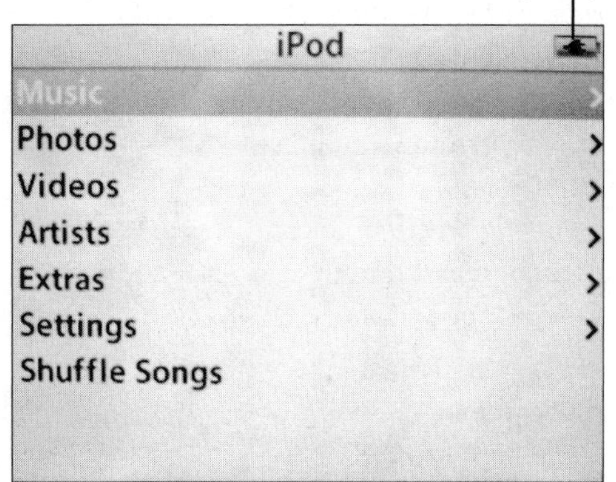

FIGURE 13.2
This iPod's battery has been fully charged via a USB cable.

When you charge your iPod's battery through a separate power adapter only, the battery icon fills the iPod's screen and flashes. When the process is complete, the battery icon remains steady, and the fully charged message appears (see Figure 13.3).

FIGURE 13.3
This iPod has been charged with a power adapter.

When you are charging a shuffle, its Power Status light (located next to the Power slider) will flash orange while the battery is charging. When it's fully charged, its light will be green.

According to Apple, it takes only 2 hours (iPod or iPod shuffle) or 1.5 hours (iPod nano) to charge a drained battery to 80% of its capacity. It can take up to 4 hours (iPod or iPod shuffle) or 3 hours (iPod nano) to fully charge a drained battery.

Getting More Life Out of an iPod's Battery

The iPod uses a lithium-ion battery. Any battery, including the iPod's, will eventually wear out and no longer provide the power it once did. In my research, most lithium-ion batteries are rated for 300–500 charges. In the iPod realm, a charge can't be precisely defined, but it does include a full discharge and then a full recharge. A partial charge doesn't "count" as much, but the precise relationship between the amount of charge and how much that charge "counts" can't be specified.

note Unlike some other rechargeable batteries, lithium-ion batteries don't have a memory, which means their performance is not degraded by not being fully discharged and then recharged each time.

Batteries like that in the iPod actually last longer if you don't let them fully discharge before you recharge them. Frequent "topping off" will not reduce the battery's life and in fact is better for your battery than letting it run very low on power before you recharge it.

Every 30 recharges or so, do run your iPod until it is completely out of power and then perform a full recharge. This will reset the battery's power gauge, which tends to become more inaccurate if the battery is never fully discharged.

It doesn't hurt the battery to do frequent and short recharges, such as by connecting the iPod to your computer every day after you are finished using it.

However, you should be sure to run the iPod on battery power for significant periods of time. If you constantly run the iPod from the power adapter or while it is in the Dock connected to a power source, the iPod's battery's performance will degrade over time.

Solving Battery Problems

Frankly, your iPod's battery will eventually wear out. You'll know this by the time it can play on battery power becoming shorter and shorter. The battery is the most likely source of any problems you might experience.

Testing Your iPod's Battery

If your iPod doesn't seem to play for a reasonable amount of time, you should test it to get an idea of what its current battery life is. Test your iPod by performing the following steps:

Because fully discharging and then recharging an iPod's battery causes wear on it, you shouldn't do this test frequently. Do it only if you suspect your iPod's battery is having problems. Or do it every 30 recharges or so to condition your iPod's power system.

1. Fully charge your iPod.
2. Remove the iPod from the charger so it is running on battery power.
3. Make a note of the current time.
4. Use the **Settings** commands to turn off the Equalizer, Shuffle, and Backlight.
5. Set **Repeat** to **All**; on the shuffle, use the slider to have music play back straight through.
6. Select an album or a playlist and play it.
7. Let the iPod play until it runs out of power. While the iPod is playing, don't use any of its controls. Anytime you cause the iPod to perform an action, you cause it to use additional power. In this test, you are attempting to determine what its maximum life is so you can compare it to its rated life.
8. When the iPod stops playing and the low power icon appears in the display (iPod or iPod nano), make a note of the time.
9. Calculate the battery life by figuring out how much time passed since you started the iPod playing. (Compare the time you noted in step 8 with that you noted in step 3.)

The rated life of iPod batteries changes regularly, but when I wrote this, the following ratings applied:

- **iPod shuffle**—Rated for up to 12 hours of playing time. If yours lasts more than 8–10 hours, your battery is in good shape. If it won't last more than 6 hours, you likely have a battery problem.
- **iPod nano**—Rated for up to 24 hours of playing time for music only or up to 5 hours for slideshows with music. If yours lasts more than 16–18 hours while playing music, your battery is probably in good shape. If it won't last more than 12 hours when playing music, you likely have a battery problem. For slideshows, if it can play for 2–3 hours, it's good to go. If it will play for only 2 hours or fewer, the battery is not performing up to snuff.
- **30GB iPod**—Rated for up to 14 hours of music playing time, 4 hours of slideshows with music, or 3.5 hours of video. If yours lasts more than 8–10

hours of music, 2–3 hours of slideshows, or more than 2 hours of video, your battery is in good shape. If it won't last more than these general guidelines, you likely have a battery problem.

- **80GB iPod**—Rated for up to 20 hours of music playing time, or 6 hours of slideshows with music, or 6.5 hours of video. If yours lasts more than 16–18 hours of music, 3–4 hours of slideshows, or 4–5 hours of video, your battery is in good shape. If it lasts for less than these general guidelines, your iPod may have a battery problem.

If you are comfortable working with electronic devices yourself, you can replace the iPod's battery on your own. How to do this is beyond the scope of this book, but you can purchase a battery and get help on the web at places such as www.ipodbattery.com and www.ipodresq.com. The cost of replacement batteries varies, and some include tools and instructions. Although it can be a bit more expensive, sending the unit back to Apple is probably a better option in most situations. (Who knows, if you have an older iPod, you even might get a newer model back in return!)

Getting Help from Apple for iPod Battery Problems

If your iPod doesn't play for the expected time, the battery might need to be replaced. If the iPod is still under warranty (1 year without the AppleCare Protection Plan or 2 years with it), Apple will replace the battery for free. If the iPod is not under warranty, Apple will replace the battery for you. (Currently this costs $59 plus $6.95 shipping.) To get more information and start this process, go to www.apple.com/support/ipod/service/battery/ and read the information about the program. Then click the **iPod service request** link.

According to Apple, your iPod will be replaced with an equivalent model (new, used, or refurbished) rather than just its battery being replaced. Make sure you have all the data you need from your iPod before you send it in for service, because the iPod you get in exchange won't have anything stored on it.

Updating or Restoring an iPod's Software

As you learned earlier, the iPod has an operating system that controls how it works. Like all other operating systems, the iPod's software can be updated. You can also restore an iPod to "start over."

Updating an iPod's Software

Apple is continually improving the iPod's software to add features, make it even more stable, and so on. When new iPod software is available and you connect your iPod to your computer, the Update button on the Summary tab of the iPod screen will become active. This indicates that you can perform an update that will place the latest version of an iPod's software onto it. An update doesn't impact the data (music, video, etc.) stored on the iPod; it changes only the iPod's operating system software.

To update an iPod, take the following steps:

1. Connect the iPod to your computer. iTunes will open (if it isn't already), the iPod will be mounted on the Source list, and the Summary tab of the iPod screen will appear (see Figure 13.4).

FIGURE 13.4
When new software is available for your iPod, the Update button on the Summary tab will become active.

At the top of the screen, you'll see the current version of the software on the iPod. iTunes will check to see whether there is a newer version available. If there is, you'll see information about the new version at the top of the Version section of the screen. The Update button will also become active.

2. Click **Update**. You'll see the iPod Software Update screen that will provide additional information about the update, such as new features it provides or whether it contains bug fixes (see Figure 13.5).

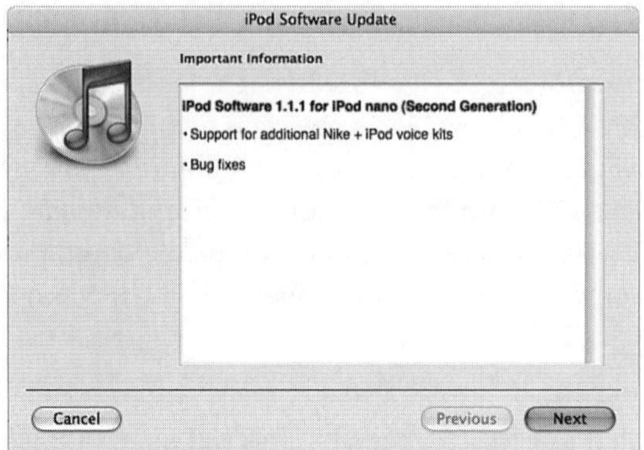

FIGURE 13.5
This window provides information about an update you are about to install on an iPod.

3. Read the information about the update and click **Next**. You'll see a license screen.
4. Click **Agree**. The update will be downloaded to your computer and installed on the iPod. How long this process takes depends on the speed of your Internet connection and the size of the update.
5. If you are prompted to authenticate yourself, enter your administrator username and password and click **OK**.

   When the update is complete, you'll see a dialog box telling you so.
6. Click **OK**. The iPod will be mounted on the iTunes Source list again. You'll see the new version information at the top of the Summary tab, and the text at the top of the Version section will inform you that the iPod is up-to-date. The Update button will be inactive, which also indicates that the iPod is running the current version of the software.

After you have updated an iPod, you can continue using it as you did before the update (except that there might be new features if they were part of the update).

Restoring an iPod's Software

When you are having major problems with your iPod or just want to completely reformat it, you can also *restore* its software to return it to factory settings. When you restore an iPod, it erases the iPod's memory and then puts the current version of the iPod operating software on it. A restore also erases *all the data* on the iPod, including any music, photos, or video.

When it's time to do an iPod redo, do the following:

1. Connect the iPod to your computer. iTunes will open (if it isn't already), the iPod will be mounted on the Source list, and the Summary tab of the iPod screen will appear.

2. Click the **Restore** button. A warning dialog box will appear. This explains that a restore completely erases an iPod.
3. Click **Restore** if you are sure you want to proceed.
4. If you are prompted to authenticate yourself, enter your administrator **username and password** and click **OK**. The restore process will start. When it's done, you'll see a dialog, explaining that the iPod has been restored to factory settings.
5. Click **OK**. The iPod will be restarted, and you'll see the iPod Setup Assistant screen.
6. Enter the iPod's name, and choose the automatic music or photos sync options you want by checking the related check boxes. (You can always change them using the tabs of the iPod screen.)
7. Click **Done**. If you've selected either of the sync options, the appropriate content will be moved onto the iPod, just as it was the first time you connected it your computer. You'll move back to the iPod screen, and the iPod will be restored to that factory-fresh feeling. This means you'll have to reconfigure its sync options to place the content you want on the iPod.
8. Reconfigure the sync options for the iPod, using the information you learned in earlier chapters of this book.

Identifying and Solving iPod Problems

Okay, I admit it. The iPod isn't perfect. Once in a while, it might not act the way you expect it to. Hey, no one or no technology is perfect, after all. In this section, you'll read some information that will help you in the event you do experience problems.

Troubleshooting iPod problems isn't all that different from troubleshooting other kinds of problems. First, observe exactly what is happening. Determine what you are doing and how the iPod is responding or not responding, as the case may be. Then use the information in the following sections to see whether you can solve the problem yourself or if you need help.

Checking the Basics

Once in a while, we all do things that can be classified as something less than intelligent. Using an iPod can result in a few of these events, so use the following list to ensure you haven't done anything to shoot yourself in the foot:

- If the iPod won't respond to any controls, make sure the Hold feature isn't active. The Hold feature does just what it is supposed to—it prevents the iPod's controls from having an effect. It can be rather embarrassing to panic about your precious iPod suffering a major failure only to realize that the Hold switch is on. (Of course, you understand that this has never happened to me, personally.) If you use an iPod or iPod nano and see orange in the Hold switch area, Hold is on. If you use a shuffle, press a control; if the status light flashes orange, Hold is on. Try turning Hold off to see whether that fixes all your problems. Also on a shuffle, make sure the Power slider isn't in the Off position.

- If the iPod won't turn on, connect it to a computer. It might simply be that the battery is out of power. Remember that the iPod uses some battery power when you aren't using it, and after 14 days or so, it might not have enough battery power to turn on. Sometimes the empty battery icon will appear when you try to turn on a fully discharged iPod—and sometimes it won't. Use the Battery Status light on a shuffle to check its charge; if the light doesn't illuminate, the shuffle must be recharged before you can use it. If an iPod is really and completely out of power, you'll have to connect it to a power source (you can also use an external power adapter) to get any response from it.
- If the iPod is on and the Hold feature isn't enabled but the iPod won't respond to commands, try connecting it to a computer. If it mounts, you probably just need to do a minor reset to get it to work again.

Resetting an iPod

If you can't get an iPod to do anything (and you've checked the Hold feature) or if it is behaving badly or locks up, try resetting it. When you reset an iPod, its temporary memory is cleared, but your data (music, photos, or video) isn't affected.

How you reset an iPod depends on the specific model you are using. Fortunately, resetting the current models is relatively easy; you have to jump through some hoops for older models. You should check the documentation that came with your iPod to see how to reset it.

To reset current iPods and iPod nanos, turn the Hold switch on and then off again. Then press and hold both the **Menu** and **Select** buttons for about 6–10 seconds until you see the Apple logo on the iPod's screen. This indicates that the reset process was effective. If the first time doesn't work, try it again. After you see the Apple logo, you know the iPod has been reset and is restarting, and in most cases, it will work normally again.

To reset a shuffle, turn it off, wait 5 seconds, and then turn it on again using the Power slider located on the bottom side of its case.

If you are using an older model and don't have its documentation, visit www.apple.com and click the **Support** tab. Then search for "reset iPod." Open one of the documents that contains information about resetting an iPod. This will either provide you with the steps you need or lead you to documentation that does.

After your iPod is reset, it should work normally. If not, you should try restoring it.

> **tip**
>
> Resetting or restoring an iPod is the solution to almost all the problems you will be able to solve yourself. Whenever you have a problem, always try to reset the iPod first. If that doesn't work, try to restore it. In the vast majority of situations, one of these will solve the problem.

Restoring an iPod

As you read earlier, you can use the Restore button on the Summary tab of the iPod screen to restore it. When you restore an iPod, its memory is erased and a clean version of its software is installed. The purpose is to configure the iPod with factory settings that will likely solve many problems you are having.

For the steps to perform a restore, see "Restoring an iPod's Software" on page **202**.

Solving the Folder/Exclamation Point Icon Problem

In some situations, your iPod will display a folder and exclamation point icon on its screen. When it does so, this indicates there is a problem and you won't be able to use the iPod until you solve it. Unfortunately, this icon doesn't relate to one specific problem but can result from an incorrect software version being installed, which is easily remedied by restoring the iPod. It can also be due to something being wrong with the iPod's disk, which will require a repair.

Fortunately, although the cause of the problem won't be clear to you, the solutions available should be. First, try to reset the iPod. If that doesn't work, try to restore it. In most cases, one of these two actions will solve the problem. If not, your iPod probably needs to be repaired or replaced. See the section "Getting Help with iPod Problems" to see what to do next.

Solving the "I Can't See My iPod in iTunes" Problem

If you connect your iPod to your computer but it doesn't appear in the Source list, this means iTunes can't find your iPod. This can happen for a number of reasons. Use the following steps to troubleshoot this problem:

1. With your iPod connected to your computer, restart the computer and then open iTunes. This will sometimes get the devices communicating again. If you see your iPod on the Source list, you are good to go. If not, continue with the next step.

2. Update the iTunes software by choosing **Help**, **Check for Updates** on a Windows computer or **iTunes**, **Check for Updates** on a Mac. Installing an iTunes update will sometimes get your computer connected to an iPod again.

   If the iPod appears on the Source list after you've installed the updated iTunes, you are good to go.

3. If the iPod still doesn't appear on the Source list, there may be a communication problem between your computer and the iPod. Try plugging the iPod into a different USB port. If the two devices still can't communicate, there is a problem either with the iPod or with your computer. You'll probably need some help to solve either of these issues.

tip

On Apple's website, you can click the iPod icons to get an explanation of what they mean and what to do about them. You'll also see solutions to the most common issues (which you've already read in this chapter). You can also select your specific model of iPod to get help with it.

Getting Help with iPod Problems

Although I probably could have added a few more pages to this book with specific problems you might encounter and potential solutions to those problems, this would have been wasteful for two main reasons. First, it is likely you will never experience the problems I would include. Second, Apple maintains an extensive iPod website from which you get detailed information about and help for iPod problems. You can use this information to solve specific problems you encounter (that aren't solved with the information in the previous sections, such as a reset or a restore).

To access this help, use a web browser to move to www.apple.com/support/ipod. On this page, you can search for help, read FAQs, and get other information that will help you solve iPod problems (see Figure 13.6).

A number of other websites might be helpful to you as well. These include www.ilounge.com and www.ipodhacks.com. You can also use www.google.com to search for iPod problems; you'll find no shortage of web pages on which those problems are discussed. It is highly likely that someone else has faced and solved the same problem you are having.

tip

You can also contact me for help with iPod problems you encounter. Visit my website at web.mac.com/bradmacosx/. Click the **Books I've Written** link, and then click the cover of this book. From this book's web page, you can click **Have an iPod or iTunes Question?** to view suggested solutions to problems other readers have reported to me. You can ask me questions via email from any of my pages by clicking the **Email Me** button.

FIGURE 13.6
Need iPod help? You got it.

The Absolute Minimum

The iPod is what we hope most technology will be—it just works and works well. Here are some pointers to help you keep your iPod in tune:

- Understand your iPod's battery, and use the practices described in this chapter to keep it maintained properly.
- Keep your iPod's software current by using the Update button on the Summary tab of the iPod screen.
- If you run into problems, you can restore an iPod to make it like new (better than new if a newer iPod software is available).
- If you do run into problems, check the last section in this chapter for help in solving them. Fortunately, most iPod problems are easy to solve with a simple reset or restore. If those don't work, lots of help is available to you.

PART 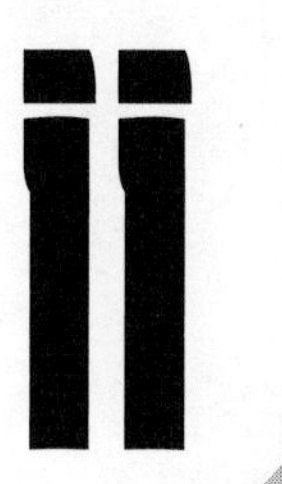

iTUNES

IN THIS CHAPTER

- Learn why iTunes will rock your world.
- Know how to speak in three-letter acronyms (TLAs), such as MP3 and AAC.
- Recognize iTunes and iPod video formats.
- Visit the iTunes Library.
- Learn the best places to get content for your own Library.
- Master your Library with playlists.
- Play with the other members of the iTunes band.

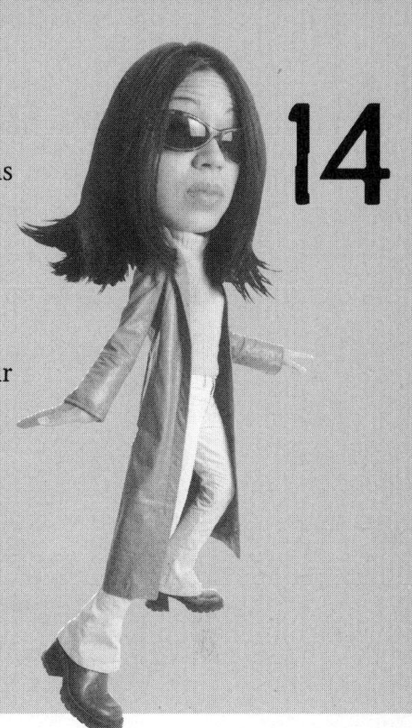

14

TOURING iTUNES

With not-very-sincere apologies to Mr. Edison, Apple's iTunes is the best thing to happen to music since the phonograph. It's also becoming the best thing to happen to video since the TV, to movies since sound was added to moving pictures, and the best thing to happen to radio since, well, the radio.... I'm sure you get the idea. This amazing application enables you to do things with music, video, movies, audiobooks, and radio that you might have never dreamed possible. Of course, you can use iTunes to listen to audio CDs, but that is certainly nothing to write home (or a book) about. Any two-bit boombox can do that. That basic task is barely a warm-up for iTunes. If you have never used iTunes before, prepare to be impressed (and if you have used iTunes before, be impressed anyway).

What You Can Do with iTunes

I could fill a book (or at least Part II of this book) with all the great things you can do with iTunes. Following are some examples just to whet your appetite:

- Listen to audio CDs.
- Listen to Internet radio and podcasts.
- Store all the music you like in a single place so you never need to fuss with individual CDs again.
- Search and organize all this music so listening to exactly the music you want is just a matter of a few mouse clicks (and maybe a few key presses).
- Create custom albums (called *playlists*) containing the specific songs you want to hear.
- Create custom albums (called *smart playlists*) that are based on a set of criteria, such as all the jazz music you have rated at four or five stars.
- Burn your own music CDs to play in those oh-so-limited CD players in your car, a boombox, or in your home.
- Share your iTunes content with other people over a wired or wireless network; you can listen to music other people share with you as well.
- Transfer photos from your computer onto an iPod so you can view them there.
- Add games to your iPod.
- Build a video library that includes music videos, TV shows, movies, and other content; watch that video in iTunes or move it onto an iPod for viewing on the move.
- Shop the iTunes Store so you can add to your music, video, and podcast collections.
- Do the Party Shuffle, iMix your music, and much more.

Audio File Formats You Might Encounter When You Use iTunes

As you work with digital music and other audio files, you'll encounter a number of file formats you need to understand. These formats are important because each offers specific benefits and limitations that impact what you do with your music and other audio. For example, some file formats offer better music quality versus file size than others. You definitely don't need to have all the specifications for each of these formats committed to memory (nor will you find them in this book); instead, all you need is to be able to distinguish between them so that you can choose the format that is the most appropriate for what you are trying to do.

Most audio file formats are *encoded*. This. This means specific compression algorithms (because this is a computer book, I am required by contract to use that word at least once) are used to reduce the size of the audio file without—we hope, anyway—lowering the quality of the resulting sound very much. The higher the compression that is used, the lower the quality of the resulting music when it is played back. Note that the words *higher* and *lower* are relative. Often, it takes a musical expert to tell the difference between encoded and unencoded music, but even if it is imperceptible to us mere mortals, it does exist.

When it comes to digital audio files, one trade-off always has to be made. And that is *file size* versus *sound quality*. When you add thousands of songs to your iTunes Library, you can easily consume gigabytes of disk space. Although you might have a humungous hard drive in your computer, you might also have other files you want to store on it, such as photos, Word documents, and so on. Even I realize that computers can be used for more than just iTunes.

To keep the amount of disk space required to store your music to a minimum, you encode it. When you do, you choose the settings you want to use to encode that music. Encoding formats with higher compression consume less disk space, but the audio quality will also be lower. Don't worry, though: It doesn't take much experimentation or much time to find a happy medium between file size and how the music sounds to you.

You'll learn about encoding music in more detail later in the book, but for now, you should read the following sections so you can become comfortable with the various audio file formats you will encounter.

CD Audio

The CD Audio format was the world's first widely used entry in the digital audio format life cycle. The creation of this format was the start of the CD revolution. Rather than vinyl albums, which were a pain to deal with and included lots of hisses, pops, and other distractions when played, listeners began enjoying digital music. In addition to being easier to handle than LPs, CDs provide a much better listening experience and are much more durable than vinyl records. They also sound much better than cassettes and are just as portable.

Eventually, CD Audio made its way to computers, which now can provide all the music-listening enjoyment of a home stereo plus much more, thanks to iTunes.

Although you can use iTunes to listen to your audio CDs, typically you will just encode those CDs into one of the newer digital formats to store their content on your computer's hard disk. That way, you don't have to bother with a CD when you want to listen to music. You can use the Audio CD disc-burning option when you put your iTunes music on your own audio CDs so you can play your iTunes music when you are away from your computer.

MP3

Even if this book is your first foray into the wonderful world of digital music, you have no doubt heard of MP3. This audio file format started, literally, an explosion in music technology that is still reverberating and expanding today.

MP3 is the acronym for the audio compression scheme called *Moving Picture Experts Group (MPEG) audio layer 3*. The revolutionary aspect of the MP3 encoding scheme was that music data could be stored in files that are only about 1/12 the size of unencoded digital music without a noticeable degradation in the quality of the music. A typical music CD consumes about 650MB of storage space, but the same music encoded in the MP3 format shrinks down to about 55MB. Put another way, a single 3.5-minute song shrinks from 35MB on audio CD down to a paltry 3MB or so in MP3 format. The small size of MP3 files opened up a world of possibilities.

For example, MP3 enabled a new class of portable music devices. Because MP3 files can be stored in small amounts of memory, devices with no moving parts can store and play a fair amount of music; these were the early MP3 players, such as the Rio. Then came other devices containing small hard drives—can you say iPod?—that could store huge amounts of music, enabling you to take your entire music collection with you wherever you went. These devices are extremely small and lightweight, and their contents can be managed easily.

Because MP3 files are relatively small, storing an entire music collection in a small amount of disk space is possible, thus eliminating the need to bother with individual CDs. Using iTunes, you can easily store, organize, and access an entire music collection on your desktop or laptop computer.

You will encounter many MP3 files on the Internet, and with iTunes, you can convert your audio CDs into the MP3 format so that you can store them in iTunes and put them on an iPod.

Although the MP3 format is still widely used, when you work with iTunes, you'll be better off using one of the newer audio formats it supports, such as AAC.

AAC

The primary successor to MP3 is called Advanced Audio Coding (AAC). This format is part of the larger MPEG-4 specification. Its basic purpose is the same as that of the MP3 format: to deliver excellent sound quality while keeping file sizes small.

However, the AAC format is a newer and better format in that it can be used to produce files that have better quality than MP3 at even smaller file sizes.

Also, as with MP3, you can easily convert audio CD files into the AAC format to store them on a computer and add them to an iPod. What's more, you can convert AAC files into the Audio CD or MP3 format when you want to put them on a CD to play on something other than your computer, such as a car stereo.

The AAC format also enables content producers to add copy protection schemes to their music. Typically, these schemes won't have an impact on you (unless, of course, you are trying to do something you shouldn't).

One of the most important aspects of the AAC format is that all the music in the iTunes Store is stored in it; when you purchase music from the store, it is added to your computer in the protected version of this format.

Apple Lossless

The Apple Lossless format is the only encoding option supported by iTunes that doesn't sport a fancy acronym. The goal of this format is maximum sound quality. As a result, files in this format are larger than they are in AAC or MP3 format. However, Apple Lossless files are slightly smaller than files in noncompressed formats.

The Apple Lossless format provides very high-quality music but also larger file sizes. If you have a sophisticated ear, high-quality sound systems, and discriminating taste in music (whatever that means), you might find this format to be the best for you. However, because storing music in this format requires a lot more space on your computer and on an iPod, you will probably use the AAC or MP3 format more often.

WAV

The *Windows Waveform (WAV)* audio format is a standard on Windows computers. It has been widely used for various kinds of audio, but because it does not offer the "quality versus file size" benefits of the MP3 or AAC formats, it is mostly used for sound effects or clips people have recorded from various sources. Millions of WAV files are available on the Internet that you can play and download.

tip

If you ever want to find a sound byte from your favorite movie or TV show, you can probably do so at one of the many WAV websites. One example is www.wavcentral.com. Interestingly enough, even the sound clips on these sites have mostly been converted into MP3.

You can load WAV files into iTunes, and you can even use iTunes to convert files into the WAV format. However, because MP3 and AAC are much newer and better file formats, you aren't likely to want to do this very often. Occasionally, you might want to add WAV files to your iTunes music collection; this can be done easily, as you will learn later in this book.

AIFF

The *Audio Interchange File Format (AIFF)* provides relatively high-quality sound, but its file sizes are larger than MP3 or AAC. As you can probably guess from its name, this format was originally used to exchange audio among various platforms and applications.

As with the WAV format, MP3 and AAC formats provide a better sound quality versus file size trade-off, so you aren't likely to use the AIFF format very often. The most typical situation in which you might want to use it is when you want to move some music or sound from your iTunes collection into a different application that does not support MP3 or AAC.

Video File Formats You Might Encounter When You Use iTunes

The most recent generations of iPod enable you to watch a video, which is really cool. Like other content you put on an iPod, you use iTunes to store a videos, TV shows, or movies so that you can download them onto an iPod. You can also watch video content within iTunes.

Like audio, video content on computers comes in a variety of file formats. However, unlike audio files, just because you can store a video file within iTunes doesn't mean you'll be able to view that file on an iPod. That's because iPods require a very specific kind of video file that has the correct resolution (size), data rate, and compression so it can be viewed on an iPod.

Video formats are more complicated than audio formats. Because more complex data is involved, the schemes used to encode and compress video data (most of which, of course, also include audio content) are more complex. The good news is that if you want to use your video content on your iPod, you really don't need to be concerned with the details of preparing that video for the iPod. If you get video from the iTunes Store, it's already in the format you need. If you get it from other sources, you'll usually use an application that supports exporting video in the iPod format. (Because iPod video is so popular, most video applications support its format, too. With one of these applications, you simply need to select the iPod format when you export the video from that application.) The bottom line is that if you just want to watch video in iTunes, you have more options with respect to file formats. If you want to watch video on your iPod too, you need to be more specific when preparing the video for your iTunes Library.

iPod Video Formats

The iPod Video supports two video formats.

The iPod Video can play video content in the H.264 format (also known as MPEG-4 Part 10 or Advanced Video Coding). The most important part of preparing video in this format is that it has a resolution of 640×480 or 320×240 pixels. Files in this format have filename extensions `.m4v`, `.mp4`, or `.mov`. Unfortunately, just because a filename has one of these extensions doesn't mean it is iPod compatible. These files can contain video with many different attributes, such as different resolutions.

On an iPod Video, you can also view content that is in the MPEG-4 format, with video rates up to 2.5Mbps and a resolution of 640×480 pixels. These files also have the `.m4v`, `.mp4`, or `.mov` filename extensions.

iTunes Video Formats

If you want to only view video content in iTunes (not export it to an iPod), the requirements are less specific. You can store and view any QuickTime or MPEG-4 movie in iTunes, such as files with filename extensions `.mov`, `.m4v`, or `.mp4`.

Fortunately, you don't really have to worry about the details of the iPod video formats explained here because you can use iTunes to convert video into the iPod's format. You'll learn how later in this part of the book.

The iTunes Library

Earlier, you read that one of the great things about iTunes is that you can use it to store all your music on your computer. If you read the previous section, you also know that you can use iTunes for video content, including TV shows and movies. There are other goodies for which you can use iTunes too, such as podcasts and audiobooks. You store all your audio and video content in the iTunes Library (see Figure 14.1). This includes music and sounds you import into iTunes, such as from audio CDs or other sources. It's also where audio and video you purchase from the iTunes Store ends up. Any podcasts to which you subscribe are stored here, too. You can also import audio or video files stored on your computer into the iTunes Library. Basically, if it's in iTunes, it's in the iTunes Library. You can then browse or search your Library to find the content you want to listen to, watch, or work with.

As you use iTunes, you will be accessing your Library frequently; it will often be your first stop when you do things with your content, such as creating playlists or burning CDs. When it comes to the iTunes Library, remember this: If you don't find it there, you won't find it anywhere (including on your iPod).

FIGURE 14.1
The iTunes Library is the one place to go for all the good audio and video in your life.

Where Do All Those Songs, Books, Podcasts, Photos, Movies, TV Shows, and Videos Come From?

You can stock your iTunes Library with audio and video content from several sources:

- **Audio CDs**—You can add music from your audio CDs to the iTunes Library. In iTunes lingo, this process is called *importing*.
- **The Internet**—You can download music, podcasts, video, and other files from the Internet and add those files to your iTunes Library.
- **Your Computer**—You can create files for the iTunes Library by using other applications on your computer. For example, you can use an application to convert a DVD movie into the H.264 format and import that file into iTunes (from which you can move it onto an iPod).
- **The iTunes Store**—Part III, "The iTunes Store," is dedicated to this source, and for good reason. With the iTunes Store, you can search for, preview, and purchase music, audiobooks, and video online. After you've downloaded content from the Store, it will become part of your Library. Content that you get from the iTunes Store has lots of benefits, but one of the most important is that it is always ready to be moved onto an iPod. You can also choose and subscribe to (in most cases, for free) podcasts from the bewilderingly large selection available.

Playlists: Customizing Your iTunes Experience

I've saved one of the best features of iTunes—playlists—for nearly last. Playlists enable you to create custom collections of music, video, and other content in your iTunes Library. (If you think of a playlist as a custom CD without the disc itself or size limitation of a disc, you'll get the idea.)

When you create playlists, you can mix and match audio or video to your heart's content. For example, you can build your own "greatest hits" collections that include multiple artists, music genres, and so on. You can repeat the same song multiple times in the same playlist, and you can get rid of songs you don't like by not including them in the playlists you listen to. What's more, you can create a playlist to include a specific amount of music from a single CD or endlessly repeat all the music in your Library. Or, if you've downloaded all the episodes of the classic TV show *Adam-12*, you can create a playlist for each season of the show so that you can easily select a season to watch.

Basically, you can use playlists to organize a collection of songs, videos, or podcasts in any way you choose. You can then listen to or watch your playlists, put them on a CD or DVD, or move them to an iPod.

You'll learn all you need to know about playlists in Chapter 19, "Creating, Configuring, and Using Playlists."

The Other Members of the Band: The iPod and the iTunes Store

When it comes to citizenship, iTunes definitely gets an A+ because it plays so well with others.

If you have read Part I, "The iPod," you know that the iPod might just be the coolest portable electronic device ever to hit the streets. Although the iPod is indeed an awesome piece of technology, it wouldn't get very far without a tool to manage the music, podcasts, photos, audiobooks, games, and video it contains. iTunes is that tool. iTunes and the iPod go together like a 1-2 combination punch, peanut butter and jelly, jalapenos on a pizza, Bing Crosby and Bob Hope (well, you get the idea). Using iTunes, you can determine which parts of your iTunes Library are on an iPod. iTunes manages moving the appropriate files to the iPod and organizing them, so the process is simple (from your perspective, anyway). In fact, iTunes manages the process for you automatically if you prefer; when you connect your trusty iPod to your computer, iTunes recognizes it and then synchronizes the content it has in your Library with that on your iPod.

When you get to Part III, you will learn in detail about the last part of the digital music triumvirate: the iTunes Store. With the iTunes Store, you can shop for music to add to your Library. When you find songs you'd like to have, you can purchase and download them into your iTunes Library with just a couple of mouse clicks. Likewise, you can find and buy video content, including music videos, TV shows (or whole seasons of them), movies, and so on. And you can do all this from within iTunes itself. It feels like the iTunes Store is just an extension of iTunes, which, in fact, it is. You access the iTunes Store from within iTunes, and the Store uses an interface that looks very similar to the iTunes interface. So, once you know iTunes, you won't have any problems with the iTunes Store.

THE ABSOLUTE MINIMUM

Now that you have met iTunes, I hope you are jazzed (pun intended) to get into it and start making its magic work for you. In the chapters following this one, you'll learn how to do everything from listening to audio CDs and Internet radio to building playlists to sharing your music over a network. Here are the major topics you learned about in this introduction to iTunes:

- You can use iTunes to do just about anything you want to with your music, from listening to CDs to putting your entire music collection on your hard drive to managing the music on an iPod.
- The primary audio file formats you are likely to use with iTunes are AAC and MP3. However, you can also use WAV, AIFF, and the Apple Lossless format when you want to maximize sound quality or for other purposes (such as to export music to another application).
- Although iTunes started out as a music tool, it's evolved into much more. You can also store and watch video content, subscribe and listen to podcasts, manage your audiobook library, and more.
- The iTunes Library is where you store and can work with all your iTunes content.
- You can get content for your iTunes Library from audio CDs, the Internet, your computer, and the iTunes Store.
- You can use playlists to create and listen to custom collections of content including music, other kinds of audio files, and videos.
- iTunes works seamlessly with iPods and the iTunes Store.

IN THIS CHAPTER

- Learn how to install and open iTunes on a Windows PC.
- Do the same on a Macintosh.
- Get comfortable with the iTunes interface; to know it is to love it.

GETTING STARTED WITH iTUNES

It's time to put iTunes through its paces so you can see and hear for yourself what it can do.

In the first part of this chapter, you'll learn how to install and launch iTunes. Although using iTunes on a Windows PC and on a Macintosh is nearly identical, there are slight differences in how you install the applications on each platform. So I've included an installation section for each kind of computer. It should go without saying, but I will say it anyway just in case: You don't need to read both installation sections. Just read the section that is applicable for the type of computer you use. (Of course, if you are fortunate enough to have both kinds of computers, you'll want to install iTunes on each and will need to read this entire chapter.)

After you have installed and launched iTunes, read the section "Getting to Know iTunes," where you'll get the grand tour of the amazing iTunes features you will be using throughout the rest of this part of the book.

Installing and Opening iTunes on a Windows PC

Over the years, Apple has produced a few applications designed for both Windows PCs and Macintoshes. Thank goodness for Windows users that iTunes is also in this group. (Few of Apple's other attempts are worthy of much mention, but iTunes is definitely a crossover hit!)

To use iTunes on a Windows computer, you must be running Windows 2000 or Windows XP. There are some other technical requirements, but if your computer is able to run either of these versions of Windows, it will meet those requirements, too. If you are running Windows 98, Me, or 95, you are out of the iTunes game. (Of course, those older versions of Windows are really old, and you should be using a newer version for more reasons than just the capability to run iTunes!)

iTunes is available as a free download from Apple's website; in addition to being free, it is also very easy to download and install the application. Because you need to have iTunes installed to be able to use an iPod, I explained how to download and install the application way back in Chapter 2 (see "Installing iTunes on a Windows PC" on page **21**). If you haven't already installed iTunes, flip back there and take care of business. You'll download and install iTunes on your computer and then perform some basic configuration courtesy of the iTunes Setup Assistant.

When you've finished installing iTunes and working through the Assistant, you need to know that there are a number of ways to open the application (if you've just completed the Assistant, iTunes will be open already) including

- Double-click the **iTunes desktop icon** (if you allowed the installer to install one, of course).
- Choose the **Start** menu, **All Programs**, **iTunes**, **iTunes**.
- Connect an iPod; by default, iTunes launches when you connect an iPod to your computer.

With iTunes open, move ahead to "Getting to Know iTunes" on page **224**.

Installing, Opening, and Configuring iTunes on a Macintosh

Because iTunes is developed by Apple, it is as integrated into the Macintosh operating system as any application can be. You have a number of ways to get iTunes installed on your Mac, including the following:

- **Install Mac OS X**—When you install Mac OS X, iTunes is also installed. If you have installed OS X on your Mac or if it came with Mac OS X, you don't need to do any installation, but you should use the Software Update tool to make sure you have the current version of iTunes installed.

- **Buy a new Mac**—Okay, this might be the most expensive option, but, hey, you get a free Mac with your copy of iTunes!
- **Download and install iTunes from the Internet**—You can always download and install the latest version of iTunes from the Internet. Just visit www.apple.com/itunes/download, check the **Mac OS X** radio button, uncheck the newsletter check boxes, and click **Download iTunes—Free**. After the application has downloaded to your Mac, run its installer and follow the onscreen instructions.

Not to push my other books (okay, to push my other books), but if you need help with Mac OS X in general, see *Special Edition Using Mac OS X Tiger.* (Catchy title, huh?)

After iTunes has been installed, there are a number of ways to open it, including the following:

- Click the **iTune**s icon on the Dock.
- Open the **Applications** folder and double-click the **iTunes** icon.
- Connect an **iPod** to your Mac; by default, iTunes will open.
- Insert an **audio CD** into your Mac; by default, iTunes is set to launch whenever you mount an audio CD.

At the risk of pummeling an already prostrate equine, make sure you are using the latest version of iTunes by running the Software Update application. To do so, select the **Apple** menu, **Software Update**. If a more current version of iTunes is available than the one installed on your computer, you will be prompted to download and install it.

The first time you open iTunes, you need to work through a basic configuration of the application. Following are the steps you need to perform:

1. Launch **iTunes**. You see yet another License Agreement screen. (I guess Apple was kidding with the others.)
2. Click **Agree**. You see the iTunes Setup Assistant, which guides you through the rest of the process.
3. Click **Next**.
4. Follow the onscreen instructions to complete the Assistant. In most cases, you should leave the default options selected and click **Next** until you reach the end of the Assistant.

   After you complete the Assistant, the iTunes window will open, and you are ready to tour the application, as you will do in the next section.

Getting to Know iTunes

The required but mundane work of installing and performing the initial configuration of iTunes on your computer is done. Now let's take a quick tour so you get the overall feel of this excellent application. In the following chapters, you'll get down and dirty (well, because we are dealing with electrons here, there isn't really any dirt, but you know what I mean) with the details.

Seeing Through the iTunes Window

The iTunes window, like a window on your house, consists of a number of panes (see Figure 15.1). Let's take a quick look at each of these.

On the far left of the iTunes window is the Source list. On this list, as you might suspect from its name, are the sources of audio and video with which you can work. To work with a source, such as a CD or the iTunes Store, you select it by clicking it. When you select a source, its contents appear in the Content pane and Browser (if you have the Browser open for a selected source). In Figure 15.1, I have selected the Music category of the Library as the source; its contents are shown in the Cover Flow Browser at the top of the window, and the list of individual songs that make up the Library is in the Content pane, which is the lower pane on the right side of the window.

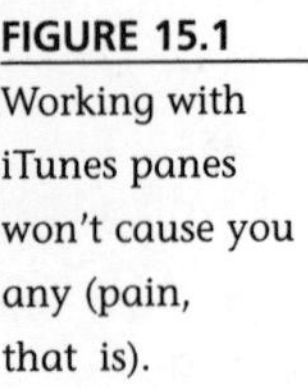

FIGURE 15.1
Working with iTunes panes won't cause you any (pain, that is).

You will use many types of sources, including Music, Movies, Podcasts, Radio, iTunes Store, audio CDs, an iPod, playlists, and more. Because there are a number of types of sources, they are organized in categories, including Library, Store, Playlists, and so on. As you work through the rest of this part of the book, you will get experience with all these kinds of sources.

At the bottom of the Source list is the Artwork or Video Viewer pane. Your music can have album artwork associated with it; this artwork is displayed in this pane based on the audio content that is either currently selected or playing. When you work with video content, this pane becomes the Video Viewer, in which you can watch that video. (You can view it at a larger size, too, as you'll learn later.) This pane can be hidden or shown.

You can see the iTunes window through three views.

The Cover Flow view, shown in Figure 15.1, enables you to view the covers of the content with which you are working. You can "flip" through the covers being displayed to browse your content.

You can change the view by using the View buttons (see Figure 15.2). The current view's button is darkened to show that it is selected.

FIGURE 15.2
The Grouped view presents an orderly view of iTunes content.

The Grouped view, shown in Figure 15.2, organizes the content with which you are working by album, TV series, podcast, and so on. For each collection, you see the contents along with the album artwork for that content.

The List view, shown in Figure 15.3, presents content in a list (like you couldn't tell that from its name!). You can easily sort the list by using any of the columns shown.

FIGURE 15.3
The List view isn't as pretty as the other two views, but it is very functional.

In the Grouped and List views, you can show or hide the Browser. (It's shown at the top of the iTunes window in both Figure 15.2 and 15.3.) The Browser is a three-column pane that presents the contents of the selected source at a summary level, by genre, artist, and album. You can view the contents of the selected source by clicking it in the appropriate column. For example, in Figure 15.3, I have selected the Blues/R&B genre. The Artist column then shows all the artists whose music I have in the selected genre. The Album column shows all the albums for the selected artists.

The Browser can be shown or hidden. For example, take a look at Figure 15.4, which shows the iTunes window with the Browser hidden.

In the center to lower part of the iTunes window (or filling it if the Browser is hidden) is the Content pane. This area lists each track (which can be a music track, podcast, TV episode, movie, music video, or other content) in the selected source. For each track, you see a variety of information, such as Name, Track #, Time, Artist, and so on. You can choose the information you see on this list. The order in which tracks are listed in the Content pane is the order in which they play when you play the selected source.

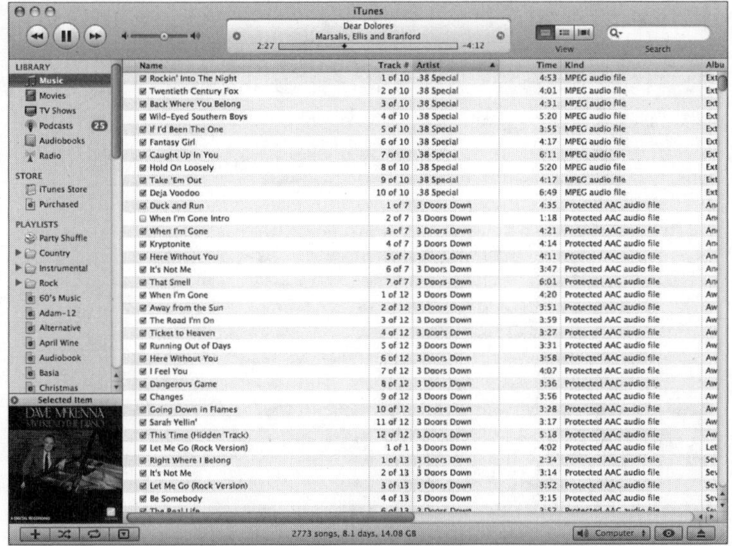

FIGURE 15.4
Where, oh where, has my Browser gone? Where, oh where, can it be?

There can be yet another pane located toward the bottom of the iTunes window, which is the iTunes MiniStore (see Figure 15.5). This provides a contextual view of content in the iTunes Store that relates to what you are working with at the moment. Notice in Figure 15.5 that I have selected a 3 Doors Down song and that other 3 Doors Down music is being shown in the MiniStore. You can access the related content in the iTunes Store by clicking the links for what you can to see; the MiniStore makes it easy to find and purchase content that is similar to the content you are currently using. You can hide or show the MiniStore by choosing View, Hide MiniStore or View, Show MiniStore.

> **tip**
>
> We will get to working with the Browser later, but for now, know that you can open and close it by clicking the **Browse** button at the bottom of the iTunes window or by selecting **View, Show Browser** or **View, Hide Browser**.

Controlling Your Music, Podcasts, and Video

Surrounding the panes of the iTunes window are the controls you use to work with and get information about the content in your Library. At the top of the window is the iTunes toolbar containing, from left to right, the following areas (see Figure 15.6):

FIGURE 15.5
The MiniStore makes it easy to build up your iTunes content by presenting you with related content that is available in the iTunes Store.

FIGURE 15.6
At the top of the iTunes window are a number of controls you can use to play and manage audio and video content.

- **Playback controls**—Here, you can see the familiar Play/Stop, Fast Forward, and Rewind buttons along with the Volume Control slider. These work as you probably expect them to.

- **Information window**—In the center of the top part of the iTunes window is the Information window. In this area, you will see a variety of information about what you are doing at any point in time. For example, when you are playing music, you will see information about the music currently being played. When you import music, you will see information about the import process. When you download music from the iTunes Store, you'll see information about the download process. You can change the information displayed in this area, as you'll learn later.
- **Search tool**—You use the Search tool to search for songs, podcasts, video, or other content in your Library.

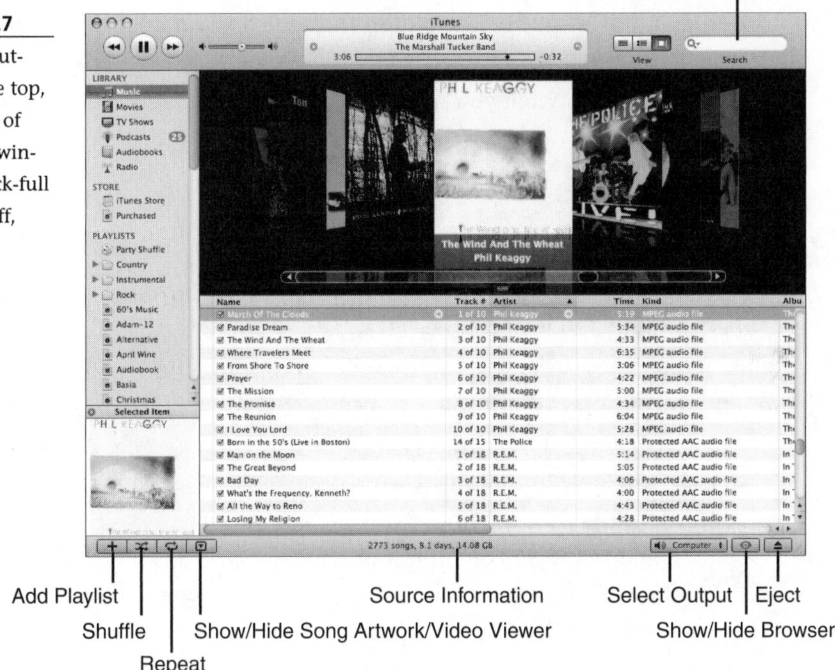

FIGURE 15.7
Not to be outdone by the top, the bottom of the iTunes window is chock-full of good stuff, too.

When you move to the bottom of the iTunes window, you see the following (see Figure 15.7):

- **Add Playlist button**—You use this button to create your own playlists.
- **Shuffle and Repeat buttons**—You use the Shuffle button to shuffle the tracks in the selected source so they don't play in the order in which they are listed in the Source list. You use the Repeat button to cause tracks to repeat within a selected source.

- **Show/Hide Song Artwork/Video Viewer button**—When you click this button, the Song Artwork/Video Viewer pane will open if it is closed or close if it is open.
- **Source information**—This information shows the number of tracks, total playing time, and disk space of the selected source. This becomes useful at certain times, such as when you are burning a CD or building a playlist.
- **Select Output menu**—This menu appears when an AirPort Express Base Station is available; you can choose to output iTunes music to your computer speakers or to a base station. When you choose a base station, you can connect powered speakers to it or connect to a stereo to hear your iTunes music in that location.
- **Show/Hide Browser button**—Click this to show the Browser if it's hidden or hide it if it is shown. The button is disabled when the Browser isn't available, such as when you use the Cover Flow view.
- **Eject button**—When you have selected an ejectable source, such as an audio CD or an iPod, you can click this button to eject it.

THE ABSOLUTE MINIMUM

You are well on your way to total iTunes nirvana. If you have read this chapter, you should be hip to the following iTunes jazz:

Installing iTunes is free and easy. Starting the application and performing basic configuration is also simple. What could be better?

- After you install iTunes, make sure you keep it up-to-date. (We'll get to that in Chapter 24, "Maintaining iTunes and Solving Problems.")
- When you first opened iTunes, you worked through several configuration settings, using the iTunes Setup Assistant. However, you can change these settings at any time by using the iTunes Preferences dialog box, which you will be working with throughout the rest of this part of the book.
- The iTunes window is an elegant mix of functionality and good interface design. As you learn more about the application, you will likely be impressed. The primary components of the iTunes window are its controls, the Information area, the Source list, the Artwork/Video Viewer pane, the Browser, the Content pane, and the MiniStore.

IN THIS CHAPTER

- Learn the basics of listening to iTunes sources by listening to audio CDs.
- Use the iTunes Information window.
- Control your tunes like a pro.
- Make iTunes be heard but not seen.
- Check out Internet radio.
- Change the size of the iTunes window.
- Configure your music with iTunes Playback preferences.

16

LISTENING TO AUDIO CDS AND INTERNET AUDIO WITH ITUNES

One of the many reasons to have and use iTunes is to listen to music and other audio, such as podcasts or Internet radio streams. That, not coincidentally, is the basic point of this chapter. Here, you will learn how to use iTunes to listen to a couple of sources: audio CDs and Internet radio. The good news is that when you know how to use iTunes to listen to these two sources, you know how to listen to other sources you will use as well, such as songs in your playlists, on an iPod, and from shared music.

After you become an iTunes-playing guru, we'll take a look at some of the ways you can configure iTunes to suit your playing preferences.

Listening to an Audio CD

What iTunes has in common with its much less sophisticated cousins the boombox and the standard CD player is the capability to play audio CDs. Although the basic function is the same, iTunes has several tricks in its bag to make listening even better. So, grab a CD and give it a try:

1. Open iTunes. Actually, this step is optional. When you insert an audio CD into your computer, iTunes opens by default, so you can just skip to step 2.
2. Insert an audio CD into your computer. In a moment, the CD will be mounted on your computer. Depending on your configuration, you might see a prompt asking whether you want to import the CD you inserted; if so, click **No** in this prompt for now. (You'll learn about the import process later in this chapter.) Then the CD will appear and be selected on the Source list in iTunes (see Figure 16.1). Notice that a new category, called Devices, has appeared on the Source list. This category is used for audio CDs, iPods, and other devices.

FIGURE 16.1
When a CD appears on the Source list, it awaits your listening pleasure.

If iTunes finds information for a CD, it remembers that information and displays it each time you insert the CD.

If you don't want iTunes to check for a CD's information automatically, you can disable this feature, as you will learn a little later in this chapter.

At the bottom of the iTunes window is the Source Information display. This will show you the total number of songs on the CD, how long it plays, and the total disc space used.

If the CD's information isn't located, you can add it yourself. (See Chapter 18, "Labeling, Categorizing, and Configuring Your Music.")

3. To play the CD, do any of the following: click the **Play** button in the upper-left corner of the window (when a CD is playing, this becomes the Pause button); select **Controls**, **Play**; or press the **spacebar**.

   The CD will begin to play. As a song plays, a speaker icon appears next to it in the Content pane to indicate it is the current song, and information about that song appears in the Information window (see Figure 16.2).

tip

By default, iTunes will automatically connect to the Internet and attempt to identify the CD you have inserted. If it finds it, it will display the CD's information, including the CD name, track names, times, artist, and genre, in the Content pane. (In Figure 16.1, you can see the CD's information has been found.) This is really cool because iTunes does most of the labeling work for you; this comes in handy when you want to search or browse for music to create playlists or just to listen to specific tracks.

FIGURE 16.2
You can tell this CD is playing because the **Play** button has become the **Pause** button and the speaker icon appears next to the song currently being played.

4. Control the volume of the sound by dragging the **Volume** slider to the left to turn it down or to the right to turn it up. You can also control the volume by selecting **Controls**, **Volume Up** or **Controls**, **Volume Down**. For yet another option, press the **Ctrl+Up arrow** and **Ctrl+Down arrow** keys on Windows PCs, or the **⌘+Up arrow** and **⌘+Down arrow** keys on Macs to set the volume from the keyboard.

   To mute the sound, select **Controls**, **Mute**. On Windows PCs, you can press **Ctrl+Alt+Down arrow**, whereas on Macs, you can press **Option+⌘+Down arrow** to do the same thing.

5. To pause a song, click the **Pause** button; select **Controls**, **Pause**; or press the **spacebar**.

That's it. You now know everything you need to listen to an audio CD. However, there are lots more ways to control the tunes, some of which are in the following list:

- Double-click any **song** to play it. When you do that, the speaker icon will jump to the song you double-clicked, and the song will play.
- Using the **Volume** slider within iTunes changes the volume of iTunes relative to your system's volume. If you can't make the music loud or quiet enough, set your system volume level and then change the iTunes volume with the slider.
- When a song is playing and you click and hold the **Rewind** or **Fast Forward** button, the song will rewind or fast-forward until you release the button.
- When a song is playing, drag the **Playhead** on the Timeline to the right to move ahead in the song, or to the left to move back in a song. When you release the Playhead, the song will resume playing at that point.
- When a song is playing, click on the **Timeline** at the point you want the song to play. The Playhead will jump to the point on which you clicked, and the song will play from that position.
- If a song is not playing or a song is playing but you single-click (but don't hold down) the **Rewind** or **Fast Forward** button, the previous or next song, respectively, will be selected. (If the previous song was playing, the next one will start to play when you jump to it.) You can also select **Controls**, **Next Song** or **Controls**, **Previous Song** to move to the next or the previous song. And for yet another method of doing the same thing, you can press the **Ctrl+Right arrow** and **Ctrl+Left arrow** keys on a Windows PC or the **⌘+Right arrow** and **⌘+Left arrow** keys on a Mac to move to the next or previous song.

- You can set a default action for iTunes to perform each time you insert a CD into your computer. You do this with the iTunes Preferences dialog box, which you will be using throughout this part of the book. Select **Edit, Preferences** (Windows) or **iTunes, Preferences** (Mac). The Preferences dialog box will appear. The Preferences dialog box has several panes that you access by clicking the related tab. Click **Advanced**. Then click the **Importing** subtab. Use the **On CD Insert** drop-down list to choose the default action iTunes should perform when it recognizes an audio CD. **Show CD** just displays the list of tracks on the CD. **Begin Playing** starts playing the CD as soon as it is mounted on your computer. (This does the same thing as clicking the Play button.) **Ask to Import CD** presents a dialog box asking you if you want to import the CD you inserted. **Import CD** adds the selected songs on the CD to your Library. **Import CD and Eject** does the same thing as Import CD, but it ejects the CD when all its tracks have been added to your Library. (You'll see the value of the last two settings in the next chapter.)
- To remove a CD from your computer, select it on the Source list and select **Controls, Eject Disc**; press **Ctrl+E** (Windows) or **⌘+E** (Macintosh); click the **Eject** button that appears next to the CD on the Source list; or click the **Eject** button located in the lower-right corner of the iTunes window.

Viewing Information While Listening to iTunes

You can view different information in the Information window at the top of the iTunes window, such as the name, artist, and album of the currently playing song. When you first view this window, it contains a timeline bar that represents the total length of the song being played (see Figure 16.3). A black diamond (the Playhead) indicates the relative position of the music you are hearing at any point in time compared to the total length of the song.

At the top of the Information window is a line of text that shows the song currently playing (even if it is paused). What appears on the second line of text changes over time; it rotates between the artist name and the album name. You can freeze this display on a specific attribute, such as album name, by clicking the text. Each time you click, the information changes from album to artist to album again. Whichever one you last clicked remains showing in the window.

When you "freeze" information in the Information window, it remains frozen until the next track is played, at which point it starts rotating again.

FIGURE 16.3
The iTunes Information window looks basic, but there is much hidden behind its quiet demeanor.

Underneath the album, artist, and song name is the Timeline. The value shown on the left end of the Timeline is always the time position of the Playhead. As a song plays, the Playhead moves to the right; the portion of the Timeline representing the amount of song that has been played is shaded (everything to the left of the Playhead). The value shown on the right end of the Timeline can be either the total time of the track or the track's remaining time (indicated by a negative value). You can choose the value that is displayed by clicking the time; if total time is shown, it will become remaining time and vice versa.

If you click the **Show Current Song** button, the song currently playing will be selected in the Content pane; this is indicated by blue highlighting. This can be handy when you are working with other music sources while listening to a song because you can click this button to quickly return to the song that is currently playing.

When you play a CD containing music from various artists, the artist will be shown on the top line of text next to the song name for each song. The artist displayed on the lower line of text will be Various Artists.

Finally, if you click the Change Display button, the display will become a graphical representation of the volume levels at various frequency groups (see Figure 16.4). You can return to the song information by clicking the button again.

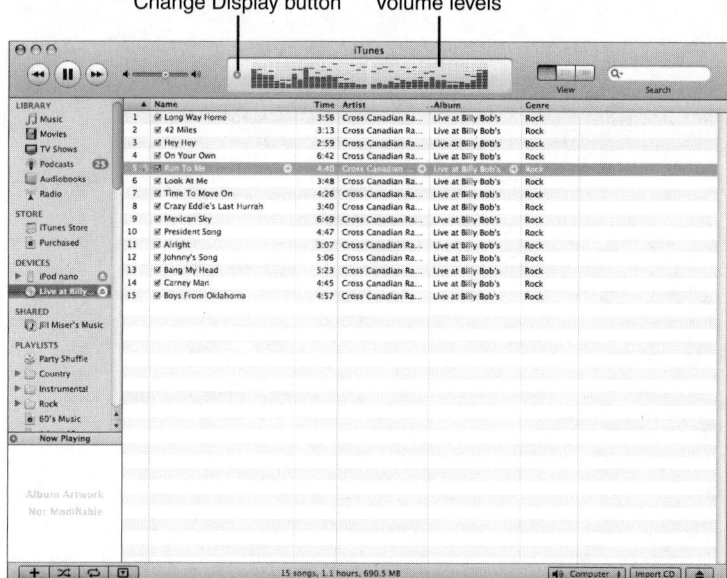

FIGURE 16.4
Why would you want to use the volume level display in the Information window? No real reason I know of, but it does look kind of cool.

Choosing the Songs You Hear

Let's face it, you might not like every song on a CD no matter how much you like the CD on the whole. With iTunes, you can choose the songs that play when you play the CD. You can cause a song to be skipped by unchecking its check box (see Figure 16.5). When the CD plays, every song whose check box is unchecked will be skipped.

To have iTunes include and thus play the song again the next time you play the CD, simply check its check box again.

Along with a CD's information, iTunes remembers the settings you make for a CD and reuses them each time you insert and play the CD. This includes skipping songs, changing the order in which they play, and so on. Cool!

Choosing the Order in Which Songs Play

iTunes determines the order in which songs play by the order in which they are shown in the Content pane, starting from the top of the pane and moving toward the bottom. By default, songs are listed and therefore play in the order they appear on the CD, from track 1 to the last track on the disc. However, you can make songs on a CD play in any order you choose. There are a couple of ways to do this.

You can change the order in which songs are listed in the Content pane (and thus the order in which they play) by dragging the songs up or down in the pane (see Figure 16.6). When you change the order of the songs in the pane, you change the order in which they will play.

FIGURE 16.5
Here, the song "President Song" will be skipped because its Select check box is unchecked. (Of course, this is only an example; all the songs on this CD happen to be excellent, and I really wouldn't skip any of them.)

FIGURE 16.6
Order! Order! Compare the order of the songs in this figure with the previous one; listening to the CD now will be an entirely different experience.

You can also change the order of tracks by sorting the Content pane by the various attributes shown, such as Track Number, Song Name, Time, Artist, and so on. You can do this by clicking the column heading of the attribute by which you want to sort the list. When you do so, the tracks will be sorted by that column (see Figure 16.7). To change the direction of the sort (from ascending to descending or from descending to ascending), click the **Sort Order triangle**; the sort direction will be reversed and the songs will be reordered accordingly. Just as they do when you move songs around manually, they play in the order in which they are listed in the pane. (This isn't so useful when you listen to a CD because many of the attributes, such as artist, genre, and album, are the same. However, when you use playlists or display more attributes, this can be very handy.)

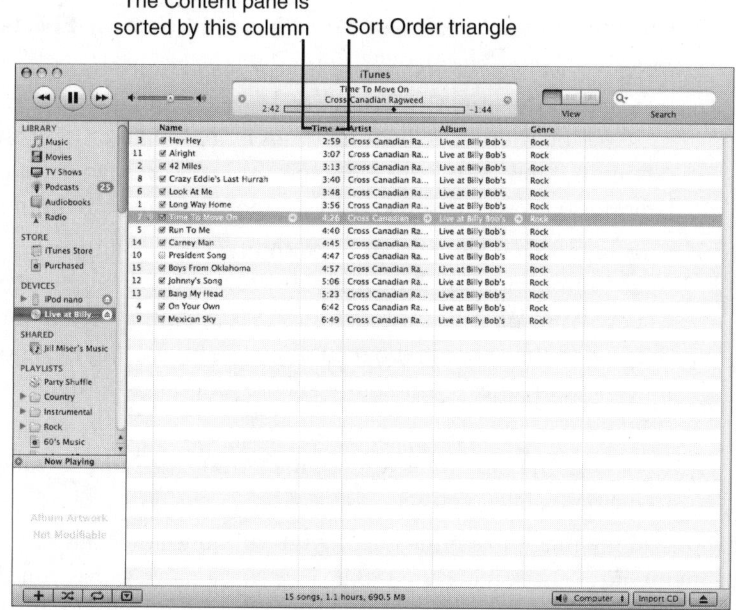

FIGURE 16.7
Now the order of the songs is based on their length; in this case, the shortest song on the CD plays first, then the next shortest second, and so on.

The column by which the pane is sorted is indicated by the column heading being highlighted in blue. This defaults to the first column, which is the Track Number (which, by the way, is the only unnamed column because it applies only to audio CDs and to no other sources). When a CD is the source, the Track Number column is always the first or leftmost column in the Content pane. When you select a different column, its heading becomes blue to show that it is the current sort column.

You can also tell which column is the current sort column by the Sort Order triangle. It appears only in the sort column. When the triangle points down, the sort is descending. When the triangle points up, the sort is ascending.

Getting Random

For a little variety, you can have iTunes play songs in a random order. This feature is called Shuffle. To use this feature, click the **Shuffle** button located at the bottom of the window (second one from the left) or select **Controls**, **Shuffle**. The songs will be reordered in the Content pane and will play in the order in which they are listed (which should be random). The Shuffle button will be highlighted in blue to indicate that it is active.

To return the CD to the order you have set for it (or its original order if you haven't changed it), click the **Shuffle** button again or select **Controls**, **Shuffle**.

You can control how the Shuffle command works by using the Shuffle preferences. Here's how:

1. Open the iTunes Preferences dialog box and select the **Playback** pane.
2. Choose how likely it is that you'll hear songs from the same artist or album by using the **Smart Shuffle** slider. Move the slider toward **more likely** to increase the chances of hearing songs by the same artist or from the same album in a row. Move the slider toward **less likely** to decrease the odds of hearing songs by the same artist or from the same album in a row.
3. Choose how you want songs to be shuffled by clicking one of the **Shuffle** radio buttons. Choose **Songs** if you want songs to be shuffled randomly. Choose **Albums** if you want iTunes to randomly select an album, play all its songs, and then choose the next album to play. Likewise, choose **Groupings** if you want iTunes to randomly choose groupings of songs to play (such as compilations).
4. Click **OK**. The next time you use the Shuffle function, it will work according to the preferences you set.

If you used the menu to shuffle a disc, you will notice that the Shuffle command on the menu has a check mark next to it. This check mark shows you that the command is currently active. When it isn't, the check mark will disappear. This is true of other settings as well, such as Repeat.

Repeating Tracks

Sometimes, you just can't get enough of the music to which you are listening. In that case, you can set iTunes to repeat an entire CD once or to repeat only a single song. To repeat your tunes, check out these pointers:

- To have iTunes repeat an entire CD, select **Controls**, **Repeat All** or click the **Repeat** button located at the bottom of the window (third one from the left). The Repeat button will become highlighted to show you that it is active, and the CD will repeat when you play it.
- To repeat only the selected song, select **Controls**, **Repeat One** or click the **Repeat** button a second time. A "1" will appear on the Repeat button to indicate that only the current song will be repeated.
- To turn off the repeat function, select **Controls**, **Repeat Off** or click the **Repeat** button until it is no longer highlighted in blue.

Controlling iTunes from the Desktop

Using the controls you have seen so far is fine, but you might not want to have the iTunes window foremost all the time. You must be able to see iTunes to control it, right? Wrong!

Controlling iTunes from the Windows System Tray

When iTunes is running on a Windows machine, an iTunes icon is displayed in the System Tray. Right-click this icon, and you will see an iTunes menu (see Figure 16.8). At the top of the menu is the Show iTunes command; select it to move into the iTunes window. Just under this command is the Now Playing section that provides information about the music that is currently playing. (If no music is playing or selected, you won't see this section in the menu.) You can use the rest of the commands on this menu just as you can from within iTunes. For example, you can skip to the next song by selecting **Next**. After you select a command, you can move off the menu and it will disappear. This is a handy way to control iTunes without having to make its window active or even being able to see it.

FIGURE 16.8
You can control iTunes even if you can't see it.

If you don't want the iTunes icon to appear in the System Tray for some reason, you can remove it. Open the **iTunes Preferences** dialog box (**Ctrl+,**), click the **Advanced** tab, click the **General** subtab, uncheck the **Show iTunes icon in system tray** check box, and click **OK**. The icon will no longer appear in your System Tray.

Controlling iTunes from the Mac's Dock

The iTunes icon on the Mac OS X Dock enables you to control iTunes at any time, even when the iTunes window is in the background, when its window is minimized, or when the application is hidden. When you Ctrl-click the **iTunes Dock** icon (or right-click if you have a two-button mouse), the iTunes menu will appear (see Figure 16.9). At the top of this menu is the iTunes command, which will move you into the iTunes window. Just under that is the Now Playing section that provides information about the song currently playing. (If no music is selected or playing, you won't see this section.) You can control iTunes by selecting a command on the iTunes Dock menu. For example, you can pause the music by selecting Pause. After you select a command, the menu will disappear, and you can get back to what you were doing.

> **tip**
>
> To keep iTunes out of the way, open it and select a source, such as an audio CD. Then configure and play the source. Minimize (Windows) or hide (Mac) the iTunes window so it no longer appears on your desktop. Then you can use the iTunes System Tray icon menu (Windows) or iTunes Dock icon menu (Mac) to control it—for example, to pause your tunes when you receive a phone call.

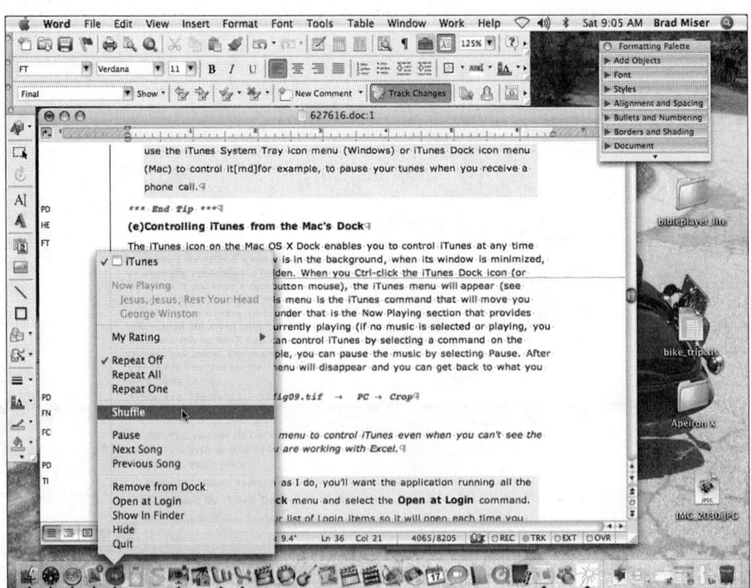

FIGURE 16.9
On the Mac, you use its Dock menu to control iTunes even when you can't see the application, such as when you are working with Word.

Controlling iTunes on a Mac with the iTunes Widget

Version 10.4 of the Mac OS introduced the cool Dashboard function that provides quick access to mini-applications called *widgets*. One of the default widgets enables you to control iTunes.

First, configure the iTunes widget to appear when you use the Dashboard by performing the following steps:

1. Press your **Dashboard** key on the keyboard; by default on desktop Macs, this is the F12 key. Mobile Macs use other keys, depending on the model you are using. The Dashboard will appear. If the iTunes widget appears, you can skip the rest of these steps.
2. Click the + located in the lower-left corner of the desktop. The Dashboard bar will appear.
3. Drag the iTunes widget from the bar onto the location on your desktop where you want it to be when you open the Dashboard.
4. Close the Dashboard by pressing the **Dashboard** key again or by clicking in an application or on the desktop.

When you want to use the iTunes widget, open the Dashboard by pressing its key. Your widgets will appear, including the iTunes widget (see Figure 16.10). Some of the controls look slightly different than they do within iTunes, but they work in the same way. Use the controls, such as rotating the Volume wheel to change volume, and then hide the Dashboard again by pressing its key or clicking someplace else.

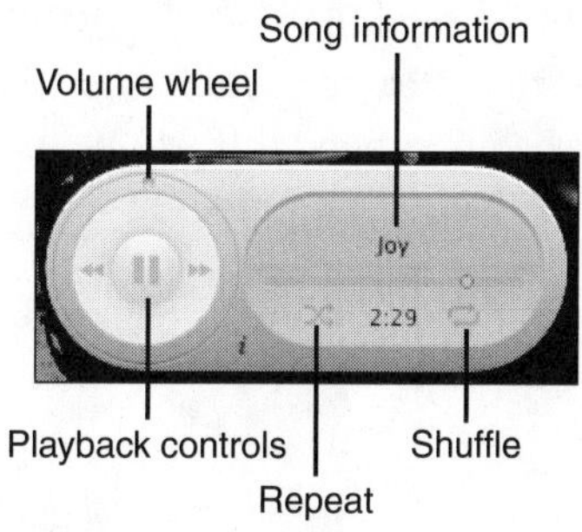

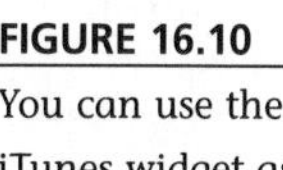

FIGURE 16.10
You can use the iTunes widget as another way to control iTunes when you aren't working with the application directly.

One control that isn't so obvious is the one that enables you to select a music source from within the iTunes widget. Open the widget and wait for a moment or two. (Just how long is a moment, anyway?) An i will appear at the bottom of the widget near its center. Click this button, and you will see a **Select a Playlist** pop-up menu. Choose a source on this menu and click **Done**. You can play the source you selected by clicking the widget's **Play** button and control the music with the widget's other controls.

Listening to Internet Radio

iTunes supports Internet "radio" stations; you can choose one of the available stations and listen to its content similarly to how you listen to a radio station over the air. (The stations are actually websites that offer streaming audio files in various formats, but they are analogous to radio, so using that as a model is a good way to think about them.) iTunes offers a number of genres from which you can choose, such as pop, classic rock, jazz, and so on. Listening to one of these stations is much like listening to a CD (or any other source for that matter).

This is likely obvious to you from the title of this section, but your computer must be able to connect to the Internet if you want to be able to listen to Internet radio.

Playing Your iTunes Radio

To tune in iTunes radio, perform the following steps:

1. Open iTunes and select the **Radio** source by clicking it. iTunes retrieves a list of all the available stations, and the Content pane will contain the list of available genres. The column headings will be updated to be appropriate to the content. For example, you will see Stream, Bit Rate, and Comment.
2. Click the **expansion triangle** for the genre in which you are interested (see Figure 16.11). iTunes will connect to the Internet to update the list of channels for the genre you selected, and the genre will expand. You will see the various channels it contains. Look at the stream name, bit rate, and comment columns for the channels to decide which you want to try. Usually, the Comment column will provide a description of the kind of music the stream contains.
3. To play a channel, select it and click **Play** or double-click the stream you want to hear. The channel will begin to play; this will be instantaneous if you have a fast connection to the Net, or there will be a slight delay if you use a dial-up connection. Just as when you play a song on a CD, the speaker icon will appear next to the channel to which you are listening.

   Also, just as when you listen to a CD, information about the channel will appear in the Information window (see Figure 16.12). This includes the stream name, the song currently playing, and the website with which the channel is associated.

tip

The name of the song currently playing is especially useful when you hear a song you like that you might want to add to your collection. Make a note of the song's name and artist. Then you can look for CDs containing that song or, even better, buy it from the iTunes Store.

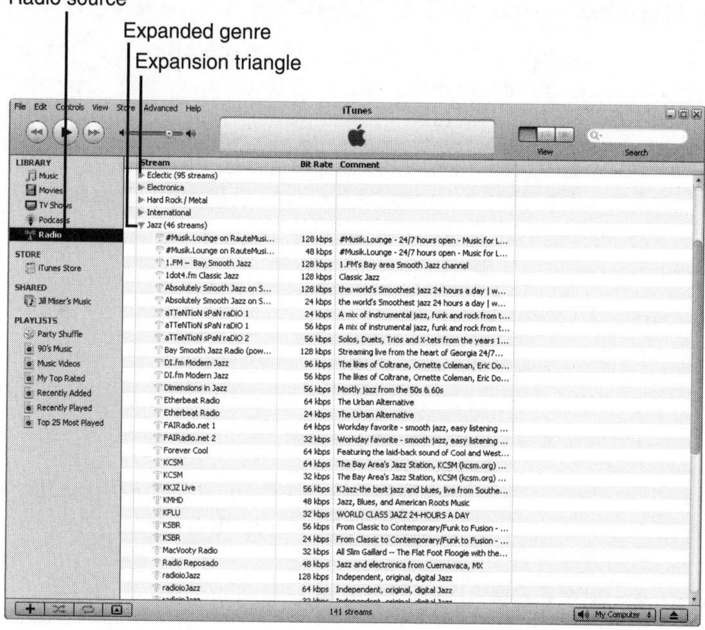

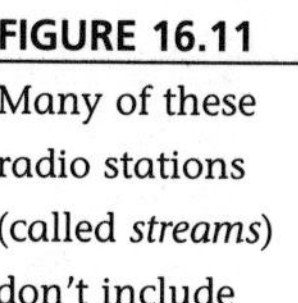

FIGURE 16.11
Many of these radio stations (called *streams*) don't include commercials.

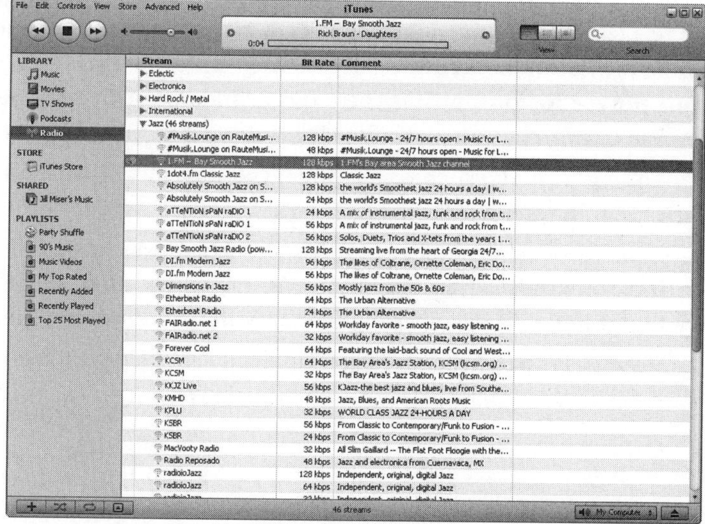

FIGURE 16.12
Smooth Jazz is an appropriate name for this stream.

You can use the Volume slider to change the volume level and the Stop button to stop playback. The Rewind and Fast Forward buttons work a little differently from what you might expect. Rather than moving you in the selected stream, they instead take you to the previous or next stream, which makes sense when you think about each stream as being like a track on a CD.

Configuring iTunes for a Slow Internet Connection

If you use a slow Internet connection, such as a dial-up account, traffic on the Internet can cause the stream of music to slow or even stop, resulting in pauses in the music, even if you choose a lower bit-rate channel, such as 32Kbps. If this is a problem for you, perform the following steps:

1. Select **Edit**, **Preferences** (Windows) or **iTunes**, **Preferences** (Mac). The Preferences dialog box will appear.
2. Click the **Advanced** tab. The Advanced pane will appear.
3. Click the **General** subtab.
4. On the Streaming Buffer Size drop-down list, select **Large**. This increases the amount of buffer space used to store a stream before it actually starts to play.
5. Click **OK**. The dialog box will close.

This should eliminate any pauses in the streams to which you like to listen. If not, choose a different stream or one with a lower bit rate.

Playing Around with Internet Audio

You can do a couple of other things with Internet radio using iTunes.

If you want iTunes to be used to play Internet audio by default, open the **Preferences** dialog box (**Ctrl+,** on Windows computers or **⌘+,** on Macs). Open the **Advanced** pane and then open the **General** subtab. Then check the **Use iTunes as the default player for audio files** check box (Windows) or click the **Set** button (Mac). When your browser hits an audio file that iTunes supports, iTunes should play it.

You can also play audio streams for which you have a URL within iTunes. To do this, use the following steps:

1. Find the URL pointing to the stream to which you want to listen. Copy the URL from the Address bar of the Web browser because that is a lot easier than trying to remember the URL or writing it down and then typing it in.
2. Select **Advanced**, **Open Stream**. The Open Stream dialog box will appear.
3. Paste or type the URL in the URL field (see Figure 16.13).
4. Click **OK**. The stream plays.

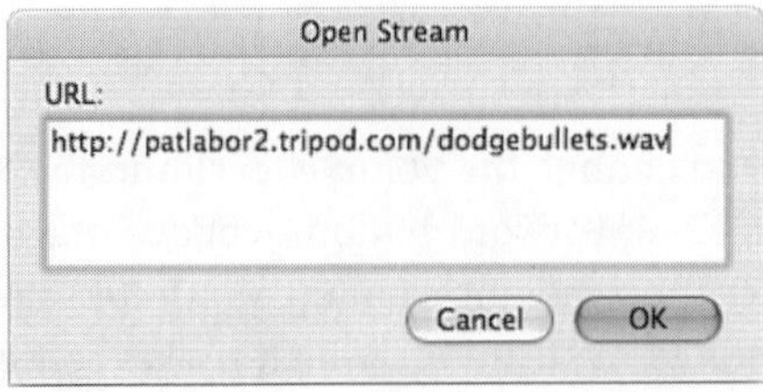

FIGURE 16.13
Here, I've pasted in a URL to an MP3 file that contains a line from the movie *The Matrix.*

If you want to play the content more than once, to which the URL points download it to your computer and add it to the Library. You'll learn how to do this in the next chapter. You can also add a stream to a playlist by selecting it and selecting **File, New Playlist from Selection**.

Customizing the iTunes Window

You can configure iTunes in various ways to suit your preferences. You can also change the size of the iTunes window in different ways.

Setting General iTunes Preferences

On the General pane of the iTunes Preferences dialog box are several settings you might want to use (see Figure 16.14):

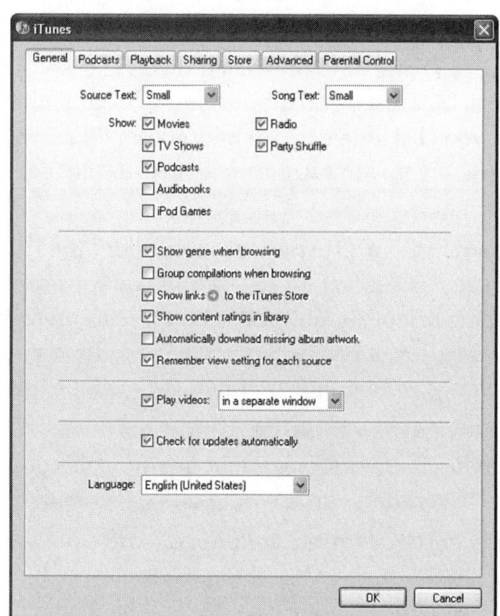

FIGURE 16.14
The General pane of the iTunes Preferences dialog box provides..., well, general preferences.

- **Source Text**—Use this drop-down list to change the font size of the sources shown in the Source list. The options are Small (default) and Large.
- **Song Text**—This setting changes the size of the text used in the Content pane. Again, your options are Small and Large.
- **Show check boxes**—These determine whether various sources appear on the Source list or not. If a source's check box is checked, it will be listed on the

Source list. If it isn't checked, the source will not appear on the list. For example, if you don't want the TV Shows source to appear, uncheck the **TV Shows** check box.

- **Show genre when browsing**—If you read the previous chapter, you learned about the Browser. This check box controls whether the Genre column appears in the Browser (the check box is checked) or not (the check box is not checked). I like the Genre column, so I leave this checked, but if you don't, you can uncheck the check box to remove that column from the Browser.
- **Group compilations when browsing**—Compilations are what iTunes calls CDs that contain music from various artists (you know, like that Greatest TV Theme Songs from the 1970s CD you like so much). If you check this check box, these compilations will be grouped as collections of music even though the artists might be different on one or more tracks. If you don't want your compilations grouped and prefer to have each track be grouped by artist, uncheck the check box.
- **Show links to the iTunes Store**—When this is checked, arrow buttons will appear next to tracks, artists, and albums in the Content pane and in other locations. When you click one of these buttons, you'll move to related music in the iTunes Store. If you don't want these links displayed, uncheck the check box.
- **Show content ratings in Library**—Content from the iTunes Store has content ratings, such as Explicit for music that contains content that might be offensive to some or not suitable for children. This preference controls whether these ratings are shown when you view content in the Content pane. If checked, the ratings will be shown. If not, they will be hidden.
- **Automatically download missing album artwork**—iTunes can automatically download album art for content in your collection that currently doesn't have any. Check this check box to allow iTunes to do this.
- **Remember view setting for each source**—There are view options you can configure in iTunes, such as the columns displayed. If you check this check box, the view settings for each source will be remembered and reused each time you select that source. If you uncheck this box, the current settings will be used for all sources you view.
- **Play videos**—You use this check box and drop-down list to configure how video content plays in iTunes. You'll learn more about this later.
- **Check for updates automatically**—This check box controls whether iTunes checks for updates and lets you know when they are available. Because it is a good idea to use the current version, you should leave this check box checked.

- **Language (Windows only)**—Use this drop-down list to choose the language you want iTunes to use.

After you've made your selections, click OK to save them and close the dialog box.

Changing Column Widths

Within the iTunes window, you can change the relative width of the Source list pane versus the Content pane or Browser, or between the Browser and the Content pane, by dragging their borders to the left or right or up or down. Move your cursor over the border; when you are in the right place to be able to drag it, the cursor will change to a vertical line with arrows coming out its side (Source pane) or a hand (Browser). When this cursor appears, drag the border to change the pane's width or height.

Changing the Size of the iTunes Window

Like the windows of other applications, you can change the size of the iTunes window. For example, you might want to make the window smaller so that it doesn't consume so much desktop space. (Remember that you can minimize or hide the window and then use its System Tray (Windows) or Dock (Mac) controls to control it.)

Changing the Size of the iTunes Window on a Windows PC

As you use iTunes, keep in mind the following tips for keeping the window out of your way:

- **Minimize/maximize the window**—Use the standard Minimize and Maximize controls in the iTunes window to hide it, allow it to be resized, or make it full-screen size.
- **Make the window smaller**—If the iTunes window is in the resize mode (click the Maximize button so the window's size is maximized and then click it again), you can drag the window's resize handle to make the window smaller until it reaches the smallest possible size. Then you can move the window out of the way, but it will still appear on the desktop.
- **Use the Mini Player**—For minimum window real estate use, put iTunes in the Mini Player mode by selecting **Advanced**, **Switch to Mini Player**; pressing **Ctrl+M**; or opening the iTunes System Tray menu and selecting **Switch to Mini Player**. The iTunes window will compress down so it is just large enough to display the playback controls and Information window (see Figure 16.15). To switch back to the normal iTunes window, use the window controls, press **Ctrl+M**, or open the iTunes System Tray menu and select **Switch to iTunes Window**.

FIGURE 16.15
Smaller is sometimes better, when it comes to window size, that is.

- If you want iTunes to be minimized to the System Tray rather than shown on the taskbar, open the **Advanced** pane and then open the **General** subtab of the Preferences dialog box. Check **Minimize iTunes window to system tray** and then click **OK**. When you minimize iTunes, it will disappear from the taskbar. (You can get to it again using its icon in the System Tray.)

Changing the Size of the iTunes Window on a Mac

When you use iTunes on a Mac, you can change the window's size in the following ways:

- **Hide the application**—Press ⌘+H to hide iTunes. Its window will be hidden from the desktop. You can control iTunes by using its Dock menu or widget. Click the **iTunes Dock** icon to show the window again.
- **Toggle the size of the window**—If you click the **Toggle Size** button (the green "light") on the window's title bar, the iTunes window will collapse so that only the playback controls and the Information window are shown (see Figure 16.16). Click the button again to open the window to its full size.

FIGURE 16.16
On the Mac, you can quickly collapse the iTunes window to this handy size.

- **Change the size of the window**—In either the full or collapsed state, you can change the size of the window by dragging its resize handle located in the bottom-right corner of the window.

Setting iTunes Playback Preferences

You can use iTunes Playback preferences to control how your music plays. For example, you can get rid of the gap of silence between songs or make songs play back at a consistent volume level. You can take advantage of these features by using the Playback pane of the iTunes Preferences dialog box. On this pane, you can configure the following preferences for your music (see Figure 16.17):

- **Crossfade playback**—This effect causes one song to fade out and the next one to fade in smoothly, eliminating the gaps of silence between songs. To activate it, check the **Crossfade playback** check box and use the slider to see the amount of fade time. If you move the slider to the left, songs fade out more quickly. If you set it to 0, there is no fading, and as soon as one song ends, the next one starts. If you move the slider to the right, songs overlap; as one song starts to fade out, the next starts to fade in so you hear them both at the same time. Click **OK**, and the effect takes effect.

  This Crossfade setting does not impact audio CDs. Because there is a physical gap between tracks on the CD, iTunes can't do anything about it. This setting applies to other sources, such as your Library and playlists. (So why cover it in the CD chapter, you ask? Because this seemed like the place to cover the other effects, so I added this one here, too.)

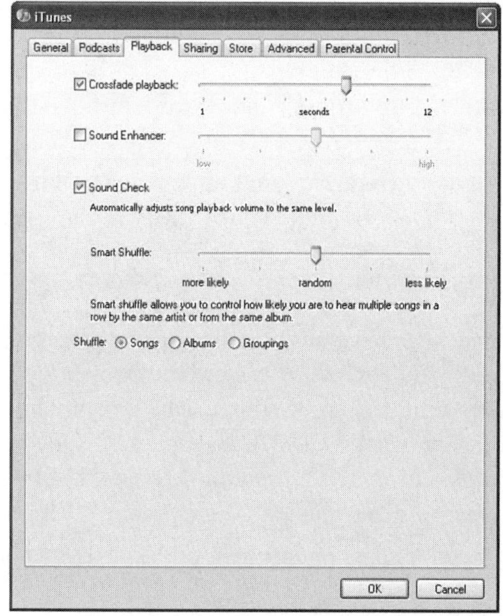

FIGURE 16.17
Control how your music sounds with the Playback preferences.

- **Sound Enhancer**—This effect is iTunes' attempt to "add depth and enliven" the quality of your music. The actual result of this effect is a bit difficult to describe, so the best thing to do is try it for yourself. Check the **Sound Enhancer** check box and use the slider to set the relative amount of enhancement. Click **OK** and then listen to some music. It if sounds better to you, increase the amount of the effect and listen again. If not, decrease it or turn it off.

- **Sound Check**—This effect attempts to set the relative volume level of all songs to be the same. It is useful if music in your Library has been recorded at different volume levels and you want to have all your music play at the same volume level (or as close to it as iTunes can get). To implement this effect, check its check box and click **OK**. (You'll learn how to change the relative volume level of songs later in this part of the book.)

The Absolute Minimum

By learning how to use iTunes to play audio CDs and Internet radio, you've picked up a lot more knowledge than you might realize. That's because you use the same steps and controls to listen to other music sources, such as your Library, playlists, and so on. In the next couple of chapters, you'll learn about these other sources; after you do, you'll be able to use the techniques you picked up in this chapter to work with them.

For now, keep the following tidbits in mind:

- Many of the controls in the iTunes window work just like similar controls on a CD player.
- The iTunes Information window doesn't look like a lot, but you'll learn to really love it when you are building your Library in the next chapter.
- If a song's check box is checked, it will play. If it's not checked, the song won't play.
- You determine the songs you want to hear and the order in which you want to hear them for all your sources by the order in which they appear in the Content pane (except for the Radio source, which you have to take as it comes). Each time you insert a CD, iTunes remembers the settings you used the last time and uses those settings again. Just wait until you get to playlists—you can take this concept to the extreme!
- You can repeat or randomize the music in any source, such as a CD or playlist.
- Don't forget about the iTunes System Tray (Windows) or Dock (Mac) menu. This is a great way to keep iTunes music going while not consuming any of your valuable desktop real estate. On the Mac, you can also use the iTunes widget to control iTunes without consuming lots of screen real estate.

continues

- You can change the width of columns within the iTunes window, and you can resize the iTunes window to make it the size you want. As you work through later chapters, you'll also learn how to customize the information you see inside the window.
- Listening to the Radio source provides access to lots of audio content available on the Internet.
- You can use iTunes Playback preferences to control the gap between songs, to equalize the relative volume of songs, and to enhance the sound you hear.
- As you view the screenshots throughout this book, you'll see examples of some of my favorite music. If you like it too, drop me an email (bradmacosx@mac.com) to let me know.

IN THIS CHAPTER

- Know the sources of all iTunes music.
- Find out where your iTunes music will be stored, and change the location if it suits your fancy.
- Maximize your music's quality/file size ratio by choosing encoding options and quality levels when you import audio CDs.
- Build your iTunes Library by importing audio CDs into it.
- Browse and search your Library like a master librarian.
- Dump music you don't want cluttering up your digital shelves.

17

BUILDING, BROWSING, SEARCHING, AND PLAYING YOUR iTUNES MUSIC LIBRARY

Are you ready for some real iTunes? If the material in the previous chapters covered good features of iTunes, which it did, then this chapter starts the coverage of the amazing, awesome [insert your own superlative here] features that make iTunes something to write a book about. Here is where we start taking your iTunes game to the next level, hitting some home runs, scoring touchdowns, and some other sports clichés that all good books use. It's time to start working with that mysterious Library I have mentioned a number of times but into which until now you have had only tantalizing glimpses.

The iTunes Library is where you can store all your music, such as that from audio CDs, from the Internet, and that you purchase from the iTunes Store; video; and other content for which you use iTunes.

Because this chapter's title references your Music Library, you can probably guess that music is the focus here. (You'll learn about the other kinds of content as you move through this part of the book.) After you have added music to your Library, you never have to bother with individual CDs again because you can access all your music from the Library. And, you can use the music in your Library in many ways, such as to create playlists, burn your own CDs, and so on.

Right now, your iTunes Library is probably sort of sad. Like a book library with no books in it, your iTunes Library is just sitting there gathering dust on its digital shelves. You will change that shortly. The first step is to add music to the Library. Then you'll learn how to browse, search, and listen to the tunes you have added there.

Gathering Your Music from All the Right Places

If you are going to add music to your Library, you have to get it from somewhere, right? The following are the three main sources of tunes for your Library:

- **Audio CDs**—Who wants to bother with audio CDs? Wouldn't it be nice if you could store all the content of your CD collection in one place so you could listen to any music you wanted to at any time just by browsing or doing a quick search? Obviously, that's a loaded question, because you already know you can use iTunes to do just that. In this chapter, you'll learn how to copy the music from audio CDs into your Library (as you'll remember from Chapter 14, "Touring iTunes," this is called *importing*) so that you never have to use the original CDs again.
- **MP3 and other audio files**—You can add audio files in just about any format to your Library. For example, there are lots of free and legal MP3 files on the web that you can add to your own Library. In this chapter, you will learn how to add music to your Library in this way, too.
- **iTunes Store**—With the iTunes Store, you can browse and search among hundreds of thousands of songs. When you find music you like, you can purchase an entire CD's worth of songs, or you can buy individual songs. (Can you say one-hit wonder?) When you buy music, it is downloaded and added to your iTunes Library. Rather than order a CD or, even worse, buy one in a physical store, you have access to your music instantly, and you don't even have to import it. Because the iTunes Store is so cool, I have devoted an entire part of this book to it (Part III, "The iTunes Store"). In that part, you will see how to build your Library by purchasing music online.

Determining Where and How the Music Library Music Is Stored

It is much easier to organize an empty room, so it is good practice to set up the organization of your iTunes Library before you fill it with music and other content. In this section, you'll learn how iTunes organizes the music in your Library. If its standard practices aren't good enough for you, you can change its ways to suit your own preferences.

Working with the iTunes Music Folder

As you import music into the Library, files are created for each song you add (whether it's from a CD, downloaded from the iTunes Store, or imported from an existing file). When you first started the application, iTunes created a folder called iTunes Music in which it stores all the music it manages for you.

The default location of this folder depends on the kind of computer you are using. On Windows computers, the folder is stored in a folder called iTunes, located within your My Music folder (that is in turn, located in your My Documents folder). On Macs, this folder is also called iTunes, but it is located in the Music folder within your Home folder.

To see the current location of the iTunes Music folder on your computer, open the iTunes Preferences dialog box, click the **Advanced** tab, and then click the **General** subtab (see Figure 17.1). At the top of this dialog box, you will see the iTunes Music folder location box. Within this box, you will see the path to your iTunes Music folder.

Just for fun, open your iTunes Music folder so you can see it for yourself. Use the path you see on the Advanced pane to find it. If you haven't added music to your Library yet, it might be pretty dull. To see what a full folder looks like, check out Figure 17.2.

As you can see, within the iTunes Music folder is a folder for each artist. Within each artist's folder, each album from which you have added music is shown. Within each of those album folders, the tracks you have added are individual files (see Figure 17.3). If you take a close look at Figure 17.3, you can see that the files have the extension `.mp3`, which means the song files for the album *The Best Of BB King* were imported in the MP3 format.

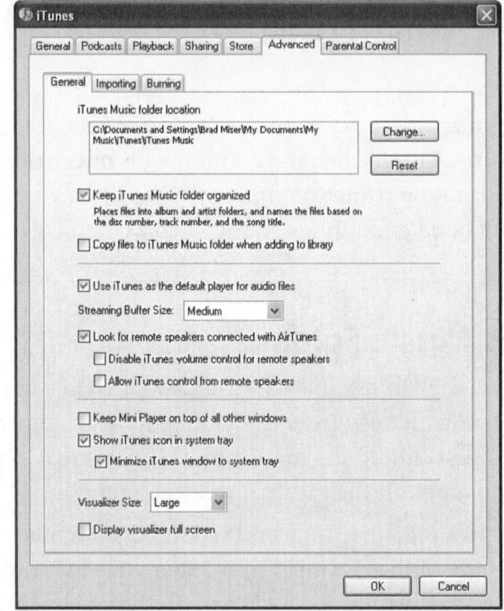

FIGURE 17.1

The current location of your iTunes folder is shown on the General subtab of the Advanced pane of the iTunes Preferences dialog box.

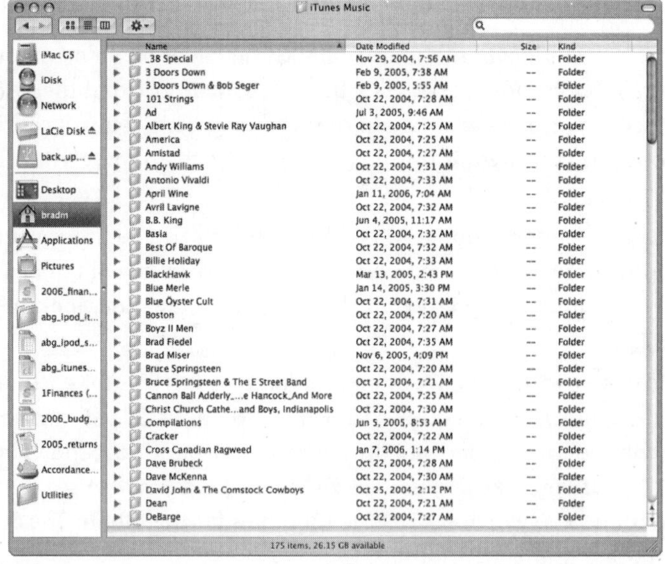

FIGURE 17.2

Don't be envious—soon your iTunes Library will be as full of good tunes as mine is.

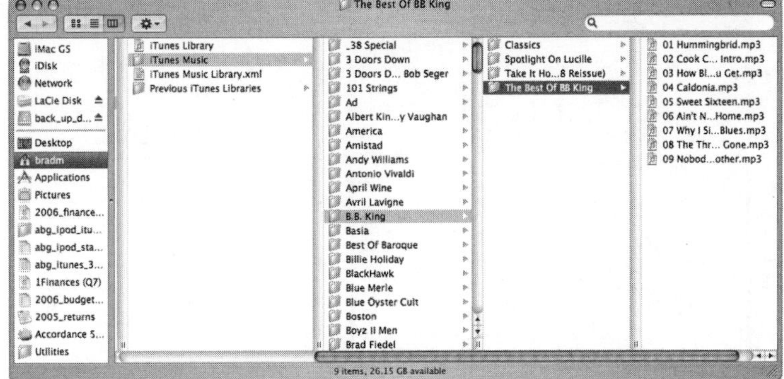

FIGURE 17.3
In this folder, you can see all the songs contained on the album *The Best of BB King* (which is an excellent album, by the way, not that I am qualified to be a music critic).

Configuring the Location of the Music Folder

In most cases, the default location of your iTunes Music folder will be fine, and you don't have to do anything about it. However, in some cases you will want to change the location of this folder. For example, suppose you have several hard drives in your computer, and the one on which the folder is currently stored doesn't have a lot of room. Even though individual song files are relatively small, you are likely to end up with thousands or tens of thousands of them in your Library. That can add up to a lot of disk space. You might want to change the location of your iTunes Music folder so it is on a drive with more room.

To change the location of this folder, do the following:

1. Open the **Advanced** pane of the iTunes Preferences dialog box and click the **General** subtab.
2. Click the **Change** button. On a Windows PC, you will see the Browse For Folder dialog box (see Figure 17.4). On a Mac, you will see the Change Music Folder Location dialog box (see Figure 17.5).

note

One of the questions I get asked frequently is how to store music on a different hard disk, such as an external hard disk. Here's the answer. Move your iTunes Music folder to the hard drive on which you want to store your music. Then use the Music Folder location preference to select the folder in its new location. From that point on, iTunes will store any music (or other content) in the folder's new location.

FIGURE 17.4
You use the Browse For Folder dialog box to move to or select a new home for your iTunes Music folder on a Windows PC.

FIGURE 17.5
The Change Music Folder Location dialog box looks a bit different from its Windows counterpart, but the purpose is exactly the same.

3. Use the dialog box to move to and select the folder in which you want your iTunes Music folder to be located. For example, if you want to move the folder to another hard drive, move to that drive and click the **Make New Folder** (Windows) or **New Folder** (Mac) button to create a new folder for your music.
4. Click **OK** (Windows) or **Choose** (Mac). You'll return to the Advanced pane, and the folder you selected will be shown in the iTunes Music Folder Location area.
5. Click **OK** to close the iTunes Preferences dialog box.

If you already have music in your Library, changing the location of the iTunes Music folder won't hurt you. When you select a new folder, iTunes remembers the location of any previous music you have added to the Library and updates its database so that music will still be part of your Library.

If you want to go back to the default location of the iTunes Music Folder, open the **General** subtab of the Advanced pane of the iTunes Preferences dialog box and click the **Reset** button.

Setting Other Organization Preferences

The location of the folder in which your music will be stored is likely the most important part of the organization preferences. However, you'll need to understand a couple more preferences that are also located on the General subtab of the Advanced pane of the iTunes Preferences dialog box:

- **Keep iTunes music folder organized**—This preference causes iTunes to organize your music as described earlier—that is, by artist, album, and song. Because this is a logical way to organize your music files, I recommend that you leave this option active by making sure this check box is checked.
- **Copy files to iTunes Music Folder when adding to library**—This preference causes iTunes to make a copy of audio files that already exist on your computer (such as MP3 files you have downloaded from the Internet) and places those copies in your iTunes Music folder, just like files you create by importing them from a CD. If this preference is inactive, iTunes uses a pointer to song files you are adding instead of making a copy of the files; it doesn't actually place the files in your iTunes Music folder. I recommend that you make this preference active by checking its check box. This way, all your music files will be in the same place, no matter where they came from originally.

  If you don't have iTunes make copies of songs when you add them to your Library and then you delete or move the song files you added, iTunes will lose track of the song and you will experience the "missing song file" problem. To learn how to solve that problem, see "Solving the Missing Song File Problem" on page **404**.

caution

If you do have iTunes copy files to your iTunes Music folder when you add them to your Library, be aware that it does actually make a copy of the file you are adding. This means you will have two files for each song you add to the Library. After you have added songs to your Library successfully, you should delete the song files from their original locations so you don't waste disk space.

Understanding Encoding and Other Important Format Options

Back in Chapter 14, you learned about the major music file formats that you need to be aware of as you use iTunes. As you will recall, the two primary formats you use when dealing with music are AAC and MP3, but the Apple Lossless format is useful when you want only the highest quality from your music. When you add music to your Library, you choose the format and then select the specific configuration of that format.

Choosing a Format Option

Although I am sure that going into the specifications for each kind of format would make for fascinating reading, there isn't really a need to get into that detail. Frankly, the benefit of using an application such as iTunes is that it manages all this complexity for you so that you don't have to be concerned with it. If you are like me, you just want to work with the music, not diddle around with complicated settings.

Generally, when you add music to your Library, you should use either the AAC or MP3 format. Because the AAC format is better (with *better* meaning that it provides higher-quality music in smaller file sizes), it is usually the best choice.

About the only case I can envision in which MP3 would be a better option is if you use a portable music player that can play only MP3 music. But because you are reading this book, you are probably using an iPod, and iPods are designed to work with the AAC format as well as the MP3 format (and all the other formats explained in this chapter as well, including the Apple Lossless format).

If you want to have the highest quality music and file size isn't a concern for you, Apple Lossless is the way to go.

Picking Quality Levels

After you select a format, you decide the quality with which the music will be encoded. Higher quality levels mean better-sounding music but larger file sizes. If file size is not a problem, choosing a higher quality setting is the way to go. If you have relatively little disk space, you might want to experiment to see which is the lowest quality setting you can choose that results in music that still sounds good to you. If you demand the absolute best in music quality and have plenty of hard drive space to spare, Apple Lossless is a good option for you.

Your computer's hard disk space isn't the only factor you need to consider when choosing a quality level. iPods also have a hard drive or flash memory, and if you use the higher-quality encoders, such as Apple Lossless, you won't be able to fit as many songs on your iPod as with a format designed to create smaller files, such as the AAC format.

Note that when it comes to music, quality is in the ear of the beholder. Also, it heavily depends on the type of music you listen to as well as how you listen to it. For example, if you listen to heavy metal rock with a low-quality pair of speakers (in other words, cheap speakers), quality will be less of an issue because you likely won't hear a difference anyway. However, if you listen to classical music on high-quality speakers, the differences in quality levels might be more noticeable.

The trade-off for quality is always file size. The higher the quality setting you choose, the larger the resulting files will be. If you don't have disk space limitations and have a discriminating ear, you might want to stick with the highest possible quality setting. If disk space is at a premium for you, consider using a lower quality setting if you can't detect the difference or if that difference doesn't bother you.

Configuring iTunes to Import Music

Before you start adding music to your Library, choose the import options (mainly format and quality levels) you want to use. Here are the steps to follow:

1. Open the **Importing** subtab of the **Advanced** pane of the iTunes Preferences dialog box (see Figure 17.6).

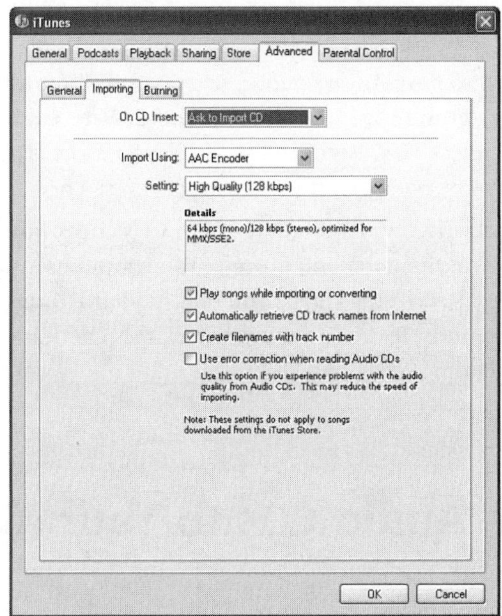

FIGURE 17.6
Here, you can see that the AAC format (the AAC Encoder) is selected.

2. Select the format in which you want to add music to your Library on the **Import Using** menu. For example, to use the AAC format, select **AAC Encoder**. To use the MP3 format, select **MP3 Encoder**. Or, select **Apple Lossless Encoder** to maximize the quality of your music. The other encoder options are WAV and AIFF, but you probably won't use those options except for special circumstances, such as when you are going to use the music you encode in a different application, in which case the AIFF encoder might be a good choice.

3. Select the quality level of the encoder you want to use on the Setting menu. The options you see in this list depend on the format you selected in step 1. If you chose AAC Encoder, you have three quality options: High Quality, Spoken Podcast, and Custom. If you chose MP3 Encoder, you have four options: Good Quality, High Quality, Higher Quality, and Custom. If you selected the Apple Lossless Encoder, you have only the Automatic option.

   In the Details box, you will see a summary of the settings you have selected. For example, you will see the data rate of the encoder, such as 128Kbps, and the processor for which the encoder has been optimized. (Do you need to worry about these details? Not really.)

   If you use the AAC encoder, the High Quality setting will likely be all you ever need.
4. If you want music you add to your Library to play while it is being added, check the **Play songs while importing or converting** check box. This is a personal preference, and it doesn't impact the encoding process significantly.
5. If you want the files that iTunes creates when you import music to include the track number in their filenames, check the **Create filenames with track number** check box. Because this helps you more easily find files for specific songs, I recommend that you keep this preference active.
6. The Use error correction when reading Audio CDs check box causes iTunes to more closely control the encoding process. You should use this option only if you notice problems with the music you add to your Library, such as crack-ing or popping sounds. If that happens, check this check box and try the import process again.
7. Click **OK** to close the dialog box.

Adding Music from Audio CDs to Your iTunes Music Library

Now that you know all you need to about configuring iTunes to build your Library, you are ready to start adding your own audio CDs to your Library.

Adding Audio CDs to Your Library

Use these steps to add a CD to your Library:

1. Configure the encoder you want to use for the import session. (See the section "Configuring iTunes to Import Music" on page **263**.)

2. Insert the CD you want to add to your Library. iTunes will attempt to identify it. When it does, the CD will appear in the Source list and will be selected (see Figure 17.7). Notice that when you have a CD mounted, the Import CD button appears in the lower-right corner of the iTunes window. Depending on your iTunes preferences, you might be prompted to import the CD; if so, click **Yes** and skip to the explanatory text in step 4.

FIGURE 17.7
iTunes is ready to add this CD to the Library.

3. If there are songs you don't want to add to the Library, uncheck their check boxes; only songs with their check boxes checked will be imported. Unless you really hate a song or disk space is at a premium, it is generally better to import all the songs. If you don't like to hear specific songs, you can use the check box in another source, such as in your Library, to cause those songs to be skipped when you play that source.
4. Click the **Import CD** button. The import process will start (see Figure 17.8).

   If you left the Play songs while importing preference active, the music will begin to play as it is imported.

   The Information window will show information related to the import process, such as the name of the song currently being imported and the rate at which the import process is happening.

   The rate of the import process depends on the hardware you are using, the import settings, and other tasks your computer might be performing. In most cases, the import process will occur at a much greater rate than the playing process. For example, with moderate hardware, you can usually achieve import rates exceeding 7x, meaning 7 minutes of music will be imported in 1 minute of time.

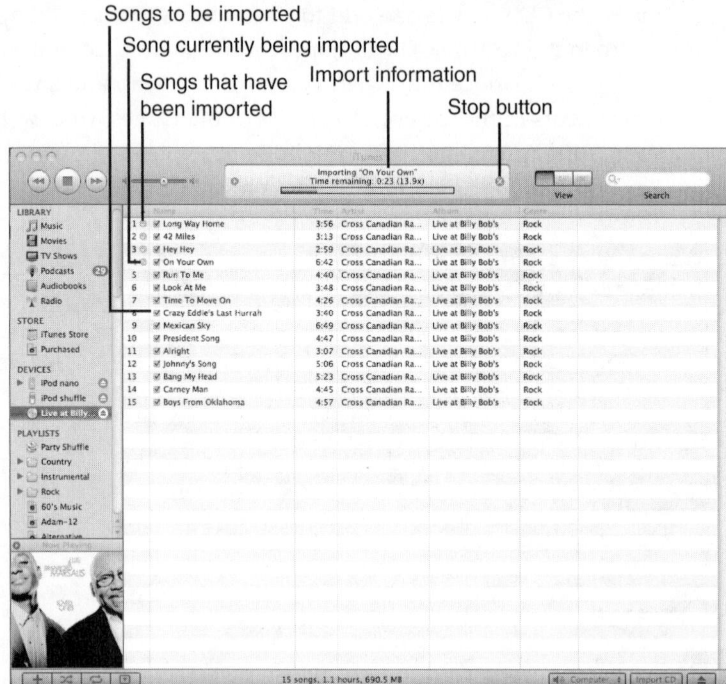

FIGURE 17.8
You can see that the import process is really speedy; it is currently moving along at 13.9× playing speed.

An orange circle with a "squiggly" line inside it marks the song currently being imported. When a song has been imported, it is marked with a green circle containing a check mark.

If you want to stop the import process for some reason, click the **Stop** button (the small *x* within a circle) in the Information window.

When the process is complete, you will hear a tone, and all the songs will be marked with the "import complete" icon.

If you have the Play songs while importing preference active, the music will keep playing long after the import process is complete (because importing is much faster than playing is). Listen for the Complete tone or keep an eye on the screen to determine when all the music on the CD has been imported.

During the import process, you don't have to listen to what you are importing. You can select a different source, such as a playlist, and play it while the CD is being imported. This will slow the import speed slightly, but probably not enough to bother you.

5. Eject the **CD** when the import process is complete. You can put the CD away somewhere because you probably won't need to use it again.

Building Your iTunes Music Library in a Hurry

The import process moves along pretty quickly, but you can make it even faster by following these steps:

1. Gather a pile of your CDs in a location close to your computer.
2. Set the import preferences (encoder and quality) for the import session.
3. Open the **Importing** subtab of the General pane of the iTunes Preferences dialog box.
4. Select **Import Songs and Eject** on the On CD Insert menu (see Figure 17.9). This causes iTunes to begin the import process immediately when you insert a CD. When the import process is complete, the CD is ejected automatically, too.

tip

You can also select **File**, **Import** or press **Shift+Ctrl+O** (Windows) or **Shift+⌘+O** (Mac) to start the import process. You will see a dialog box that enables you to move to and select the CD you want to import.

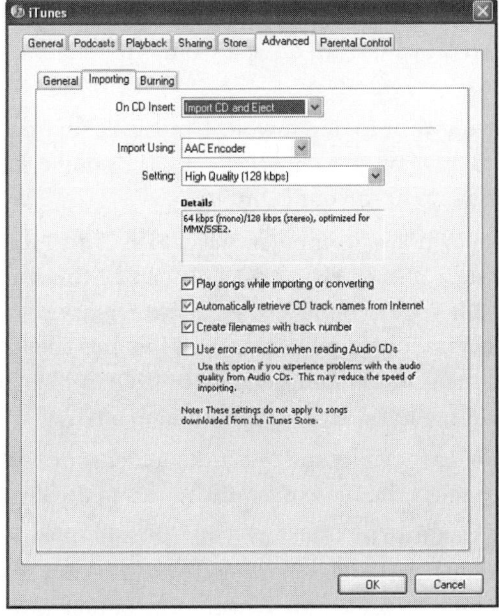

FIGURE 17.9
Choosing the Import Songs and Eject option makes adding lots of CDs to your Library as fast as possible.

5. Click **OK** to close the dialog box.
6. Insert the first **CD** you want to import. iTunes will start importing it automatically. When the process is complete, the CD will be ejected automatically.

7. Insert the next **CD** you want to import. Again, iTunes will import the music and eject the disc when it is done.
8. Repeat step 7 until all the CDs you want to be able to use in iTunes have been imported. You'll be amazed at how quickly you can build a complete iTunes Music Library, even if you have a large number of CDs.

When you are finished batch importing your CDs, you might want to reset the On CD Insert menu to **Show Songs** to prevent unintentionally importing a CD more than once.

Importing Audio Files into Your Library

Another potential source of music for your Library is the Internet. There are millions of audio files there, and you can download these files and add them to your Library.

Or, you might have lots of MP3 files on your computer already. You can add all these to your iTunes Library so you can use that music from within iTunes as well.

Make sure you don't download and add illegal files to your Library. In addition to this being the wrong thing to do, you can be prosecuted for downloading files illegally. Make sure any websites from which you get files has those files legally with permission of the files' creators.

You can add music stored on your hard drive to your iTunes Library by following these steps:

1. Locate the **files** you want to add to your Library. For example, find the MP3 files on your hard drive or go to a website that has audio files, such as MP3 files, and download them to your computer.
2. Using iTunes on a Windows computer, select **File**, **Add File to Library** to add individual music files or **File**, **Add Folder to Library** to add a folder full of music files. If you used the Add Folder to Library command, you'll see the Browse for Folder dialog box. If you used the Add File to Library command, you'll see the Add to Library dialog box. On a Mac, select **File**, **Add to Library**. You'll see the Add To Library dialog box.
3. Use the dialog box to move to and select the folder containing the files you want to add or to select the files you want to add to the Library.
4. Click **Open**, **OK**, or **Choose**. (The name of the button you see depends on the command you use.) The files you selected will be imported into your Library. If you selected a folder, all the songs it contains will be added to your Library. The files will be added in their original format; in other words, if the files are in the MP3 format, they won't be encoded again when you add them to the Library.

Browsing and Searching Your Music Library

It won't be long until you have a large Library with many kinds of music in it. In fact, you are likely to have so much music in the Library that you won't be able to find songs you are interested in just by scrolling up and down the screen. In this section, you'll learn how to find music in your Library, first by browsing and then by searching. When you browse, you can choose to use three views: List, Grouped, and Cover Flow.

Browsing in the Library with the List View

You've already seen the Browser a couple of times. Now it is time to put it to work:

1. Click the **List view** button, which is the View button closest to the Information window.
2. Select **Music** on the Source list. This focuses iTunes' attention on the music content in your collection.
3. If the Browser isn't showing, click the **Browser** button, which is located in the lower-right corner of the iTunes window. (It contains something that looks like an eye.) The Browser will appear (see Figure 17.10). It has three columns: Genre, Artist, and Album. The columns start on the left with the most general category, Genre, and end on the right with the most specific category, which is Album.

FIGURE 17.10
The Browser offers a good way to find songs in your Library.

If you don't see the Genre column in the Browser, open the **General** pane of the iTunes Preferences dialog box and check the **Show genre when browsing** check box.

The contents of the "path" selected in the Browser are shown in the Content pane that now occupies the area below the Browser. At the top of each Browser column is the All option, which shows all the contents of that category. For example, when All is selected in the Genre column, you will see the contents of all the genres for which you have music in the Library.

At the bottom of the screen, you will see Source Information for the selected source. Again, in Figure 17.10, you can see that the 303 songs shown in the Content pane will play for more than 19 hours and consume 1.23GB of disk space.

3. To start browsing your Library, select the **genre** in which you are interested by clicking it. When you do so, the categories in the other two columns are scoped down to include only the artists and albums that are part of that genre. (See Figure 17.11, which shows the Jazz genre in my Library.) Similarly, the Content pane now includes only jazz music. Notice in Figure 17.11 that the Source Information has been updated, too.

FIGURE 17.11
Because Jazz is selected in the Genre column, the Artist and Album columns and Content pane contain only the jazz that is in my Library.

4. To further limit the browse, click an **artist** in which you are interested in the Artist column. The Album column will be scoped down to show only those albums for the artist selected in the Artist column (see Figure 17.12). Also, the Content pane will show the songs on the albums listed in the Album column.

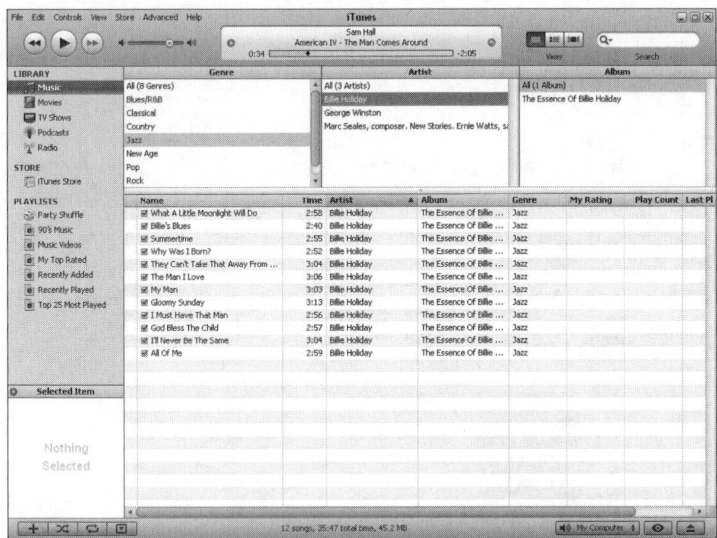

FIGURE 17.12
Now I am browsing all my music in the Jazz genre that is performed by Billie Holiday.

5. To get down to the most narrow browse possible, select the **album** in which you are interested in the Album column. The Content pane will now show the tracks on the selected album.
6. When you have selected the genre, artist, and album categories in which you are interested, you can scroll in the **Content** pane to see all the tracks included in the music you are browsing.

To make the browse results less narrow again, select **All** in one of the Browser's columns. For example, to browse all your music again, click **All** in the Genre column.

I hope you can see that you can use the Browser to quickly scan your Library to locate music you want to hear or work with. As you use the Browser more, you will come to rely on it to get you to a group of songs quickly and easily.

Browsing in the Library Using the Grouped View

The List view is useful, but it doesn't really provide you with a good sense of the collections of music you browse because the tracks appear in a list with no respect to how the tracks are collected. Use the Grouped view to browse the Music source while seeing the groups of music you are browsing:

1. Click the **Grouped view** button, which is the middle View button. The music in the Content pane will now be grouped by album or collection, and you'll see the artwork associated with each group (see Figure 17.13).

FIGURE 17.13
Using the Grouped view, you get to see how the music you are browsing is grouped, along with its artwork.

2. Use the Browser to narrow the music you are browsing to find what you are looking for (see Figure 17.14). It works just as it does in List view.

FIGURE 17.14
Now I'm browsing my Johnny Cash music.

Browsing in the Library with the Cover Flow View

I admit that browsing music only in a digital format does lose something when compared to looking through a collection of CDs. There's something appealing about flipping through a set of CDs, especially when you stumble upon one you haven't listened to in a while. If you like to do this, the Cover Flow view will appeal to you. To use it to browse your music, perform the following steps:

1. Click the **Cover Flow view** button, which is the rightmost View button. The Browser will be replaced by the Cover Flow browser (see Figure 17.15). Here, you'll see the "album" art associated with the music you're browsing; this will look similar to a collection of CDs. The album facing the screen directly is associated with the music at the top of the Content pane. (This is the music currently in focus.) You'll see the album name and artist just below the album in focus. The covers to the right of this one represent music lower in the Content pane, whereas the covers to the left represent music higher in the Content pane.

FIGURE 17.15
The Cover Flow view enables you to "flip" through your music collection to browse it.

2. To browse "ahead" in your music, click an album cover to the right of the one in focus; to browse "back" in your music, click a cover to the left of the one in focus. The farther to the left or right you click, the more covers to which you'll jump ahead or back, depending on which direction you click. For example, if you click on an album immediately next to the one in focus, you move ahead or back one album. If you click all the way to the edge of the screen, you jump ahead or back by multiple albums.

   As albums come into focus, you can see their content at the top of the browser (see Figure 17.16).

FIGURE 17.16
The Cover Flow view enables you to "flip" through your music collection to browse it.

3. When music comes into focus that you want to hear, double-click it to start playing it.

As you flip through albums, music you happen to be playing continues to play as you bring other music into focus. If you don't play the music you are browsing, after a couple of seconds of inactivity, the covers flip back to the music currently playing so that it comes back into focus.

Searching Your Music Library

You can use iTunes' Search tool to search for specific content. You can search for content (music, audiobooks, video, and so on) by any of the following criteria:

- Artist
- Album
- Composer
- Song (track name)

To search for music in your Library, perform the following steps:

1. Select the source you want to search. (For example, click the **Music** source to search your entire music collection.) As you might surmise, you can search

any source in the Source list—such as a CD, playlist, and so on—by selecting it and then performing a search.

2. To choose a specific attribute by which to search, such as Album, click the **Magnifying Glass** icon and choose the **search attribute** on the drop-down list that appears. If you don't choose a specific attribute, All is used, which searches all the available attributes.
3. Type the data for which you want to search in the Search tool (see Figure 17.17). As you type, iTunes searches the selected source and presents the songs that meet your criterion in the Content pane. It does this on the fly, so the search narrows with each keystroke. As you type more text or numbers, the search becomes more specific.

FIGURE 17.17
This search is finding music with "cross" in any of the searchable attributes.

4. Keep typing until the search becomes as narrow as you need it to be to find the content in which you are interested.
5. To refine your search by attribute, open the **Magnifying Glass** icon and choose the attribute to which you want to limit the search. For example, if you want to see only results that have your search

tip

The current search attribute is marked with a check mark on the Magnifying Glass drop-down list.

term as the Artist attribute, choose **Artist**. The search results will be limited to only those tracks that match the current criteria (what you typed and what attribute you selected).

By the way, searching works the same way regardless of the current view.

After you have found content with a search, you can play it, add it to playlists, and so on.

To clear your search, click the **Clear Search** button that appears in the Search tool after you have typed in it (refer to Figure 17.17). The songs shown in the Content pane will again be determined by your selections in the current view.

Playing Music in Your Music Library

Remember earlier when I said that you use the same listening techniques to listen to music in your Library as you do when listening to a CD? Now it's time to prove my words.

When you listen to music in your Library, you start by choosing the scope of the music you want to hear. You do this by browsing or searching for music. (If you don't know how to do this, here's a hint: Read the previous two sections.)

After you have the group of songs to which you want to listen showing in the Content pane, use the listening tools you learned about in the previous chapter to listen to your music. For example, you can click Play to play the songs, use the Repeat button to repeat them, sort the Content pane by one of the column headings to change the order in which the songs play, and so on.

If it helps to think about it like this, think of the Library as a giant CD containing all your music. You can play this CD just like the physical discs. (If it doesn't help to think about the Library like this, then don't think about it this way.)

Removing Tunes from the Music Library

Not all that glitters is gold, nor are all tunes that are digital good. Sometimes, a song is so bad that it just isn't worth the hard disk space it consumes.

To remove songs from your Library, ditch them with the following steps:

1. Find the songs you want to delete by browsing or searching.
2. Select the songs you want to trash. They will become highlighted to show you they are selected.
3. Press the **Delete** or **Backspace** key. You will be prompted to confirm that you really want to delete the song you have selected.

4. If you see the warning prompt, click **Remove** to confirm the deletion. You will see another prompt asking whether you want the selected files to be moved to your Recycle Bin (Windows) or Trash (Mac), or you want to keep the files on your computer. (If you have disabled the warning prompt, you'll move directly to the second dialog box.)
5. Click **Move to Recycle Bin** (Windows) or **Move to Trash** (Mac) to move the files so you can get rid of them entirely. The selected songs will be deleted from your Library, and their song files will be moved to the appropriate trash receptacle on your computer. The next time you empty that receptacle, those songs will be gone forever.

   If you just want to remove the references to files from the iTunes Library but not delete the song files, click **Keep Files**. The songs will be removed from the Library, but the song files will remain in their current locations (and so you could always add the songs to your Library again later).

You should never delete music you purchased from the iTunes Store unless you are absolutely sure you will never never never want it again or you have that music backed up elsewhere. You can download music you purchased from the store only one time. After that, you have to pay for it to download it again.

Of course, songs you delete probably might not really be gone forever. You can always add them back to the Library by repeating the same steps you used to place them in there the first time. This assumes you have a copy somewhere, such as on a CD or stored in some other location. If you imported the music from your hard disk and had iTunes move the song files to your iTunes Music folder, your only copy will reside in your iTunes Library, so make sure you have such music backed up before you delete it if you might ever want it again.

THE ABSOLUTE MINIMUM

Although it might not smell like a book library, your iTunes Library is at least as useful and is a heck of a lot easier to get to. In this chapter, you learned how to build and use your iTunes Music Library. Before we move on to the next great thing about iTunes, check out some related points of interest (well, my interest anyway; I hope they will be yours, too):

- Through the Audible.com service (accessible via the iTunes Store), you can also add audiobooks to your iTunes Library to listen to them on your computer, and you can add them to an iPod. Working with audio bookcontent is similar to working with music. Unfortunately, covering the details of doing so is outside the scope of this book.

continues

- You learned that you can choose the import encoder and quality settings when you import music from audio CDs to your Library. You can import the same songs at different quality levels to experiment with various settings or to create different versions of the same song. For example, you might want a higher-quality version to play from your computer and a lower-quality version with a smaller file size for a portable device. To create another version of a song, you can change the import settings and import it from a CD again. You can also reimport a song already in the Library by setting the encoding settings and importing its file (which will be located in the iTunes Music folder) to the Library, just like other music files stored on your computer.
- Although we focused on the AAC and Apple Lossless Encoder formats in this chapter, in some cases you might want to use the WAV or AIFF format. For example, suppose you want to use part of a song as a sound byte in an application that doesn't support either of the primary formats but does support WAV files. You could choose the WAV format and then import the song you want to use in that format. The WAV file, which would be located in your iTunes Music folder, could then be added to the other application you are working with.
- If you are listening to music while doing something else, such as browsing your Library, you might move away from the song that is currently playing. If you want to move back to it again, select **File**, **Show Current Song** or press **Ctrl+L** (Windows) or **⌘+L** (Mac). You can also click the **Show Current Song** button in the Information area to return to the music currently playing.
- You can use the Browser with any source (but you can't use it with the Cover Flow view), although it defaults to being closed with CDs and some playlists because it usually isn't that useful in those contexts (especially when the source is a single CD). To open it for any source, just select the source you want to browse and click the **Browser** button.

In This Chapter

- Get to know and love tags.
- Get the details for your music.
- Label your music so you can do cool things with it, such as creating playlists based on musical attributes.
- Rate your songs, set the relative volume level, and hear only the parts you want to hear.
- Add lyrics to your music so you really know what you are saying when you sing along.
- Don't miss out on album artwork just because you have gone digital.
- Work the Content pane like a pro.

18

Labeling, Categorizing, and Configuring Your Music

It's confession time. I admit it. This topic might not seem too exciting at first glance. Who wants to spend time labeling and categorizing music? That is a fair question, but I hope by the time you read through this chapter, you answer that question with an enthusiastic, "I do, that's who!" Of course, I would be almost as happy even if your response is, "It might not be as fun as building my Library, but it will make my iTunes world a lot better." Think of this chapter as learning the nuts and bolts of how iTunes works so you can become an iTunes wizard later.

After you have worked through the labeling content in this chapter, I think you will find the ability to configure the tracks in your Library to be pretty exciting because that is where you really start bending iTunes to your will (which isn't as dramatic as it sounds because iTunes is really pretty easy to command).

Understanding Song Tags and Knowing Why You Should Care About Them

In the previous chapter, you saw how you can browse your iTunes music collection by genre, artist, and album. This makes finding music fast and easy, even if you have thousands of songs in your Library. This functionality is enabled because each track in your Library has data—also called *tags*—that categorize and identify that track for you. Genre, artist, and album are just three of the possible tags for each track in iTunes. There are many more items of information that iTunes manages.

Tags fall into two groups: tags that iTunes assigns for you and that you can't change, and tags that you or iTunes assigns and that you can change.

Tags that iTunes assigns and that you can view but can't change include the following:

- **Kind**—This identifies the type of file the track is, such as Protected AAC audio file, AAC audio file, MP3, and so on.
- **Size**—The amount of disk space required to store the track.
- **Bit Rate**—The quality level at which the track was encoded. Larger numbers, such as 128Kbps, mean the track was encoded at a higher quality level (and also has a relatively larger file size).
- **Sample Rate**—The rate at which the music was sampled when it was captured.
- **Date Modified**—The date on which the track file was last changed.
- **Play Count**—The number of times the track has been played.
- **Last Played**—The last time the track was played.
- **Profile**—A categorization of the track's complexity.
- **Format**—The format in which the track was encoded, such as MPEG-1, Layer 3.
- **Channels**—Whether the track is stereo or mono.
- **Encoded with**—The tools used to encode the track, such as the version of iTunes used, the version of QuickTime, and so on. This applies only when you use iTunes to encode the track.
- **ID3 Tag**—ID3 tags are data formatted according to a set of specifications. If a track's data has been formatted with this specification, the ID3 version number will be shown.
- **Purchased by, Account Name, and FairPlay Version**—If a track was purchased from the iTunes Store, this information identifies who purchased the music and which account was used. The FairPlay version information relates to the means by which the track is protected.

- **Owner, Narrator, Published**—This information is provided for audiobooks that you add to your Library, such as those from Audible.com. The owner is whoever purchased the book. The narrator is who reads the book. Published identifies when the book was published.
- **Where**—This shows a path to the track's file on your computer along with its filename.

Tags collected for songs that you can change include the following:

- **Name**—The name of the track.
- **Artist**—The person or group who performs the track.
- **Album**—The name of the album or compilation from which the song comes.
- **Grouping**—A label you can assign to group tracks together. You can then organize tracks by their group, collect them in playlists, and so on.
- **Composer**—The person who is credited with composing the track.
- **Comments**—A free-form text field in which you can make comments about a track.
- **Genre**—This associates a track with its genre, such as Jazz or Classical.
- **Year**—The year the track was created.
- **Track Number**—The track's position on the CD from which it came, such as "2 of 12."
- **Disc Number**—The number of the CD or DVD. This is meaningful for multiple-disc sets.
- **BPM**—The track's beats per minute.
- **Part of a Compilation**—When checked, this check box indicates that the track is part of a compilation, meaning a CD or other grouping that contains tracks from a variety of artists.

When you add a song to your Library, no matter how you add it, iTunes will add as much of this data as it can find for each song.

When you insert a CD, iTunes attempts to get that CD's information from an online CD database, which is why it connects to the Internet. If iTunes finds the CD in this database, the information for that CD is applied to the CD and carried into the Library if you import the tracks from that CD into iTunes. If you purchase music from the iTunes Store, it also contains many of these tags. If content you add to your Library doesn't have tags, you'll have to add them yourself (which isn't hard to do, as you'll soon see).

Even if content you add does have tags, you can add or change the data in the previous list.

So, why should you care about all these tags? There are a couple of reasons.

The first is that, as you already know because you learned how to browse and search your Library in the previous chapter, tags can be used to find music in which you are interested. That reason alone should be enough to convince you that these types of data are important to you. But wait, there's more.

The second reason is that when it comes time to create playlists (which you will learn about in Chapter 19, "Creating, Configuring, and Using Playlists"), you can use tags to determine which tracks are included in your playlists. For example, you can configure a playlist to include the last 25 songs you have played from the Jazz genre. This is just a basic example—you can get much more sophisticated than this. In fact, you can include several combinations of tags as criteria in playlists to create interesting sets of music to listen to.

Viewing Song Information

Now that you understand the types of tags that can be associated with tracks in your Library, it's time to learn how to view that information. You have three basic areas in which to view track information: the Browser, the Content pane, and the Info window.

Viewing Tags in the Browser

If you read through the previous chapter, you have already used this technique. When you view the Browser, you see the Genre, Artist, and Album tags associated with the tracks you are browsing (see Figure 18.1).

FIGURE 18.1
Each column in the Browser displays a tag associated with tracks in your Library.

Viewing Tags in the Content Pane

Even if you don't realize it, you have also seen tags in the Content pane. The column headings you see in the Content pane are actually the tags associated with the tracks you are viewing (see Figure 18.2).

FIGURE 18.2
Each column heading in the Content pane is a tag.

You can determine which columns (tags) are shown in the Content pane, as you will learn later in this chapter.

Viewing Tags in the Info Window

The Info window is probably the only area in which you might not have seen tags yet. To view the Info window, select a track in your Library and select **File**, **Get Info** or press **Ctrl+I** (Windows) or **⌘+I** (Mac). The Info window will appear; at the top of the window, you'll see the name of the track whose information you are viewing (see Figure 18.3). This window has five panes that you will be using throughout the rest of this chapter and a sixth that you'll see when we get to working with video content in iTunes.

The Summary pane (shown in Figure 18.3) provides a summary view of the track's tags (that you can't change), starting at the top with any album art associated with the track and including its name, length, artist, and album. (Again, if you are viewing a track of another type, you'll see a slightly different set of tags.) In the center part of the pane, you see the data that iTunes manages. (You can view this data, but you can't change it.) At the bottom of the pane, you can see the path to the track's file on your computer.

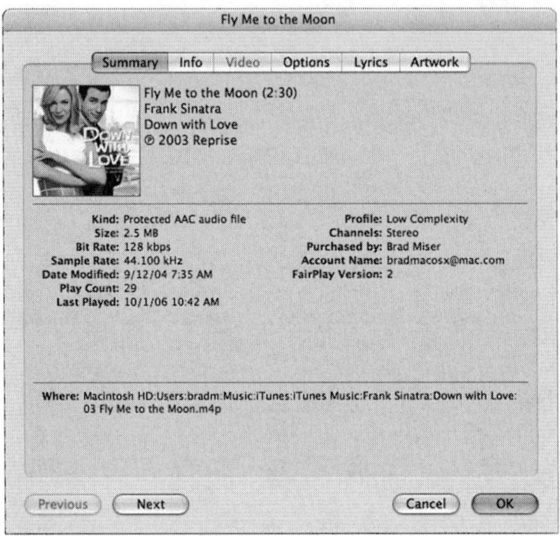

FIGURE 18.3
The Info window enables you to view the tags associated with tracks, and you can change many of them.

When you click the **Info** tab, you will see the tags you can change (see Figure 18.4). You'll learn how to change this data in the next section.

The other three panes of the window that relate to music content—Options, Lyrics, and Artwork—are used to configure specific aspects of a track. (We'll get to these topics in a few pages.)

You can view information for other tracks in the selected source without closing the window. Click **Next** to move to the next track in the source you are viewing (such as your Library) or **Previous** to move to the previous track. When you do so, the next or previous track's information will be displayed in the Info window.

You can also open the Info window by opening a track's contextual menu (by right-clicking the track) and choosing **Get Info**.

To close the Info window, click **OK**.

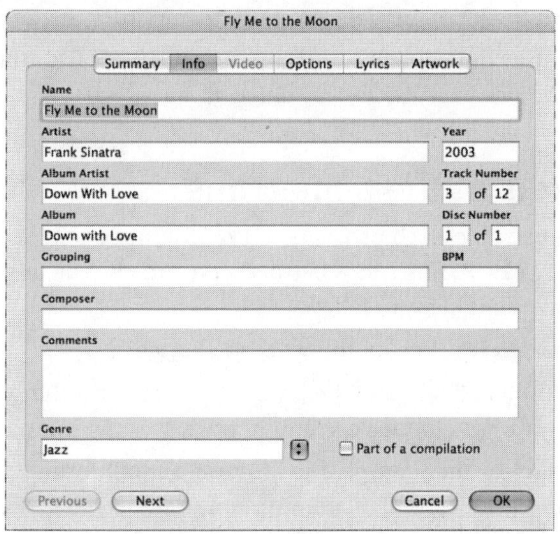

FIGURE 18.4
Although you can't change the tags shown on the Summary pane, you can change those on the Info pane.

Labeling Your Tracks

You can change a track's tags in a couple of ways.

Labeling a Track in the Info Window

Typically, if you have imported a CD or purchased music from the iTunes Store, you shouldn't change the data that came from the source, such as name, artist, album, track number, and so on. Occasionally, a CD's information will include an error when it is added (such as a misspelling in the artist's name); you'll probably want to fix such mistakes. You can certainly add data to empty fields.

You can use the Info window to change a track's tags, as you can see in the following steps:

1. Open the **Info** window for the track that has tags you want to add or change.
2. Click the **Info** tab, and the Info pane will appear.
3. Enter or change the **information** shown in the various fields. For example, you can change the track's name or artist. Or you might want to add comments about the track in the Comments box.

4. To change a track's genre, select the new genre from the Genre menu.
5. When you are done entering or changing tags, click **OK**. The Info window will close, and any changes you made will be saved.

Tagging Multiple Tracks at the Same Time

You can change some tags, such as Genre, for a group of tracks at the same time. This can be a faster way to enter tags because you can change multiple tracks in one window. Here are the steps to follow:

1. Select the tracks whose tags you want to change.
2. Open the Info window. You'll be prompted to confirm that you want to change the information for a group of tracks.
3. Click **Yes** to clear the prompt. The Multiple Song Information window will appear (see Figure 18.5). The information and tools in this window work in the same way as they do for individual tracks. The difference is that the information and settings apply to all the tracks you have selected.

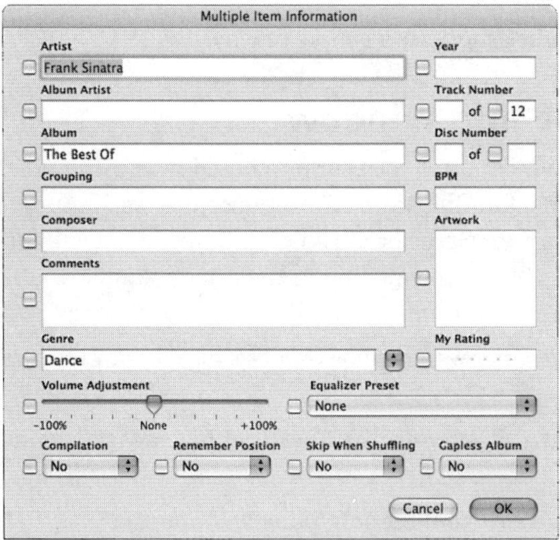

FIGURE 18.5 You can use this window to change the data for multiple tracks at the same time.

4. Enter data in the fields, make changes to existing data, or use the other tools to configure the tracks you have selected. As you change information, the check box next to the tag will become checked to show that you are changing that tag for all the selected tracks.
5. When you are finished making changes, click **OK**. The window will close, and the changes you made will be saved.

Most of the fields in the Multiple Item Information dialog box are pretty straightforward, such as Artist, Album, and so on. You'll learn about others when you read about changing a track's options in a bit. The same options apply as for an individual track; you can just change multiple tracks at the same time by using the Multiple Item Information dialog box.

Setting Tags in the Content Pane

You can also edit tags within the Content pane:

1. Click once on a track to select it.
2. Click once on the tag you want to edit. The tag will become highlighted to show that it is ready to be edited (see Figure 18.6).

FIGURE 18.6
You can also change tags from the Content pane. In this example, the album name is highlighted and can be changed (not that I really would because it's correct as is).

3. Type the new information, choose a value on the tag's drop-down list (such as to set equalization for a track), or click to set a value (for example, to rate a track).
4. Press **Enter** (Windows) or **Return** (Mac). The changes you made will be saved.

Configuring a Track's Options

You can configure a number of options for the tracks in your Library, including the following:

- **Relative Volume**—You can change a track's relative volume so it is either louder or quieter than "normal." This is useful if you like to listen to tracks recorded at a variety of volume levels, because the volume remains somewhat similar as you move from track to track.
- **Equalizer Preset**—You can use the iTunes Equalizer to configure the relative volume of sound frequencies. When you set an Equalizer preset for a track, the settings in that preset will be used each time the track plays.
- **My Rating**—You can give tracks a rating from one to five stars. You can use ratings in various ways, such as to create criteria for playlists (for example, include only my five-star songs) or to sort the Content pane.
- **Start and Stop Time**—You can configure tracks to start or stop playing at specific times in the track. This can be useful if you don't want to hear all of a track, such as when a track has an introduction you don't want to hear each time it plays.
- **Remember Playback Position**—When this option is enabled, iTunes (and an iPod) will start playing a track from the point at which you last played it. This is an incredibly useful option for tracks that are audio-books, podcasts, or videos because you can stop playing that content and do something else, such as listen to or watch other content. When you come back to a track with this option enabled, iTunes and an iPod will pick up where you left off. This prevents you from hearing or seeing the same content again or from searching for the point at which you stopped listening or watching.
- **Skip when Shuffling**—If this option is enabled for a track, the track will be skipped when you play iTunes in the Shuffle mode. This is useful for tracks you don't want to hear when you shuffle (such as those that make sense only in the content of the album from which they come)

> **note**
>
> iTunes is pretty smart and makes your listening and viewing life as easy as possible. For example, when you add podcasts, video, or audio books from the iTunes Store to your Library, the Playback Position, Skip, and Gapless options are set appropriately. If you add this kind of content from other sources, you should make sure these options are set the way you want them to be.

or for content that doesn't make sense when you shuffle (such as episodes of a podcast or an audiobook).

- **Part of a gapless album**—Some tracks are designed to be heard with no gap between them, such as those from a live album. When a track is part of such an album, checking this option removes any gap between songs. iTunes recognizes most gapless albums automatically, but you can manually configure this setting if you need to.

Configuring Track Options in the Info Window

You can configure a track's options in the Info window by performing the following steps:

1. Select the track whose options you want to set.
2. Open the Info window.
3. Click the **Options** tab (see Figure 18.7).

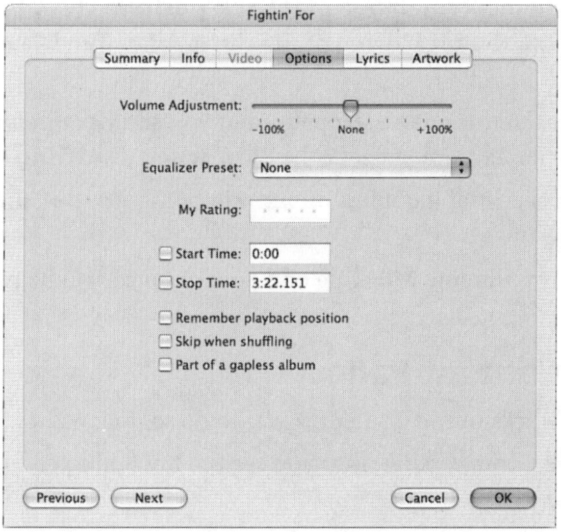

FIGURE 18.7
Using the Options tab, you configure a track's optional settings.

4. To set the track's relative volume, drag the **Volume Adjustment** slider to the left to make the track quieter or to the right to make it louder.
5. To apply an equalizer preset to the track, choose the preset you want to be used when the track plays on the Equalizer Preset menu. On this menu, you'll see a large number of presets that are available to you. When you choose one, the track's playback will be adjusted accordingly. For example, if you choose Bass Booster, the relative volume of the bass frequencies will be increased.

6. To rate the track, click the dot representing the number of stars you want to give it in the My Rating field. For example, to give the track three stars, click the center (third) dot. Stars will appear up to the point at which you click. In other words, before you click, you'll see a dot. After you click a dot, it becomes a star, as do the rest of the stars to its left.
7. To set a track's start time, check the **Start Time** check box and enter a time in the format *minutes:seconds*. When you play the track, it will start playing at the time you enter. The default value is 0:00, which makes sense because that is the starting point for a track.
8. To set a stop time, check the **Stop Time** check box and enter a time in the format *minutes:seconds*. When you play the track, it will stop playing at the time you enter. The default stop time is the total track length, which also makes sense. Notice that the default stop time is very precise, even going to two decimal places beyond a second.
9. If you want iTunes or an iPod to remember the point at which you stopped playing a track and to start playing the track at that point the next time you play it, check the **Remember playback position** check box. If you always want the track to start playing at the current Start Time, leave the box unchecked.
10. If you want the track to be skipped when you shuffle (when the track is an audiobook, for example), check the **Skip when shuffling** check box.
11. If the track is part of a gapless album, check the **Part of a gapless album** check box.
12. Click **OK**. The window will close and your changes will be saved.

Rating Tracks in the Content Pane

You can also rate tracks in the Content pane. To do so, follow these steps:

1. Scroll in the Content pane until you see the My Rating column (see Figure 18.8).
2. Select the track you want to rate. Dots will appear in the My Rating column for that track.
3. Click the dot representing the number of stars you want to give the track. The dots up to and including the one on which you clicked will become stars.

FIGURE 18.8
You can also rate tracks in the Content pane.

Adding Lyrics to Tracks

In the Info window, you've seen that there is a Lyrics tab. As you probably can guess, you can store lyrics, or any other text for that matter, for a track on this tab. You can then view the text you store there by using the Info window, or you can display the lyrics on an iPod.

Adding Lyrics to a Track

The first step is to find or create the lyrics you want to associate with a track. Although it might be lots of fun figuring out the lyrics for tracks by listening to them and writing them down yourself, I'm going to assume you have better things to do with your time. In that case, it's easy to look up lyrics for most artists on the web.

Most of the lyrics available on the web come from a person who listened to the music (as opposed to the published source). This means that there can be errors in the lyrics you find. You can correct them yourself or look for a more reliable source.

You can then copy and paste the lyrics you find onto the Lyrics tab. Here's how:

1. Open your web browser and move to www.google.com.
2. Search for *artistname* and lyrics, where *artistname* is the name of the artist with which the track is associated. The result will likely be several sites that provide lyrics for that artist.
3. Click a link to move to one of the sites. These sites typically organize lyrics by album (see Figure 18.9).

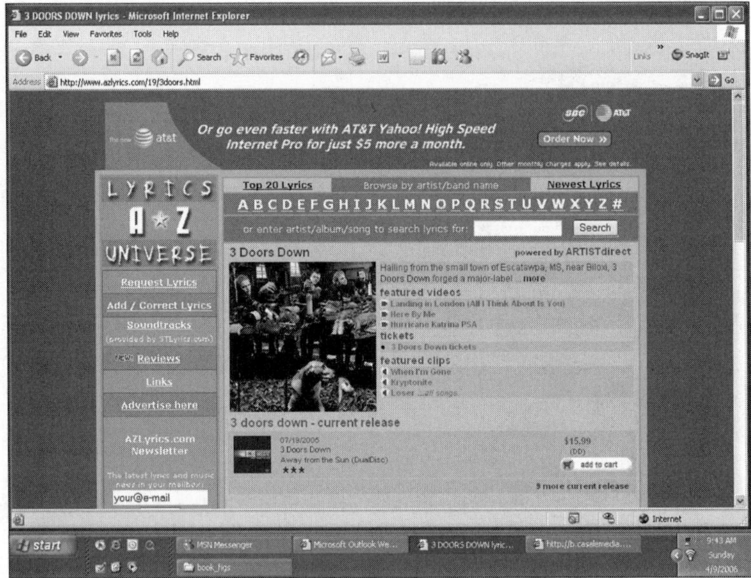

FIGURE 18.9
This site has plenty of lyrics for the group 3 Doors Down.

4. Find the track for which you want lyrics, and click it. The lyrics will appear.
5. Select the lyrics and copy them to your computer's Clipboard.

Now that you have the lyrics, you can apply them to a track by performing the following steps:

1. In iTunes, open the Info window for the track whose lyrics you just copied.
2. Click the **Lyrics** tab.
3. Paste the lyrics you copied into the Lyrics pane (see Figure 18.10).
4. Click **OK**. The lyrics will be saved with the track.

Viewing Lyrics for a Track

After you have added lyrics for a track, you can view those lyrics in iTunes by selecting the track and opening the **Lyrics** pane of the **Info** window. You can also view lyrics on newer iPod models by clicking the **Select** button until the lyrics are displayed on its screen.

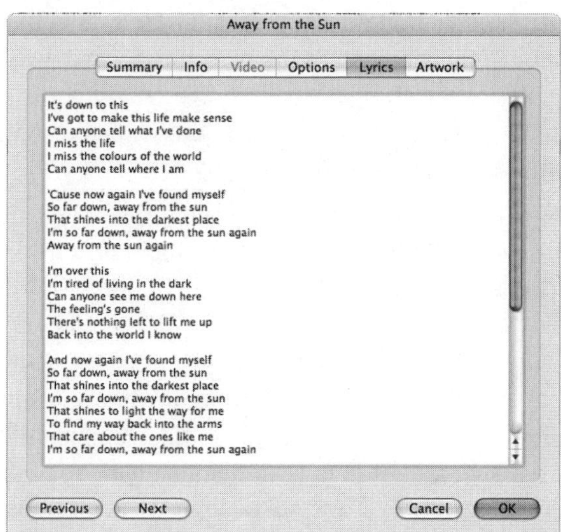

FIGURE 18.10
I've pasted the lyrics for the song "Away from the Sun" into the Lyrics tab.

Adding and Viewing Album Artwork

Many CD and album covers are works of art (though many aren't!), and it would be a shame never to see them just because your music has gone digital. With iTunes, you don't need to miss out, because you can associate artwork with tracks and display that artwork in the iTunes window.

To enjoy artwork with your tunes, you need to first associate artwork with your music. There are a number of ways to do this. All the music you purchase from the iTunes Store includes artwork, so any music you buy will have artwork automatically. And, if you have an iTunes Store account, iTunes can be configured to automatically download artwork for music you add to your Library in other ways, such as when you import an audio CD. If the artwork for music isn't in the iTunes Store because the music itself isn't there, you can add artwork to music manually or semi-automatically.

After artwork has been added to your music, you can easily view it in iTunes.

You can also view album artwork on an iPod or iPod nano.

If you burn discs for your music, having artwork associated with your music is good because you can use iTunes to print jewel case covers that include this art. You'll learn how to print with iTunes in Chapter 22, "Burning Your Own CDs or DVDs."

Configuring iTunes to Download Album Artwork Automatically

One of the cool features of iTunes is that it will automatically download artwork from the iTunes Store. As you read earlier, when you purchase music from the store, its art comes with it. What you might not expect is that as long as you have an iTunes Store account, iTunes will also download art associated with music you add to the Library from other sources, such as audio CDs you import.

To learn how to obtain and configure iTunes with an iTunes Store account, see "Obtaining an iTunes Store Account" on page **422**.

After you have configured your iTunes Store account, open the iTunes Preferences dialog box, click the **General** tab, check the **Automatically download missing album artwork** check box, and click **OK**. iTunes will automatically retrieve artwork for all the albums in your Library that it can. As you add other music to your Library by importing it, iTunes will retrieve any artwork it can automatically, too.

The limitation to this cool feature is that for iTunes to automatically download an album's artwork, that album must be available in the iTunes Store. This isn't a big limitation because a huge amount of music is available there, so the odds are good that any music you add to your Library will be there, which means most of your music will get artwork automatically.

Adding Artwork for Songs Manually

If music isn't available in the iTunes Store, you can add artwork to it manually. Or you might want to associate artwork that isn't the default album cover with a track. For example, you might want to add the artist's picture or some other meaningful graphic to tracks.

You can add one or more pieces of art to tracks by using the following steps:

1. Prepare the **artwork** you are going to associate with a track. You can use graphics in the usual formats, such as JPG, TIFF, GIF, and so on.
2. Select the **track** with which you want to associate the artwork.
3. Open the **Info** window, and then click the **Artwork** tab (see Figure 18.11). If the selected track has artwork with it, you will see it in the Artwork pane.
4. Click **Add**. A dialog box that enables you to choose an image appears.
5. Move to and select the image you want to associate with the track.
6. Click **Open** (Windows) or **Choose** (Mac). The image will be added to the Artwork pane of the Info window (see Figure 18.12).

You can also add artwork to a track by dragging the image file from your desktop onto the Artwork pane of the Info window or onto the Artwork pane of the iTunes window.

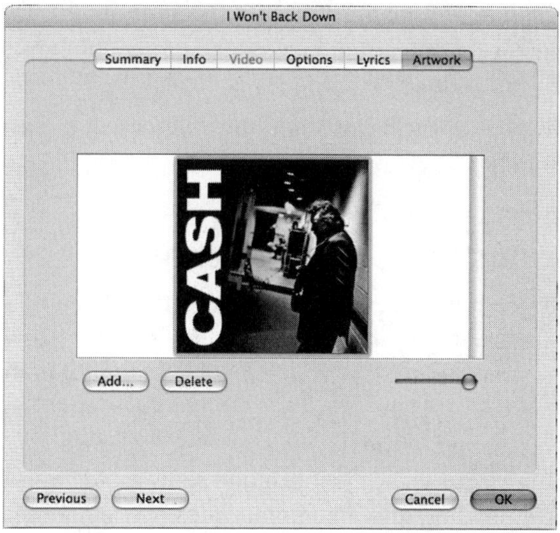

FIGURE 18.11
You use the Artwork pane to add artwork to a song.

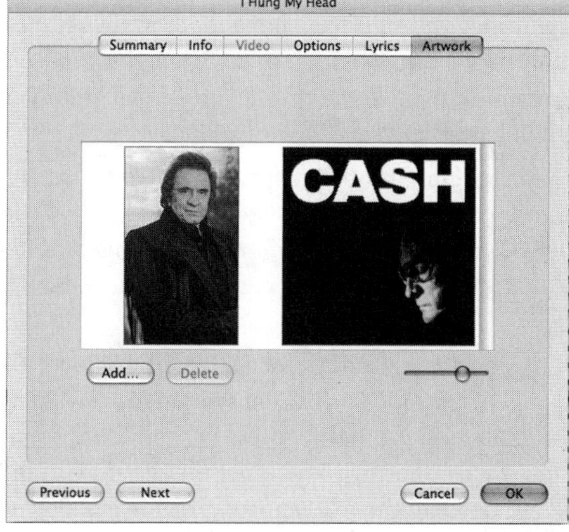

FIGURE 18.12
This track now has two graphics associated with it, which are the album cover and a photo of the man in black.

You can use the slider under the image box to change the size of the previews you see on the Artwork pane. Drag the **slider** to the right to make the image larger or to the left to make it smaller. This doesn't change the image; instead, it only impacts the size of the image as you currently see it in the Info window. This is especially useful when you associate lots of images with a track because you can see them all at the same time.

7. Repeat steps 4–6 to continue adding images to the Artwork pane until you have added all the images for a track.

8. To change the order of the images, drag **them** around in the image box. If a track has more than one graphic, place the image that you want to be the default on the left side of the image box.
9. Click **OK**. The window will close, and the images will be saved with the song and will be ready to view.

Adding Artwork to Songs Semi-Automatically

The odds are that if you have an iTunes Store account and you allow iTunes to download artwork automatically, most of your music will have artwork associated with it. If not, in the previous section, you learned how to manually add artwork to tracks. The results are cool, but the process is kind of laborious. There's a path between fully automatic and manual, which is what I've cleverly called semi-automatic. What this means is that you can add software to your computer that will assist you in downloading artwork for your music. These tools use different sources of album artwork than the iTunes Store, such as Amazon.com, so you might be able to obtain artwork that isn't available in the store.

Because I'm on a tight page count, I don't have room to review all the available tools or show you how they work. What I can do is tell you how to find them and show you how my personal favorite works as an example. Then you can find and use the one that you like best.

Use Google to search for "automatic artwork for iTunes." You'll get lots of results for Windows and Macintosh computers. Read about them and choose the one you want to try; most are freeware or shareware, so you can try lots of them for free. Some of these tools are standalone applications, some plug into iTunes, and others are widgets/gadgets.

My current favorite is Amazon Album Art Widget by The Widget Factory (www.widget-foundry.com) for Mac OS X. After you add this widget to the Mac OS X Dashboard, you can easily add art to any tracks in your Library based on the tracks you have selected, the track currently playing, or the album currently playing. When you open the widget, it looks up the related artwork on Amazon.com and copies it into the widget (see Figure 18.13). You then click the **Set as album art in iTunes** link to save the art in iTunes for the selected or playing music. With this cool tool, it takes only about ten seconds and three mouse clicks to add art to tracks.

Viewing Album Artwork

To view a track's artwork, do one of the following:

- Click the **Show/Hide Song Artwork** button located under the Source list. The Artwork pane will appear and display the artwork associated with either the currently playing song or the currently selected song (see Figure 18.14).

At the top of the artwork, you will see **Selected Song**, which indicates you are viewing the artwork associated with the selected track, or **Now Playing**, which indicates you are viewing artwork associated with the track currently playing.

FIGURE 18.13
The Amazon Album Art widget has found artwork for this Johnny Cash album.

FIGURE 18.14
You can view the artwork associated with a track in the Artwork pane.

- Move the pointer over the artwork and click when the pointer becomes the hand icon to see a larger version in a separate window (see Figure 18.15). The title of the window will be the name of the track with which the artwork is associated.

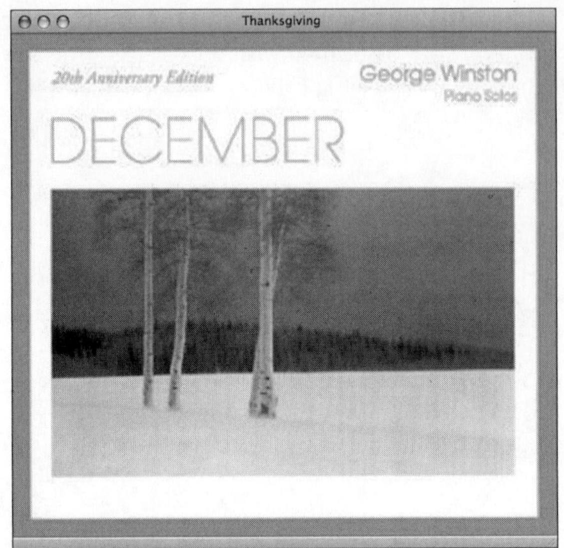

FIGURE 18.15
You can view a large version of a track's artwork in a separate window.

- To choose between viewing artwork associated with the selected track or the track currently playing, click the arrow button or text at the top of the Artwork pane. The artwork will change to the other option (for example, if you click Now Playing, it will become Selected Song), and you will see the artwork for that track.
- If you select the **Now Playing** option, the artwork will change in the Artwork pane and in the separate art window as the next track begins playing (unless, of course, the tracks use the same artwork, and even then the track title in the separate artwork window will change). When nothing is playing or selected, you'll see a message saying so in the Artwork pane.
- If the track has more than one piece of artwork associated with it, click the arrows that appear at the top of the pane to see each piece of art (see Figure 8.16). You can click on each image to open it in a separate window, too.

FIGURE 18.16
You can tell this track has multiple images associated with it by the arrows at the top of the Artwork pane. Click an arrow to see its other images.

Customizing the Content Pane

There are a number of ways to customize the columns (tags) that appear in the Content pane. What's more, you can customize the Content pane for each source. The customization you have done for a source (such as a CD or playlist) will be saved and used each time you view that source.

To be able to save the view settings for each source, open the iTunes Preferences dialog box, click the **General** tab, check the **Remember view setting for each source** check box, and click OK. If you don't check this box, all sources will use the same view setting.

You can select the tags (columns) that are shown for a source by using the following steps:

1. Select the **source** whose Content pane you want to customize. Its contents will appear in the Content pane.
2. Select **View**, **View Options** or press **Ctrl+J** (Windows) or **⌘+J** (Mac). You will see the View Options dialog box (see Figure 18.17). At the top of the dialog box, you'll see the name of the source for which you are configuring the Content pane. You'll also see all the available columns that can be displayed. If a column's check box is checked, that column will be displayed; if not, it won't be shown.

FIGURE 18.17

You can set the columns shown in the Content pane with the View Options dialog box.

3. Check the check boxes next to the columns you want to see.
4. Uncheck the check boxes next to the columns you don't want to see.
5. Click **OK**. When you return to the Content pane, only the columns you selected will be shown (see Figure 18.18).

FIGURE 18.18

If you could view all the columns in this Content pane, you would see that they correspond to the check boxes checked in the previous figure. (You trust me, right?)

If you can't see all the columns being displayed, use the horizontal scrollbar to scroll in the Content pane. You can also use the vertical scrollbar to move up and down in the Content pane.

Not all columns apply to all types of content. For example, the Season column is intended for TV shows to display what season a particular track (episode) appeared in. iTunes doesn't limit the columns available in the View Options dialog box based on the source you've selected. If you include a column for a source that doesn't really apply, just open the View Options dialog box again and uncheck its check box.

Following are some other ways to customize the Content pane:

- You can change the width of columns in the Content pane by pointing to the line that marks the right boundary of the column in the column heading section. When you do, the cursor will become a vertical line with arrows pointing to the left and right. Drag this to the left to make a column narrower or to the right to make it wider. The rest of the columns will move to accommodate the change.
- You can change the order in which columns appear by dragging a column heading to the left or to the right. When you release the mouse button, the column will assume its new position, and the other columns will move to accommodate it.
- As you learned when playing a CD, you can sort the Content pane, using any of the columns, by clicking the column heading by which you want the pane to be sorted. The tracks will be sorted according to that criterion, and the column heading will be highlighted to show it is the current sort column. To change the direction of the sort, click the **Sort Order triangle**, which appears only in the Sort column. When you play a source, the tracks will play according to the order in which they are sorted in the Content pane, starting from the top of the pane and playing toward the bottom (unless you have the Shuffle feature turned on, of course).

THE ABSOLUTE MINIMUM

I hope this chapter turned out to be more exciting than you might have expected based on its title. Although labeling the content of your iTunes Library might not be fun in itself, it does enable you to do fun things. Setting options for your music enables you to enhance your listening experience, and adding and viewing lyrics and artwork is fun. Finally, you saw that the Content pane can be customized to your preferences. As we leave this chapter, here are some nuggets for you to chew on:

continues

- If iTunes can't find information about a CD, you can enter that information yourself by using the Info window you learned about in this chapter.
- If you want to check for information about a CD on command, select **Advanced**, **Get CD Track Names**. iTunes will connect to the Internet and attempt to get the CD's information.
- Occasionally, iTunes will find more than one CD that seems to be the one it looked for. When this happens, you will see a dialog box that lists each candidate iTunes found. Select the information you want to apply to the CD by clicking one of the candidates.
- You can submit track names for a CD. First, label the CD and select it. Then select **Advanced**, **Submit CD Track Names**. The CD's information will be uploaded to the CD database and will be provided to other people who use the same CD.
- Adding lyrics to tracks in your Library is currently a manual operation. If you really enjoy seeing the lyrics in iTunes or on an iPod, it might be worth your time and effort to add them. One can hope that lyrics will be included for songs you purchase from the iTunes Store at some point in the future.
- You can view album artwork in iTunes and on an iPod. When you purchase content from the iTunes Store, artwork is included, and if you have an iTunes Store account, iTunes will retrieve artwork for you automatically. If that doesn't work, you can also add artwork to any tracks in your Library manually or semi-automatically.
- When adding artwork to songs, you aren't limited to just the related album cover. You can associate any kind of graphics with your tracks. For example, you can use pictures of the artists, scenes that relate to the music, pictures you have taken that remind you of the music, and so on.
- Look for a tool that adds artwork to your Library semi-automatically with just a few mouse clicks so it is easy to have artwork for all your music, even if iTunes can't find the artwork for you.
- Use the View Options dialog box to choose the columns that are displayed in the Content pane of a source. You can also further customize a source's Content pane by changing the width of columns, changing their order, and sorting the content by any of the available columns.

IN THIS CHAPTER

- Learn why playlists might just be the best of iTunes' many outstanding features.
- Collect your favorite music in a standard playlist so you hear only what you want to hear when you want to hear it.
- Change your playlists whenever the spirit moves you.
- Become an iTunes master by creating your own smart playlists to make iTunes choose music for you to listen to based on your criteria.
- Keep your Source list neat and tidy.
- Work with oh-so-special playlists, including the Party Shuffle.

19

CREATING, CONFIGURING, AND USING PLAYLISTS

Of all the cool features iTunes offers (and as you have seen, there are lots of cool features), this chapter's topic—playlists—just might be the coolest of them all. Playlists enable you to listen to exactly the music you want to hear, when and how you want to hear it. Do you love a CD but hate a song or two on it? Fine, just set up a playlist without the offensive song. Wish you could hear different songs from a variety of albums in your own greatest hits collection? Make a playlist and be the judge of what is great and what isn't. How about keeping things interesting by creating collections of music whose contents automatically change as your music collection does? No problem. Ever thought it would be neat if you could pick a style of music and hear your favorite tunes in that style? What about if the tunes you hear are selected for you automatically based on your preferences? With iTunes playlists, you can do all this and more.

Understanding Playlists

Simply put, playlists are custom collections of tracks that you create or that iTunes creates for you based on criteria you define. After a playlist has been created, you can listen to it, put it on a CD, move it to your iPod, share it over a network, and more.

There are two basic kinds of playlists: standard playlists and smart playlists.

The Standard-But-Very-Useful Playlist

A *standard playlist* (which I'll usually call just a *playlist* from here on) is a set of songs you define manually. You put the specific songs you want in a playlist and do what you will with them. You can include the same song multiple times, mix and match songs from many CDs, put songs in any order you choose, and basically control every aspect of that music collection (see Figure 19.1).

FIGURE 19.1
Here is a standard playlist that contains a variety of tunes from an assortment of artists.

Playlists are useful for creating CDs or making specific music to which you might want to listen available at the click of the mouse. With a playlist, you can determine exactly which songs are included and the order in which those songs play. Playlists are also easy to create, and they never change over time—unless you purposefully change them, of course.

The Extra-Special Smart Playlist

A *smart playlist* is smart because you don't put songs in it manually. Instead, you tell iTunes which kind of songs you want included in it by the attributes of that music, such as genre or artist, and iTunes picks those songs for you (see Figure 19.2). For example, you can create a playlist based on a specific genre, such as Jazz, that you have listened to in the past few days. You can also tell iTunes how many songs to include.

FIGURE 19.2

On the surface, a smart playlist doesn't look all that different from a playlist, but when you take a closer look, you will see that a smart playlist lives up to its name.

The really cool thing is that smart playlists can be dynamic, meaning the songs they contain are updated over time based on criteria you define. As you add, listen to, or change your music, the contents of a smart playlist can change to match those changes; this happens in real time so the songs included in a smart playlist can change, too. Imagine you have a smart playlist that tells iTunes to include all the music you have in the Jazz genre that is performed by Kenny G, the Pat Metheny Group, Joe Sample, and Larry Carlton. If you make this a "live" smart playlist, iTunes will automatically add any new music from any of the artists to it as you add that music to your Library. The content of a live smart playlist changes over time, depending on the criteria it contains.

> **caution**
>
> Creating smart playlists depends on your music being properly tagged with information, such as genre, artist, song names, and so on. Sometimes music you add to your Library, such as MP3 files that are stored on your hard drive, won't have all this information. Before you get going with smart playlists, make sure you have your music properly labeled and categorized. Chapter 18, "Labeling, Categorizing, and Configuring Your Music," explains how to do this.

Building and Listening to Standard Playlists

Although they aren't as smart as their younger siblings, standard playlists are definitely useful because you can choose the exact songs included in them and the order in which those songs will play. In this section, you will learn how to create, manage, and use playlists.

note Whether it's a standard playlist or a smart playlist, the playlist is the starting point for many iTunes activities, such as burning a CD.

Creating a Standard Playlist

You have two ways to create a playlist. One is to create a playlist that is empty (meaning it doesn't include any songs). The other is to choose songs and then create a playlist that includes those songs.

The place you start depends on what you have in mind. If you want to create a collection of songs but aren't sure which specific songs you want to start with, create an empty playlist. If you know of at least some of the songs you are going to include, select them first and then create the playlist. Either way, creating a playlist is simple, and you'll end up in the same place.

Creating an Empty Standard Playlist

You can create an empty playlist from within iTunes by using any of the following techniques:

- Selecting **File**, **New Playlist**.
- Pressing **Ctrl+N** (Windows) or **⌘+N** (Mac).
- Clicking the **Create Playlist** button (see Figure 19.3).

Whichever method you use will result in an empty playlist whose name will be highlighted to show you that it is ready for you to edit. Type a name for the playlist and press **Enter** (Windows) or **Return** (Mac). The playlist will be renamed and selected. The Content pane will be empty because you haven't added any songs to the playlist yet. You will learn how to do that in the section "Adding Songs to a Playlist" on page **XX (this chapter)**.

Creating a Standard Playlist with Songs in It

If you know some songs you want to place in a playlist, you can create the playlist so it includes those songs as soon as you create it. Here are the steps to follow:

1. Browse or search the Library to find the songs you want to be included in the playlist. For example, you can browse for all the songs in a specific genre or search for music by a specific artist.

FIGURE 19.3
This playlist has been created and is ready to be renamed.

2. In the Content pane, select the songs you want to place in the playlist.
3. Choose **File, New Playlist from Selection**. A new playlist will appear on the Source list and will be selected. Its name will be highlighted to indicate that you can edit it, and you will see the songs you selected in the Content pane (see Figure 19.4).

FIGURE 19.4
Because I created a playlist from selected songs, the new playlist contains the songs I selected when I created it.

iTunes will attempt to name the playlist by looking for a common denominator in the group of songs you selected. For example, if all the songs are from the same artist, that artist's name will be the playlist's name. Similarly, if all the songs are from the same album, the playlist's name will be the artist's and album's names. Sometimes iTunes picks an appropriate name, and sometimes it doesn't.

4. While the playlist name is highlighted, edit the name as needed and then press **Enter** (Windows) or **Return** (Mac). The playlist will be ready to listen to and for you to add more songs.

tip

When you add a new album to your Library, use this technique to quickly create a playlist to make it easy to listen to. Select all the songs in the album and then use the New Playlist from Selection command. You can use the resulting playlist to easily select the new album for your listening pleasure.

Adding Songs to a Playlist

The whole point of creating a playlist is to add songs to it. Whether you created an empty playlist or one that already has some songs in it, the steps to add songs are the same:

1. Select **Music** as the source.
2. Browse or search the **Music Library** (or other source) so that songs you want to add to the playlist are shown in the Content pane.
3. Select the tracks you want to add to the playlist by clicking them. (Remember the techniques to select multiple tracks at the same time.) To select all the tracks currently shown in the Content pane, press **Ctrl+A** (Windows) or **⌘+A** (Mac).
4. Drag the selected songs from the Content pane onto the playlist to which you want to add them. As you drag, you'll see the songs you have selected in a "ghost" image attached to the

tip

For still another way to create a playlist, try this: Select a group of songs and drag them onto the Source list. When you do so, iTunes will do the same thing it does when you create a playlist with the New Playlist from Selection command.

tip

You can add the same song to a playlist as many times as you'd like to hear it.

pointer. When the playlist becomes highlighted and the cursor includes a plus sign (+), release the mouse button (see Figure 19.5). The songs will be added to the playlist.

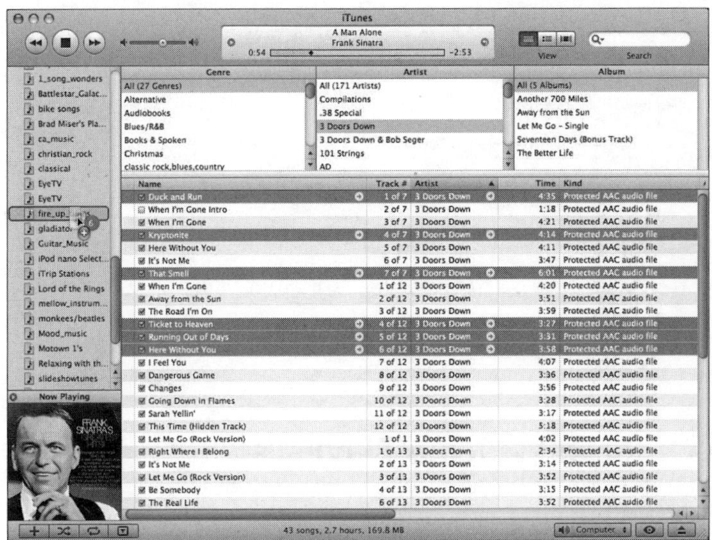

FIGURE 19.5
You can add songs to a playlist by dragging them from the Content pane onto the playlist in the Source pane.

5. Repeat steps 2–4 until you have added all the songs you want to include in the playlist.
6. Select the playlist on the Source list. Its songs will appear in the Content pane (see Figure 19.6). Information about the playlist, such as its playing time, will appear in the Source Information area at the bottom of the iTunes window.

The Source Information area becomes very important when you are creating a CD because you can use this to make sure a playlist will fit onto a CD.

Removing Songs from a Playlist

If you decide you don't want one or more songs included in a playlist, select the songs you want to remove in the playlist's Content pane and press the **Delete** key. A warning prompt will appear. Click **Yes**, and the songs will be deleted from the playlist. (If this dialog box annoys you as it does me, check the **Do not ask me again** check box. You will never have to see it again.)

FIGURE 19.6
This playlist, called "Songs to Ride By," are tunes that are a good companion while traveling on my motorcycle.

Setting the Order in Which a Playlist's Songs Play

Just like an audio CD, the order in which a playlist's songs play is determined by the order in which they appear in the Content pane. (The first song will be the one at the top of the window, the second will be the next one down, and so on.) You can drag songs up on the list to make them play earlier or down in the list to make them play later.

You can also change the order in which songs will play by sorting the playlist by its columns. You do this by clicking the column title in the column by which you want the Content pane sorted. You can set the columns that appear for a playlist by selecting **View**, **View Options**, as you learned to do in the previous chapter.

When you delete a song from a playlist, it *isn't* deleted from the Library. It remains there so you can add it to a different playlist or listen to it from the Library. Of course, if it is included in other playlists, it isn't removed from those either.

Listening to a Standard Playlist

After you have created a playlist, you can listen to it by selecting it on the Source list and using the same controls you use to listen to a CD or music in the Library. You can even search in and browse playlists just as you can the Library or CDs. (That's the real beauty of iTunes; it works the same way no matter what the selected source is!)

You can use the iTunes Shuffle feature with playlists just as you can with other sources. For example, to hear the songs in a playlist in a random order, select the playlist you want to hear and click the Shuffle button. The songs will play in random order. If you like that order and want it always to be used for a playlist, select that playlist, open its contextual menu (by right-clicking it), and choose **Copy To Play Order**. The "random" order will be saved for the playlist.

Likewise, you can repeat all the songs in a playlist or just one of them by using the **Repeat** commands or button.

You can't change the order of tracks in a playlist by dragging songs up or down unless the playlist is sorted by the Track Number column (always the first column in the Content pane unless you are viewing the Library, in which case it is always the first column with information in it). If songs "bounce back" when you try to reorder them, click the Track Number column to make it the sort column. Then you'll be able to drag songs around to change their order.

Deleting a Standard Playlist

If you decide you no longer want a playlist, you can delete it by selecting the playlist on the Source list and pressing the **Delete** key. A prompt will appear; click **Yes**, and the playlist will be removed from the Source list. (Be sure to check the **Do not ask me again** check box if you don't want to be prompted in the future.) Even though you've deleted the playlist, the songs in the playlist remain in the Library or in other playlists for your listening pleasure (or not).

Becoming a Musical Genius with Smart Playlists

The basic purpose of a smart playlist is the same as a standard playlist—that is, to contain a collection of tracks to which you can listen, put on a CD, and so on. However, the path that smart playlists take to this end is completely different from that of standard playlists. Rather than choose specific songs as you do in a standard playlist, you tell iTunes the kind of tracks you want in your smart playlist, and it picks out the tracks for you and places them in the playlist. For example, suppose you want to create a playlist that contains all your classical music. Rather than picking out all the songs in your Library that have the Classical genre (as you would do to create a standard playlist), you can use a smart playlist to tell iTunes to select all the classical music for you. The application then gathers all the music with the Classical genre and places that music in a smart playlist.

Understanding Why Smart Playlists Are Called Smart

You create a smart playlist by defining a set of criteria based on any number of tags. After you have created these criteria, iTunes chooses songs that match those tags and places them in the playlist. Another example should help clarify this. Suppose you are a big-time Elvis fan and regularly add Elvis music to your Library. You could create a playlist and manually drag your new Elvis tunes to that playlist. But by using a smart playlist instead, you could define the playlist to include all your Elvis music. Anytime you add more Elvis music to your Library, that music would be added to the playlist automatically so it always contains all the Elvis music in your Library.

You can also base a smart playlist on more than one attribute at the same time. Going back to the Elvis example, you could add the condition that you want only those songs you have rated four stars or higher so the smart playlist contains only your favorite Elvis songs.

As the previous example shows, smart playlists can be dynamic; iTunes calls this *live updating*. When a smart playlist is set to be live, iTunes changes its contents over time to match changes to the music in your Library. If this feature isn't set for a smart playlist, that playlist will contain only those songs that met the criteria at the time the playlist was created.

Finally, you can also link a smart playlist's conditions by the logical expression All or Any. If you use an All logical expression, all the conditions must be true for a song to be included in the smart playlist. If you use the Any option, only one of the conditions has to be met for a song to be included in the smart playlist.

Creating a Smart Playlist

You can create a smart playlist by performing the following steps:

1. Select **File**, **New Smart Playlist** or hold down the **Shift** (Windows) or **Option** (Mac) key and click the **New Playlist** button, which becomes the **New Smart Playlist** button when the Shift or Option key is pressed down. You will see the Smart Playlist dialog box (see Figure 19.7).
2. Select the first tag on which you want the smart playlist to be based in the **Tag** menu. For example, you can select **Artist**, **Genre**, **My Rating**, or **Year**, among many others. The Operand menu will be updated so that it is applicable to the attribute you selected. For example, if you select **Artist**, the Operand menu will include contains, does not contain, is, is not, starts with, and ends with.

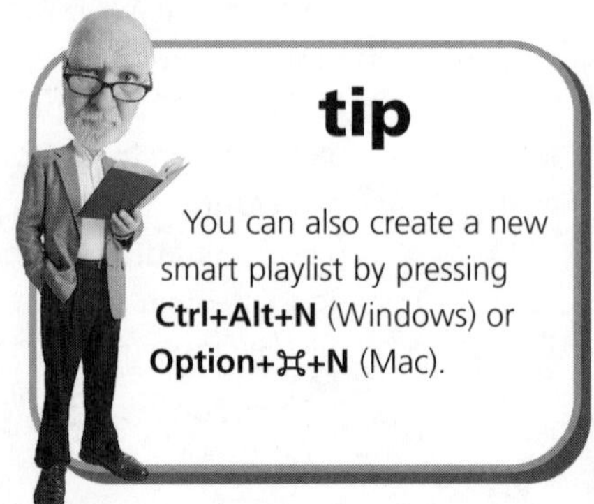

You can also create a new smart playlist by pressing **Ctrl+Alt+N** (Windows) or **Option+⌘+N** (Mac).

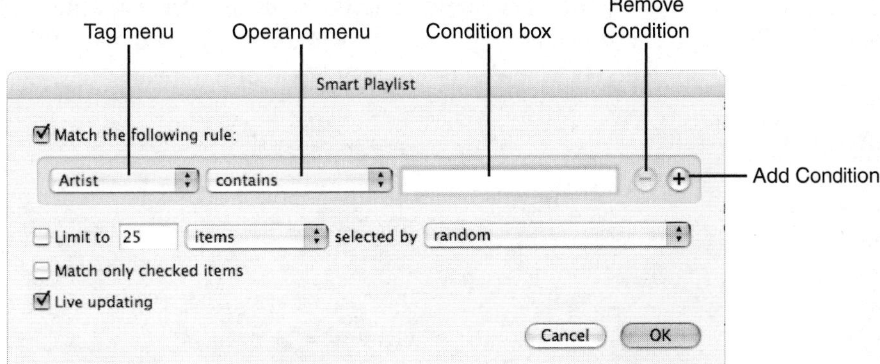

FIGURE 19.7
The Smart Playlist dialog box enables you to create playlists based on a single tag or on many of them.

3. Select the operand you want to use on the **Operand** menu. For example, if you want to match data exactly, select **is**. If you want the condition to be more loose, select **contains**.
4. Type the condition you want to match in the Condition box. The more you type, the more specific the condition will be. As an example, if you select **Artist** in step 1, select **contains** in step 2, and type **Elvis** in this step, the condition would look like the one shown in Figure 19.8 and would find all songs that include Elvis, Elvis Presley, Elvis Costello, Elvisiocity, and so on. If you typed **Elvis Presley** in the Condition box and left the **contains** operand, iTunes would include only songs whose artist includes Elvis Presley, such as Elvis Presley, Elvis Presley and His Back-up Band, and so on.

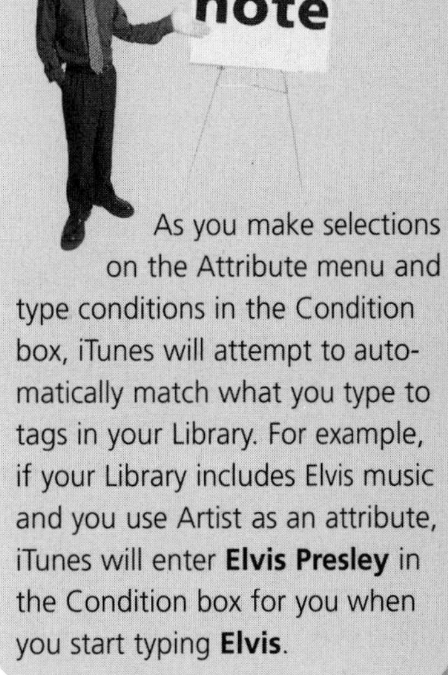

As you make selections on the Attribute menu and type conditions in the Condition box, iTunes will attempt to automatically match what you type to tags in your Library. For example, if your Library includes Elvis music and you use Artist as an attribute, iTunes will enter **Elvis Presley** in the Condition box for you when you start typing **Elvis**.

FIGURE 19.8
This smart playlist is getting smarter.

5. To add another condition to the smart playlist, click the **Add Condition** button. A new, empty condition will appear (see Figure 19.9). At the top of the dialog box, the all or any menu will also appear.

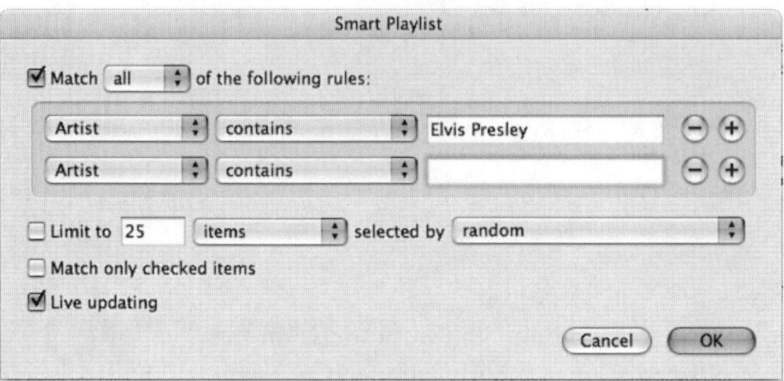

FIGURE 19.9
This smart playlist now contains two conditions; both are currently based on Artist.

6. Select the second tag on which you want the smart playlist to be based in the second condition's **Tag** menu. For example, if you want to include songs from a specific genre, select **Genre** on the menu.
7. Select the operand you want to use in the Operand menu, such as **contains**, **is**, and so on.
8. Type the condition you want to match in the Condition box. For example, if you selected Genre in step 6, type the genre from which the music in the playlist should come. As you type, iTunes will try to match the genre you type with those in your Library.
9. Repeat steps 5–8 to add more conditions to the playlist until you have all the conditions you want to include (see Figure 19.10).

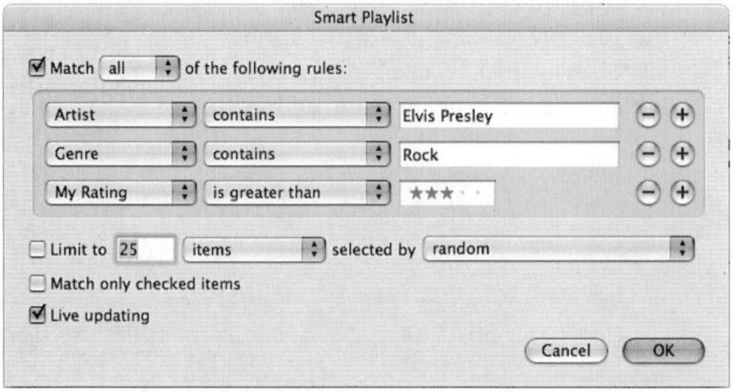

FIGURE 19.10
This smart playlist is approaching the genius level; it now includes three conditions.

10. Select **all** on the menu at the top of the dialog box if all the conditions must be met for a track to be included in the smart playlist, or select **any** if only one of them must be met. For example, you could create a smart playlist based on multiple Artist conditions, and the playlist would feature music by those artists. In this case, you would choose **any** so that if a song were associated with *any* of the artists for which you created a condition, it would be included in the playlist. As a contrasting example, if you want the playlist to include songs you have rated as three stars or better by a specific artist, you would want to use both of these conditions by selecting **all** in the menu so that both conditions would have to be met for a song to be included. (A song is both by the artist and is rated with three or more stars.)

    You can limit the length of a smart playlist to a maximum number of songs, the time it plays, or the size of the files it includes. You set these limits using the **Limit to** check box and menus.

tip

If you want to remove a condition from a smart playlist, click the **Remove** button (the minus sign) for the condition you want to remove.

11. If you want to limit the playlist, check the **Limit to** check box. If you don't want to set a limit on the playlist, leave the check box unchecked and skip to step 15.
12. Select the **parameter** by which you want to limit the playlist in the first menu; by default, this menu has items (which are actually songs if you are working with music) selected (see Figure 19.11). Your choices include the number of items, the time the playlist will play (in minutes or hours), or the size of the files the playlist contains (in MB or GB).

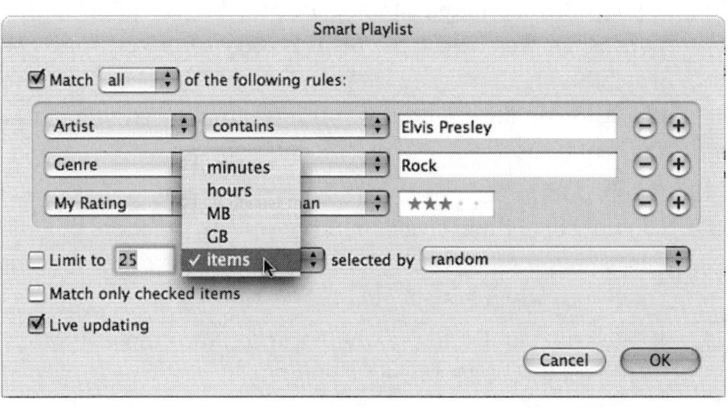

FIGURE 19.11
You can choose to limit a smart playlist to a number of songs, a length of time, or by disk space.

13. Type the data appropriate for the limit you selected in the **Limit to** box. For example, if you selected **minutes** in the menu, type the maximum length of the playlist in minutes in the box. If you selected **items**, enter the maximum number of songs (or other items, such as episodes of a TV series) that can be included in the playlist.
14. Select how you want iTunes to choose the songs it includes based on the limit you selected by using the **selected by** menu. This menu has many options, including to choose songs randomly, based on your rating, how often the songs are played, and so on (see Figure 19.12).

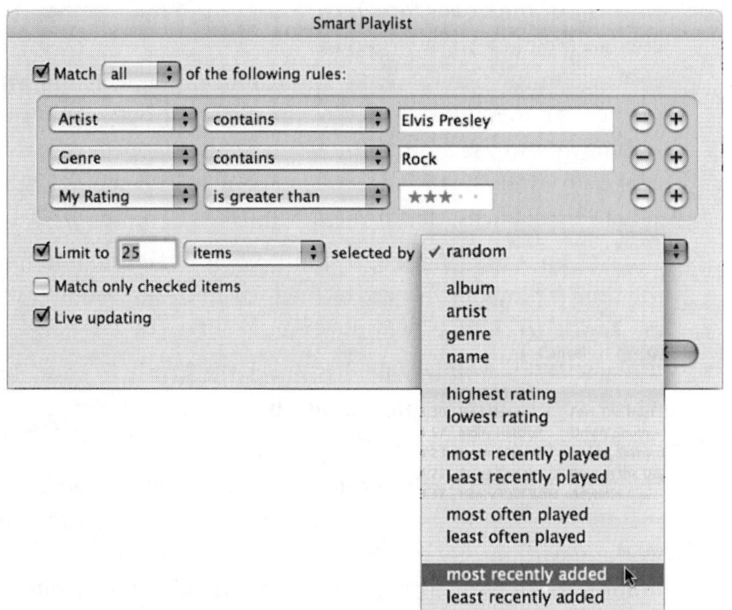

FIGURE 19.12
These options tell iTunes how you want it to choose songs for a smart playlist when you limit that playlist's size.

15. If you want the playlist to include only songs whose check box in the Content pane is checked, check the **Match only checked items** check box. If you leave this check box unchecked, iTunes will include all songs that meet the playlist's conditions, even if you have unchecked their check boxes in the Content pane.
16. If you want the playlist to be dynamic, meaning that iTunes will update its contents over time, check the **Live updating** check box. If you uncheck this check box, the playlist will include only those songs that meet the playlist's conditions when you create it.
17. Review the playlist to see whether it contains the conditions and settings you want (see Figure 19.13).

FIGURE 19.13
This playlist will include up to 25 songs of the best (rated at four stars or more) of my Elvis Presley music from the Rock genre that I have most recently added to my Library; as I add music that meets these conditions to my Library, it will also be added to this playlist.

18. Click **OK** to create the playlist. You will move to the Source list, the smart playlist will be added and selected, and its name will be ready for you to edit. Also, the songs in your Library that match the criteria in the playlist will be added to it, and the current contents of the playlist will be shown in the Content pane.

19. Type the playlist's name and press **Enter** (Windows) or **Return** (Mac). The smart playlist will be complete (see Figure 19.14).

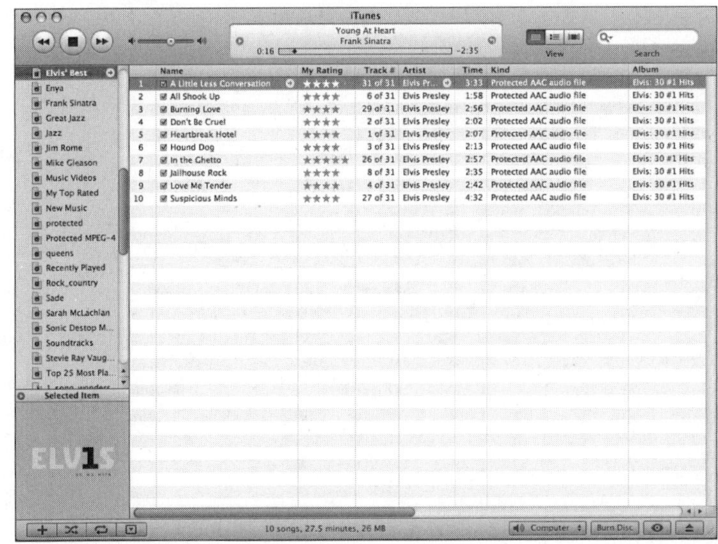

FIGURE 19.14
If you compare the songs in this smart playlist to the criteria shown in the previous figure, you will see they match.

Listening to a Smart Playlist

Listening to a smart playlist is just like listening to other sources: You select it on the Source list and use the playback controls to listen to it. The one difference is that, if a smart playlist is set to be live, its contents can change over time.

Changing a Smart Playlist

To change the contents of a smart playlist, you change the smart playlist's criteria. (Remember that iTunes automatically places tracks in a smart playlist based on your criteria.) Use the following steps to do this:

1. Select the **smart playlist** you want to change.
2. Select **File**, **Edit Smart Playlist**. The Smart Playlist dialog box will appear, and the playlist's current criteria will be shown.
3. Use the techniques you learned when you created a playlist to change its criteria (see Figure 19.15). For example, you can remove a condition by clicking its Remove Condition button. You can also add more conditions or change any of the other settings for the playlist.

tip

You can also edit a smart playlist by selecting it and opening the Info window (which also opens the Smart Playlist dialog box). Plus, you can open the playlist's contextual menu by right-clicking (two-button mouse) or Ctrl-clicking it (one-button mouse) and selecting **Edit Smart Playlist**.

FIGURE 19.15
I changed the conditions on this smart playlist so that only five-star songs are included and also removed the limit on number of songs included.

4. Click **OK**. Your changes will be saved, and the contents of the playlist will be updated to match the current criteria.

You can also change a smart playlist by using the same techniques you use on other sources, such as sorting it, selecting the columns you see when you view it, and so on.

tip

To delete a smart playlist, select it on the Source list and press **Delete**. Confirm the deletion at the prompt (if you see it), and the playlist will be removed from the Source list. Again, this doesn't change the music in the Library in any way; it only deletes the playlist.

Organizing Your Playlists

As you use iTunes, you are likely to create lots of playlists. Over time, your list of playlists can get huge, making your Source list long and unwieldy. Fortunately, you can create folders to organize your playlists and then drag your playlists into the folders you create to organize them. By doing this, you can keep your Source list neat and tidy and also make your playlists easier to use.

Just like folders on your desktop, you can create folders for any kind of playlist on your Source list. You might want a folder for all your playlists from specific genres or maybe another folder for all your playlists that contain albums.

To create a folder, choose **File**, **New Folder**. A new folder will appear on the Source list; its name will be highlighted to indicate it's ready for you to give it a name. Type the folder name and press **Return** or **Enter** to save it (see Figure 19.16).

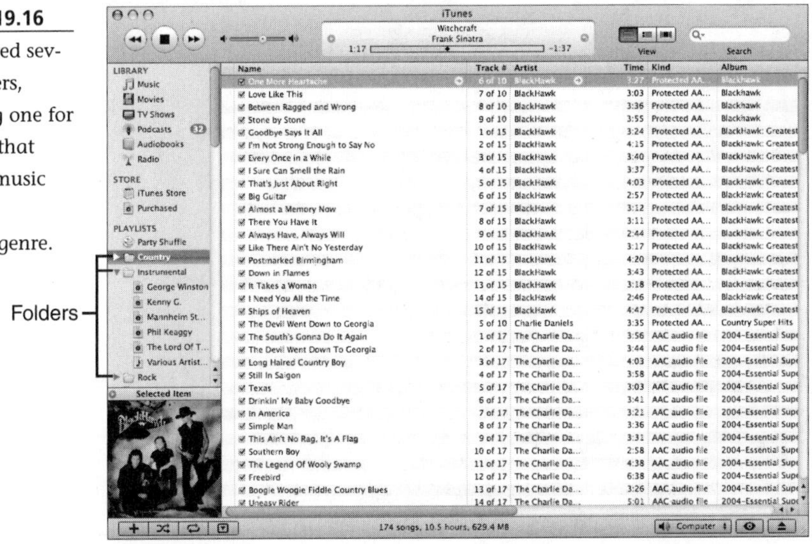

FIGURE 19.16
I've created several folders, including one for playlists that contain music from the Country genre.

Folders

To place a playlist within a folder, drag its icon onto the folder until that folder's icon becomes highlighted. Then release the mouse button. The playlist will be moved into the folder; as soon as you add at least one playlist to a folder, an expansion triangle will be added to the folder's icon. You can click this to expand or to collapse the folder so that you see or don't see the playlists it contains.

> **tip**
>
> You can also create a new folder by pressing **Ctrl+Shift+N** (Windows) or **Option+Shift+⌘+N** (Mac).

A folder can contain both kinds of playlists, and they can even contain playlists containing different types of content. For example, you can create playlists of rock music videos and include them in a folder you've created for your playlists that also include rock music.

Just because you can create folders for your playlists, that doesn't mean you have to do so. You can place some playlists in folders and leave others at the top level of the Source list. The point is that you can use folders to organize your Source list however you see fit.

When you select a folder's icon on the Source list, the contents of all the playlists it contains will be displayed in the Content pane (see Figure 19.17). You can play all the content in a folder just as you can a playlist; select the folder and use the playback controls to play it. You can also sort it, choose its view options, and perform all the other amazing iTunes tricks that you've come to know and love.

FIGURE 19.17
You can use folders just like playlists; for example, you can play the contents of a folder by selecting it and clicking **Play**.

On the Source list, your folders will appear between the "special playlists" (you'll learn about these in the next section) and the playlists that aren't in folders. Folders are listed in alphabetical or numerical order based on their names.

Within folders or not, playlists are listed in alphabetical order based on their names (just like folders). You can make your playlists and folders be listed in another order by appending numbers before their names, such as adding "1." before the name of the playlist you want to appear at the top of the list. You could add "2." to the one you want to be listed next, and so on. (Remember that you can change the name of a folder or playlist by selecting it, clicking the name so it becomes highlighted, changing the name, and then pressing the **Return** or **Enter** key.)

Using the Special iTunes Playlists

On the Source list, you'll see a number of special "playlists" (some really are playlists, whereas others are tools) organized by type (Library, Store, Devices, and Playlists). These are the following:

- **Music**—As you well know by now, you choose the Music source to work with the music in your iTunes Library.
- **Movies**—This source enables you to work with your movie content. See Chapter 21 for more information on this one.
- **TV Shows**—Have you added TV shows to your Library? Use this source to work with them. See Chapter 21, "Working with iTunes Video," for the skinny on this one, too.
- **Podcasts**—This special playlist is used to manage your podcasts. You'll learn all about podcasts in Chapter 20, "Subscribing to and Listening to Podcasts."
- **Audiobooks**—This sources contains your audiobook content.
- **Radio**—This playlist contains Internet "radio" stations to which you can listen; it's covered in Chapter 16, "Listening to Audio CDs and Internet Audio with iTunes," as I am sure you recall.
- **Store**—Although it looks like a typical source, it isn't. Rather, it's the source you select to work with the iTunes Store. You'll get the scoop in Part III, "The iTunes Store."
- **Purchased**—This playlist contains music and videos you purchase from the iTunes Store; it's also explained in detail in Part III.
- **CDs, iPods, and other ejectable sources**—As you've seen, when you have a CD mounted in your computer, it appears on the Source list. Its icon is a playlist containing the tracks on the disc. Likewise, when you have an iPod connected to your computer, its icon is a playlist that shows the playlists and other content it contains.

- **Shared sources**—iTunes makes it easy to share content over a local network. In the Shared section, you'll see sources of shared content that you can access. You'll get generous with iTunes in Chapter 23, "Sharing iTunes."
- **Party Shuffle**—You'll learn how to do the party shuffle a little later in this chapter.

Configuring the Special Playlists on the Source List

You can turn some of the special playlists off (meaning they aren't shown on the Source list) or on (meaning that they are shown on the Source list). To configure your special playlists, perform the following steps:

1. Open the iTunes Preferences dialog box.
2. Click the **General** tab (see Figure 19.18).

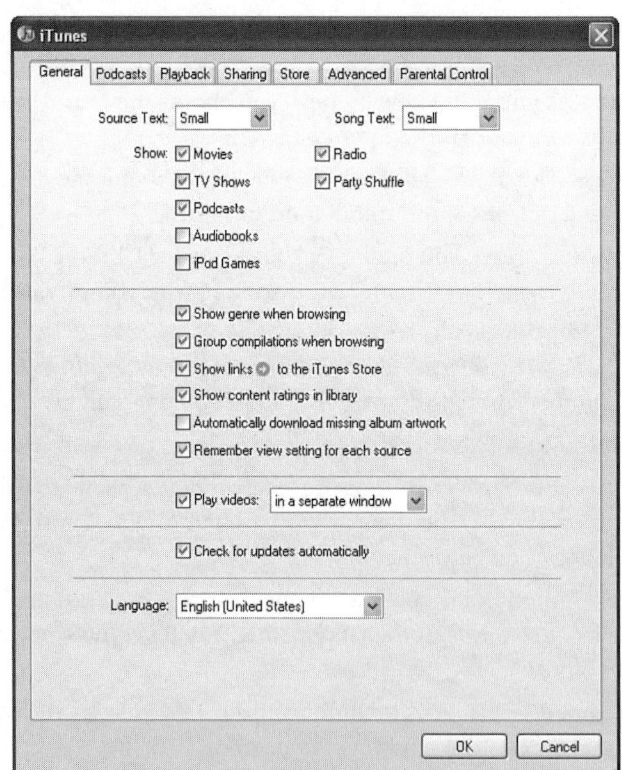

FIGURE 19.18

By checking or unchecking the Show check boxes, you can show or hide sources on the Source list.

3. Uncheck a source's check box if you don't want it to appear on your Source list. For example, if you don't have audiobook content, uncheck the Audiobooks check box to remove it from the Source list.

4. Check the **Show** check box for those sources that you do want to appear on the Source list.
5. Click the **Parental Control** tab (see Figure 19.19).

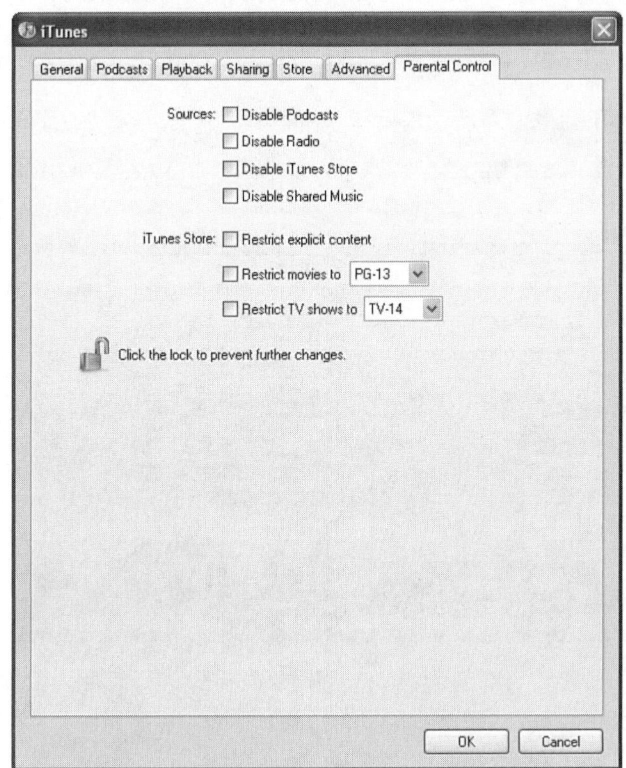

FIGURE 19.19
You can disable a number of special playlists with the Parental Control pane.

6. Check the **Disable Podcasts**, **Disable Radio**, **Disable iTunes Store,** or **Disable Shared Music** check boxes if you don't want any of those sources to appear on the Source list.
7. Click **OK**. When you return to the Source list, you won't see any of the special playlists you've chosen not to show or to disable (which in effect does the same thing).

Doing the Party Shuffle

One of the coolest special playlists is the Party Shuffle. This playlist enables you to play a source you select in shuffle mode; you can also set several options to liven things up even more. If you like to keep things interesting, the Party Shuffle is a good way to do so because you can hear the songs in any source in a random order without having to change the source itself. After you try this special playlist, you'll probably use it as often as I do, which is to say, quite a lot. To do the party shuffle, follow these steps:

1. Select **Party Shuffle** on the Source pane. You'll see a dialog box explaining what the Party Shuffle is; read it, check the **Do not show this message again** check box, and click **OK**. You'll see songs fill the Content pane, and some controls will appear at the bottom of that pane (see Figure 19.20).

FIGURE 19.20
The Party Shuffle source might seem odd to you at first, but once you get to know it, you'll love it.

2. Select the source of music you want to shuffle on the Source pop-up menu. You can choose your Library, any playlist (standard or smart), or any folder (that contains standard or smart playlists). The playlists and folders appear in alphabetical order, and the different kinds of playlists look the same on the menu.
3. If you want songs you have rated higher to be played more frequently, check the **Play higher rated songs more often** check box. This causes iTunes to choose songs with higher star ratings more frequently than those with lower or no star ratings.

note

The Party Shuffle is one item for which the Source Information data doesn't make a lot of sense. Because the list is always changing, the source information doesn't really mean a lot. It simply shows information based on the songs currently shown in the Content pane, which changes after each song is played.

4. Use the two Display pop-up menus to choose how many songs are shown that have been played recently and that are upcoming. Your choices range from 0 to 100 on both menus. When you make selections, the songs shown in the Content pane will reflect your choices.

   The current song is always highlighted in the Content pane with a blue bar. Songs that have played are grayed out and are listed above the current song. Songs that will be played are in regular text and appear below the current song.

5. If you want to change the order in which upcoming songs will play, drag them up or down in the Content pane.
6. When you are ready to hear the tunes, use the same **playback controls** that you use with any other source.

The Party Shuffle source will play forever. After it plays a song, it moves one of the recently played songs off the list, moves the song it just played into the recently played section, highlights and plays the next song, and adds another one to the upcoming songs section. This process will continue until you stop the music.

As the Party Shuffle plays, you can keep moving upcoming songs around to change the order in which they will play. You can also press the right-arrow key to skip to the next song.

In addition, you can add songs manually to the Party Shuffle. View a source to find the song you want to add. Open the song's contextual menu by right-clicking it (see Figure 19.21). Select **Play Next in Party Shuffle** to have the song play next, or select **Add to Party Shuffle** to add the song to the end of the upcoming songs list.

tip

One interesting command on a track's contextual menu is the Show in Playlists command. Choose this to see a list of all the playlists in which a song is contained.

FIGURE 19.21
To add a song to the Party Shuffle, use one of the Party Shuffle commands on its contextual menu.

THE ABSOLUTE MINIMUM

Playlists are a great way to customize the contents of your Library for listening and viewing purposes, to create a CD, or to manage the music on an iPod. As you learned in this chapter, playlists include a specific collection of songs that you choose, whereas iTunes chooses the songs in a smart playlist based on the conditions you specify.

Playlists are a great way to select specific music to which you want to listen. You can make them as long or as short as you like, and you can mix and match songs to your heart's content.

You can use folders to keep your playlists organized on the Source list.

Don't forget about the special playlists on the Source list. For example, you can use the Party Shuffle playlist to spice up your music experience by keeping it fresh.

Smart playlists can really enhance your listening experience. Following are some ideas you might find interesting for your own smart playlists:

- Be diligent about rating your songs. Then create smart playlists for favorite genres and artists that also include a rating condition. Enable these playlists to be updated live. Such playlists will always contain your favorite songs in those genres and artists, even as you add more songs to your Library.

- Create a smart playlist based only on genre and allow it to be updated live. This playlist makes it easy to listen to that genre, and it always contains all your music in that genre.
- Create a smart playlist that includes several of your favorite artists (remember to choose **Any** in the top menu), and limit the number of songs to 20 or so. Have iTunes select the songs in a random order. Playing this playlist might provide an interesting mix of music. If you include a My Rating condition, you can cause only your favorite music to be included in this group. Make a dynamic list, and it will change over time as you add music to your Library.
- Create a smart playlist for your favorite artists and allow it to be updated live. As you add music by the artists to your Library, just play the related playlist to hear all the music by that artist, including new music you've added to your collection.
- If you like to collect multiple versions of the same song, create a playlist based on song name. Allow it to be updated live, and this playlist will contain all the versions of this song you have in your Library.

IN THIS CHAPTER

- Use podcasts to enjoy a mind-boggling array of audio and video content from the comfort of your computer or iPod.
- Set your podcasting preferences.
- Learn how to add all the best podcasts to your Library.
- Listen to and manage your podcasts like you've been doing it all your life.

20

SUBSCRIBING TO AND LISTENING TO PODCASTS

You know that a technology has arrived when new words are created because of it. *Podcast* is one of those words that shows the iPod is big. Really big.

Podcasts are radio-like audio or TV-like video you can add to your iTunes Library. Podcasts exist for just about any topic you can think of and are created by individuals or organizations. Some podcasts are informative in nature, such as news podcasts, while others are for entertainment only. People and organizations create podcasts for all sorts of reasons; I suspect you'll choose to listen to and watch them for all kinds of reasons, too.

You add podcasts to your iTunes Library by subscribing to them from the iTunes Store. You can also find thousands more podcasts on a variety of websites; for example, many radio shows also provide their content in podcasts that you can download from the show's website.

Like radio and TV shows, most podcasts are provided in episodes. When you want to be able to listen to or view a podcast, you subscribe to it; subscribing to a podcast causes it to be downloaded to your computer and added to your iTunes Library automatically. You can also choose to download previous episodes if you want to. (You can't subscribe to all podcasts; some are provided as individual files that you download to your computer and then add to your iTunes Library.)

After you have downloaded podcasts, you can listen to or watch them on your computer, move them to an iPod, and so on.

Setting Your iTunes Podcast Preferences

You should set some podcast preferences before you start working with podcasts. Do so with the following steps:

1. Open the iTunes Preferences dialog box and click the **Podcasts** tab (see Figure 20.1).

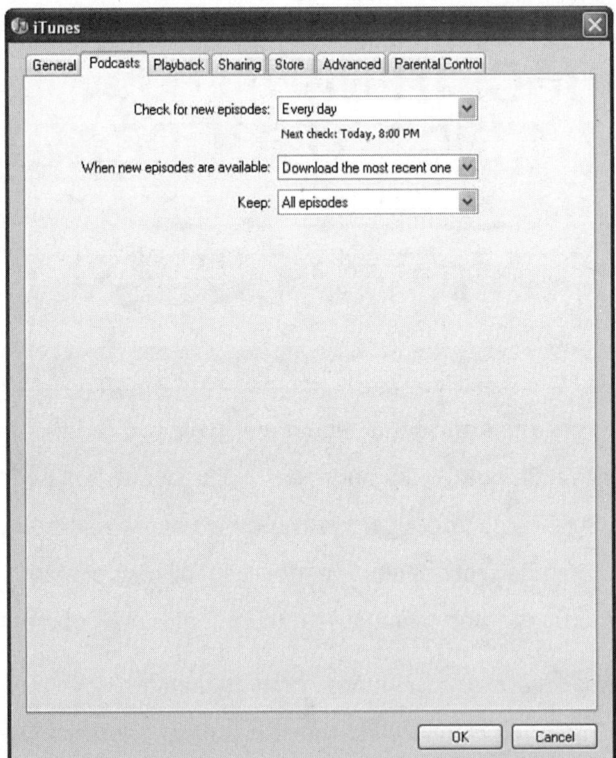

FIGURE 20.1
Use the Podcasts preferences to determine how you want your podcast subscriptions to be managed.

2. Choose how often you want iTunes to check for new episodes, using the **Check for new episodes** drop-down list. The options are Every hour, Every day, Every week, or Manually. iTunes will check for new episodes according to the timeframe you select—unless you select Manually, in which case you must check for new episodes manually.

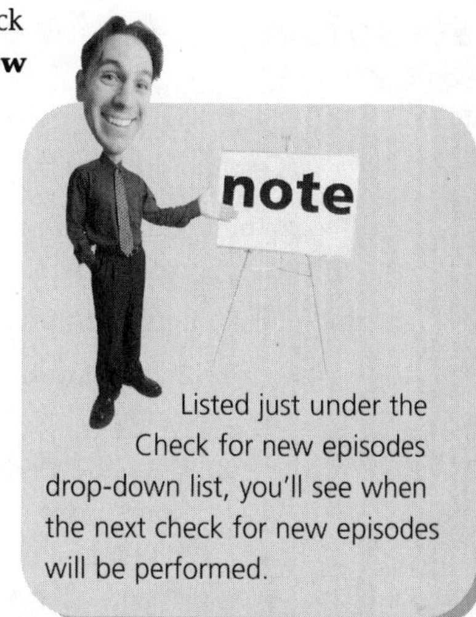

Listed just under the Check for new episodes drop-down list, you'll see when the next check for new episodes will be performed.

3. Use the **When new episodes are available** drop-down list to determine what iTunes does when it finds new episodes of the podcasts to which you are subscribed. Select **Download the most recent one** if you want only the newest episode to be downloaded. Select **Download all** if you want all available episodes downloaded. Select **Do nothing** if you don't want any episodes to be downloaded.
4. Use the **Keep** drop-down list to determine whether and when iTunes deletes podcast episodes. Select **All episodes** if you don't want iTunes to automatically remove any episodes. Select **All unplayed episodes** if you want iTunes to remove episodes to which you have listened (via iTunes or on an iPod), or select **Most recent episode** if you want iTunes to keep only the most recent episode even if you haven't listened to all of them. Select **Last *X* episodes**, where ***X*** is 2, 3, 4, 5, or 10, to have iTunes keep only the selected number of episodes.
5. Click **OK**. The dialog box will close, and your podcast preferences will be set.

Adding Podcasts to Your Library

Like other iTunes content, the first step toward enjoying podcasts is to add the podcasts you want to enjoy to your iTunes Library. You can do this in one or more of the following three ways:

- Subscribe to podcasts via the iTunes Store
- Subscribe to podcasts via a website
- Download episodes of a podcast and add them to your Library manually

As you might suspect, you'll learn how to do each of these tasks in the following sections.

Subscribing to Audio or Video Podcasts from the iTunes Store

In addition to lots of great music, TV shows, and movies, you can access thousands of podcasts via the iTunes Store. Most of these podcasts are free, and you don't even need an iTunes Store account to gain access to them.

When you access the podcasts section of the iTunes Store, you can browse or search for podcasts to which you can then subscribe.

First, check out these nifty browsing steps:

1. Select **iTunes Store** on the Source list. The iTunes Store will fill the Content pane.
2. Click the **Podcasts** link in the iTunes Store box. You'll move to the Podcasts home page (see Figure 20.2).

FIGURE 20.2
Want podcasts? The iTunes Store has them!

3. Scroll down the window until you see all of the Categories section. Here, you can access podcasts based on various categories, such as Arts, Business, Comedy, and so on.
4. Click a category in which you are interested, such as Technology, and then click the **Browser** button located in the bottom-right corner of the iTunes window. The Browser will open, and you'll see the subcategories of podcasts available under the category you selected (see Figure 20.3). The podcast Browser works just like the Browser when you browse your Library or other sources.
5. If the category has subcategories, you'll see them in the rightmost pane of the Browser; click the **subcategory** in which you are interested. The Content pane will show all podcasts in the categories selected in the Browser (see Figure 20.4).

FIGURE 20.3
As you can see in the Browser, I am browsing podcasts in the Technology category.

FIGURE 20.4
Here, I've selected Software How-To; the Content pane shows the podcasts available in that subcategory.

6. Use the scrollbar in the Content pane to browse all the podcasts available. For each podcast, you'll see the name, time, artist, album, genre, and price information (which is free for most podcasts).
7. When you find a podcast in which you are interested, you can listen to it by selecting it and clicking the **Play** button. The podcast will begin to play.
8. When you find a podcast that you would like to try, click its **Subscribe** button. You'll see a confirmation dialog box; click the **Subscribe** button to subscribe to the podcast. Under the iTunes Store source, you'll see the Downloads

icon that displays the progress of file downloads, including the number of episodes being downloaded. You can continue to subscribe to other podcasts until you've subscribed to all those that are of interest to you. The podcasts to which you subscribed will download in the background as you use iTunes.

9. When you are ready to start working with your podcasts, click the **Podcasts** source in the Source list. You'll move to the Podcasts source in your Library, and the podcasts to which you have subscribed will be shown (see Figure 20.5). These will be downloaded according to the preferences you set earlier.

FIGURE 20.5
Here, I've subscribed to the Geekspeak podcast. The most recent episodes are being downloaded to my computer.

10. Click the **Podcast Directory** link located at the bottom of the Content pane to go back to browse for and subscribe to more podcasts. You'll return to your previous location in the store.

You can also search for specific podcasts in the iTunes Store by following these steps:

1. Select the **iTunes Store** source.
2. Enter **search text** in the Search iTunes Store tool located at the top of the iTunes window, and press the **Enter** or **Return** key. The entire iTunes Store will be searched, and the Search Results screen will appear (see Figure 20.6). You'll see all the results that matched your search, only some of which will be podcasts.

tip

Like most other screens in the iTunes Store, most elements are links that will take you to more details about a podcast, to the podcasts within specific categories, and so on. Click around until you find ways that you like to navigate around the store .

3. Click the **Podcasts** button. The search results will be refocused to show only podcasts (see Figure 20.7).

FIGURE 20.6
Searching for podcasts in the iTunes Store is easy.

FIGURE 20.7
Here are the podcasts related to iTunes that my search found.

4. Click the arrow button next to a podcast's name. You'll move to the details screen for that podcast (see Figure 20.8). You'll see a description of the podcast along with customer reviews. In the Content pane, you'll see a list of episodes for that podcast.

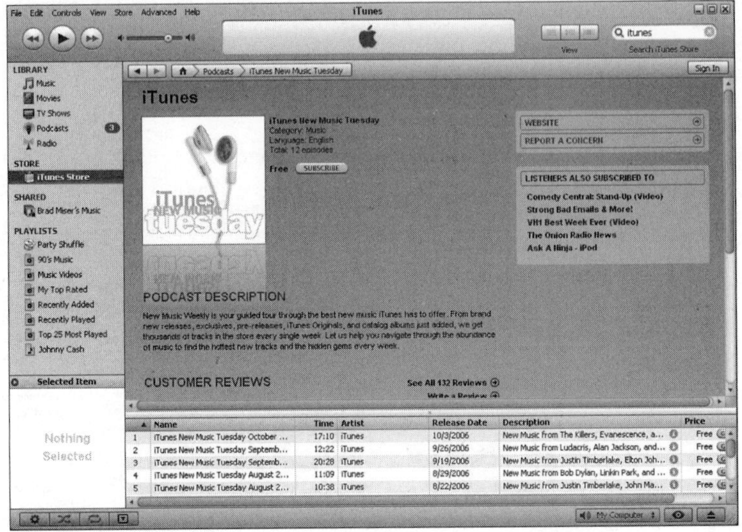

FIGURE 20.8
When you drill down into a podcast, you get to see all its details.

5. To preview an episode, select it and click **Play**. A segment of the podcast will play.
6. To subscribe to the podcast, click its **Subscribe** button. Its episodes will be downloaded according to the preferences you set earlier.

> **tip**
>
> If you want to move to the website to which a podcast is related, click its **Website** link.

To learn how to work with podcasts to which you have subscribed, refer to "Listening to and Managing Podcasts" on page **340**.

Subscribing to Podcasts from Websites

Although accessing podcasts via the iTunes Store is definitely the easiest way to get to them, not all podcasts are available there (although with the tremendous quantity available there, that's hard to believe). Podcasts are available all over the Internet, and you can subscribe to these to listen to them and download them to your Library and iPod. The most challenging part is finding podcasts that are worth the time to listen to, but that judgment is, of course, in the ear and eye of the beholder.

> **tip**
>
> You can download individual episodes of the podcast without subscribing to it by clicking the Get Episode button for the episodes that you want to download. This is a great way to preview podcasts to which you might want to subscribe later.

There are two general sources of podcast websites on the Internet. One includes websites whose sole purpose is to provide access to podcasts. The other includes websites from specific organizations, such as radio shows, that provide podcasts related to those organizations. Subscribing to podcasts from either source is similar.

The following steps show you how to subscribe to a podcast accessed from a specific podcast collection website. You can use similar steps to find other podcast sites.

1. Open a web browser and move to a website that provides podcast information. For example, www.podcastalley.com contains information about thousands of podcasts.
2. Browse or search the website for podcasts that interest you. Most provide tools that enable you to browse categories or podcasts or search for specific ones.
3. Click the **Subscribe** link for a podcast in which you are interested. You'll move to an information page that provides a URL for you to subscribe to the podcast (see Figure 20.9).

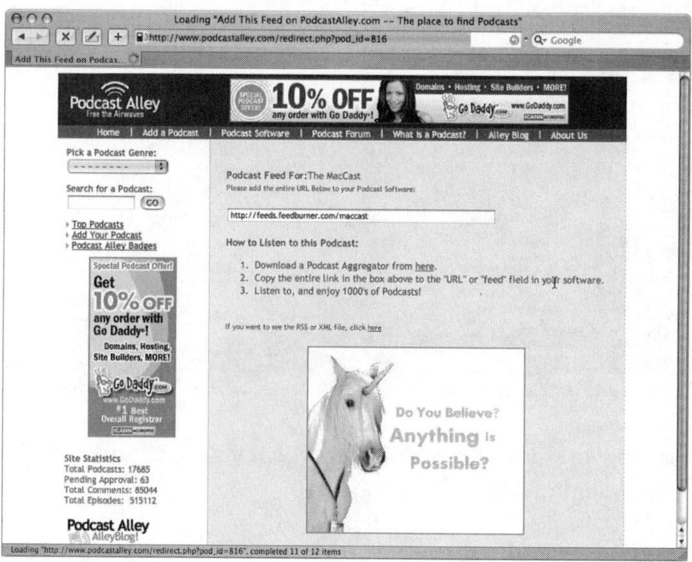

FIGURE 20.9
Here I am viewing the URL for a podcast called The MacCast.

4. Copy the URL that is displayed.
5. Move into iTunes.
6. Select **Advanced, Subscribe to Podcast**. You'll see the Subscribe to Podcast dialog box.
7. Paste the **URL** you copied in step 4 into the dialog box (see Figure 20.10).

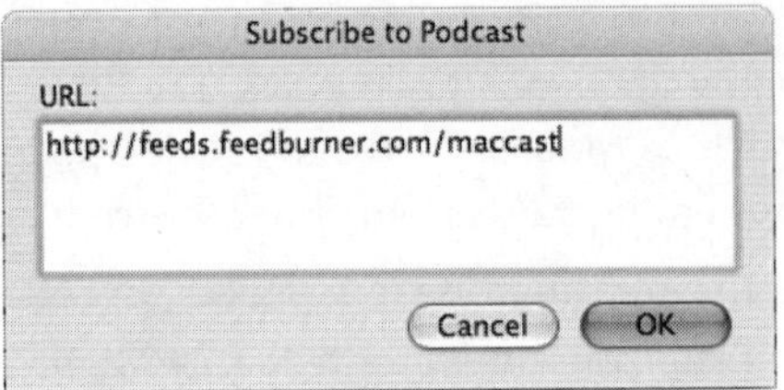

FIGURE 20.10
Paste the URL for a podcast into the Subscribe to Podcast dialog box to subscribe to that podcast.

8. Click **OK**. The dialog box will close and you'll move into the Podcasts source. You'll see the podcast to which you subscribed in the Content pane and its episodes will be downloaded to your computer (see Figure 20.11).

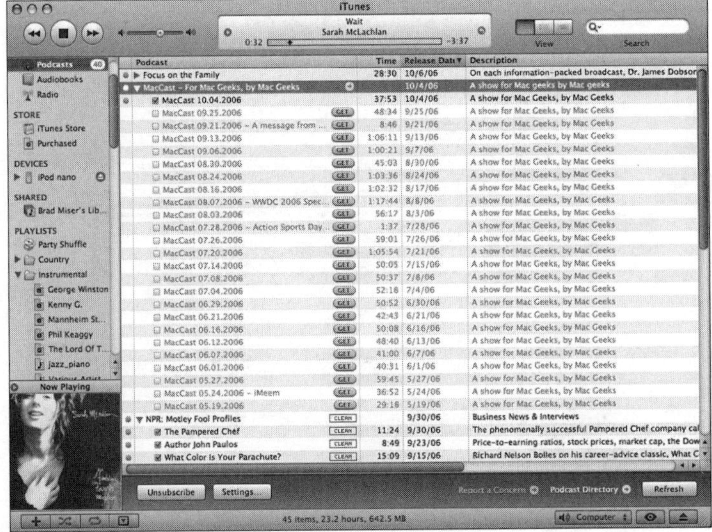

FIGURE 20.11
If you're a Mac geek, check out the MacCast podcast. (I admit it, I'm a geek.)

To learn how to work with podcasts to which you have subscribed, refer to "Listening to and Managing Podcasts" on page **340**.

Adding Podcasts You Download as Files to Your Library

Subscribing to podcasts is cool because after you've subscribed, you don't need to do anything to manage their content. Episodes are downloaded automatically according to your preferences (unless your preference is to manually download them, of course) and added to your Library so that you can access them quickly and easily.

Some podcasts, most notably those provided by national radio shows, don't work with the subscription model. Rather than subscribe to episodes so that iTunes handles the download process for you, you have to download individual episodes to your computer and manually add them to your Library.

To add this kind of podcast to your Library, perform the following steps:

1. Move to the website where the podcast is located.
2. If the podcast is provided for a fee, register an account on that site. After you've completed the registration process, you'll receive a username and password.
3. Locate the episode of the show that you want to download as a podcast.
4. Use your web browser to download the podcast, which will usually be provided as an MP3 file, to your computer (see Figure 20.12).

FIGURE 20.12
Most downloadable podcasts are provided as MP3 files.

5. Repeat steps 3 and 4 until you've downloaded all the podcast files to your computer.
6. Move into iTunes.
7. Choose **File**, **Add File to Library** (Windows) or **File**, **Add to Library** (Mac).
8. Use the resulting dialog box to move to and select the podcast files that you downloaded, and then click **Open** (Windows) or **Choose** (Mac). The files will be copied into your Library.
9. Select and play the podcast. You do this just as you do for other tracks in your Library.

tip

One way to make it easy to listen to a file-based podcast is to create a smart playlist with the podcast's artist as its search criteria. Make the playlist update live. Each time you add a podcast episode to your Library, it will be added to the playlist automatically.

Moving to a website to manually download podcasts is a pain. Fortunately, many of these sites provide applications that automate the download process for you. You can download and install their "download" application and set its preferences. It will then download the episodes of the podcast as they become available for you automatically. You'll still have to add them manually to your iTunes Library, but at least the download part of the process is automatic.

In the next section, you'll learn how to listen to and manage podcasts. However, the information in that section doesn't apply to podcasts not provided under the subscription model. You listen to podcasts provided as MP3 or other files just like music or other content you've manually added to your Library, such as tracks from a CD that you've imported. The Podcast source and other iTunes' podcast tools don't apply to these non-subscription podcasts.

For example, using the Podcast Keep preference, you can set iTunes to delete episodes automatically when you are finished listening to them or to set iTunes to keep only a specific number of episodes. When you download episodes and add them to your Library manually, there is no way iTunes can automatically delete the episodes after you've listened to them. You'll have to delete manually the episodes you no longer want to keep in your Library.

Listening to and Managing Podcasts

After you have subscribed to podcasts, you can listen to them in iTunes or on an iPod. You can also manage the podcasts to which you have subscribed.

To work with your podcasts, click **Podcasts** on the Source list. You'll see the podcasts to which you have subscribed in the Content pane (see Figure 20.13).

To perform various podcast actions, refer to the following list:

- To see all the episodes available for a podcast, click its **expansion triangle**. All the available episodes will be shown. The episodes that have been downloaded to your computer and to which you haven't listened will have a blue dot next to them. Those that you have downloaded and listened to do not have the blue dot. Those that haven't been downloaded yet will be grayed out, and the Get button will be shown.

note

Unlike other sources, you can't choose the column by which the Podcasts source is sorted; podcasts are listed in alphabetical order. Episodes of a podcast are always sorted by Release Date. You can change the sort order, however, so that episodes of podcasts are listed from oldest to newest or vice versa.

FIGURE 20.13
Use the Podcasts source to work with the podcasts to which you have subscribed.

- To download an episode, click its **Get** button. The episode will be downloaded to your computer. When that process is complete, it will be marked with a blue dot, and you will be able to listen to it. The Information area will present information about the download process.
- To play an episode of a podcast, select it and click the **Play** button. The other iTunes playback controls work similarly to how they do for other sources.
- To get information about an episode, click its **Information** button, which is located at the end of the description. You'll see the Podcast Information window that presents a summary of the episode (see Figure 20.14).
- To move to a website associated with a podcast or to the podcast in the iTunes Store, click the **Website** or **Store** button (the circle containing an arrow) in the Podcast column. If the podcast came from the iTunes Store, you'll move to its page in the Store. If it came from outside the iTunes Store, you'll move to the podcast's home page on the web.

tip

Remember that you control how many episodes are downloaded to your computer and saved automatically by using the Podcasts preferences you learned about earlier in this chapter.

FIGURE 20.14
Here I am viewing information for an episode of the MacCast podcast.

- Click the **Podcast Directory** link at the bottom of the Content pane to move to the Podcast home page in the iTunes Store.
- Set the Keep preference so that iTunes automatically keeps or deletes the episodes for each podcast. For example, choose the **All unplayed episodes** option so that iTunes automatically deletes episodes to which you have listened.

tip
You can click the Settings button to jump to the Podcasts pane of the iTunes Preferences dialog box.

- To delete an episode from your Library (whether it's been downloaded or not), select it and press the **Delete** key. If the file has been downloaded to your Library, click the **Move to Recycle Bin** (Windows) or **Move to Trash** (Mac) button to delete the podcast's files from your computer and from the Library or the **Keep Files** button to remove the podcast from your Library but leave its files on your computer.

- To unsubscribe from a podcast, select the podcast (not an individual episode) and click the **Unsubscribe** button. Episodes of the podcast will no longer be downloaded to your computer, although episodes that you have downloaded will remain in your Library, and you can listen to or delete them. You can subscribe again by clicking the Subscribe button that will appear next to the podcast to which you used to be subscribed. If you don't regularly listen to a podcast, you should unsubscribe from it so you aren't wasting disk space storing episodes to which you'll never listen.

tip

You should periodically review your Podcast preferences to ensure they match your current podcast habits, such as how you want episodes to be downloaded and kept.

- To remove a podcast from your Library, select it and press the **Delete** key. Click the **Move to Recycle Bin** (Windows) or **Move to Trash** (Mac) button to delete the podcast's files from your computer and from the Library or the **Keep Files** button to remove the podcast from your Library but leave its files on your computer.
- Click the **Refresh** button located in the bottom-right corner of the iTunes window to refresh the list of episodes available for each podcast to which you are subscribed. The podcast's episodes will be downloaded to your computer according to your Podcast preferences. And episodes will be removed based on your Keep preference. (For example, if you've elected to keep only unplayed episodes, all the episodes to which you've listened will be deleted.)
- If a podcast has an exclamation point icon next to it, that podcast has a problem, such as no content being available. If you want to report the problem, select the podcast and click the **Report a Concern** link, which is available only for podcasts that are in the iTunes Store. If the exclamation point appears next to an episode, but the Get button is enabled, there was a problem downloading that episode. Click the **Get** button to try to download it again.

THE ABSOLUTE MINIMUM

Podcasts are a great feature because they enable you to listen to and view a huge amount and variety of content. Much of this content is free, too. Here's a reminder of the podcast info you learned in this chapter:

- Podcasts are similar to radio or TV except that you can store episodes in your iTunes Library so you can listen to or view them from your computer at a time of your choosing or move them to an iPod so you can listen and watch on the go. iTunes includes all the tools you need to subscribe to, manage, and listen to any podcasts you can find.
- Set your podcast preferences so that iTunes manages your podcasts for you, such as keeping only episodes that you haven't listened to yet and deleting those you have heard or seen.
- You can subscribe to any of the thousands of podcasts available in the iTunes Store. (You don't need even need an account to subscribe to the free ones there.) It's easy to search or browse for podcasts on specific topics or from specific people or organizations.
- You can also subscribe to podcasts from websites that provide repositories of podcasts or from websites that actually produce the podcasts. This is only slightly harder than subscribing from the iTunes Store.
- Some podcasts are available only outside the iTunes subscription model. To access these, you have to download the episode files to your computer and add them to the Library manually. iTunes' Podcast tools don't work on these kind of podcasts, but its other tools do work on them just like other content in your Library. For example, you can add them to playlists just like tracks you've imported from a CD.
- Use the Podcasts source to manage all the podcasts to which you've subscribed. You can listen to or watch episodes, download them, and so on.

IN THIS CHAPTER

- Purchase and download video from the iTunes Store to build up your iTunes video Library.
- Add a digital video recorder to your computer so you can add any TV show to your Library.
- Rip DVD content to move it onto an iPod.
- Download video from the Internet so you can watch it on an iPod, too.
- Watch video within iTunes.
- Manage your iTunes video content like a pro.

21

WORKING WITH iTUNES VIDEO

iTunes isn't just for audio any more; you can also use iTunes to store and view video content. If you have an iPod capable of video display, you can move the video from your iTunes Library onto that iPod so you can watch it anywhere, anytime.

Working with video in iTunes isn't all that different from working with audio. The first step is to add video content to your Library. As soon as it's there, you can enjoy it within iTunes, and you can move it onto an iPod. You can also use iTunes to manage your video collection.

Adding Video to Your iTunes Library

Just like audio content, you need to get video into your iTunes Library to view it there or move it to an iPod. There are a number of ways to get video into your Library, including

- **Buying it from the iTunes Store**—This is the easiest method because you can add video to your Library with just a couple of mouse clicks. The video you purchase here is already in the format required for an iPod, too, so you don't need to be concerned about the details of the format. The primary downside is that the amount and variety of video content currently available in the iTunes Store is somewhat limited (when compared to what's on DVD, anyway), although both continue to increase rapidly. You can purchase movies, TV shows, music videos, and other content here.
- **Recoding video from an external source**—There are TiVo-like devices that you can connect to your computer that enable you to watch and record cable or other kinds of TV on your desktop. The software for the best of these devices will automatically export recorded content into your iTunes Library. This enables you to add easily any content available via your TV to iTunes and an iPod.
- **Converting DVD content**—This method provides you access to a huge amount of content, which is basically anything on DVD. However, you need to use an application that converts the DVD content into a format that iTunes (and an iPod) can use. This is usually a fairly time-consuming process, but some applications make it easy to choose the correct formats to use.
- **Downloading video from other sources**—Many websites enable you to download all sorts of video content. You can add this content to your Library and onto an iPod, with the caveat that the video has to be in the required format for iTunes and an iPod. Whether it is or not depends on the source from which you download the video. You can also subscribe to and download video podcasts from the iTunes Store (see Chapter 20, "Working with iTunes Video," for the details).

Although the end result—video in your iTunes Library and on your iPod—for each method is similar, each has pros and cons. Some are easier to do than others. Some involve learning new software. Some require hardware and software or just software. In the following sections, you'll get an overview of each method along with some examples of how that method works.

To set your expectations, it's time for a disclaimer/confession. Working with video to get it into iTunes can range from trivially easy (iTunes Store) to somewhat difficult (converting DVD content), depending on the specific tools you use. The disclaimer is that there are a large number of different hardware and software tools that you might end up using for these tasks. The confession is that there isn't room in this chapter to provide details about all or even many of these tools. What you will find is an explanation of each method, an overview of how it works, its pros and cons, tips on how to locate what you need, and an example. It is my hope that this information equips you to choose the methods you want to try and understand what you need to get started. If you need detailed help from there, you'll need to rely on the documentation provided with the hardware and software you choose to use.

Purchasing and Downloading Video from the iTunes Store

Along with music, audiobooks, and podcasts (audio and video), you'll find plenty of video content on the iTunes Store. This includes music videos, movie shorts, feature-length movies, and TV shows (by the episode or by the season) (see Figure 21.1).

FIGURE 21.1 The number of TV shows available in the iTunes Store continues to grow rapidly.

Adding video content from the iTunes Store is no different from adding music or audiobooks from it. With an iTunes Store account, you log into the store. When you find the content you want, you click on it to purchase and download it to your Library.

This method has three main benefits, including the following:

- **It's easy**—With a couple of mouse clicks, you can add video content to your Library. Because the video in the iTunes Store is already in the required formats, you can view it from iTunes or move it onto an iPod. No fuss or muss required.
- **It's inexpensive**—For example, most video content (except for movies) is $1.99, such as $1.99 per episode of a TV series (the cost is less per episode if

you buy an entire season's worth). Movies currently range from $9.99 to $14.99.

- **It's built in**—You don't need anything besides iTunes and an iTunes Store account.

There is one primary downside to this method, which is the somewhat limited amount and variety of video content available in the iTunes Store. Although it continues to grow rapidly, the amount of video in the store pales in comparison to what is available on DVD or on cable or satellite TV networks.

There is another potential drawback to video from the iTunes Store, which also happens to be one of its benefits. That is that it is already in the format the iPod requires. Although this makes moving it to an iPod simple, the format is a fairly low resolution in today's world of HD. This is fine for viewing in iTunes or on an iPod, but it's probably not so good if you want to put the content on a DVD and watch it on a large screen TV in the HD format. If you intend to use video content primarily outside of iTunes or an iPod, I don't recommend that you obtain it from the iTunes Store. Use one of the other methods instead so that you can convert the same source into the format that best matches how you are going to use it.

To learn how to purchase video content from the iTunes Store, see Part III, "The iTunes Store." In no time, you'll be building up the video side of your Library (see Figure 21.2).

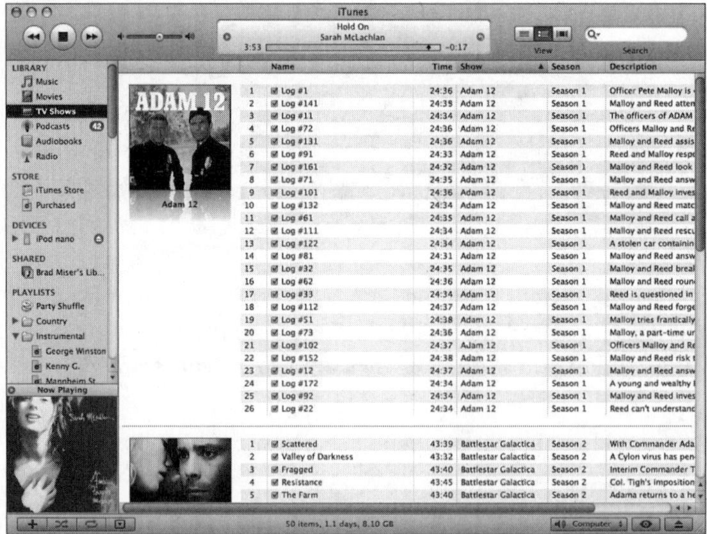

FIGURE 21.2
The classic police series *Adam-12* is available in the iTunes Store.

As soon as video from the iTunes Store is in your Library, you can use the information in "Using iTunes to Watch Video" on page **353** to watch it and "Managing Video in iTunes" on page **358** to work with it.

Recording Video from an External Source for Your Library

When you connect a digital video recorder (DVR) to your computer, you can watch TV from an antenna, cable, or satellite on your computer. That can be useful. Even better, you can also record programs in a digital format to play back at your convenience (during which you can avoid watching commercials, which is a very good thing). Many of these systems also enable you to export the shows you record in different formats. If this includes formats that are compatible with iTunes or iPods, you can move this content into your Library for viewing or for moving onto an iPod. This means that you can literally add anything you can view to your iTunes Library and then move it onto an iPod.

note

Some computers might have DVR capability built in when you purchase them. If so, you obviously don't need to buy additional hardware, which is also a good thing.

The general steps to get started are the following:

1. Purchase the DVR for your computer. The package will include hardware and software.
2. Connect the hardware to the source of the TV signal, such as cable or satellite, and to the appropriate input on your computer. Some DVRs are cards that you physically install inside the computer. Some are external boxes that you connect to your computer via USB or FireWire ports.
3. Install the DVR software on your computer.

After you install the hardware and software, you can record content and add it to your Library by following these general steps:

1. Choose the shows you want to record. Better systems include an online guide that shows you the schedules for all the channels to which you have access (see Figure 21.3).
2. Export the show you want to move to your Library in an iTunes/iPod compatible format. How you do this will depend on the specific software your system uses. The best systems will perform this step for you automatically or provide an iPod format option. For example, EyeTV includes an iPod option. When you select this for shows you record, the system automatically exports the recorded show in the iPod format and adds it to your iTunes Library.

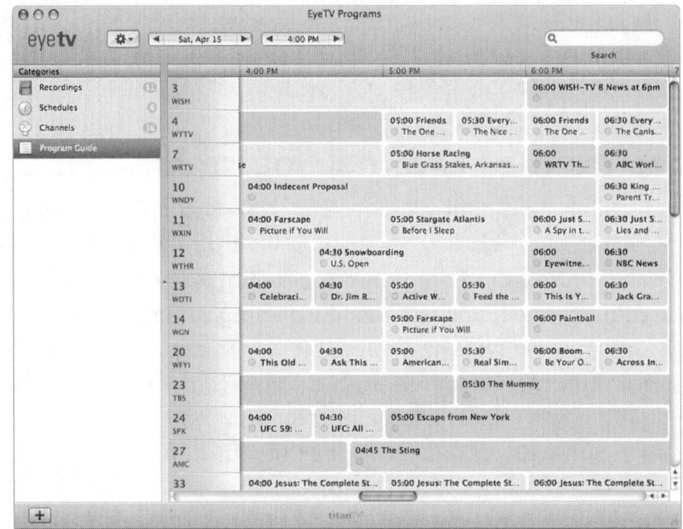

FIGURE 21.3 With EyeTV, you can click the **Record** button for any show on the schedule shown in its Program Guide to record it on your computer.

3. If the software for your DVR doesn't add the content it records to iTunes for you automatically, move into iTunes and use the **Add to Library** command to add the recorded content to your Library.

The main benefits of this approach include

- **Lots of content**—You can add any content you can watch to your iTunes Library. If you have cable or satellite TV, you probably have lots of channels from which to choose. You can record any of this content and add it your Library.
- **Low cost per show**—After you have purchased the hardware and software, you can add any show to your iTunes Library for free.
- **Can be easy to do**—This benefit depends on how well the system you use is designed and how well it works. The best systems make the process as simple as clicking a program's Record button. From that point, the system does the rest, from recording the show to exporting it in the iPod format to adding it to your iTunes Library.

Better DVR systems also enable you to schedule shows to record by show, time and channel, and so on.

The main drawback of this method is that unless the hardware and software were included with your computer, you have to purchase them. The least expensive systems cost about $100, but you should expect to pay more than this for a better-quality system.

Other drawbacks will depend on the system you end up using. Some work really well, whereas others don't. If you end up with a system that doesn't work so well, it can be a hassle to use, or it might not be able to export content in the format you need to view it on an iPod.

To find systems that are available for your computer, check with your favorite electronics retailer or perform a Google search for "recording tv for iPod" to start researching the devices available for your system.

After video you've recorded is in your Library, you can use the information in "Using iTunes to Watch Video" on page **353** to watch it and "Managing Video in iTunes" on page **358** to work with it.

Adding Video from a DVD to Your Library

Wouldn't it be nice if you could put movies and TV shows you already have on DVD on your iPod? The answer is yes. The good news is that this is possible to do. The bad news is that it requires a bit of work.

To do this, you need to convert the content of a DVD into the iTunes/iPod format and then add that content to your iTunes Library. Assuming your computer has a DVD drive, all you need is the software that will rip the DVD content into the format that you need for an iPod.

After you install the software on your computer, you can convert the DVD into the iPod format by following these general steps:

1. Insert the DVD you want to convert into your computer.
2. Launch the DVD ripping software.
3. Select the content on the DVD you want to convert.
4. Configure the conversion process, such as by choosing the iPod format.
5. Rip the content (see Figure 21.4). The result will be a file in an iPod-compatible format.
6. Use the iTunes **Add to Library** command to add the converted file to your Library.

Make sure you don't violate copyright laws when you convert DVDs for an iPod. You should only convert DVDs you actually own and should keep the files you create to yourself.

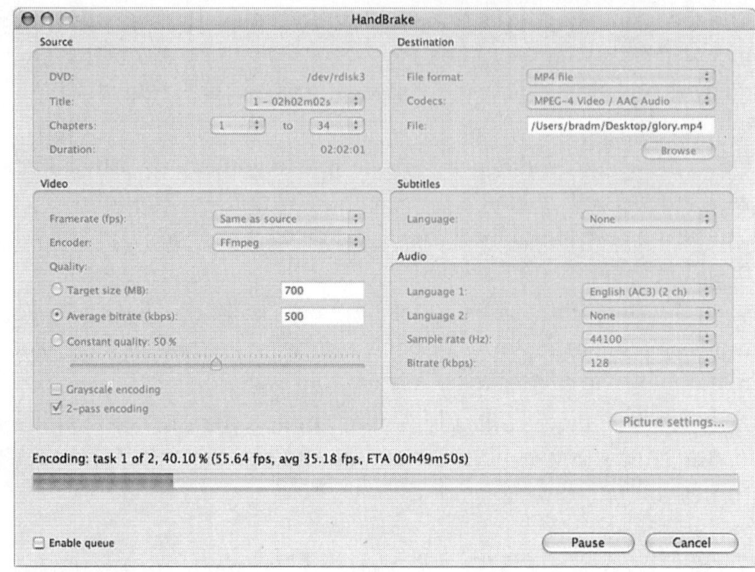

FIGURE 21.4
Here I'm converting the movie *Glory* into an iPod-compatible file by using the HandBrake application.

Converting DVD content for an iPod has several benefits, including the following:

- **Lots of content**—If you have it on DVD, you can add it your iTunes Library and move it to an iPod.
- **Can be easy**—Assuming the software you use is well designed, the conversion process is usually simple and requires just a few mouse clicks.
- **Inexpensive**—Many DVD ripping applications are freeware or are available for a low cost. After you have the software and DVD, there's no cost to convert DVD content into the iPod format.

This method really doesn't have significant downsides. There are two things you need to be aware of, though. One is that the conversion process usually takes a fairly long time to complete; however, because your computer does all the work, this isn't a big deal. The other is that converted movie files are large. If your system is low on disk space, you might not have room to store many converted files.

To find software for your system, perform a Google search for "convert dvds for iPod." You'll get lots of hits that you can explore to find software to try.

After you've added video that you've converted to your Library, you can use the information in "Using iTunes to Watch Video" on page **353** to watch it and "Managing Video in iTunes" on page **358** to work with it.

Downloading Video from Other Sources for Your Library

There are many places from which you can download video content on the Internet. Many are legit, many are not. Since the rise of the iPod Video, the number of sites that provide video content for them continues to grow. For example, some TV networks provide their shows so that you can download them and add them to your iTunes Library for free. The downside with some of these is that you can't avoid the commercials that come with them, so I'm not a fan of this, but you might want to check it out.

The general steps you use to download video and add it your Library are the following:

1. Move to the Internet site providing the video you want to download.
2. Download the video to your computer.
3. Convert the video into the iPod format if it isn't already in that format. You'll need an application that can do this conversion for you, such as Apple's QuickTime Pro.
4. Add the file you downloaded and converted to your iTunes Library.

It's impossible to describe pros and cons to this method because it all depends on which specific website you use and the formats and cost for the videos it provides. In an ideal case, the video content is free and is already available in the iPod format, so you just have to download it and add it your Library. In other cases, you'll need to pay for the downloads and then convert them into the format you need to put the content on an iPod.

After video you've downloaded is in your Library, you can use the information in "Using iTunes to Watch Video" on page **353** to watch it and "Managing Video in iTunes" on page **358** to work with it.

Using iTunes to Watch Videos

After you've added video content to your Library, you can use iTunes to watch the content you've added. But for the second time in this chapter, I need to confess. This time, I'm confessing that although being able to watch video in iTunes is okay, in most cases, the real reason you add video to your Library is to move it to an iPod so you can watch it wherever you use your iPod. If you don't want to move video to an iPod, there isn't really any need to move it into iTunes. That's because most of the methods described in this chapter to get

To learn how to move video in your iTunes Library to an iPod, see Chapter 10, "Using an iPod to Watch Video."

video into your Library also enable you to better watch that content outside of iTunes, without the work to add it to your Library. For example, if you aren't going to add a movie to an iPod, it's a lot easier to use your computer's DVD viewing application to watch it than it is to convert it for iTunes so you can watch it there.

That said (or more literally, written), there are two reasons you might want to watch video in iTunes. One is that you download video from the iTunes Store, such as episodes of a TV show. Because this is fast, easy, and inexpensive to do, watching that content in iTunes can be useful. The other reason you might want to watch video in iTunes is to preview it before you move it to an iPod.

You can choose how video content plays in iTunes. The options are in a separate video window, full screen, or in the Video Viewer pane. Because you'll probably want to use the full screen option most of the time, set that as your preference. Open the iTunes Preferences dialog box and click the **General** tab. On the Play videos drop-down list, choose **full screen**. Click **OK**. When you play video content, it will fill your computer's screen. (If you have more than one display attached to your computer, the video will fill the screen on which iTunes is located.)

If you choose **in a separate window**, when you play video content, a new window will appear, and you can watch the content there. If you choose **in the main window**, video content will play in the Video Viewer pane (also known as the Album Artwork pane).

The remainder of this section assumes you have selected the full screen option. Watching video using one of the other options is similar.

To watch video in iTunes, perform the following steps:

1. Select the source of the video you want to watch on the Source list, such as **Movies** or **TV Shows** (see Figure 21.5).
2. Choose the view in which you want to browse your video content; these are the same three views that you can use with the Music source. (The Cover Flow view is shown in Figure 21.5, whereas the Grouped view is shown in Figure 21.6.)
3. No matter which view you choose (even the somewhat plain List view), use the **Browsing tools** to browse for video you want to watch or use the **Search tools** to search for it. These work in the same way as they do for music.

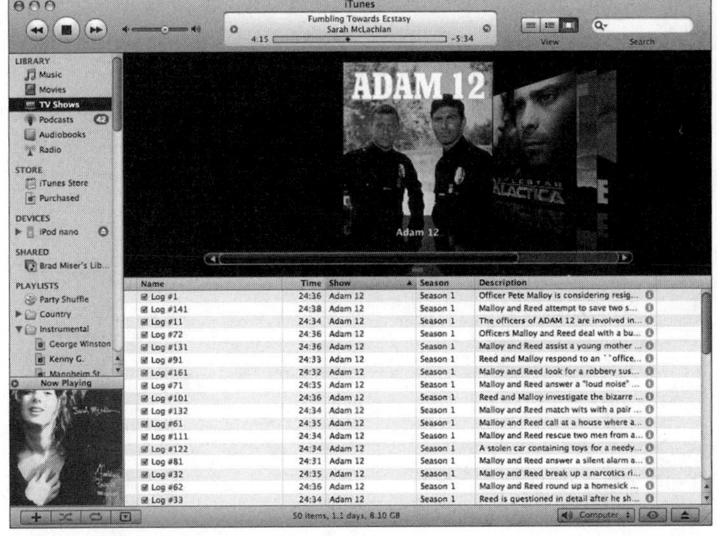

FIGURE 21.5 When you select the TV Shows source, you'll see all the TV show content in your Library.

FIGURE 21.6 You can also view your video content in the Grouped view.

4. When you find a video you want to watch, select it. It will appear in the Album Artwork/Video Viewer pane if Selected Item is set in that pane (see Figure 21.7).
5. Click **Play** or press the **Spacebar**. iTunes and other windows open on your computer will be replaced with the video content as it starts to play (see Figure 21.8). (If you select one of the other viewing options, the video will appear according to the option you set, such as in a separate window.)

FIGURE 21.7
Here, I've selected an episode of the excellent *Battlestar Galactica* series that I purchased from the iTunes Store.

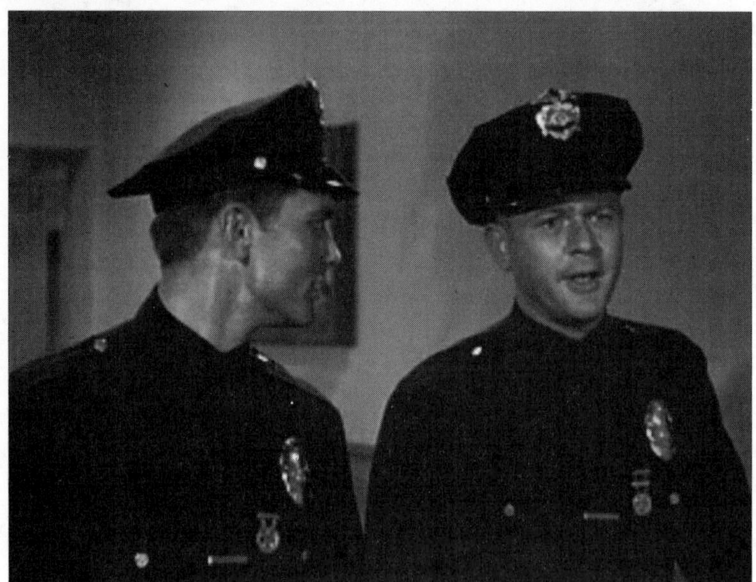

FIGURE 21.8
When you view video content in the full screen mode, it fills your screen.

6. When you want to control the video, move your mouse. This will cause the control bar to appear (see Figure 21.9).
7. Use the playback controls in the control bar to control the video, such as to fast forward, rewind, and so on. These work as you probably expect them to. For example, to increase the volume, move the Volume slider to the right. To fast forward, click and hold on the Fast forward button.

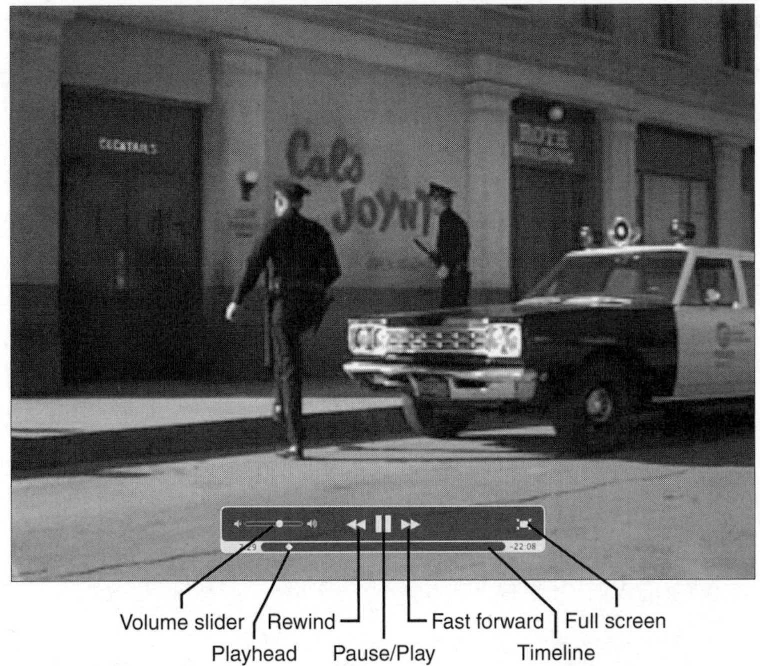

FIGURE 21.9
When you move your mouse, the iTunes control bar appears.

As video plays, the Playhead moves along the Timeline. You can jump to any point in the video by dragging the Playhead to the position you want.

The Full screen button behaves differently, depending on the view in which you are. When you are watching video in the Full screen mode, clicking this button turns off Full screen mode, which stops the video from playing and returns you to the iTunes window. To play video again, click the Play button, and you go right back to where you left off.

> **tip**
>
> In any view, you can drag the control bar around the screen to change its location. When you use the separate window view, you can drag the video window's Resize handle (located in the lower-right corner of the window) to change its size.

If you use the Separate window option, clicking this button moves you into the Full screen mode. Clicking it again returns you to the video window, and the video will continue to play.

8. To stop the video playback and return to iTunes, click the **Full screen** button or press the **Esc** key. (If you are using the separate window option, just close the window.)

Managing Video in iTunes

Managing the video content in your iTunes Library isn't that different from managing the other content you have there. Consider the following pointers:

- You can add videos to audio playlists and vice versa, although iTunes will warn you when you do this.
- Just as with audio content, you can use the Info window to change the tags associated with video. You access the Info window in the same ways that you do for music content.
- Video content is classified as Movie, TV Show, or Music Video. This classification determines which source contains the video. You can change how a video is classified by selecting the video, opening the Info window, and clicking the Video pane. Use the **Video Kind** menu to choose the classification. (You won't be able to change the classification of video you get from the iTunes Store.) If the video is from a TV show, you can also include tags for the show's name, season number, episode name, and episode number. When you are finished making changes, click **OK**.

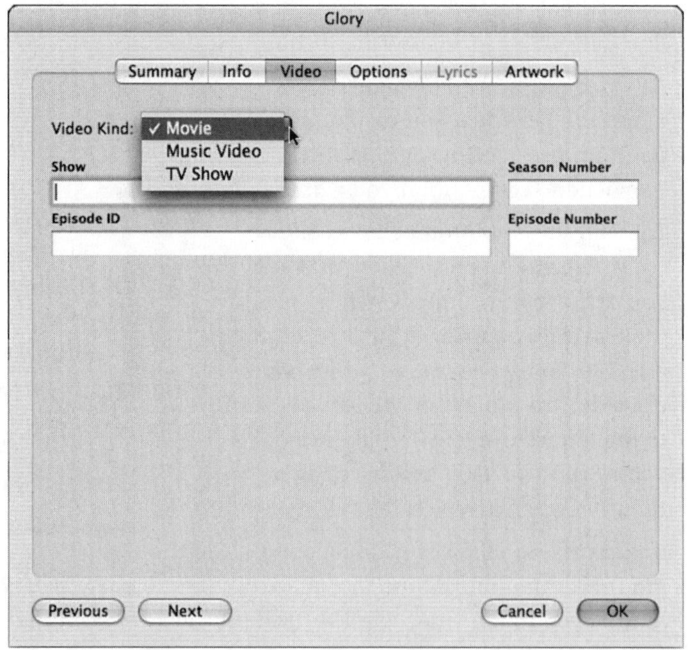

FIGURE 21.10
Here, I've selected an episode of the excellent *Battlestar Galactica* series that I purchased from the iTunes Store.

- Video files are large. For example, a 1-hour (about 45 minutes of playing time without commercials) show you purchase from the iTunes Store will be about 200MB. If you add video content that you won't want after seeing it once, delete it from your Library to recover the disk space it consumes. Make sure you don't delete content you've purchased from the iTunes Store unless you are very, very sure you won't want it again. You can download video you purchase from the iTunes Store only one time. You'd have to pay for it again to download it again. (You should back up any content you purchase from the iTunes Store, as you'll learn later in this part of the book.)

The Absolute Minimum

Because it does a lot more than music, I wonder if Apple will rename iTunes to be iMedia someday? That would make more sense because as iTunes has continued to evolve, its capabilities have gotten better and better. As you've seen in this chapter, you can add video content to iTunes to watch it there, and, more importantly, move it onto a video-capable iPod. Here's a recap of the most important points:

- The first step in working with video in iTunes is adding video content to your iTunes Library.
- The fastest and easiest way to add video is to purchase it from the iTunes Store. There, you'll find lots of TV shows, movies, and music videos you can purchase and download. In addition to being relatively inexpensive (for example, it's $1.99 per video or less if you buy a full season of a show), videos you purchase here are ready for an iPod.
- Using a DVR, you can record broadcast, cable, or satellite TV and add that content to your iTunes Library. You'll need hardware and software to record the video and convert it into the correct format, but by using this method, you can add any cable or satellite content to your Library and an iPod.
- Using a DVD ripping application (it isn't as painful as it sounds), you can convert movies and TV shows you have on DVD into an iTunes/iPod compatible format and add them to your Library.
- You can also download video content from the Internet to add to your Library. How easy/hard or cheap/expensive this is depends on the specific site from which you download video.
- After you've added content to your iTunes Library, you can watch it in iTunes in the Video Viewer pane, a separate video window, or in Full screen mode.
- You can use almost all the iTunes tools you're learning about in this part of the book to manage video in your Library. One of the great things about iTunes is that it works similarly with different kinds of content, including music and video.

IN THIS CHAPTER

- Know the three disc formats that you can burn.
- Prepare your computer to burn.
- Burn, baby, burn.
- Make that disc look simply marvelous.

22

BURNING YOUR OWN CDs OR DVDs

When you are at your computer, you'll likely use iTunes to listen to your music or other audio because you can easily get to the specific content to which you want to listen, such as by using your Library, creating standard playlists and smart playlists, and so on. When you are on the move, you'll probably use your iPod to listen to your tunes or watch video content such as TV shows. At other times, you might want to put music on a CD to take with you, such as when you are traveling in a car equipped with a standard CD player. And, you definitely should back up your music, video, and other content on CDs or DVDs to keep your collection safe. Using iTunes, you can quickly and easily burn the CDs or DVDs you need.

Understanding the Types of Discs You Can Burn

You can burn several types of disc formats with iTunes, and each of these formats is useful for specific purposes. With iTunes, you can burn the following types of discs:

- **Audio CD**—When you burn a CD in this format, you can play it in any CD player, such as the one in your car, a boombox, or a home theater. And that is the primary benefit of this format: CD players are ubiquitous, so you can play audio CDs you create with iTunes just about anywhere.
- **MP3 CD**—You can place your audio content on a CD in the MP3 format and then play those discs in any player that can handle MP3 music. Many newer CD players for cars and home theater systems can play MP3 CDs, so this is a good thing. The benefit of using the MP3 format is just what you might think it is: You can put about three times as much music on a single disc as you can with a disc that uses the Audio CD format.
- **Data CD or DVD**—This format is the same that's used to store audio and video files on your computer's hard drive. In fact, when you choose this format, you simply replicate the files in your iTunes Library as they are on your computer on a CD or DVD disc. The primary purpose of this format is to back up your Library's content to protect it from loss should something go horribly wrong with your computer. You can also use data discs you create to move content from one computer to another.

note There's actually a fourth type of disc you can burn, which is a backup disc. This just might be the most important type of all. You'll learn about this type in Chapter 24, "Maintaining iTunes and Solving Problems."

Getting Your Computer Ready to Burn

To burn CDs or DVDs, your computer must have a drive capable of writing to CD or DVD. Fortunately, almost all newer computers include a CD-RW (CD-Rewritable) drive you can use to burn CDs. Most also include a DVD-R, DVD-RW, DVD+R, or DVD+RW drive you can use to create DVDs.

To determine whether your computer is ready to burn, open the iTunes Preferences dialog box, click the **Advanced** tab, and then click the Burning sub-tab (see Figures 22.1 and 22.2). At the top of this pane, you'll see the text `CD Burner`. If iTunes can find one or more drives capable of burning CDs or DVDs, they will be shown here. If iTunes does recognize at least one drive that is capable of burning discs, you are good to go and can proceed to the next section.

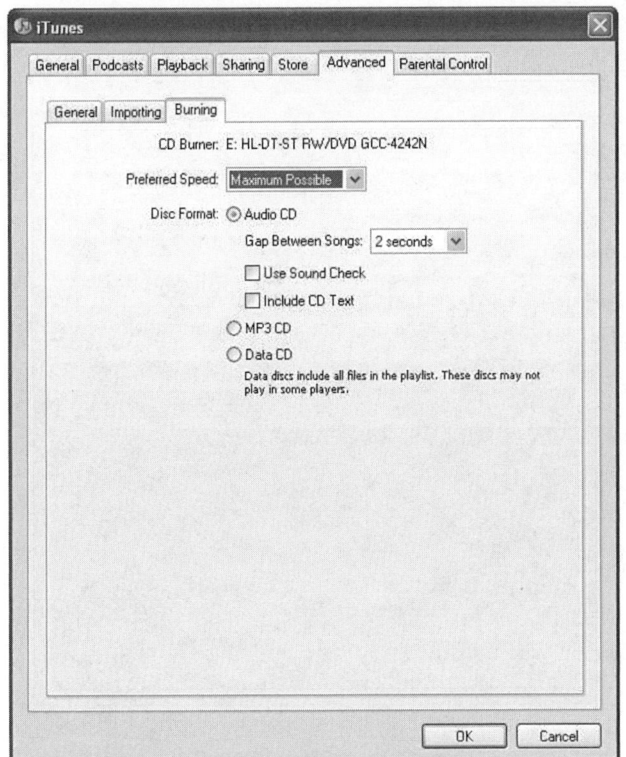

FIGURE 22.1 This Windows computer has a CD burner that is ready to go.

If a drive is not shown on this pane, there are two possibilities. One is that a capable drive is installed but is not functioning correctly, so it's not recognized by iTunes. The other is that your computer doesn't have a capable drive.

If your computer does have a drive capable of writing to a disc but it is not recognized by iTunes, it is likely that your drive is not working. You'll have to use troubleshooting techniques to repair and configure the drive to get it working again. I don't have room in this book to cover this topic because it can be complicated. If you don't know how to do this or you don't know someone who does, you can consult one of the many books available on this topic to help you get the drive working properly.

Selecting and installing a writable CD or DVD drive in your computer is beyond the scope of this book. If your computer doesn't have at least a writable CD drive, it is likely a fairly old machine because these drives have been standard on most computers for several years. Most current machines include a writable DVD drive, too. If you don't want to purchase a new computer that includes a writable drive, you can purchase an external or internal CD or DVD drive and use it with your computer fairly easily.

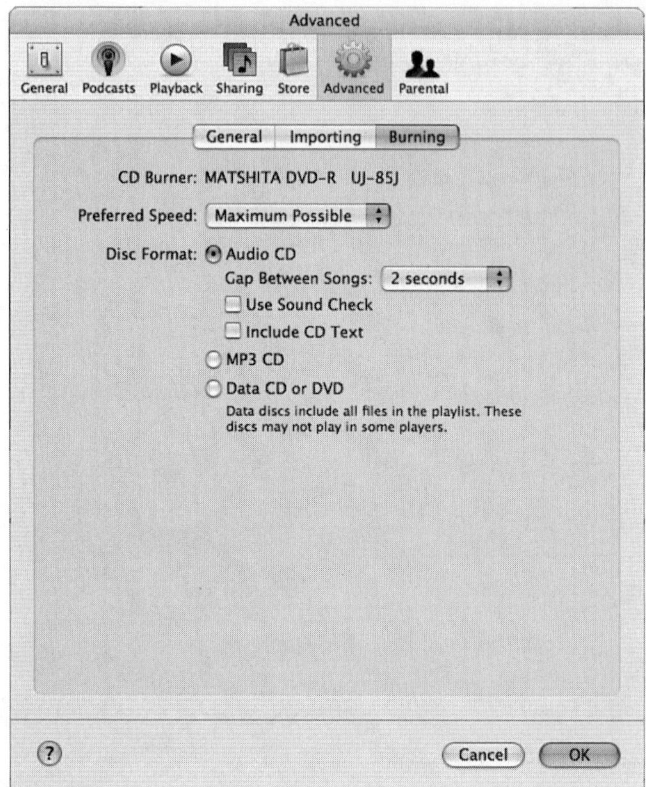

FIGURE 22.2
This Macintosh includes a SuperDrive that can be used to burn CDs or DVDs.

Burning Discs

Burning a disc from iTunes is quite straightforward, as you will see from the information in this section.

Preparing Content to Burn

The first phase in the process is to choose the content you want to place onto a disc. You do this by creating a playlist. In Chapter 19, "Creating, Configuring, and Using Playlists," you learned everything you need to know about creating and using playlists, so I don't need to repeat that information here.

One thing you need to keep in mind as you create a playlist for CD or DVD is the size of the playlist. Obviously, you can't put more music on a CD or DVD than there is room to store files on the disc. How large a playlist can be to be put on a disc depends on the format you will be using. If you are burning an Audio CD, you can get about 70 minutes of music on the disc. If you are creating an MP3 disc, you can store about 210 minutes on a disc. If you are creating a data CD, you can store about 750MB of data per disc. On a data DVD disc, you can store at least 5.2GB of files in the single-sided format.

When you are creating an audio CD, use the play time to judge the size of the playlist; keep it to 70 minutes plus or minus a couple minutes. For the other formats, use file size. (For example, a CD can typically hold 750MB of data.)

tip

If you click once on the time displayed in the Source Information area, you'll see the exact time to the second instead of the rounded-off time. Click again to return to the rounded-off time.

These are estimates because the actual amount you can store on a disc will depend on the specific type of drive and disc media you use. For example, if you use a system (drive and discs) that supports dual-layer DVDs, you'll be able to store between 8 and 10GB per disc.

In any case, use the Source Information area to check the playlist to make sure it will fit on the type of disc you are going to create (see Figure 22.3).

FIGURE 22.3
This playlist contains 1.1 hours of music, which will be just right for a CD in the Audio CD format.

The name of the playlist will become the name of the CD or DVD, so if you don't want the current playlist name to be used, change it to be what you do want the disc to be called. (To do this, click the playlist name once and pause. It will be highlighted to show you can change it. Type the new name and press **Return** or **Enter**.)

Preparing for a Burn Session

Next, configure the burn session, during which you will create a disc by opening the **Advanced** pane of the iTunes Preferences dialog box and then clicking the **Burning** subtab. Choose the format you want to use for the burning session by clicking the appropriate radio button (see Figure 22.4).

If you choose Audio CD, there are three options you can configure. One is the gap between songs, which you choose by making a selection on the **Gap Between Songs** menu. Your options are none, which causes one song to begin immediately after the previous one ends;
1 second, which places 1 second of silence between tracks; 2 seconds, which places 2 seconds of silence between songs; and so on, up to 5 seconds.

The exact amount of music you can fit on a disc depends on your drive and the discs you use. The best way to figure out a maximum limit is to experiment until you find the upper limit for your system and the discs you use. Fortunately, iTunes will help you by telling you when you have selected more than will fit on a disc.

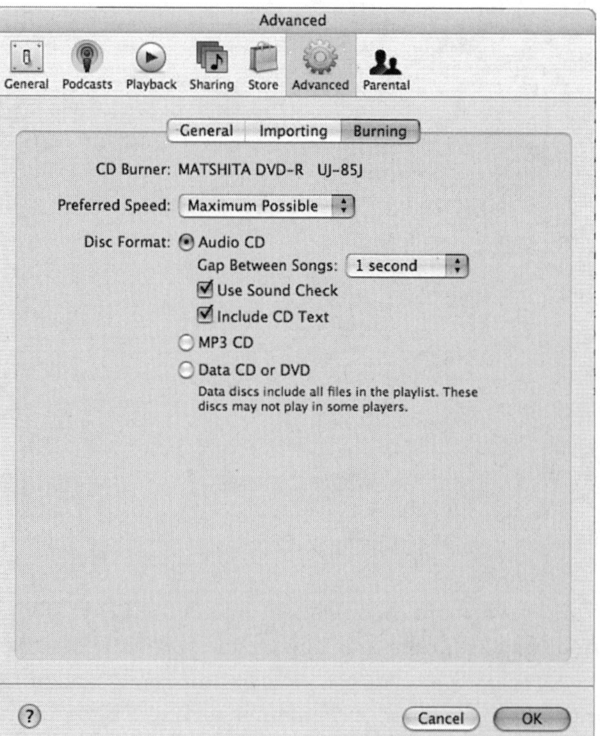

FIGURE 22.4
Because the Audio CD radio button is selected, the next CD will be burned in that format.

The second option is the **Use Sound Check** box. If you check this box, iTunes applies its Sound Check feature to the music it places on a disc. (If you don't remember from earlier in the book, this feature causes iTunes to attempt to set the relative volume of the songs you play to the same level.)

The third option is the **Include CD Text** check box. This causes iTunes to place CD text on the CD when it is burned. This text can be displayed on some CD players when you listen to the CDs you create.

To select either the MP3 CD or the Data CD or DVD format, click the appropriate radio button. There are no additional options to configure with either of these formats.

Click **OK** to close the iTunes Preferences dialog box and prepare the burn session.

If you are going to burn a disc in the MP3 CD format, you must make sure all the music in the playlist you want to put on disc is in the MP3 format before you can burn the MP3 CD disc. If you are going to create a disc in one of the other formats, you can skip the rest of this section.

To convert songs into the MP3 format, perform the following steps:

1. Open the **Importing** subtab of the Advanced pane of the iTunes Preferences dialog box.
2. Select **MP3 Encoder** on the Import Using menu.
3. Click **OK** to close the dialog box.
4. Select the songs you want to convert and right-click (multiple-button mouse) or Ctrl-click (single-button mouse) them to open their contextual menus.
5. Select **Convert Selection to MP3**.

tip

If you are putting live music on a disc, be sure you select none on the Gap Between Songs menu. Otherwise, the roar of the crowd will be interrupted by the silent gaps, which causes the live feeling to be lost.

caution

Burning an MP3 disc is the most difficult option because all the music in the playlist must be capable of being converted to the MP3 format before it can be placed on a disc. If music is in the protected AAC format, such as music you purchase from the iTunes Store, you can't put it directly on an MP3 disc because you can't directly convert it into the MP3 format. You can burn that music to a disc in the Audio CD format and then reimport that music in the MP3 format into your iTunes Library. Then you can place the MP3 versions of the songs in the playlist you are going to burn. But, that is a lot of trouble to go through just to create a disc. And, don't do this if your use of the MP3 versions will violate the license to which you agreed when you purchased the music.

Copies of the songs you selected will be made in the MP3 format.

6. Find the MP3 versions of the songs you selected in step 4. Use the Kind information to do this; look for those songs with MPEG audio file as their Kind.
7. Place the MP3 versions of the songs in the playlist you are going to put on an MP3 CD.

> **tip**
>
> You can also select songs and select **Advanced**, **Convert Selection to MP3** to accomplish the same thing.

Burning a Disc

After you have selected the content and prepared the burning session, actually burning the disc is rather anticlimactic. You burn a disc with the following steps:

1. Select the playlist you want to burn to a disc.
2. Click the **Burn Disc** button. iTunes will prompt you to insert a blank disc; if your computer has a disc tray, it will open (see Figure 22.5). If your computer uses a tray-loading drive, the tray will open so you can insert a disc.
3. Insert the appropriate **disc** into the drive. If you selected the Audio CD or MP3 CD format, use a CD. If you selected the Data format, use a CD or DVD. iTunes will check the disc you inserted. If everything is ready to go, the disc burning process will start.

   Depending on the type of disc you are attempting to burn, iTunes might present a dialog box asking you to confirm what you are asking it to do (such as when you burn a data DVD). Click **OK** to confirm and enable iTunes to proceed.

   If the disc can't be burned for some reason, such as there being too much in the selected playlist to fit onto the type of disc being burned, iTunes will let you know what is wrong. You'll have to correct the situation before you can complete the burn. In the case of your selecting too much music for the selected disc format, you'll have the option to burn the playlist on multiple discs.

   iTunes will start the burn process and display information about the process in the Information window (see Figure 22.6).

> **tip**
>
> You can add the Kind column to the Content pane by using the **View**, **View Options** command to make finding the MP3 versions easier.

FIGURE 22.5
iTunes is ready to burn.

FIGURE 22.6
The selected playlist is being burned onto an audio CD.

If you are burning across multiple discs, iTunes will eject discs as they become full and prompt you to insert new ones.

When the process is complete, iTunes will play a tone to let you know. The disc you just burned will appear on the Source list and will be selected (see Figure 22.7).

tip
To stop the burn before it completes, click the **Stop** button. If you do this, the disc you are trying to burn might be ruined.

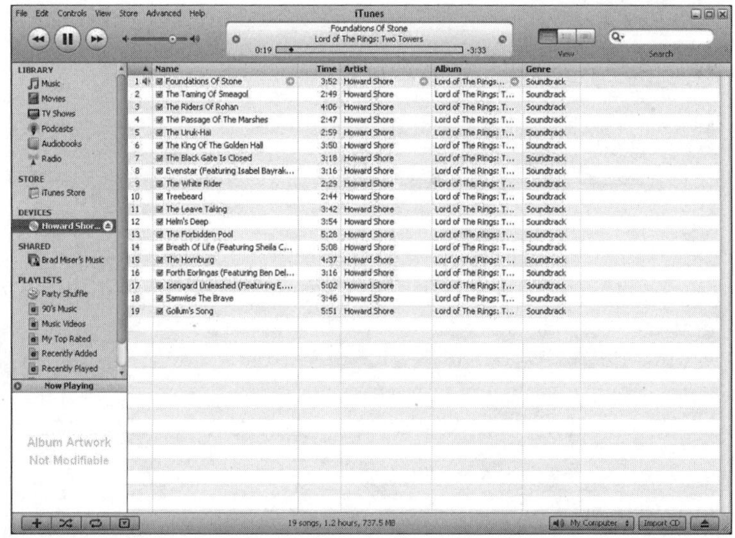

FIGURE 22.7

I can play this audio CD I created in iTunes in any old CD player, such as the one in my car.

4. To eject the disc, click the **Eject** button. You can then use the disc you created in any player or drive that is compatible with its format.

Labeling Your Discs

Now that you can create your own CDs and DVDs, you will probably want to make labels for them to keep them organized and make them look cool. The good news is that iTunes can do some of this for you. The bad news is that it can't do all of it.

Printing Disc Labels

Unfortunately, iTunes can't help you print disc labels—yet. I hope this capability will be added in a future version. For now, if you want to label your discs, you'll need to use a different application. You can use just about any graphics application to create a CD or DVD label; you can also use a word processor to do so. However, to make the process easier and the results better, consider investing in a dedicated disc label creator. If you use a Windows computer, many labeling applications are available, such as AudioLabel CD Labeler. If you use a Mac or a Windows computer, Discus will enable you to create just about any disc label you can imagine (see Figure 22.8).

To print labels, you'll also need a printer and CD labels to print on. For the best results, you should use a color printer, but black-and-white labels can look stylish, too.

Most CD labeling applications contain templates for specific labels (identified by brand and label number) you purchase. If you choose the right template for the labels you use, the labels you print will be exactly the same as the labels you design.

caution

Any audio or video content you purchase from the iTunes Store should be backed up in at least one way, such as on a CD or DVD. You can download audio or video from the iTunes Store only once. If something happens to that content on your computer so it becomes unusable (such as with a hard drive problem), you will have to pay for it again to be able to download it again. To protect your investment, create a CD or DVD of all the audio and video you purchase. For example, you can burn the Purchased playlist on disc. If something should happen to your computer, you can restore your purchased audio and video from the backup disc. If you don't do this, it can be a costly mistake. In Chapter 24, you'll learn how to use the iTunes backup function to do this quite easily.

To get more information about AudioLabel CD Labeler, go to www.audiolabel.com. To get more information about Discus, visit www.magicmouse.com.

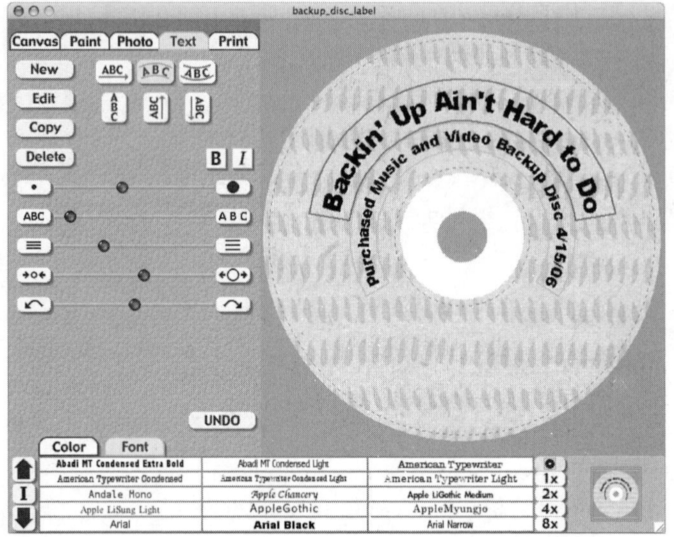

FIGURE 22.8

Discus is a good tool to create disc labels if you use a Macintosh or a Windows computer.

Printing Disc Inserts

Although iTunes can't help you with disc labels, it can help you create cool disc inserts so you can label the jewel case in which you store your discs.

For best results, associate artwork with the songs you put on a disc. (As you learned in Chapter 18, "Labeling, Categorizing, and Configuring Your Music," iTunes can do this for you automatically most of the time.) When you create and print a disc insert, the artwork associated with the songs on the disc will become part of the insert. Refer to Chapter 18 to learn how to do this manually if necessary.

tip

For the ultimate disc labels, consider purchasing a disc burner that can print directly on a disc or etch label information onto the disc's surface. An example of the latter is the LaCie LightScribe external DVD-RW drive.

To create a disc insert, perform the following steps:

1. Select the playlist or other source for which you want to create a disc insert; obviously, this should be the same one you used to burn the disc you are labeling.
2. Select File, Print. You'll see the Print "*source*" dialog box, where *source* is the name of the playlist or other source you selected in step 1 (see Figure 22.9).

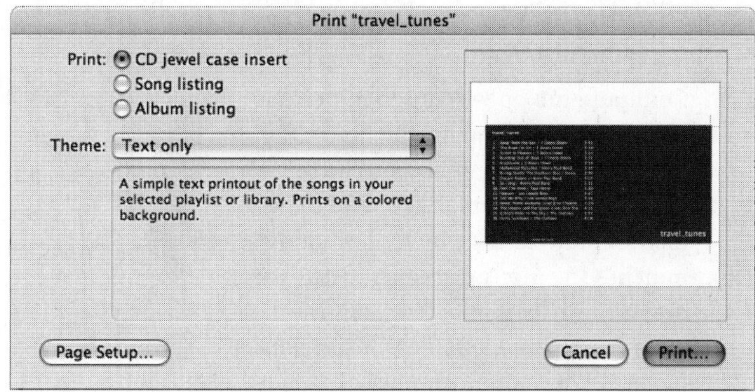

FIGURE 22.9
Use the Print dialog box to choose the type of jewel case insert you want to print.

3. Click the **CD jewel case insert** radio button.
4. Use the **Theme** pop-up menu to select the type of insert you want to print. Some of the more useful options are explained in the following list:
   - **Text only**—This prints a listing of the songs on the disc on the back of the insert over a colored background.
   - **Mosaic**—This prints a collage of the artwork associated with songs in the playlist on the front and a list of the songs on the back. This is a color insert.
   - **White Mosaic**—This is similar to Mosaic, except it prints on a white background.
   - **Single cover**—This places a single graphic on the front; the graphic of the currently selected song is used, or if no song is selected the artwork for the first song on the playlist is used instead. It also includes a list of songs on the back.
   - **Large playlist (Black & White)**—It doesn't include any artwork, but it does place the list of songs on the front and back of the insert. As you can tell by its name, it is intended for large playlists that have too many songs to be listed on the back of the other insert types.
   - **Black & White versions**—These exist for some of the color types in case you don't use a color printer or like the look of black-and-white inserts.

If you choose a mosaic label and the songs included in the playlist have only a single piece of artwork (such as if they are all from the same album), that graphic will fill the front of the insert.

5. Click **Page Setup**. You'll see the Page Setup dialog box.
6. Configure the page setup to match the paper you are using for the insert. If you are using paper designed specifically for this purpose, you might have to experiment a bit to know which selection best matches the insert paper on which you are printing. Unfortunately, iTunes doesn't support specific CD insert paper by brand and insert number as a dedicated disc label application does. Maybe in a future version....
7. When you have configured the page setup, click **OK**. You'll move back to the Print dialog box.

> **tip**
>
> Even though iTunes doesn't natively support specific brands and "models" of jewel case covers, you can use the custom option in most print dialog boxes to create and save the specific settings for the jewel case covers you use. It's a pain to set up the first time, but each time thereafter, you only have to select the custom setting you created.

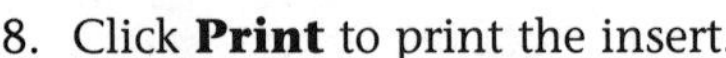

8. Click **Print** to print the insert.
9. Cut or tear out the insert and place it in the jewel case. Prepare to be impressed!

Printing Song and Album Listings

In some cases, you might not want to use a disc insert; instead, you might want to create just a listing of songs on playlists or even in your entire Library. iTunes can help you do this easily. Here's how:

1. Select the source for which you want to print a listing.
2. Select **File**, **Print**. You'll see the Print "*source*" dialog box, where *source* is the name of the source you selected in step 1.
3. Click the **Song listing** radio button to print a listing of songs in the selected source or the **Album listing** radio button to print songs grouped by their albums.
4. If you selected the Song listing option, select the theme for the list on the Theme drop-down list. The options are the following:
   - **Songs**—Prints the song name, length, artist, and album.
   - **User Ratings**—Adds your rating to the data in the Songs option.
   - **Dates played**—Includes all the information in the Songs option, plus the play count and date.

- **Custom**—Prints the data shown in the current view of the selected source. You can change the data included in the list by changing the View options for the source. (If you don't remember how to do this, refer to Chapter 18.)

tip
When you use the Album listing option, any artwork associated with an album appears on the list.

5. If you selected the Album listing option, select the theme for the list on the Theme drop-down list. The options are the following:
   - **Songs by album**—Prints the list with songs grouped by album.
   - **List of albums**—Prints the contents of the source, grouped by artist and album; it doesn't include the songs on each album.
6. Click **Print**. The listing will be printed to the printer you have selected (see Figure 22.10).

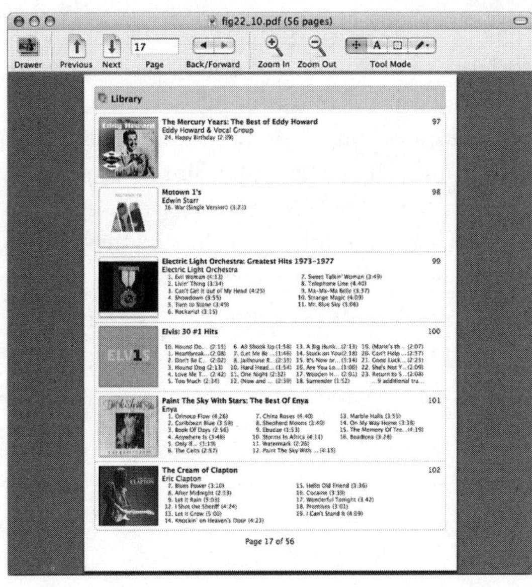

FIGURE 22.10
Printing song or album lists is useful to keep track of the content you have; in this case, I printed the album listing for My Library.

THE ABSOLUTE MINIMUM

Burning a CD or DVD is useful when you want to listen to music apart from iTunes or your iPod or to back up your iTunes media on disc. It is a relatively simple process, as you have seen in this chapter. As you burn, keep the following points in mind:

- There are three types of discs you can burn with iTunes: Audio CD, MP3 CD, and data CD or DVD discs.
- To prepare your computer to burn discs, you use the Burning subtab of the Advanced pane of the iTunes Preferences dialog box to check that you have a compatible drive.
- To burn a disc, create or select a playlist (even the special ones, such as Purchased) containing the content you want to put on disc, configure the settings for the burn session, and then burn the disc.
- The format for a burn session must be compatible with the format of the music you are using. The most likely case that might cause you problems is when you attempt to burn a CD in the MP3 format but the music you are attempting to place on a disc is in the AAC format (such as what you purchase from the iTunes Store). In this case, iTunes can't burn the disc because you are trying to place music that is in the AAC format on an MP3 disc. These are different and incompatible formats. If this happens, use the Audio CD or Data CD format instead. Or, if you simply must put AAC music on an MP3 disc, convert the music into the MP3 format before you try to burn the disc. (You'll have to burn it to an Audio CD and then reimport it in the MP3 format.)
- Although iTunes can't help you print disc labels, it does a great job with jewel case inserts and album or song lists.

IN THIS CHAPTER

- Learn how iTunes can share with other computers on a network and on multiple user accounts on one computer.
- Get generous and share your iTunes Library with others.
- Listen to and watch content other people share with you.
- Share your audio content over the air with AirTunes and an AirPort Express Base Station.

23

SHARING ITUNES

With such a great collection of content in your iTunes Library, I'm sure you don't want to keep this good stuff to yourself. So be generous and share the contents of your iTunes Library with others. And, enjoy content that is shared with you.

If two or more computers are connected via a local network—and with the broad use of high-speed Internet connections, networks are becoming common even in homes these days—you can share your iTunes Library with other people on your network. They can listen to music and watch video almost as if it were stored in their own Libraries. Of course, assuming other folks on your network are also generous, you can listen to and watch content they share with you as well.

If you use the multi-user features of Mac OS X, you can also share your music with other people who use your computer in the same way. (If you use a Windows computer, sharing your iTunes Library with other people who use your computer is a bit harder, but it isn't something you can't handle with a little help, which you'll find later in this chapter.)

If you want to share your audio content even with non-computer devices, you can use AirTunes and an AirPort Express to do so.

Understanding How iTunes Sharing Works

When iTunes computers can communicate with each other over a network, they can access the iTunes Library stored on each computer; on Macs, they can access each user account's iTunes Library, too. This means that you can see the content in other iTunes Libraries and other computers can see the content in your Library (assuming that iTunes sharing is enabled on each computer).

When an iTunes Library is shared with you, the Shared section will appear on the Source list. You'll see one source in this section for each iTunes Library that is being shared with you. When you share your Library with others, it will appear as a source in the Shared section on their Source lists. In either case, the person using the computer can select the shared source and listen to and watch its content, using the same tools used to listen to and watch other sources, such as CDs and playlists.

Even better, Windows and Macintosh users can share with each other on networks that include both kinds of computers.

To share with others on your network, you configure iTunes to share its Library, which is covered in the next section. To access shared music, you configure iTunes to look for Libraries being shared with you; that is the topic of the "Using iTunes Libraries Being Shared with You" section, later in this chapter.

Sharing iTunes on the Same Computer and over a Network

Setting up an iTunes computer to share its Library is a two-step process. The first step is to enable your iTunes Library to communicate with other iTunes Libraries, whether those are on the same computer or on different computers connected through a network. The second step is to configure iTunes to share your content.

You can also use iTunes to see who is accessing the content you have shared.

Sharing Your iTunes Library with Other People Who Use Your Windows PC

As of iTunes version 7.0.1, on which this chapter was based, you can't share your iTunes Library among the user accounts on a Windows XP computer because iTunes can be running under only one user account at a time.

To access another user account's iTunes content, you have to import that content into the iTunes Library under each user account from which you want to be able to access it. This process doesn't actually use the iTunes Sharing feature, but it places iTunes content to be shared among users in a single location that all the user accounts can access. Users then add the content they want to share into the iTunes Library under their own user accounts. This, in effect, enables all the users on one computer to access the same content. Each user will be able to add the shared content into his or her own iTunes Library, which isn't really the same thing as sharing content among user accounts, but it ends up doing something similar.

After the content is imported into each Library, each user can create individual playlists to organize and manage all accessible content.

If you want to share iTunes content among different user accounts on the same Windows computer, refer to http://docs.info.apple.com/article.html?artnum=93195. If you don't want to also share iTunes content over a network, you can skip the rest of this section, because you don't need to use the iTunes Sharing feature to do this. You can move onto the section called "Sharing Your iTunes Audio Anywhere with AirTunes and an AirPort Express Base Station" later in this chapter.

I hope this difference between the Windows and Macintosh version of iTunes will be corrected soon and Windows users will be able to enjoy the same sharing among user accounts on one computer that Mac users do.

Sharing Your iTunes Library with Other People Who Use Your Mac

If you use a Mac, each user account can share its music with the other user accounts on the same computer (and on the network to which that Mac is connected). Shared iTunes Libraries on the same Mac act just like Libraries stored on different computers that you access via a network. Using the Fast User Switching feature, you can leave iTunes running under one user account, and someone else can log in under another user account and use iTunes to listen to music or watch video that you share. Likewise, if another user shares her iTunes Library and leaves iTunes running while you log in to your user account, you can access her shared music and video, too.

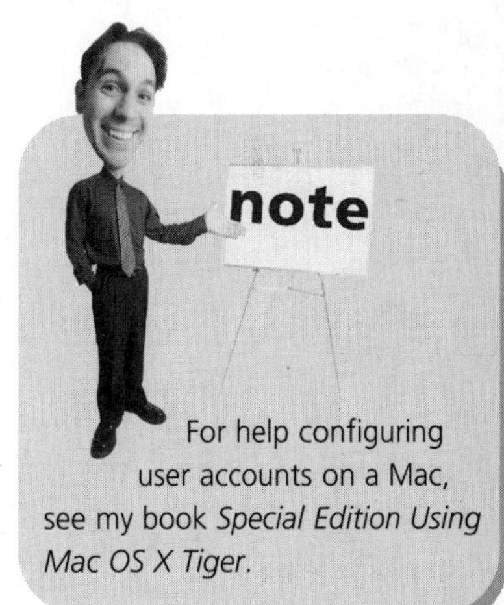

For help configuring user accounts on a Mac, see my book *Special Edition Using Mac OS X Tiger*.

Connecting an iTunes Computer to a Network

As I wrote in an earlier note, this is not a book on networking, so I can't provide the information you need to connect computers on a network. However, to enable iTunes sharing over a network, you must be connected to a network, which makes sense because the computers have to have some way to communicate with one another.

The network over which you share iTunes music can be wired, wireless, or both, and it can include Windows and Macintosh computers. If you have such a network and your iTunes computers are connected to it, you are ready to share your music. Otherwise, you will need to build the network before you can share your iTunes content.

Sharing Your iTunes Content

To allow other people to access your iTunes Library, perform the following steps:

1. Open the iTunes Preferences dialog box and then open the **Sharing** pane (see Figure 23.1).

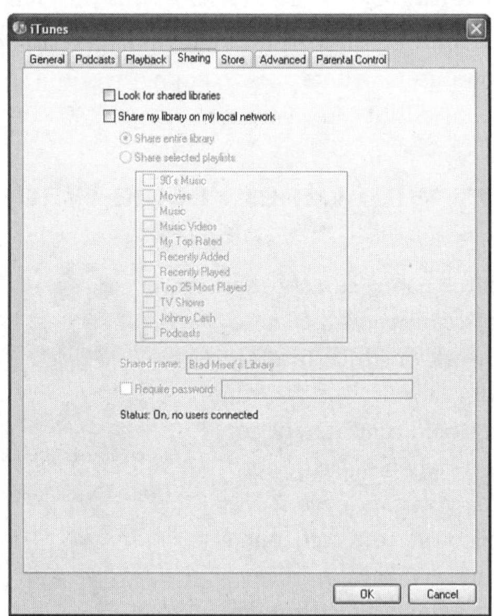

FIGURE 23.1
Using the Sharing pane of the iTunes Preferences dialog box, you can allow other people on your network to access your iTunes content.

2. To enable sharing on your computer, check the **Share my library on my local network** check box.

   When you share your library, you have two options for the content you share: You can share your entire Library, or you can share only selected playlists.

3. To share your entire Library, click the **Share entire library** radio button.

   To share only specific playlists, click the **Share selected playlists** radio button and then check the check box next to each playlist you want to share. You can scroll through the list of available playlists by using the scrollbar located on the right side of the list of available playlists.

4. Enter the name of your shared content collection in the **Shared name** field. By default, this will be the name of your user account on the computer with *'s* Library added to it. However, you can enter any name you'd like. This name will be how others identify your shared content on their Source Lists.

5. If you want to require that people enter a password before they can access your shared content, check the **Require password** check box and enter the password they will have to use in the box.

6. Click **OK**. The first time you do so, you will see a prompt reminding you that sharing is for personal use only; click **OK** to clear the prompt. The content you elected to share will become available to others on your network.

7. If you require a password to let others access your music, provide them with the password you created.

> **tip**
>
> If you make changes to the sharing configuration in iTunes while other people are accessing your Library, such as changing your sharing name or requiring a password, those users might have to restart their iTunes to be able to access your shared content again.

Knowing How Many People Are Using Your iTunes Content

You can monitor how many people are accessing the content you are sharing by opening the Sharing pane of the iTunes Preferences dialog box (see Figure 23.2). At the bottom of the pane, you will see the current status of sharing (On or Off) and how many users are currently connected to your Library.

The Status section shows only those users who are actually accessing your music by selecting it on their Source Lists. If they don't have your music selected, they won't be shown as being connected, even if they can see your shared content on their Source Lists.

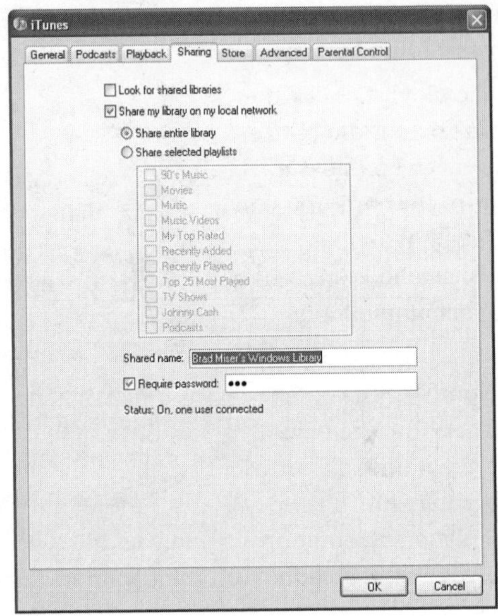

FIGURE 23.2
At the moment, the Status information at the bottom of the Sharing pane shows that one user is sharing this iTunes Library.

Using iTunes Libraries Being Shared with You

Two steps are required to access iTunes content being shared with you. The first one, which must be done only once, is to tell iTunes to look for any music being shared with you. The second one is to access shared sources and listen to or watch content being shared.

Accessing iTunes Content Being Shared with You

To have iTunes look across the network and across user accounts on a Macintosh computer to locate shared content that is available to you, open the **Sharing** pane of the iTunes Preferences dialog box. Then check the **Look for shared libraries** check box and click **OK**.

When you return to the iTunes window, you will see each source that is being shared with you in the Shared section on your Source List (see Figure 23.3).

If a shared source requires that you provide a password to listen to it, you will see the padlock icon in the lower-right corner of its icon. If you see this, you'll need to know the password for this source before you can listen to its content.

To view the content of a shared source, select it. If the source is protected by a password, you'll see the Shared Library Password dialog box (see Figure 23.4). Enter the password for the shared source. If you want iTunes to remember the password so that you don't have to enter it again, check the **Remember password** check box. Click **OK**.

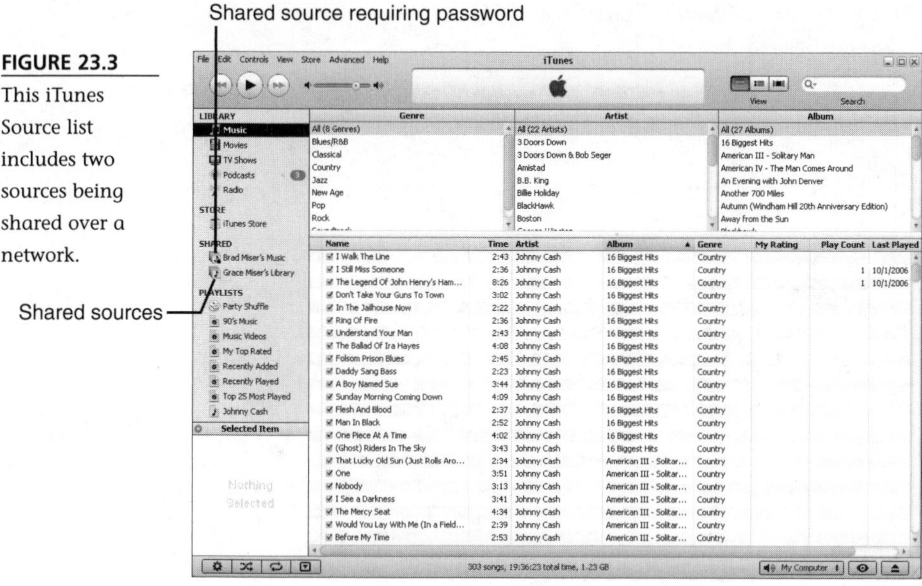

FIGURE 23.3
This iTunes Source list includes two sources being shared over a network.

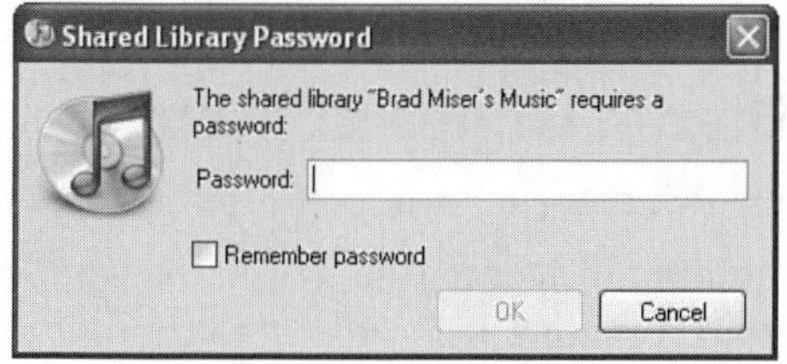

FIGURE 23.4
When you access a shared source that is password protected, you'll see this dialog box.

After iTunes has accessed the shared source that you selected, you'll see its content in the Content pane, and an Expansion triangle will appear next to the source that you are accessing (see Figure 23.5).

The Shared Music source will have an expansion triangle next to it. Click this **triangle** to expand the Shared Music source to see each of the sources being shared with you. Likewise, click the expansion **triangle** next to each shared source to view the playlists being shared (see Figure 23.5).

If a source has been loaded in your iTunes, it will have an expansion triangle next to it. If this triangle doesn't appear, this means that although the source is available, you haven't accessed it.

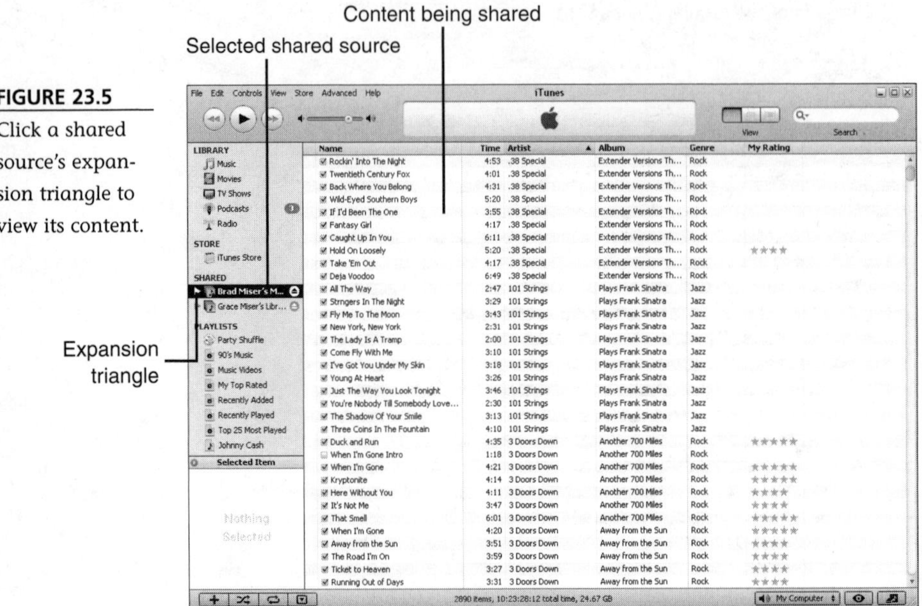

FIGURE 23.5
Click a shared source's expansion triangle to view its content.

Listening to and Viewing Shared iTunes Content

To listen to shared audio or watch shared video, perform the following steps:

1. Select the source containing the content to which you want to listen or watch by clicking its icon. Your computer will attempt to connect to that music source if it isn't already connected (if it is connected, you'll see an expansion triangle next to the source's icon).
2. If the source is protected by a password, you will be prompted to enter the password for that source. Do so and click **OK**.

   After you have entered the correct password, or if no password is required, the shared source information will be loaded, and its icon will be shown on the Source list. If the shared source has lots of content, it can take a minute or so for it to load on your Source list. You know this process is complete when the expansion triangle appears next to the shared source and its content appears in the Content pane.

tip

Check the **Remember password** box in the Shared Library Password prompt to have your computer remember the password for a source so that you don't have to enter it each time to access that source.

3. Click the expansion triangle next to the shared source's icon. When it expands, you will see the folders and playlists it contains (see Figure 23.6).

FIGURE 23.6
The Brad Miser's Music source is selected, and its content appears in the Content pane; the playlists and folders it contains are shown under its icon.

4. Select a playlist under the shared source, and its content will be shown in the Content pane (see Figure 23.7).

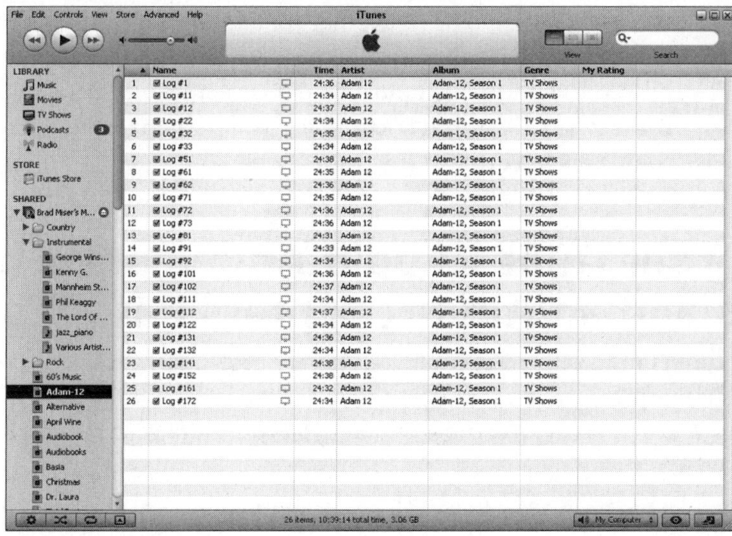

FIGURE 23.7
The shared source Brad Miser's Music has a number of playlists available; the Adam-12 playlist (which contains episodes of the TV show *Adam-12*) is selected.

5. Play content on the shared source just as you play the content in your Library—such as by selecting it and clicking Play. Other playback tools, such as sorting the Content pane to change the order in which songs play, also work just as they do when you are working with your own Library.

note

If a shared source includes shared folders (which have a folder icon on the Source list), you can click their expansion triangles to see and access their contents.

There are some differences between shared content and content in your iTunes Library, including the following:

- You can view shared content in only the List view. The other view buttons are inactive.
- You can't view artwork associated with shared content. The Artwork pane will contain the message "Album Artwork Not Modifiable" instead of the artwork.
- You can't copy shared content into your Library, such as to add it to your own playlists or burn it to disc. Shared content is "read only" to you, meaning that you can listen to or watch it, but you can't change or organize it.
- You can't organize shared content in any way, such as by adding it to a playlist. You have to take shared content as it comes.
- If shared content has been purchased from the iTunes Store, the computer you use to listen to or watch that content must be authorized to do so. This requires that you enter the user account information (account name and password) under which that content was purchased before you will be able to listen to or view it. You'll learn all about authorizing (and deauthorizing) computers in Part III, "The iTunes Store."

Sharing Your iTunes Audio Anywhere with AirTunes and an AirPort Express Base Station

Sharing music with other computers is very cool, but what if you want to listen to your music someplace that doesn't have a computer? Using an AirPort Express wireless hub and iTunes' AirTunes feature, you can share your music with audio devices such as a home stereo.

You can use an AirPort Express for a lot more than just sharing your iTunes music. It is a full-featured wireless hub—not that you would ever guess so because it's very small. It also enables you to wirelessly share USB printers and so on. The focus of this section is sharing iTunes audio with a non-computer device; explore the AirPort Express documentation to learn about its other features.

The general steps to use an AirPort Express to share iTunes content with an audio device are the following:

1. Obtain and install an AirPort Express on your network.
2. Connect your AirPort Express to a home stereo, a set of powered speakers, or other audio device.
3. Use the AirPort Express Assistant to set up a new network.
4. Set iTunes to broadcast audio to that network.
5. Listen to the music or other audio from the device to which it is being broadcast.

Obtaining and Installing an AirPort Express

note
If it is to share iTunes content with an audio device using AirPort Express, your computer must have access to a wireless network so it can broadcast its music to the AirPort Express.

You can purchase an AirPort Express at any retail location that carries Apple products, such as the online Apple Store (see Figure 23.8). At press time, an AirPort Express costs $129, which is quite a bargain considering its small size and excellent features.

After you have obtained an AirPort Express, use the installation CD that comes with it to install the AirPort Express software on your computer. This also installs AirTunes, the software required to broadcast iTunes content.

FIGURE 23.8
An AirPort Express is a full-featured wireless hub that is just slightly larger than a deck of cards.

Connecting the AirPort Express to an Audio Device

As you can see in Figure 23.8, on the bottom of the AirPort Express are three ports. You can use the Ethernet port to connect the device to a cable modem, DSL modem, or wired network so you can use the AirPort Express as a hub. You can use the USB port to share a USB printer wirelessly. Finally, you can use the Line Out port to connect the AirPort Express to any audio device that has an input port or to powered speakers.

After you have installed the AirPort Express software, connect the Line Out port on the AirPort Express to the Line In port on an audio device. For example, connect the output cable for a set of power speakers to this port. Or, use a mini-jack to RCA stereo cable to connect the AirPort Express Output port to audio input ports on a stereo receiver.

Then plug the AirPort Express into a wall outlet. It will become active, and you'll see its activity lights turn on.

That is all the installation that is required. How simple is that?

Setting Up a New AirTunes Network

To broadcast your music to an AirPort Express, you first set up a network for that device:

1. Launch the AirPort Express Assistant. On a Windows PC, select **Start**, **All Programs**, **AirPort**, **AirPort Express Assistant**. On a Mac, open **Applications**, **Utilities**, **AirPort Express Assistant**. The Assistant will open, and you'll see an information window explaining what you can do.
2. Click **Continue**. Depending on how your current wireless network is set up, you might or might not see prompts that ask you to configure your current wireless connection. These prompts should be self-explanatory, so work through them until you see the Introduction screen in the Assistant.
3. Click the **Set up a new AirPort Express** radio button, and click **Continue**.
4. If you have an existing wireless network, click **Connect to my current wireless network**. If not, click **Create a new wireless network**. The rest of these steps assume you are creating a new network; using an existing network isn't much different. The computer will scan for the AirPort Express, and you will see all available AirPort Express units on the Network Setup screen.

You can connect to multiple AirPort Express units at the same time. For example, you could connect one to a stereo in the basement and another to one in the living room. You can also broadcast to more than one at a time.

5. Click **Continue** to use the AirPort Express that was found. If multiple Express units were found, select the **AirPort Express** you want to use and click **Continue**. The Assistant will begin configuring the AirPort Express for the existing network. When it finds the network, you will be prompted to connect to it and will see the Network Setup screen.
6. Enter the name of the network you are creating, along with a name for the AirPort Express; then click **Continue**.
7. Continue following the instructions in the Assistant until the AirPort Express is fully configured. The exact steps you use depend on your specific network configuration. Fortunately, the Assistant makes it pretty easy in most situations. When the Assistant has completed its work, your AirPort Express will be ready to use.

Configuring iTunes to Broadcast to a Network

After your AirPort Express has been configured, you set iTunes to broadcast to it.

1. Open the **General** subtab of the **Advanced** pane of the iTunes Preferences dialog box (see Figure 23.9).

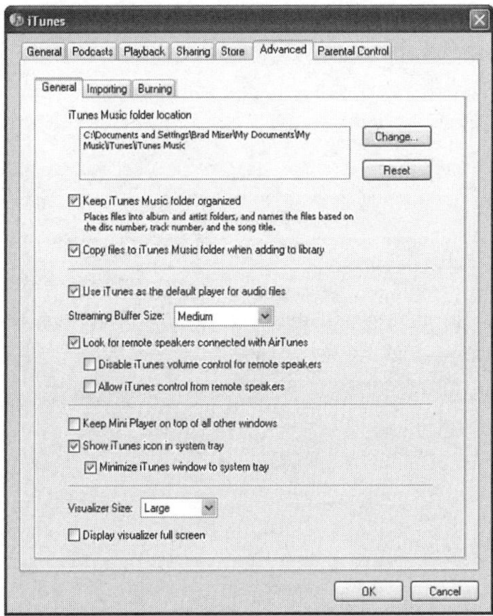

FIGURE 23.9
Use the Look for remote speakers connected with AirTunes check box to broadcast iTunes content to other devices.

2. Check the **Look for remote speakers connected with AirTunes** check box.
3. Check the **Disable iTunes volume control for remote speakers** check box if you don't want the position of the Volume slider in iTunes to impact

the volume of the audio device to which you are broadcasting. Generally, this is a good option so that you don't accidentally change the volume at the remote device when you are using iTunes.

4. Check the **Allow iTunes control from remote speakers** check box if you have a device connected to the AirPort Express that can control iTunes remotely. For example, if you connect an iPod Hi-Fi speaker set to an Express Base Station, you can control iTunes volume from the speakers.
5. Click **OK** to close the Preferences window. You'll return to the iTunes window.

Listening to Broadcasted Audio

Now you can listen to your iTunes audio from the remote audio device. Follow these steps:

1. Choose the remote device on which you want to play music on the **Speaker** pop-up menu that appears in the lower-right corner of the iTunes window when the AirTunes software is running (see Figure 23.10). You'll see several options on this menu. The My Computer option is used to play via the computer on which iTunes is running. Below that, you'll see each Express Base Station with which iTunes can communicate. At the bottom of the menu, you'll see the Multiple Speakers option that enables you to play content over more than one device at the same time.

FIGURE 23.10

On this menu, choose the location at which you want to enjoy iTunes content.

Speaker pop-up menu (appears when iTunes can connect to an Airport Express)

2. Select the option that you want to use. If you want to broadcast to a single location, choose the name of the Base Station connected to the audio device you want to use and skip the next step. If you want to broadcast to more than one device, choose **Multiple Speakers**. You'll see the Remote Speakers window (see Figure 23.11).

FIGURE 23.11
Check the check box for each device on which you want to hear iTunes music.

3. Check the check box for each base station to which you want to broadcast content; if you want to hear the content on your computer too, leave the **My Computer** check box checked (if not, uncheck it). Close the Remote Speakers window.
4. Play the audio you want to hear, such as a playlist, a podcast, a CD, or your Library. You can choose a shared source to broadcast just like any source in your own Library.

   In the Information window, you'll see a message telling you that iTunes is connecting to the selected speakers. When that process is complete, music will begin playing over the device to which the AirPort Express is connected.
5. Use the audio device's volume control to adjust the volume. (If you didn't check the Disable iTunes volume control for remote speakers check box, you can also control the volume with the iTunes Volume slider).

If the base stations on your current network don't support playback as a group, you'll be able to choose only one at a time.

If you choose to broadcast to an AirPort Express Base Station that doesn't have any speakers (or a stereo) connected to it, you'll see a warning message when you connect to that device.

Because the music source is iTunes, you control music playback from the computer streaming music to the AirPort Express, such as to start or stop it, change the source, and so on. You can control only the volume from the audio device, such as by muting it, increasing it, and so on.

To hear iTunes music on the computer again, select **My Computer** on the Speaker pop-up menu.

Interestingly, if your wireless hub also connects wired computers to your network, you can broadcast music from any computer with iTunes connected to the wired network.

THE ABSOLUTE MINIMUM

The ability to share your iTunes content with other computers on your network and listen to the music on other people's computers is pretty cool, don't you think? If you use a Mac, you can just as easily share your content with everyone who has a user account on your computer. And, using an AirPort Express Base Station, you can even share your iTunes audio by broadcasting to other devices, such as a home stereo receiver.

Following are some points to keep in mind to help your sharing:

- To share music, the computer sharing it must be turned on and cannot be in Standby (Windows) or Sleep (Mac) mode. If the computer goes to one of these modes or is turned off, the shared content will no longer be available.
- Similarly, iTunes must be running for it to share content. If you quit iTunes while sharing, the content you were sharing will no longer be available to others.
- When it comes to sharing, iTunes doesn't care whether a machine is a Windows computer or a Mac. You can share or access shared content from both kinds of computers.
- If you use a Mac, configure Fast User Switching to be active so other people can access shared content in your Library (leave iTunes running whenever you are logged in) when they use your computer.

- When you access shared content, you can only listen to or watch it. You can't add it your Library, put it in playlists, change its information, put in on a disc, or perform other tasks that you can with the content in your own Library.
- You can share your content with up to five computers at the same time.
- If you access shared content that was purchased at the iTunes Store, you must validate that you have permission to listen to that music by authorizing it. Content that you purchase from the iTunes Store can be used on only five computers at a time, and someone sharing content you purchased counts as one of those five. To be able to use shared content from the iTunes Store, you must be able to provide the account and password under which it was purchased. You'll learn about this in more detail in Part III, "The iTunes Store."
- You can connect an AirPort Base Station to your network to broadcast your iTunes music to other devices, such as a set of powered speakers or to a home stereo system.
- If you broadcast music using AirTunes, the Party Shuffle can be a good source to use because it will play for a long, long time if you use it with sources containing lots of music. And since it shuffles the tunes, they don't get stale.
- When you use AirTunes to broadcast iTunes content, you control playback from iTunes. If the computer on which it is running is far away, this can be a pain because you have to go back to it to change songs, change the source, and so on. There are remote control devices that connect to an AirPort Express Base Station so that you can control the music using the remote. One of these devices is the Keyspan Express Remote (see www.keyspan.com for more information).

IN THIS CHAPTER

- Take care of iTunes, and it will take care of you.
- Limit the type of content that can be accessed in iTunes.
- Be safe, not sorry (potentially very, very sorry) by backing up your iTunes Library.
- Get help with those very rare, but possibly annoying, iTunes problems.

MAINTAINING iTUNES AND SOLVING PROBLEMS

As an application, iTunes is so well designed that you aren't likely to have many problems with it. And that is a good thing, because who wants problems? However, you can minimize iTunes' problems by keeping the application updated to the current release. You can also protect people who use iTunes from content that might not be appropriate. You should also keep your iTunes collection backed up just in case something really bad happens to your computer.

In the rare case that you do have troubles, you can usually solve them without too much effort.

Keeping iTunes Up-to-Date

iTunes is one of Apple's flagship applications, especially because it is the only current Apple application that runs on both Macintosh and Windows computers. Apple, therefore, is continually refining the application to both make it even more trouble free and to enhance its features. You should keep your copy of iTunes current; fortunately, you can set up iTunes so it maintains itself.

Keeping iTunes Up-to-Date on Any Computer Automatically

Setting up iTunes so that it keeps itself current automatically is simple. Open the **General** pane of the iTunes Preferences dialog box. Then check the **Check for updates automatically** check box (see Figure 24.1). Click **OK**.

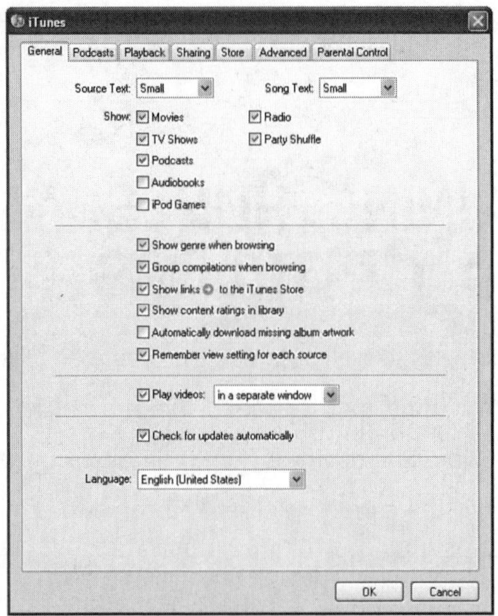

FIGURE 24.1
Using the General pane of the iTunes Preferences dialog box, you can have iTunes keep itself current.

Once per week, iTunes will connect to Apple's servers and check for updates. When it finds an update, you will be prompted to download and install it on your computer. As you can probably guess, iTunes needs to connect to the Internet to perform this task.

caution

For iTunes to perform this check, it must be stopped and started once during the week. In other words, if you never quit iTunes, it will never perform this check.

The benefit of this is that you don't have to remember to check for updates yourself. There isn't really a downside, because you have the opportunity to decline to install the update if you don't want it installed for some reason.

Keeping iTunes Up-to-Date on a Windows PC Manually

You can check for an iTunes update manually any time you think one might be available or if you prefer to do manual updates for some reason. You can check for iTunes updates manually on a Windows computer by selecting **Help**, **Check For Updates**. iTunes will connect to the Internet and check for a newer version of itself. If a new version is available, you will be prompted to download and install it. If a newer version is not available, you will see a dialog box telling you that you are using the current version.

Keeping iTunes Up-to-Date on a Macintosh

Because both Mac OS X and iTunes are Apple products, iTunes is one of the applications tracked by Mac OS X's Software Update feature.

If you have set Software Update to check for updates automatically, it will check for iTunes updates according to the schedule you set. When it finds an update, you will be prompted to download and install it.

To manually check for updates, select **Apple menu**, **Software Update**. If an iTunes update is available, you will see it in the Software Update window. You can then select it and download it to your Mac. iTunes will then be updated to the latest and greatest version.

Configuring Parental Controls

You can limit the type of content that iTunes users can access to protect children and others from some of the not-so-wholesome products that are available through a number of sources. While this isn't technically iTunes maintenance and troubleshooting (the topic of this chapter), it can be the prevention of problems for the people who use iTunes, which is why it's included here. To configure parental controls, perform the following steps:

1. Open the **Parental Control** tab (Windows) or the **Parental** tab (Mac) of the iTunes Preferences dialog box (see Figure 24.2).

To be able to keep others from changing iTunes Parental Controls, you must be using a user account on your computer that has administrator privileges.

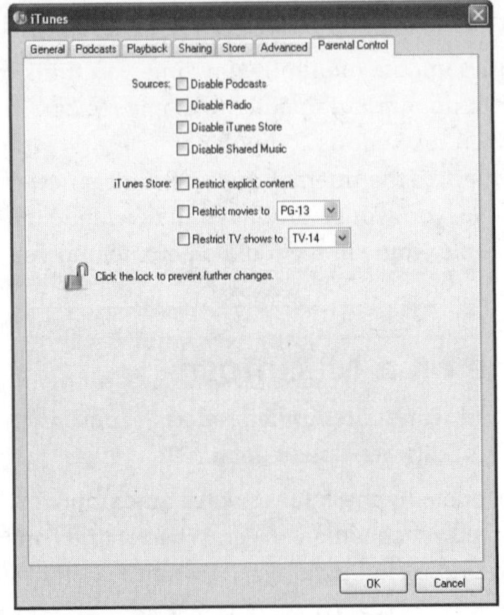

FIGURE 24.2
You can use the Parental Controls to limit the type of content available in iTunes.

2. Check the check boxes for the content you want to limit. Use the following list to understand each option:
   - **Disable Podcasts**—If you select this option, the Podcasts source will no longer be available, nor will the podcast functionality. If you don't want other users to access podcasts, some of which are not suitable for all audiences, use this function to prevent this.
   - **Disable Radio**—Check this box to remove the Radio source.
   - **Disable iTunes Store**—Use this to remove access to the iTunes Store.
   - **Disable Shared Music**—This one prevents iTunes from accessing shared music.
   - **Restrict explicit content**—This option prevents users from accessing content marked as being explicit in the iTunes Store.

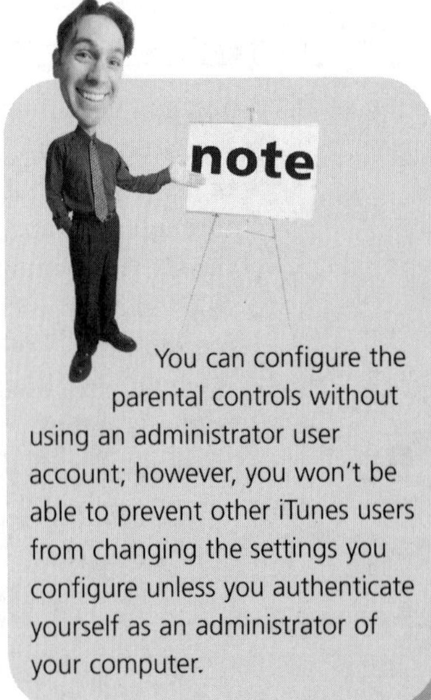

You can configure the parental controls without using an administrator user account; however, you won't be able to prevent other iTunes users from changing the settings you configure unless you authenticate yourself as an administrator of your computer.

- **Restrict movies to**—If you check this box, you can select a movie rating on the drop-down list to limit the movies that can be accessed in the iTunes Store based on their rating. For example, if you check the box and choose PG-13, R-rated movies won't be available.
- **Restrict TV shows to**—This performs a similar function to the movie check box. Check the box and choose a rating on the drop-down list to limit access to TV shows in the iTunes Store based on ratings.

3. Click the **Lock** icon.
4. Enter your computer user account's username and password.
5. Click **OK**. If you entered account information for an administrator user account, you'll return to the Preferences dialog box. The Lock icon will be closed to show that changes to the settings are currently prevented. If the user account information you entered is not for an administrator user account, you'll see an information prompt telling you so. Click **OK** to close the prompt; parental controls will be set, but there's no reason someone else can't change them again.
6. Click **OK**. The Preferences dialog box will close. Any changes you made will be reflected on the Source list, such as the Podcasts source disappearing if you disabled podcasts.

iTunes' Parental Controls are independent for each user account on your computer. So you can set the parental controls on an account someone else uses on your computer, and those controls won't impact your use of iTunes. For example, if you share your computer with children, you can set the Parental Controls while using iTunes under their user account to block explicit iTunes Store content. That setting won't impact iTunes when you use it under your user account.

> **caution**
>
> Backing up is especially critical for music, audiobooks, and video you purchase from the iTunes Store. If something happens to that content, you can't download it again without paying for it again. If you lose files you have purchased and don't have a backup, they are gone forever—unless you pay for them a second time, that is. Consider this your first warning. (It won't be your last.)

Backing Up Your iTunes Library

I hope you have and use a good backup system to protect all your files, including your iTunes Library. If so, you get extra points from me and can skip the rest of this section (although you should read on to learn how to use iTunes to back up your Library).

If you don't use a backup system to protect yourself, shame on you. However, you can earn some points back by choosing and doing one of the following backup options:

- Use the iTunes backup feature to protect your entire iTunes Library.
- Back up your purchased content.
- Back up your entire iTunes Library.
- Back up your entire iTunes folder.

Backing Up with iTunes

iTunes includes a backup function that you can use to burn your iTunes Library onto CDs or DVDs. If your Library includes video content, you'll want to be able to use DVDs because video content requires a lot of storage space. To back up with iTunes, perform the following steps:

1. Choose **File**, **Back Up to Disc**. You'll see the iTunes Backup dialog box (see Figure 24.3).

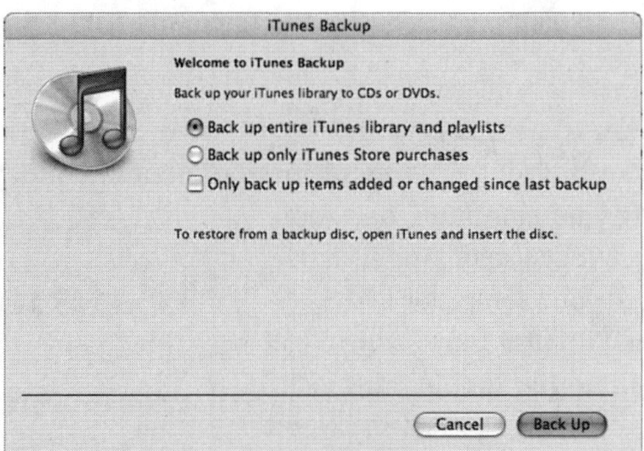

FIGURE 24.3
With iTunes, backing up isn't hard to do.

2. Click **Back up entire iTunes library and playlists** if you want to be able to restore all your iTunes content, or click **Back up only iTunes Store purchases** if you want to back up only content you've purchased from the iTunes Store. If you have a very large library, choosing the first option can require lots of discs and time, but it's likely worth it if you think about the time it took for you to build your Library. I recommend that you choose the first option all the time. You can use the incremental backup feature to limit the number of discs you use.
3. To enable iTunes to perform incremental backups, check the **Only back up items added or changed since last backup** check box. I recommend that you check this box, because after the first time iTunes backs up your

Library, it will back up only changed items from then on, which saves you discs and time during later backups.

4. Click **Back Up**. You'll be prompted to insert a blank disc.
5. Insert a blank DVD or CD. (Use DVDs if your computer has a DVD burner, because it will require a lot fewer discs.) iTunes will determine what needs to be backed up.

   If some content can't be back up, you'll see a warning dialog showing how many files can't be backed up. You can expand this to see the specific tracks that can't be backed up and the reason they can't be. You can review this information to determine whether or how to fix the problem. Click **OK** to close the warning dialog box and continue the backup process.

   If the backup will require more than one disc, you'll see a prompt explaining this is the case. Click **Data Discs** to continue.

   iTunes will start the backup process and begin burning content to the disc you inserted.

   As it fills up discs, the full discs will be ejected, and you'll be prompted to insert a new blank disc.
6. Remove and label each **disc** as iTunes ejects it and insert a new blank **disc**. You should label the **disc** so that you'll know it's an iTunes backup disc. You also need to number the **disc** and you should also include the date on which you burned it.
7. Repeat step 6 until the backup process is complete. How long this will take depends on the size of your Library (or how much content you've purchased from the iTunes Store), the speed of your computer, whether you use CDs or DVDs, and so on.

   The first time you back up, this process will likely take a long time and consume many discs. Fortunately, because iTunes can back up incrementally, subsequent backups will require much less time and fewer discs.

   If you get impatient, remind yourself how bad it would be to lose your iTunes Library, especially if you lose the content you've purchased from the iTunes Store.

   The good news is that you can continue to use your computer while the backup process is underway. You can even continue using iTunes to listen to or watch content while you are backing up.

   When the process is complete, you'll hear a tone, and a dialog box will appear on the screen explaining that the backup is done.
8. Click **OK**. Store the discs in a safe place where you'll be able to find them if you ever need them.

Following are some pointers to help you keep your iTunes content safe:

- If you breezed over my advice about labeling each disc, you may have a hard time restoring content because you won't know which disc to insert. Label each disc carefully so you'll know when you need to use it during the restore process.
- Unfortunately, with the current version of iTunes, the backup process is manual, meaning you have to start it by choosing a command. (I hope that, in a future version, you'll be able to set a schedule for iTunes backups.) You should perform a backup periodically to make sure you've saved your latest and greatest Library.
- You should backup immediately after buying content from the iTunes Store to make sure you never lose it.
- You can use backup discs only to restore content; you can't play content from them.
- Audiobook content you've purchased from the iTunes Store *is not* backed up with the iTunes tool. You need to use one of the other options explained in this section to back up that type of content.
- Every so often, you should perform a full backup and store those discs at a different location. This will ensure your iTunes Library is safe even if something really bad happens and you lose a set of backup discs.

Restoring Your iTunes Content

If something happens to the iTunes content on your computer (perhaps you accidentally delete your iTunes folder, or your hard drive crashes), you can restore your content by performing the following steps:

1. Reinstall iTunes if necessary and open it.
2. Insert the first disc in your current backup set. iTunes will mount the disc, and you'll see a prompt asking whether you want to restore from the disc (see Figure 24.4).

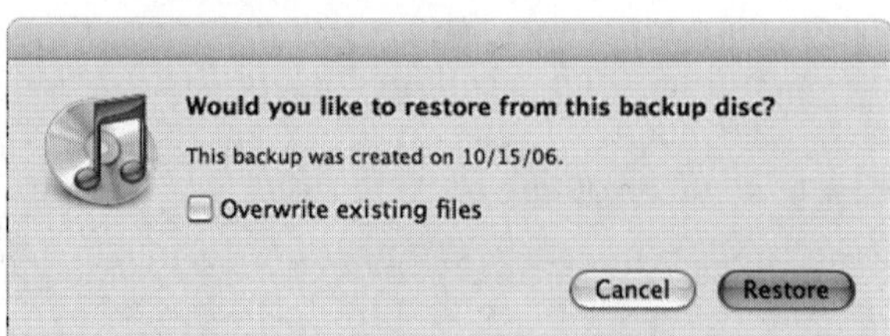
Would you like to restore from this backup disc?
This backup was created on 10/15/06.
Overwrite existing files
Cancel
Restore

FIGURE 24.4
Being able to restore your iTunes Library is a very, very good thing.

3. If you want to replace existing files with the versions in the backup, check the **Overwrite existing files** check box. If you don't check this box, only files that currently don't exist in your Library will be written to your computer.
4. Click **Restore**. iTunes will restore your Library if you backed up the entire thing (including all your playlists and preferences) or just the purchased content if you selected that option. As the restore occurs, you'll be prompted to insert the discs containing the content that needs to be restored. When the process is complete, your content will be back where it belongs.

Backing Up Your iTunes Folder on a Hard Disk

Using the iTunes Back Up feature requires a lot of time and discs. You should do this periodically so you make sure that your important content is protected.

> **tip**
>
> There are many programs that enable you to back up files automatically on your computer. If you include the iTunes folder in your backups, this can make the process easier and more automatic, which means it is more likely that you'll have more current backups.

If you have more than one hard disk available to you, you might also want to perform more frequent backups by copying the iTunes folder from your startup disk to a backup disk.

The iTunes folder contains all the content in your Library, along with the iTunes database file. Because it contains so much data, this folder is relatively large if you have a substantial amount of content in your Library.

The iTunes folder's default location on a Windows computer is in your My Music folder. On a Mac, its default location is the Music folder within your Home folder. If you ever need to restore your iTunes configuration, you can do so by using your backup of the iTunes folder. In addition to your content, this will also restore your playlists, settings, and most other aspects of your iTunes configuration.

If multiple user accounts on your computer use iTunes, you need to back up each account's content (from within iTunes) or, better, the iTunes folder (from the desktop). That's because each user account on your computer has its own iTunes folder, so you'll need to make sure each is protected with a backup.

If you do back up to hard disk, you should also back up to DVD or CD. Hard drives can fail, and some causes of failure can take out all the hard drives attached to your computer (such as a major power surge), in which case having a backup on a hard drive will be of no help.

The bottom line is that you need to keep important content (such as your iTunes Library) backed up in more than one way.

Solving iTunes Problems

iTunes is about as trouble-free as any application gets; this is especially amazing because iTunes offers so many great features. However, even the best application is bound to run into a few hiccups.

> **caution**
>
> iTunes depends on QuickTime to work. If you remove QuickTime from your system, iTunes will stop working. You'll have to reinstall QuickTime or run the iTunes Installer to get it working again.

Because the odds of my including a specific problem you might experience in this book are small, it is more profitable for you to learn where you can access help with problems you might experience. So I've included the solution to the one problem you are most likely to encounter here. Then you'll learn how to get help for other problems should you experience them. (You probably won't.)

Solving the Missing Song File Problem

One problem you might encounter occasionally has nothing to do with iTunes not working properly. This problem occurs when something happens to the file for a song, audiobook, or video in your Library. When this happens, iTunes doesn't know what to do because it can't find the content file. To show its confusion, iTunes displays an exclamation point next to any content whose files it can't find when you try to play them—or do anything else with them, for that matter (see Figure 24.5).

> The most likely cause of the missing file problem is that the content's file has been moved or deleted outside of iTunes.

To fix this problem, you have to reconnect iTunes to the missing file. Here are the steps to follow:

1. Double-click a song or other content next to which the exclamation point icon is shown. You will see a prompt telling you that the original file can't be found and asking whether you would like to locate it (see Figure 26.6).
2. Click **Yes**. You will see the Choose File dialog box.

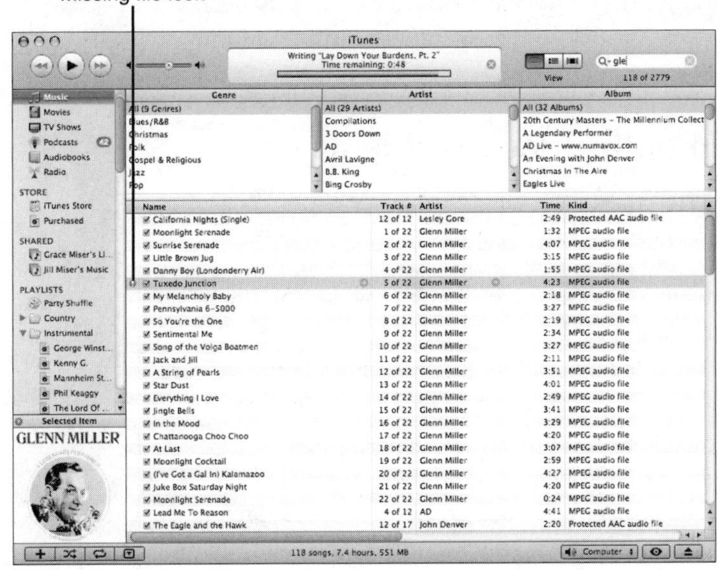
Missing file icon
iTunes
Tuxedo Junction
118 songs, 7.4 hours, 551 MB

FIGURE 24.5
The missing file icon next to the song "Tuxedo Junction" means iTunes can't find the file for that song.

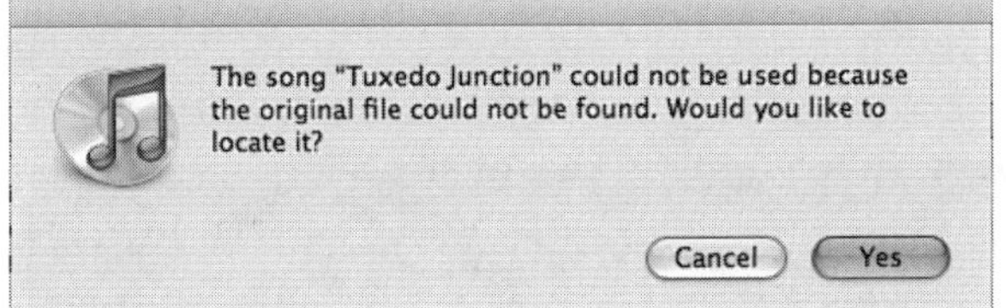
The song "Tuxedo Junction" could not be used because the original file could not be found. Would you like to locate it?
Cancel
Yes

FIGURE 26.6
When you see this dialog box, iTunes can't find a file it needs.

3. Move to the missing file, select it, and click **Open**. You'll return to the iTunes window, and the content will begin to play. This will also restore the link from the iTunes Library to the song's file, and you will be able to play it again as you could before it was lost.

If the problem was that the file had been moved, you might want to cause iTunes to place it back within the iTunes Music folder to keep your music files nicely organized. To do this, select **Advanced**, **Consolidate Library**. In the resulting prompt, click **Consolidate**. iTunes will place a copy of any

note

If you can't find a file anywhere on your computer (probably because it has been deleted), you will have to reimport that song into your iTunes Library. (Because you have backed up your iTunes content, this isn't a problem. Right? Right!)

missing files you have reconnected manually back into the proper location (within your iTunes Music folder).

Getting Help with iTunes Problems

When you run into a problem you can't solve yourself, the first place to go for help is Apple's iTunes Support website, located at www.apple.com/support/itunes/. This page provides solutions to common problems, and you can search for specific problems you might experience (see Figure 24.7).

Many other websites contain useful iTunes troubleshooting help. To find them, go to www.google.com and search for the specific problem you are having. This will often lead you to a forum or other place in which you can find information, including a solution, for many problems.

You can also get help with iTunes problems that other readers have asked about by visiting my website at web.mac.com/bradmacosx/. Click the **Books I've Written** button, and then click the image of the cover of this book. From the resulting webpage, you can move to a list of common questions and answers to get help. You can also ask me questions via email by clicking the **Email me** button.

FIGURE 24.7
Need help? Apple's iTunes Support website has it.

The Absolute Minimum

Heck, who wants to spend time solving problems with an application when the whole point is to spend time enjoying what you can do with it? Not me, that's for sure. Fortunately, iTunes is designed and implemented so well that you aren't likely to experience any problems. If you do, help is available to you on the web and from other sources.

- Of course, you can lower the chances that you will ever have problems with iTunes by keeping the application up-to-date. Fortunately, you can set iTunes to do this for you automatically.
- Just in case the worst happens, keep your Library safe by keeping it backed up separately from your computer, such as on CD or DVD. With the iTunes Back Up feature, this is easy to do, so there isn't any reason to risk losing your iTunes content.
- You aren't likely to need to solve many problems. You might occasionally run into the "missing song file" problem. Fortunately, you learned how to solve that one.
- If you experience problems with iTunes, you can also access the application's help system. You can get help from the Apple Support website, other websites, or by emailing me.

PART III

The iTunes Store

In This Chapter

- Learn why the iTunes Store is so great.
- Get an overview of how the store works.
- Know what you can do with the music, audiobooks, and video you buy.

25

Touring the iTunes Store

The iTunes Store might just be the best thing to happen to music and video, well, since iTunes and the iPod. The iTunes Store gives you online access to hundreds of thousands of songs and thousands of albums by thousands of artists. (That's a lot of thousands!) You can also purchase audiobooks and subscribe to podcasts. (Most are free, although some have a subscription fee.) There's also a large and growing collection of music videos, movies, and TV shows you can purchase. You can search or browse for content in many ways. When you find something that interests you, you can preview it to see whether it seems to be up your alley. If it is, you can buy it immediately and download it into your iTunes Library. This all works so well because access to the iTunes Store is built in to iTunes, so you can make the most of the store with the iTunes tools you already know so well.

Why the iTunes Store Rocks

There are many reasons the iTunes Store is great. To get you pumped up, here are a few:

- **The one hit wonder**—You know what I mean—that group or artist who put out one great song and that's it. Before the iTunes Store, if you wanted to own such a song, you usually had to buy a CD with 11 less-than-good songs to get the one you wanted. Not so with the iTunes Store. You can buy individual songs, so you only pay for the music you want.
- **Video that's iPod ready**—All the videos in the iTunes Store, including movies, TV shows, and music videos, are ready to go directly onto an iPod with no fuss or muss.
- **Season pass**—You can purchase a season pass for TV series that are currently in production. As soon as a new episode becomes available (usually the day after it airs), it is downloaded to your Library.
- **Try before you buy**—You can preview any content in the store to make sure you know as much as possible about it before you actually buy it. For example, you can watch part of a TV show to be sure you really want to add it to your collection.
- **It's legal**—Unlike many other sources of online audio and video content, the iTunes Store contains only content that is legal for you to buy and download.
- **It's convenient**—Because you access the iTunes Store through iTunes, shopping for audio and video is easy and convenient.
- **You can find the audio and video you want**—You can search for specific content or browse entire genres, artists, and more.
- **Immediate gratification**—Because content is immediately downloaded to your computer, you don't have to wait for a CD or DVD to be delivered to you. You don't even need to drive to a store.
- **It's cheap**—Individual songs are only $.99. When you buy a CD's worth of songs, the price gets even lower and is usually less than you would pay elsewhere. Music videos and episodes of TV shows are $1.99; if you buy an entire season of a series, the cost per episode is even less. Movies range in price from $9.99 to $15.99. Plus, there are no shipping costs.

Ever hear a song on a commercial or TV show that reminds you that you like that song? You can often find and buy such a song in just a few minutes.

- **Allowances**—You can create iTunes Store allowances that enable someone to purchase up to a certain amount per period (such as $20 per month). This is a great way to enable someone to make purchases from the store while also putting a cap on the spending amount.
- **Gift Certificates**—You can purchase iTunes Store gift certificates and send the gift of music, audiobooks, or video via email to someone who uses iTunes. This is a great way to buy gifts for people even if you aren't sure of the music or video they already have. They can jump into the iTunes Store and purchase exactly what they want.
- **Audiobooks**—You can add lots of audiobooks to your iTunes Library so that you can listen to them on your computer or, even better, on an iPod.
- **iPod Games**—In the store, you'll find games you can purchase and then play on your iPod.
- **Podcasts**—In the iTunes Store, you can subscribe to thousands of podcasts and download them to your iTunes Music Library and an iPod. Most of these are free.
- **Pick and choose**—Because you can buy individual songs or episodes of TV shows, you can pick and choose, such as by selecting among songs from a specific artist. Even when you like an artist, sometimes collections from that artist might have only a few songs you like. Rather than getting stuck with several you don't like, you can buy only those you do like.

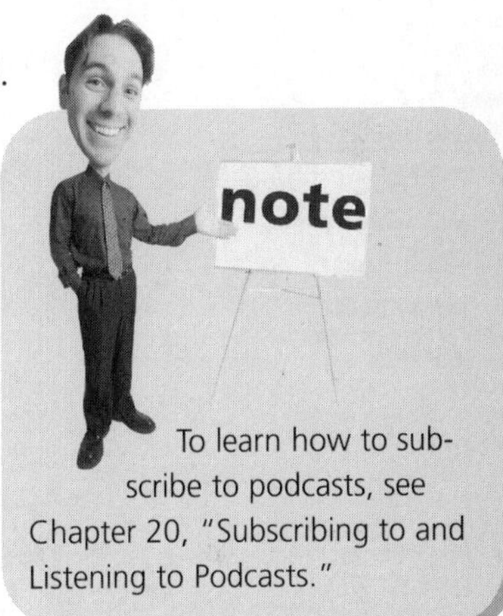

To learn how to subscribe to podcasts, see Chapter 20, "Subscribing to and Listening to Podcasts."

How the iTunes Store Works

Through the rest of the chapters in this part of the book, you will learn how to use the iTunes Store in detail. For now, read through the following sections to get an overview of this amazing tool.

Getting an Account

To purchase content from the iTunes Store, you need an account. (You don't need an account to subscribe to most podcasts or to browse the store or preview music, audiobooks, or video.) This account lets you charge what you purchase and prevents you from having to enter your information each time you visit the store. After you create and configure your iTunes Store account, you sign in to the store automatically, so you don't need to think about it again.

tip

You can use your iTunes Store account to log in to the store from any iTunes-equipped computer.

Accessing the Store

Accessing the store is as easy as clicking the iTunes Store source in the iTunes Source List (see Figure 25.1). The iTunes Store will fill the Content pane, and you can begin browsing or searching for content in which you are interested.

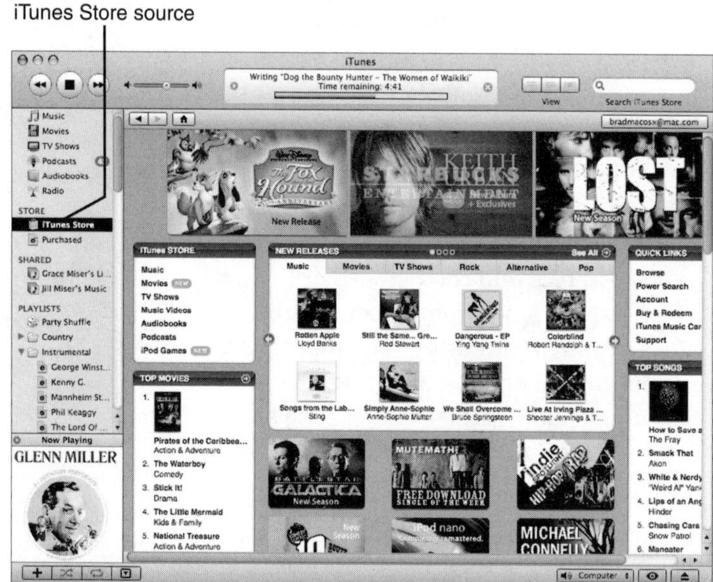

FIGURE 25.1
When you shop at this store, you don't need to worry about parking.

Browsing or Searching for Content

You can use the iTunes Store's tools to browse for content by type, genre, artist, or other attributes. This is a good way to explore the store to look for audio or video you might be interested in but might not be aware of. You can also search for content with the iTunes Search tool, which becomes the Search iTunes Store tool when the iTunes Store Source is selected (see Figure 25.2).

FIGURE 25.2
You can use the familiar iTunes Search tool to search for content in the iTunes Store.

Previewing Content

When you find a song, audiobook, podcast, or video in which you are interested, you can play a preview of it. The preview typically consists of 30 seconds of the content. This can help you decide whether something is really worth your money before you buy it.

Buying and Downloading Content

When you find songs, audiobooks, or videos you want to add to your iTunes Library, you can buy and download them with a few mouse clicks. The content you buy is automatically placed in a special playlist called Purchased (see Figure 25.3).

What Happens to Content You Buy?

When you purchase content, it is automatically placed in your iTunes Library. From there, with a few minor exceptions, you can do the same things with iTunes Store music as you can with music from CDs or video that you import.

FIGURE 25.3
As you can see, I have had no trouble finding music and video to purchase from the iTunes Store.

What Can You Do with Content You Buy from the iTunes Store?

The answer to this question is, just about anything you can do with any other content in your iTunes Library. Of course, "just about" means that there are some limitations on the music, audio, and video you get from the iTunes Store. However, you aren't likely to find these very limiting (unless you are trying to do something you shouldn't be doing anyway). So, following are the exceptions that make iTunes Store content slightly different from the content you add in other ways, such as music you import from a CD:

- **You can listen to music or watch video that you purchase from the iTunes Store on up to five computers or iPods at the same time**—For most people, this isn't a limitation, because they don't have more than five computers or iPods anyway. Even if you have more than five computers, you can easily authorize

note

Although the iTunes Store has an enormous amount of music and video available in it, it doesn't contain music or video from every artist. Some music companies have chosen not to place their music or video in the iTunes Store—for now. The inventory in the iTunes Store is continually increasing, and because of its dramatic success, my guess is that most of the few holdouts will eventually join the party.

and deauthorize computers to enable them to play iTunes Store content as needed.

- **You can burn the same playlist containing iTunes Store to a disc up to seven times**—So, you can create up to seven copies of the same CD or DVD. You aren't ever likely to really want to create that many copies of a disc, so this isn't much of a limitation either. Besides, all you have to do is change one song in a playlist, and then you can burn the changed playlist onto seven more discs.
- **You are supposed to use the music, video, and other content you purchase for personal use only**—Of course, this is the same limitation for the audio CDs and video DVDs you buy, too.

That's about it. You likely will never encounter any of these limits in your regular use of iTunes Store content.

The Absolute Minimum

The iTunes Store is one of the best things to happen to music and video, ever. Personally, in the first few months the iTunes Store was available, I purchased more music than I did in several of the previous years. That's because I have fairly eclectic tastes and don't often want to purchase full CDs because I like only a few songs by some artists. That said, I have purchased a number of full CDs as well. I've also added some video to my Library, such as classic TV shows and movies. Since the iTunes Store opened, I haven't ventured into many other online or brick-and-mortar music retailers. My guess is that as soon as you start using the iTunes Store, you, too, might find it to be the only audio and video store you need.

- When you shop in the iTunes Store, you can try any song, audiobook, or video before you buy it!
- To shop in the store, you need to set up an account. This can be done in just a few minutes, and you set up your account with iTunes.
- To visit the iTunes Store, simply click the iTunes Store source.
- You can browse and search the store for specific music, audiobooks, or podcasts you want to hear. You can do the same for music videos, movies, and TV shows.
- After you buy content and download it into your Library, you can do all sorts of things with it, such as listening to and watching it (duh), moving it onto an iPod, adding it to playlists, burning it to disc, and so on.

IN THIS CHAPTER

- Choose the shopping method that works best for you.
- Configure your iTunes Store account.
- Create allowances or purchase certificates for other iTunes lovers.
- Configure iTunes to suit your shopping preferences.

26

CONFIGURING iTUNES FOR THE iTUNES STORE

Before you burst through the iTunes Store's doors, it is a good idea to configure iTunes for the store so that when you do get there, you can focus on finding and buying cool stuff to add to your collection. And that is the point of this chapter—to help you understand your shopping options and create and configure your iTunes Store account.

Understanding Your Shopping Options

When it comes time to buy in the iTunes Store, you have two basic options: 1-Click or Shopping Cart. The 1-Click option works best when you have a broadband connection to the Internet. The Shopping Cart method works well for everyone but is primarily intended for people using a slow Internet connection, such as a 56K dial-up account.

1-Click Shopping

This method is aptly named. When it's active, you can click the contextual **Buy** button to purchase an item. That item can be an album, in which case the button will be Buy Album; a song, which has the Buy Song button; an episode of a TV show, which has the Buy Episode button; a season of a TV show, which has the Buy Season or Buy All Episodes button; and so on (see Figure 26.1). The item you elected to buy (a collection of songs, such as an album, a single song, an episode of a TV series, a whole season of a TV series, and so on) is immediately purchased and downloaded to your iTunes Library. The process requires literally one click (which is where the name came from, I suppose).

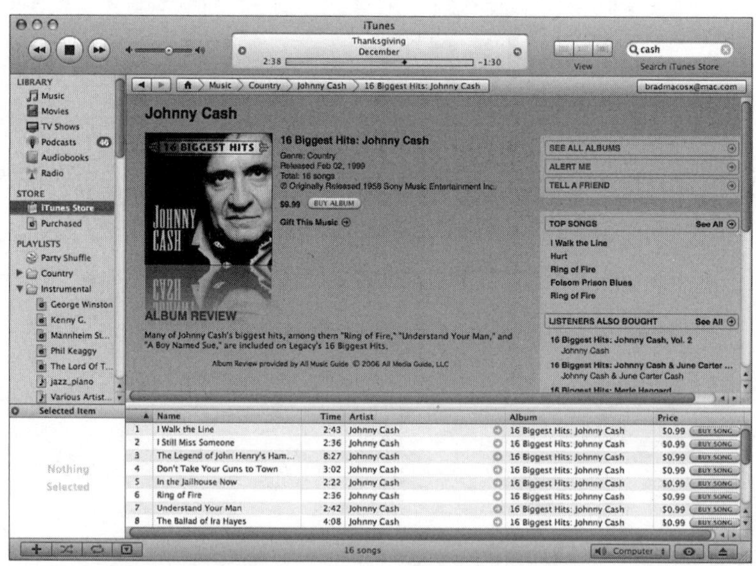

FIGURE 26.1
The Buy Album button enables you to purchase and download an album with a single mouse click; the Buy Song button does the same for individual songs.

If you have a broadband Internet connection, such as cable or DSL, this is a useful option because it makes buying content fast and easy. You can click a button, and the purchase and download process takes place in the background while you do something else, such as look for more music or videos.

If you have a slow connection, such as a dial-up account, this is probably not a good option for you. Because downloading content will consume your connection's bandwidth, you won't be able to do anything else while that content is being downloaded. You will have to wait until the download process is complete before continuing to shop. In this case, you should probably use the Shopping Cart method instead.

Shopping Cart Shopping

When you use this method, content you select is moved into the Shopping Cart, which serves as a holding area for that content until you are ready to purchase and download it. When you find music you want to buy, you click the Add Album or Add Song button. Likewise, if you are interested in video, you can click the Add Episode or Add Season button. The item whose button you click is moved into your Shopping Cart, which appears on the Source List underneath the iTunes Store source in the Store section. When you select the Shopping Cart, you will see the content you have added to it (see Figure 26.2). From there, you can purchase the content by clicking the Buy Album button for albums, the Buy Song button for songs, the Buy Episode button for episodes of TV shows, and so on, at which point the content you purchase is downloaded to your computer and placed in your Library. You can also click the Buy Now button to purchase everything in your Shopping Cart.

FIGURE 26.2
The Shopping Cart holds the audio and video you are interested in.

If you have a slow Internet connection, the Shopping Cart method is useful because you can place content in the cart and then continue shopping for music, audiobooks, or video in the store without being hampered by the content being downloaded to your computer. When you are finished shopping, you can pop back to the cart and purchase content and then do something else while that content is downloaded to your computer.

Although the Shopping Cart is designed for slow connections, you can use this method with a fast connection in the same way. The benefit of this is that you can gather a collection of content without actually purchasing it. When you are ready to check out, you can move to the cart and select the content you do actually want to buy. In other words, you can use the Shopping Cart as a holding area for items you find that you might want to buy. When you are ready to purchase items, you move back to your cart and click the Buy buttons for the specific content you want.

Configuring Your iTunes Store Account

To purchase content in the iTunes Store, you need to have an account and configure that account on your computer.

Obtaining an iTunes Store Account

If you already have an account with AOL, the Apple online store, or .Mac, you already have an account with the iTunes Store because it can use any of those accounts.

If you don't have one of these accounts, you can obtain an account in the iTunes Store by following these steps:

1. Select the **iTunes Store** source. The iTunes Store will fill the Content pane (see Figure 26.3).
2. Click the **Account** button, which is labeled Sign In when you are not signed in to an account. You'll see the Account Login dialog box (see Figure 26.4).
3. Click the **Create New Account** button. You will return to the Content pane, which will be filled with the first of the screens you use to create an account.
4. Read the information on the first screen and click the **Agree** button. (The information on the first screen contains the terms of service to which you must agree if you want to use the iTunes Store.)
5. On the next screen, enter an email address, which will be your account's username (called an Apple ID), and password. Then enter a security question, enter your birth date, and select any information you want to be emailed to you. Then click **Continue**.

6. On the third screen, enter your credit card information and address and then click **Done**.

FIGURE 26.3
To sign in to the iTunes Store, you click the Account button.

FIGURE 26.4
The Account Login dialog box enables you to log in to an existing account or create a new one.

7. If you are prompted to enter any additional information, do so and click the **Continue** or **Done** button. When the process is complete, you will see a completion screen. You will then be logged in to your new account. Click **Done**. You will return to the iTunes Store, and you can start shopping (see Figure 26.5).

FIGURE 26.5
When your iTunes Store account appears in the Account button, you are logged in to your account and can start shopping for tunes and other content.

Logging In to Your iTunes Store Account

To be able to purchase content from the iTunes Store, you must log in to your iTunes Store account first. To log in to an existing iTunes Store account, perform the following steps:

1. Click the **Account** button. (This will be labeled Sign In when you aren't signed in to your account.) You'll see the Sign In dialog box (see Figure 26.6).
2. If you use an Apple ID to sign in to the store, click the **Apple** button. (This is selected by default.) If you use an AOL account to sign in, click the **AOL** button.
3. Enter your Apple ID in the Apple ID field or your AOL screen name in the AOL Screen Name field.
4. Enter your password in the Password field.
5. Click **Sign In**. You will be logged in to your account. When you return to the iTunes window, you will see your Apple ID or AOL screen name in the Account field. After you are signed in, you'll be able to make purchases in the store.

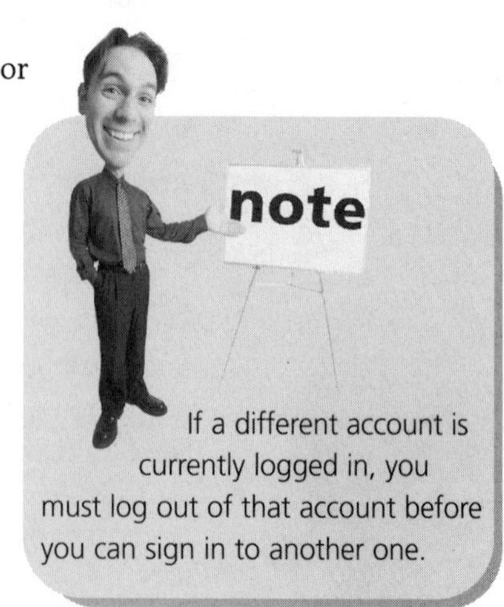

If a different account is currently logged in, you must log out of that account before you can sign in to another one.

FIGURE 26.6
You can sign in to your iTunes Store account by entering your Apple ID or AOL account information in this dialog box.

Logging Out of Your iTunes Store Account

To sign out of your account, click the **Account** button, which shows your Apple ID or AOL account name when you are logged in to your account. The Sign In dialog box will appear; click **Sign Out**. You will return to the iTunes Store, and the Account button will again be labeled Sign In.

When you click the AOL button, the Apple ID field becomes the AOL Screen Name field.

Changing and Viewing Your iTunes Store Account

Times change, and sometimes so does your personal information, such as your address or the credit card you want to use in the iTunes Store. If such changes occur in your life, you can change your Apple ID account information by using the following steps:

If you can't remember your password, click the **Forgot Password** button. You will move to a website that will help you retrieve your password.

1. Click your iTunes Store account name, shown in the Account button, as if you want to sign out. The Sign In/Sign Out dialog box will appear.
2. Enter your password. (Your account name will be filled in already.)
3. Click **View Account**. The Content pane will be replaced by the Apple Account Information screen. On this screen, you will see a number of buttons that enable you to change your account information and to manage various aspects of your account.

4. To change your account information (such as your address), click the **Edit Account Info** button and follow the onscreen instructions to change your information.
5. To change your credit card information, click **Edit Credit Card** and follow the onscreen instructions to change your credit card information.
6. If you want to change the country with which your account is associated (and sometimes the version of the store you use if the country you select has a different version of the store), click the **Change Country** button and follow the onscreen instructions.
7. To view your purchase history, click the **Purchase History** button. The screen will be filled with a detailed list of all the transactions for your account (see Figure 26.7). Use the **Preview** and **Next** buttons to move among the various transactions you've made. Review the list and click **Done**.
8. When you are finished making changes or viewing information about your account, click **Done**. You will return to the iTunes Store.

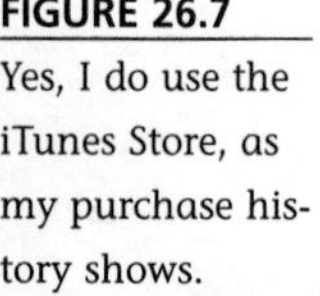

FIGURE 26.7

Yes, I do use the iTunes Store, as my purchase history shows.

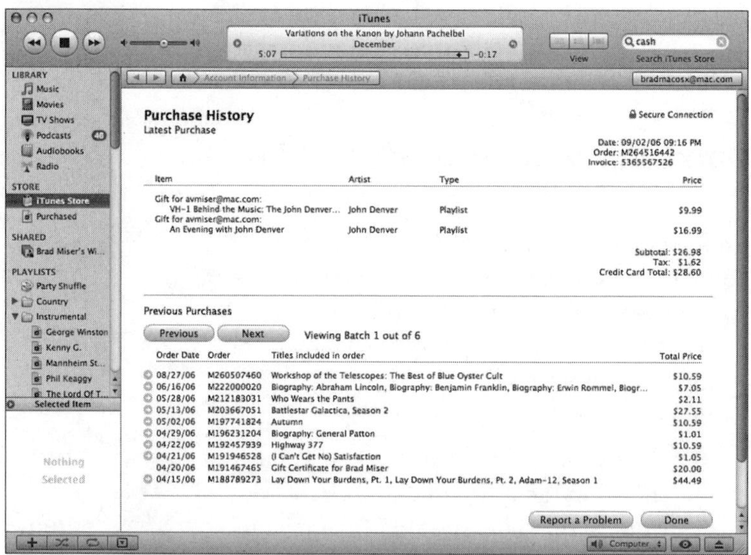

Setting Up and Managing Allowances

You can create an allowance for an iTunes Store account. This enables someone using that account to purchase a certain amount from the store per month. This can be useful if you have kids who you want to be able to buy content at the store and you want to provide a limited amount of credit for them to use.

If the person to whom you are going to provide an allowance already has an Apple account, you will need her iTunes Store ID. Or, you can create an account for that person when you assign an allowance to her if she doesn't already have one.

To create an allowance, perform the following steps:

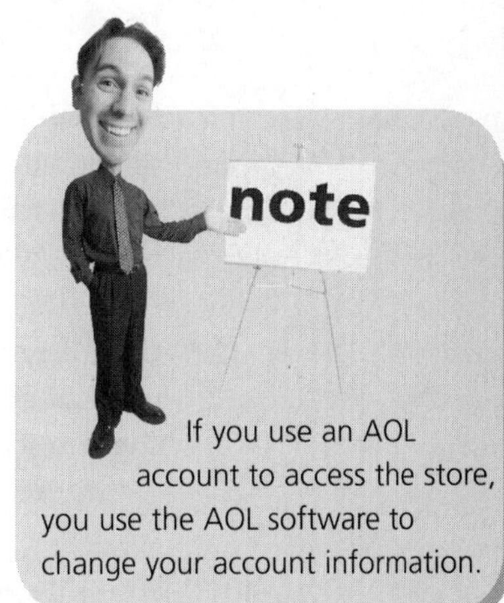

If you use an AOL account to access the store, you use the AOL software to change your account information.

1. Access the **Account Information** screen for your account. (See the previous section for the steps to do this.)
2. Click **Setup Allowance** or **Manage Allowances**. (The button you see depends on whether you created at least one allowance or not.) You'll see the Set Up an iTunes Allowance or the Manage Allowances screen.
3. Click **Create New Allowance**. You'll see the Set Up an iTunes Allowance screen.
4. Enter your name in the Your Name field.
5. Enter the recipient's name in the Recipient's Name field.
6. Choose the amount of money the recipient will be able to spend each month in the Monthly Allowance menu—this amount will be applied to the recipient's account on the first day of each month. You can choose an amount from $10 to $200 per month in $10 increments between $10 and $100 or in $50 increments from $100 to $200.
7. If you want the allowance to become available immediately, click the **Send now, and on the first of next month** radio button. (This is the default option.) If you want the allowance to start on the first day of the next month, click the **Don't send now, wait until the first of next month** button instead.
8. If the recipient already has an Apple ID, check the **Use recipient's existing Apple Account** radio button and enter the Apple ID in the two **Apple ID** fields. (One is a verification field.) If the recipient does not have an Apple ID, click the **Create an Apple Account for Recipient** radio button and enter an Apple ID for that person in the two fields.
9. If you want to provide a personal message about the allowance, write it in the **Personal Message** field.
10. Click **Continue**. If you indicated you wanted to create a new account, you'll move to the Create an Apple Account screen. If you chose to use an existing Apple ID, you'll move to a purchase confirmation screen that summarizes the allowance you are setting up, and you can skip to step 12.

11. Complete the information for the new Apple account you are creating. This includes the recipient's email address, first name, last name, birthday, and password. When you have entered this information, click **Create**. You'll move to the purchase confirmation screen.

12. Click **Buy** to start the allowance, **Back** to move back to the previous screen so you can change the information for the allowance, or **Cancel** to stop the transaction.

    You will see a screen that confirms that the allowance has been completed.

13. Click **Done** to complete the process, or click **Set Up Another** if you want to set up another iTunes allowance. When you finish setting up allowances, you'll return to the Manage Allowances screen, on which you'll see each allowance you've created under your account. Click **Back to Account** to return to your account information.

If the recipient doesn't spend an entire month's allowance, the balance carries over to the next month.

On the Manage Allowances screen, the current status of the allowance is indicated by the colored dot next to each one. A red dot means the allowance is suspended, and a green dot means the allowance is active.

The allowance's recipient will receive an email containing information about the allowance you set up, including the Apple account username and password, if you created one for this person. When the recipient signs in, her current balance will be shown next to the username in the Account box. This balance always reflects the amount left for the current month. When the recipient has spent all of this, the account won't be able to purchase more content until the following month.

To change your allowances, return to the Apple Account Information screen. When you have set up at least one allowance, this screen will contain the Manage Allowances button. Click this, and you'll move to the Manage Allowances screen. Here, you have the following options:

- You can suspend an allowance by clicking the **Suspend** button. The allowance will remain configured, but any future allowances will be disabled.

- You can restart a suspended allowance by clicking the Activate button. The allowance will receive the allotted amount on the first of the next month.
- You can change the amount of an allowance by selecting a new amount on the pop-up menu (which is active only for current allowances).
- You can remove an allowance entirely by clicking the **Remove** button. Do this only when you are sure you will never use the allowance again.
- You can create a new allowance by clicking the **Create New Allowance** button.

tip

Gift certificates are handy when you want to purchase content for someone but don't know what he has already or even what his preferences are. They are also useful to put yourself on an iTunes Store budget. Each month, you can purchase a gift certificate for yourself and apply it to your account. When you use up the certificate's amount, you'll be done spending in the store for that month. The next month, you can purchase another certificate.

Purchasing and Using Gift Certificates

If you know people who use iTunes, you can create gift certificates for the iTunes Store so the gift recipient can purchase music, audiobooks, and video there. These work similarly to allowances, except that gift certificates are for a set amount and expire when that amount has been spent.

To purchase a gift certificate, move to the iTunes Store home page and click the **Buy & Redeem** link in the Quick Links box. You'll see the Gift Certificates screen. In the Gift Certificates section on the resulting screen, click the **Buy** button and follow the onscreen instructions to purchase the certificate. You can choose to have the certificate delivered via email, you can print it yourself, or you can have it sent via U.S. Mail. Click the button for the option you want and follow the onscreen instructions to complete the purchase process.

After the recipient receives the certificate, or if you've created one for yourself, the certificate can be used by performing the following steps to apply the certificate's amount to your or the recipient's iTunes Store account:

1. Open the certificate, whether it came view email, snail mail, or as a hard copy. The most important part is the Certificate Code, which is a string of characters that identify the certificate in the iTunes Store.
2. Select the **iTunes Store** source.
3. Click the **Buy & Redeem** link.
4. In the Buy or Redeem Gift Certificates section, click **Redeem**. You'll see the Redeem an iTunes Gift Certificate screen.

5. Enter the code exactly as it is shown on the certificate.
6. Click **Redeem**. A confirmation prompt will appear. In the prompt, you'll see the account to which the certificate's amount will be credited.
7. Click **Redeem Gift Certificate**. The certificate's amount will be applied to the account, and a screen will appear to confirm the certificate. Its amount will be shown as a credit next to the Account button (see Figure 26.8). You can purchase any content in the store against this amount until the credit amount is consumed.

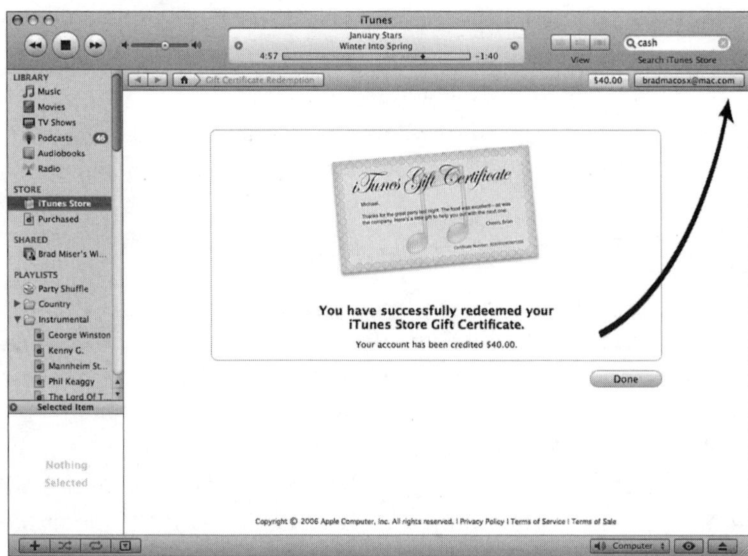

FIGURE 26.8

Thank you... thank you very much!

Managing Your Artist Alerts

If you are interested in specific artists, you can receive an email when new content from that artist is added to the iTunes Store.

To create an artist alert, click the **Alert me** link from the artist's home page in the iTunes Store and then click **OK**. When content from that artist is added to the store, you'll receive an email letting you know.

To remove an artist alert, click the **Manage My Alerts** button on the Apple Account Information screen. You'll see the Manage My Alerts screen. Here, you'll see each artist for whom you will receive alert emails. To remove an alert, uncheck the artist's check box and click **Save Changes**. You'll no longer be notified about that artist.

Choosing Your Shopping Preferences

The final step in preparing to shop is to configure your shopping preferences. To do so, follow these steps:

1. Open the iTunes Preferences dialog box.
2. Click the **Store** tab to open the Store pane (see Figure 26.9).

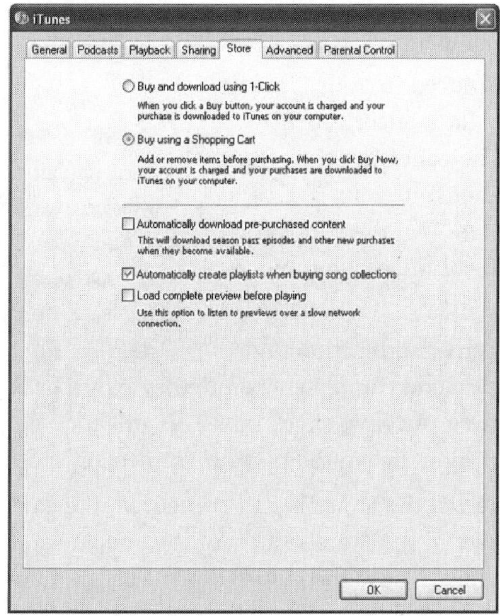

FIGURE 26.9
You can customize your iTunes Store experience by using the Store pane of the iTunes Preferences dialog box.

3. Choose your shopping method by clicking either the **Buy and download using 1-Click** radio button or the **Buy using a Shopping Cart** radio button.
4. Check the **Automatically download pre-purchased content** check box if you purchase content before it is actually available in the store (such as a season pass for a current TV show). As soon as the content you have purchased becomes available in the store, it will be downloaded to your computer automatically.
5. If you want iTunes to create playlists automatically for collections that you purchase, such as iMixes or iTunes Essentials, check the **Automatically create playlists when buying song collections** check box. This is useful because iTunes will automatically keep the contents of these collections in playlists that are the same as the collections that you purchase. For example, if you buy an iMix containing songs by 15 different artists from several genres, iTunes will create a playlist with that iMix's name and place all the songs

it contained when you purchased it in the new playlist. You can listen to the iMix just as you purchased it by playing its playlist.

If you don't enable this option, content in these collections will be "scattered" across your Library according to the tags applied to the songs that the collections contain. Going back to the iMix example, with this option disabled, the songs in the iMix you purchase would be placed in your Library only by each song's tags, such as artist, genre, and so on. The collection that was the iMix would not exist in your iTunes Library as a collection. (All the songs that the iMix contained would be available in your Library.)

If you want to hide the iTunes Store source so it can't be used, open the Parental Control (Windows) or Parental (Mac) pane and check the **Disable iTunes Store** check box. After you click **OK**, the store will no longer be visible on the Source list.

6. If you use a slow Internet connection and want previews to download completely before they play, check the **Load complete preview before playing** check box. This will enable the preview to play without pauses that might be caused by your connection speed (or lack thereof).
7. Click **OK**. If you selected the Shopping Cart method, the cart will appear below the iTunes Store in the Store section of the Source list. If you selected the 1-Click method, you'll see only the iTunes Store. You are now ready to shop!

The Absolute Minimum

Shopping at the iTunes Store is better than it is at any other music store I have ever seen, and its supply of video and audiobook content gets better all the time. Here are some more shopping points to keep in mind:

- When you shop in the iTunes Store, you can choose the 1-Click or Shopping Cart method. The 1-Click method is faster but is designed for a broadband connection to the Internet. The Shopping Cart method is better for slow Internet connections or if you prefer to collect content in a holding area before making purchases.
- To buy content from the store, you need to obtain and configure an iTunes Store account.
- You can browse, search, and preview content in the iTunes Store without an account. You can also subscribe to podcasts without an account.
- After you have an account, you configure iTunes to shop according to your preference.
- The music you buy from the iTunes Store is in the Protected AAC audio file format. This is the same AAC format in which you can import music into your Library, but it also includes some protections against copyright violations. As you learned in the previous chapter, the limits imposed by the protection are not very limiting; it is unlikely you'll ever notice the difference between the protected and nonprotected formats (except for authorization, which you'll learn about later in this part of the book).
- Other types of content, such as movies, are also in protected formats. You aren't likely to encounter problems because of these protection schemes (unless you are trying to do something not allowed by the terms of service to which you have to agree to be able to use the store).
- The best thing about music or video you buy from the iTunes Store might be that you don't have to unwrap a CD or DVD. I hate trying to pry them out of their plastic wrapping!

IN THIS CHAPTER

- Enter the iTunes Store and prepare to be amazed.
- Browse the iTunes Store for great tunes.
- Peruse the store for video.
- Search for the music, video, or other content you want.
- Preview—try before you buy.
- Buy what you want, when you want it.
- Link your Library with the iTunes Store.
- Use iMixes to see what other people like, and let them know what you like.
- Shop the iTunes MiniStore.

SHOPPING IN THE iTUNES STORE

Now that you have an account in the iTunes Store and have configured iTunes to use it, it is time to start shopping. You can browse or search for content, preview it, and then buy what you like—all with just a few mouse clicks and keystrokes. To shop in the iTunes Store, you use the following general steps:

1. Go to the store (no parking required).
2. Browse or search for music, video, audiobooks, or other goodies.
3. Preview content in which you are interested.
4. Buy it.

Going into the iTunes Store

You learned this in the previous chapter, but I've included it again in this chapter just for completeness's sake. To move into the store, select the iTunes Store source on the Source List. The iTunes Store will fill the Content pane (see Figure 27.1). If your account is shown in the Account button, you are signed in and ready to go. If not, click the **Sign In** button to sign in to your account (refer to Chapter 26, "Configuring iTunes for the iTunes Store," for help signing in to the store).

As you move around the store, know that just about everything in the iTunes Store window is a link, from the album covers to the text you see to the ads showing specific artists. Just about anywhere you click will move you someplace else.

FIGURE 27.1 Shopping in the iTunes Store won't make your feet tired.

Browsing for Tunes

The iTunes Store is all about music. (Well, it's also about video, audiobooks, and podcasts, too, but music is its primary focus.) Browsing for tunes can be a great way to discover music you might be interested in but don't know about yet. You can click through the store to explore in various ways; when you aren't looking for something specific, browsing can help you find lots of great music, of which you might not have even been aware.

tip

Unlike brick-and-mortar stores, when you shop in the iTunes Store, you can forget the elevator music, because you can listen to other sources in your Source List while you are shopping.

Browsing the iTunes Store Home Page

You have several ways to browse for music from the iTunes Store home page.

You will see several special sections titled New Releases, Top Songs, Top Albums, Just for You, What's Hot, and Staff Favorites; these categories of content are relatively self-explanatory. (For example, Top Songs is a list of the top 10 songs at the time you access the store.) Within some of these categories, the music is organized by genre; click a genre to see music in that genre within the category. Some sections are also broken out by content, such as Music, Movies, TV Shows, and so on. To scroll through the content available in these areas, click the scroll arrows or buttons (see Figure 27.2). When you do so, you will see the next set of content in that category. If you see content that interests you, click it. You will see the details of the content (such as an album) on which you clicked (see Figure 27.3). When you get to something that interests you, you can preview and purchase it.

tip

Remember that you can make the Source List narrower by dragging its border to the left. This can be helpful so that you can see more of the iTunes Store without scrolling.

tip

Clicking the **See All** link in the upper-right corner of any section's window enables you to see all the content in that category.

FIGURE 27.2
You can browse the categories on the home page by using the scroll tools; here I'm browsing the What's Hot section.

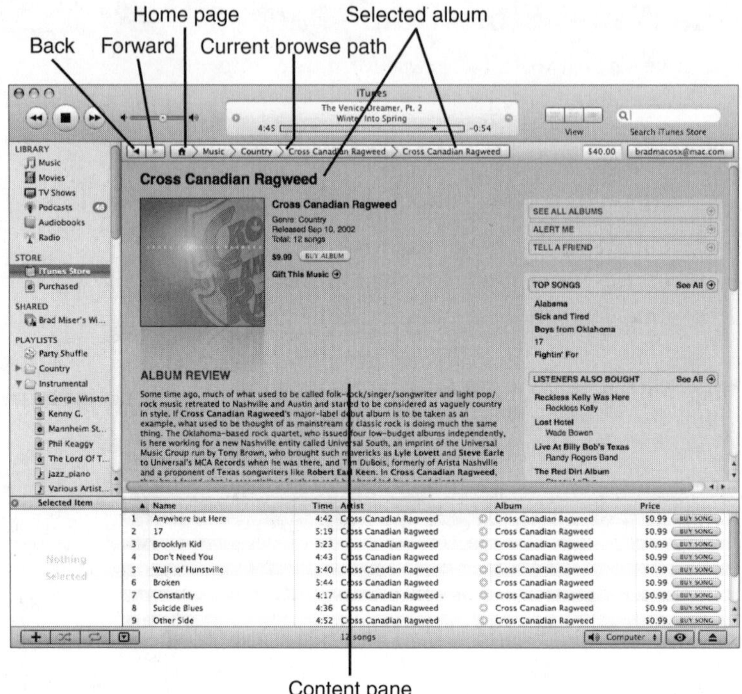

FIGURE 27.3
Here I've browsed to a specific album; at the bottom of the Content pane, you can see the songs in the album you are browsing.

You can also browse the iTunes Store home page by using the various lists presented on the screen, such as the Top Songs, Top Albums, and others. To browse a list, you can click its title or any of the songs or artists in the list. For example, to see the most downloaded albums, click the title text of the **Top Albums** list. You will see a screen that shows the albums that have been downloaded most on the day you visit the store (see Figure 27.4). You can click an album to view its contents.

tip
To return to the iTunes Store home page at any time, click the **Home page** button.

In the upper-left area of the home page, you will see the iTunes Store section, which enables you to focus on specific kinds of content, including Music, Movies, TV Shows, Music Videos, Audiobooks, and so on. Just click a link to move to the related area.

Also on the home page are a number of ads that change over time. These ads feature specific artists, the current sales promotion, and so on. Just click an ad to move to its content.

FIGURE 27.4
Checking the Top Albums list is a good way to see what other people are finding in the iTunes Store.

You can also browse the iTunes Store by clicking the Browse button. The Browser pane will appear above the Content pane just as it does when you are browsing your Library. Select the genre you want to browse, and you'll be able to browse for content using the Browser, which works just as it does when you browse your Library. Click the **Browse** button or the **Home page** button to return to the normal store interface.

Browsing by Genre

Browsing by genre is a good way to find music by its style. Starting from the iTunes Store home page, click the **Music** link in the iTunes Store section and then click a genre in the Genres section. The home page will be refreshed, presenting music only in the genre you selected (see Figure 27.5). The tools on the home page will be the same; the content of the music you see will be entirely focused on the genre of music you are browsing.

When you browse by genre, think of the resulting page as the "home page" for that genre.

FIGURE 27.5
If you like jazz, as I do, browsing the Jazz genre is a great way to find new music.

Browsing for Video

As you learned earlier, the iTunes Store also has a large and growing collection of video content that you can preview and purchase. This content includes movies, TV shows, and music videos. Browsing for video in the store is similar to browsing for music.

One way to browse for video in the iTunes Store is by using the video links in the iTunes Store section on the store's home page, as the following steps highlight:

1. Select the **iTunes Store** source. The iTunes Store will fill the Content pane.
2. If you don't move to the home page, click the **Home** button to move there. The iTunes Store remembers your last location in the store if you haven't quit iTunes since you were last there. If you have, you'll move back to the home page when you select the iTunes Store source.
3. Click the link for the kind of video you want to browse in the iTunes Store section of the home page. The options are **Movies**, **TV Shows**, and **Music Videos**. You'll move to the home page for the kind of video you selected (see Figure 27.6). As you do on the iTunes Store home page, you'll see content organized into various sections, categories, and lists.
4. Use the icons and links to browse the content that is available. As you browse, you'll move down into the content; after a few clicks, you'll move to video content that you can preview and purchase (see Figure 27.7).

FIGURE 27.6

Here I'm browsing the TV Shows home page.

FIGURE 27.7

I've drilled into the TV Show category to see individual episodes of the second season of the series *Battlestar Galactica*.

Searching for Specific Tunes, Video, and Other Content

Browsing is fun, but it can be time-consuming and might not lead you to the specific content in which you are interested. When you want something specific, use the iTunes

Store Search tools to search for it. The two kinds of searches are basic search and power search.

When you do a *basic* search, you search by one search term. Basic searches are fast and easy but can sometimes find a lot of content you aren't interested in. When you perform a *power* search, you can combine several search terms to make searching more precise.

Performing a Basic Search

You have already learned how to search with iTunes, so you also know how to perform a basic search in the iTunes Store. To perform a basic search, follow these steps:

1. Select **iTunes Store** as the source. You will see the iTunes Store home page.
2. In the Search iTunes Store box, type the text or numbers for which you want to search.
3. Press **Return** or **Enter**. The search will be performed, and you will be presented with the Search Results pane. What you see in this pane will depend on the specific search you performed.

   If you search for and find content from a specific artist, you'll see that artist's albums at the top of the Search Results pane. You can click an album to view its details. You can click the artist's link in the Artists section to move to the artist's home page. In the Content pane at the bottom of the iTunes window, you'll see all of the content related to your search.

   If you search using a term than is broader that just a specific artist, or you search for an artist but don't find that artist referred to exactly like your search term, you'll see a slightly different Search Results pane (see Figure 27.8). At the top of the pane, the Search bar will appear; you can use this to refine the results by type of content, such as Music, Movies, TV Shows, and so on. Under the Search bar, you'll see the content that met your search criteria organized into various categories, such as by albums, artists, content type (such as video or podcasts), and so on. At the bottom of the window, the Content pane lists the specific content that meets your search criteria. If your search results include different kinds of content, all those types will be included in the results.

tip

If your search term is narrow, the Search bar might not appear. If it doesn't and the content you wanted to find isn't included in the results, click the **If you were not searching for** link. This will open the Search bar and make your search broader.

FIGURE 27.8
In this search, I found all the content related to "doors down."

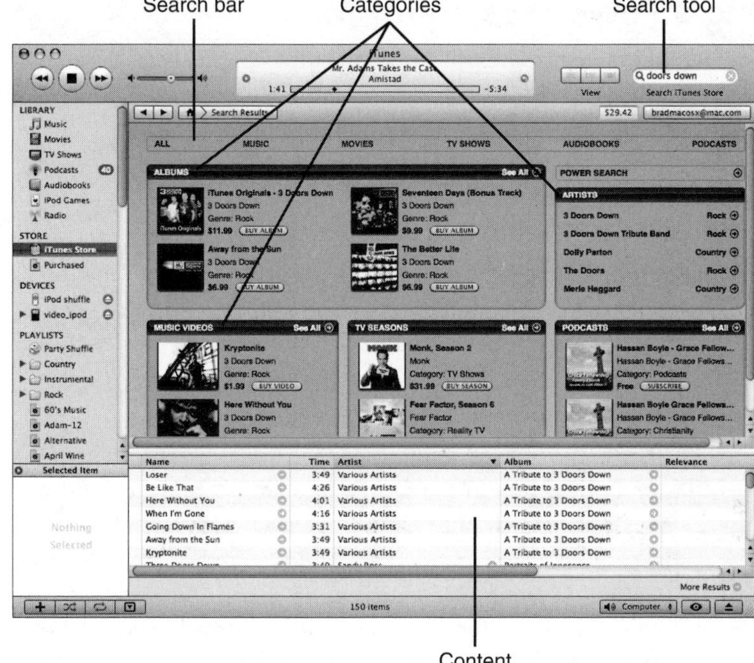

4. Use the **Search bar** to refine the results of your search. For example, if you want to see only music, click the **Music** link. The results will be refreshed so that only music is included. Likewise, you can choose a different tag to limit the results being displayed by clicking its button. For example, if you want to see only podcast content that has your search term associated with it, click **Podcasts**.
5. To drill down into the details of your search results, click an album, artist, or other link.
6. Use the standard controls in the Content pane to change your view of the content being displayed at any time. For example, you can sort the content by any of the column headings by clicking the one by which you want to sort the list. For example, click **Artist** to sort the results by the Artist tag.

After you have performed a search, you can click albums to view their contents, preview songs and video, purchase content, and so on.

To clear a search, click the **X** button in the Search tool. You can leave a term in the Search tool and browse if you'd like.

Performing a Power Search for Music

Sometimes a basic search just doesn't cut it. Fortunately, you can use a power search if you want to find very specific content. With a power search, you can search by more than one attribute at the same time, such as by artist and composer. To search with power, do the following steps:

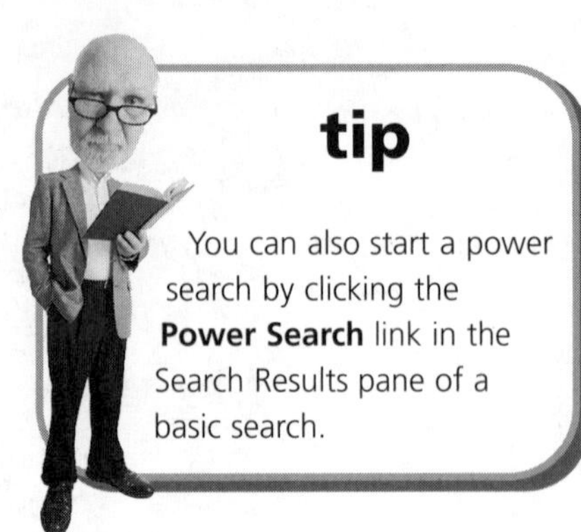

tip

You can also start a power search by clicking the **Power Search** link in the Search Results pane of a basic search.

1. From the iTunes Store home page, click the **Power Search** link located in the Quick Links section. You'll see the Power Search window (see Figure 27.9).
2. Choose the type of content for which you want to search by clicking the appropriate link in the Search bar. For example, to search for music, click **Music**; to search only for movies, click **Movies**. When you limit the search by content, the search boxes change to reflect the kind of content you selected. In Figure 27.9, you see the search boxes presented for a music search. Searches for other types of content will use similar or fewer search attributes.
3. For the first attribute for which you want to search, enter text or numbers in its box. For example, to search by artist, enter the artist's name in the **Artist** box for a music search.

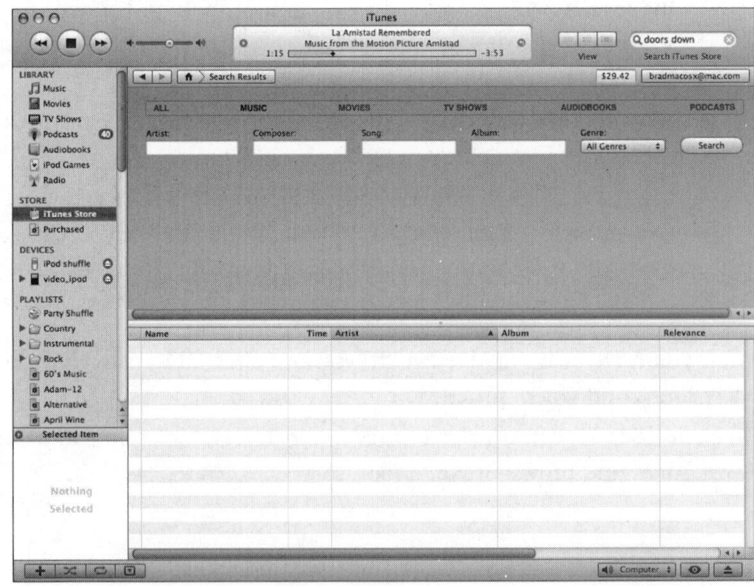

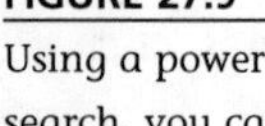

FIGURE 27.9

Using a power search, you can perform searches based on more than one attribute.

4. Repeat step 3 for each attribute for which you want to search. You can search by all of the attributes in the search tool or by only some of them.
5. Choose options presented on menus if they appear for the type of content for which you are searching. For example, if you want to limit a music search to a specific genre, select the genre in which you want to search from the **Genre** menu.
6. When you have configured the search, click **Search**. The window will be refreshed, and you will see the results of your search (see Figure 27.10). The search tools will remain at the top of the pane. Just under the search tools, you will see the categories of content that matched your search. For example, if you search for music, you'll see albums, artists, and music videos related to your search criteria. At the bottom of the window, you will see the content that met your search in the Content pane.

> **tip**
>
> Any of the link buttons (black circles with arrows inside them) are links to other places in the store (refer to Figure 27.10). For example, click the link button next to the artist to move to that artist's home page.

Just as you can with a basic search, after you have performed a power search, you can click the links you see to explore the content you found. For example, in a music search, click the albums to view their contents, preview songs, purchase albums or songs, and so on.

FIGURE 27.10
Here I have searched for the song "Kryptonite" from the group 3 Doors Down.

Previewing Content

One of the great things about the iTunes Store is that you can preview any content before you buy it. These 30-second previews help you be more sure that what you are thinking about buying is really something you want. For example, you can compare alternative versions of the same songs, listen to songs by artists who are new to you, or watch part of a video.

To preview a song, video, podcast, or audiobook, select it in the Content pane of the iTunes Store and click the **Play** button or double-click what you've selected (see Figure 27.11). The preview will begin to play, again just like content in another source, such as a playlist. You can preview as much content as you'd like, and you can preview the same selection as many times as you want. When you are previewing content, the controls work just as they do when you are working with content in your Library. For example, you can preview video in a separate window or in the Video Viewer pane.

FIGURE 27.11
You can preview any content in the iTunes Store, such as video, so you can decide to buy it (or not).

When you have drilled down to an individual content item, such as a music video, you can also click its **Preview** button to preview it.

Buying Tunes, Video, or Audiobooks

After you have found content you want to add to your Library, you can purchase it. How you do this depends on which shopping method you selected: 1-Click Shopping or the Shopping Cart method. (If you don't know what I am talking about, refer to Chapter 26.)

Buying Content with the 1-Click Method

The 1-Click method is aptly and literally named. It really does require only a single click. To purchase an album, you click the **Buy Album** button next to the album you want to purchase. To purchase a song, you click the **Buy Song** button. To purchase an episode of a TV show, you click **Buy Episode**. To purchase an entire season of episodes, you click **Buy Season**. I could go on, but I suspect you get the idea.

In any case, whatever you selected will be immediately purchased and downloaded to your Library. As soon as it starts to download, the Download tool will appear below the Purchased playlist in the Store section. Click this to see the progress of the download (see Figure 27.12). (Because you entered credit card information when you configured your iTunes Store account, you don't need to provide any payment information—after you click the relevant **Buy** button, the store automatically gets the information it needs to complete your purchase.) After the download process is complete, the content you purchased will be in your Library and in the Purchased playlist. From then on, it's yours to listen to, put on a CD, watch, and so on.

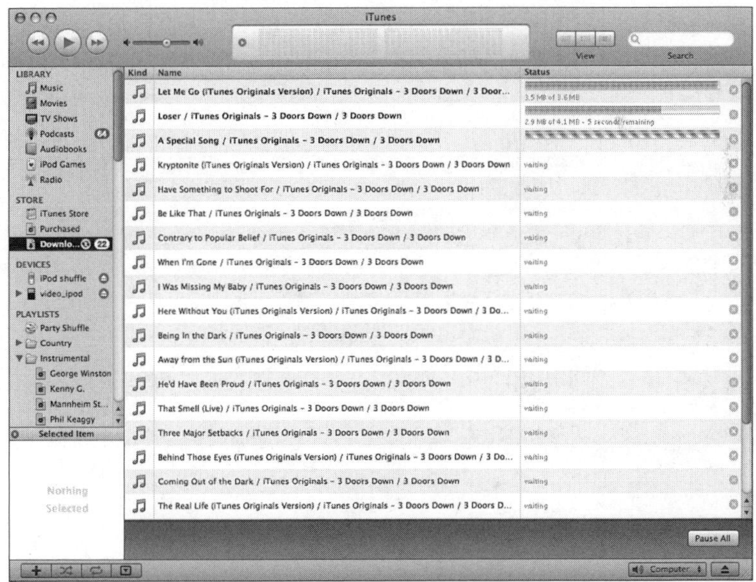

FIGURE 27.12
I've selected the Download source to view the progress of an album I purchased.

If you like the idea of 1-Click shopping but want to be able to gather content in one place so that you can think about it before you purchase it, you can create a "holding" playlist and put content from the store in it. Then you can preview and purchase that music from the playlist on your Source list. To create your own holding area, perform the following steps:

1. Create a playlist and name it anything you'd like.
2. Find content in the store you want to evaluate, and drag it from the store onto the playlist you created.
3. Select your holding playlist to preview its content, and use the **Buy** buttons to purchase anything it contains.

Of course, you can do the same thing with the Shopping Cart method, so if you find yourself doing this often, you might want to use the Shopping Cart instead.

Buying Content with the Shopping Cart Method

Whereas the 1-Click method requires a single click to purchase something, the Shopping Cart method requires all of two or three clicks to accomplish the same result—that being to add new content to your Library.

When you find content in which you are interested, click the relevant **Add** button to add that content to your Shopping Cart. For example, click the **Add Album** button to place an entire album in your cart or the **Add Episode** button to add an episode of a TV series there. When you do so, you will see a message in the Information window telling you that the item you selected has been added to your Shopping Cart (see Figure 27.13). Continue adding content to the Shopping Cart as long as you like.

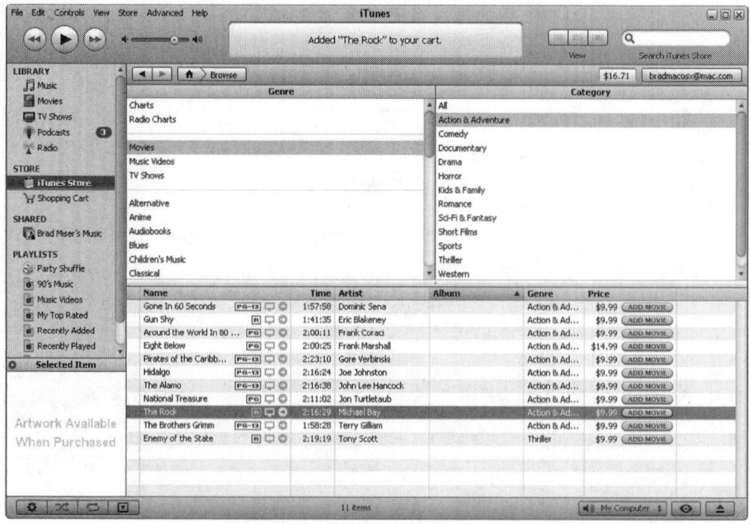

FIGURE 27.13
Here you can see that I added the movie *The Rock* to my Shopping Cart.

When you are ready to buy content you've added to your cart, select the **Shopping Cart** source on the Source List. You will see all the content you have added to the cart but not purchased (see Figure 27.14).

FIGURE 27.14
Here I have added lots of goodies to my Shopping Cart, including songs, albums, TV shows, and movies.

You can preview content in your Shopping Cart just as you can content in the store. Just select an item and click the **Play** button.

You can view individual songs on an album or episodes in a TV series you've added to the cart by clicking that album's or series' expansion triangle. This will expand whatever you clicked to show its contents. However, if you've added a collection of items, such as an entire album, to your cart, you can't purchase individual items, such as songs, it contains, although you can preview them. To purchase an individual item, you'll need to add that item to your cart separately.

You can purchase individual items, such as albums, songs, or seasons, by clicking the item's **Buy** button. The item whose button you clicked will be purchased and downloaded to your Library. (Just like the 1-Click method, you don't need to enter payment information because that is stored as part of your iTunes Store account and is submitted for you automatically.)

tip

To remove an item from the cart, click its **Remove** button (the **x** next to the item's Buy button). The item will be deleted from the cart, and the cart's cost information will be updated.

You can also purchase the entire contents of the cart by clicking the **Buy Now** button located in the bottom-right corner of the Content pane. (The total cost of all the items in your cart is shown just to the left of the Buy Now button.) Everything in the cart will be purchased and downloaded to your Library.

After the download process is complete, the content you bought will be part of your Library so that you can listen to or watch it, add it to playlists, and so on.

Linking Your iTunes Library with the iTunes Store

The contents of your Library can be linked to the iTunes Store. When you select or play an item in your Library, the iTunes Store links will appear for that item. The value of this is that you can click a link to quickly find content in the store that is related to content in your Library (see Figure 27.15). For example, click the **iTunes Store link** for an artist to move to that artist's page in the iTunes Store, which lets you easily get more music from artists whose music you already have. Clicking the link for a song will take you to that song in the store; this can sometimes help you find similar music or to purchase the album from which the song came. Clicking an album's link will take you to that album if it is available in the store or to an album that is similar if the exact one isn't contained in the store. The links for other kinds of content work in a similar way.

By default, the iTunes Store links are enabled. If you don't want these links to appear, you can hide them. To do so, open the **General** pane of the iTunes Preferences dialog box and uncheck the **Show links to the iTunes Store** check box. Click **OK**. The links will no longer appear.

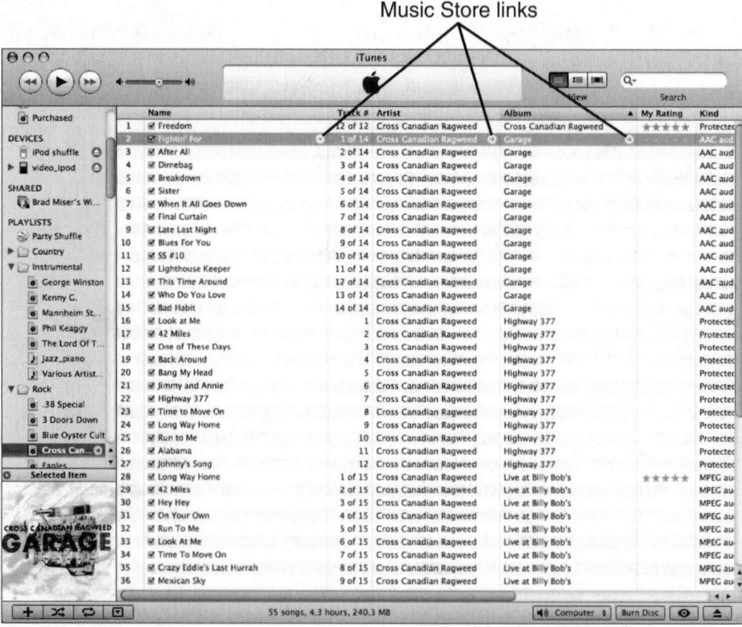

FIGURE 27.15
These links enable you to quickly move to related content in the iTunes Store.

iMixing It Up

iMixes are collections of content (including audio or video content) that are created by iTunes users and published to the iTunes Store. Anyone viewing an iMix can purchase individual items in the iMix or buy all of them at once.

Working with iMixes

There are a couple of ways you can access others' iMixes. One is when someone who knows you sends you a link to it. The other is to browse or search for available iMixes. To work with iMixes, use the following steps as a guide:

1. Move to the **home page** for the kind of content in which you are interested, such as the Music home page for music. (Some types of content allow you to get to iMixes, but some don't.)
2. Click the **iMix** link. (On the Music home page, it is located in the More in Music section.) You'll move to the iMix home page (see Figure 27.16). Existing iMixes are grouped into various categories, including Top Rated, Most Recent, and Featured.
3. To view one of the iMixes shown in the categories on the iMix home page, click its icon. You'll move to iMix's page and can skip to step 7.

FIGURE 27.16
iMixes can be useful when you are looking for new music for your Library.

4. To see all the iMixes in a category, click its **See All** link. You'll move to the home page for the category and can browse all the iMixes it contains. To view an iMix, click its icon. You'll move to the iMix's page and can skip to step 7.

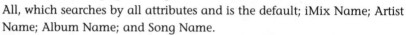

5. To search for content included in iMixes (as an alternative to browsing for it), select the **attribute** for which you want to search on the pop-up menu at the top of the iMix home page. The options are All, which searches by all attributes and is the default; iMix Name; Artist Name; Album Name; and Song Name.

tip

When an iMix page contains more iMixes than can be displayed on a single screen, use the vertical scroll-bar to view all of the iMixes on that page.

6. Enter the text or numbers for which you want to search in the **Search for** box and click the **Search** button, which has the magnifying glass icon. iMixes that contain music that meets your search criterion will appear. Click an iMix's icon to view its contents.

7. When you are viewing an iMix, you can preview the content it contains just as you can other content in the store (see Figure 27.17). At the top of the screen, you'll see the iMix's name, its average rating, and notes for the iMix that its publisher created.

8. Use the **Buy** tools (if you use 1-Click) or **Add** tools (if you use a Shopping Cart) to purchase any content in the iMix. For example, you can purchase individual songs or all the music in the iMix if all the songs it contains are available for individual purchase in the store. If all the content in the iMix is available for purchase individually, the total cost of the iMix is shown at the top of the window next to the Add All Songs or Buy All Songs button. If either of these buttons is not shown, that means at least one track in the iMix can be purchased only when the entire album is purchased; you'll see the View Album button next to such songs instead of the more common Buy or Add button.

9. To see other iMixes created by the same person, click the **See all iMixes by this user** link or click the **iMixes by this user** button in the path area just above the iMix. You'll move to a page showing all iMixes published by the same person.

tip
You can sort music in an iMix just as you can other sources in iTunes.

FIGURE 27.17
This iMix was published by yours truly.

10. To rate an iMix, click the button for the number of stars you want to give to the iMix and then click **Submit**. The rating buttons will disappear, and your rating will be shown. You can rate an iMix only once.
11. To send information about the iMix to other people, click the **Tell a friend** link. You'll see a form on which you enter email addresses (separated by commas), your name, and a message. When you have completed the form, click **Send** to send it. An email containing a link to the iMix will be sent to each recipient. Click **Done** to move back to the iMix.

Publishing Your Own iMixes

You can publish your own iMixes that include content stored in your Library. Then other people can access the iMixes you publish using the steps in the previous section.

When you create an iMix, be aware that only content that is available in the iTunes Store will be included in the iMix; for example, music you import from audio CDs that aren't available in the store will be removed from an iMix when you publish it.

To publish an iMix, perform the following steps:

1. Create a playlist containing the music you want to publish in an iMix. You can create an iMix from both kinds of playlists (standard or smart).
2. Select the **playlist** you created, and click the **iTunes Store** link that appears next to it on the Source list. You'll be prompted whether you want to create an iMix or give the contents of the playlist to someone.

3. Click **Create iMix**. You'll see another prompt explaining what an iMix is; because you are reading this, you already know, so click **Create**. You'll move onto the iTunes Store and will see the Sign in to publish your iMix dialog box.
4. Enter your password and click **Publish**. The iMix will be created, and you'll see an edit screen that enables you to add information to the iMix (see Figure 27.18). The content in the playlist that is available in the iTunes Store will be shown in the Content pane.

FIGURE 27.18

Use this screen to add information to your iMix, including its title and description.

5. Type the name of the iMix in the Title box; by default, this will be the name of your playlist.
6. Enter a description of the iMix in the Description box.
7. To create a standard iMix, leave the **iMix** radio button checked; to create a sport iMix, click **Sport iMix**. (Sport iMixes are collected in a special iMix section but are otherwise the same as regular iMixes.)
8. When you are ready to publish the iMix, click the **Publish** button. (You might have to scroll down in the top pane to see it.) Your iMix will be created, and you'll see a confirmation screen explaining that you'll be notified by email when your iMix is available in the iTunes Store.
9. Click **Done** to close the confirmation screen and return to the iTunes Store.

When your iMix has been published, you'll receive a confirmation email (see Figure 27.19). This email includes a link to the iMix, its name, the notes you entered, and a listing of its contents. You can click the link to visit your iMix, send the email or the link to others to invite them to view it, and so on. You can also invite people to your iMix by clicking its link in the email and then using the Tell a Friend link on the iMix screen.

tip

After you publish a playlist to an iMix, you can click the arrow button that will appear next to that playlist to move to the iMix you created from the playlist.

iMixes remain available for one year after you publish them.

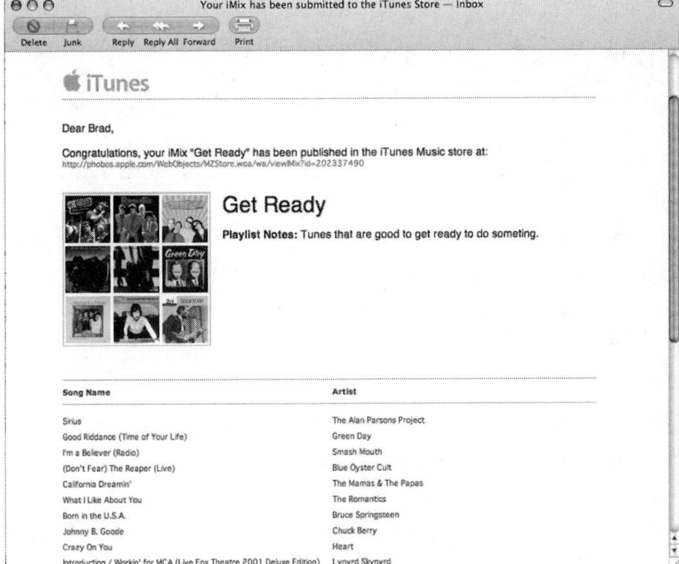

FIGURE 27.19
An email like this means your iMix is ready for visitors.

Using the iTunes MiniStore

The iTunes MiniStore is yet another pane that you can add to the iTunes window. In this pane, you'll get, well, a mini-version of the iTunes Store. The content of this pane will change over time to reflect the context of what you are doing. For example, you'll see music related to music to which you are listening. ("Related" is a relative term. Sometimes the relationship between what you are doing and the contents shown in the MiniStore is tenuous at best.)

You must enable the MiniStore to use it. Choose **View**, **Show MiniStore**. The MiniStore will open; if you've not used it before, click the Turn on MiniStore button. The MiniStore will appear below the Content pane (see Figure 27.20).

FIGURE 27.20
The MiniStore showed music related to the group 3 Doors Down because that was the music I was listening to when I created this figure.

Use the links in the MiniStore to perform various actions related to its contents. For example, click the links in the **More from** section to move to music from the same artist in the iTunes Store. Click a song on the list of songs to move to it on the store. Use the links in the **Listeners Also Bought** section to see music in the store that other people bought who also purchased the music you are working with.

When you are done with the MiniStore, you can hide it again by choosing **View, Hide MiniStore**.

THE ABSOLUTE MINIMUM

You now have all the skills you need to find, preview, and buy content from the iTunes Store. If you are like me, you will be hooked after your first trip. Following are some pointers to help you shop like an iTunes Store master:

- Using the iTunes Store is mostly a matter of clicking around. Start by clicking the iTunes Store source. You can browse for music, video, and other content by clicking what you see.
- You can also search for specific content, using a basic or power search.
- When you search and iTunes can't find any content that matches your search, it will prompt you with its best guess about what you meant to search for. For example, if you search for music from the group Lynyrd Skynyrd and searched for "lynnrd" (who could ever spell that name right, anyway), iTunes

continues

will present a prompt in the search results asking whether you meant to search for "Lynyrd" because it can match that to its database. If you click the search text in the prompt, iTunes will search for that term instead.

- You can preview any content you see in the store. When you do, you'll get to enjoy 30 seconds of that content, whether it's music, an audiobook, video, or a podcast.
- You can shop using the 1-Click or Shopping Cart process.
- No matter which shopping method you use, the price for everything is listed next to the buttons you use to purchase the song or album or to add it to your Shopping Cart. Songs are $.99 each. The cost of albums varies, but in most cases, the price per song works out slightly less when you buy an album than when you buy the same music by the song. Most TV shows are available for $1.99, with the cost per episode being slightly less if you purchase an entire season. Movies currently range in price from $9.99 to $15.99. (There is a fair amount of free content in the store, too. This includes many podcasts, and there are sometimes special promotions for specific artists who provide free songs.)
- Some albums are available only as a partial album; this is indicated by the term "Partial Album" next to the album. This means you can purchase one or more of the songs on the album, but not all the songs on the album or the album itself.
- Some songs are available only as part of an album. This means you can purchase the song only by buying the album of which it is a part. Songs in this category are indicated by the text "Album Only" in the Price column of the Content pane.
- Even if you have a fast connection, you might like the Shopping Cart shopping method because you can use the cart as a holding area for the content you might want to buy. This gives you a chance to think about it before you complete the purchase. Be aware that when you use the 1-Click method, as soon as you click the related **Buy** button, the deal is done.
- Your Library is linked to the iTunes Store by default. These links make it easy to find content in the store that is related to content in your Library.
- You can put your own mark on the iTunes store by publishing an iMix there. You can also use other people's iMixes.
- The MiniStore might help you build your Library by presenting content related to whatever you are doing at any point in time.

IN THIS CHAPTER

- Learn what really happens when you buy from the iTunes Store.
- Know and love the Purchased playlist.
- Understand how to enable a computer to play—or prevent it from playing—purchased content.
- Move purchased content to other computers.
- See all the content you have purchased.
- Back up what you bought.

28

WORKING WITH PURCHASED CONTENT

The title of this chapter is somewhat misleading because it implies there is a lot different about working with content you have purchased from the iTunes Store than with other content in your Library, such as music you've imported from audio CDs. Although there are some unique aspects of audio and video you purchase from the iTunes Store, mostly you can use it in the same way as any other content you have added to your own iTunes Library. But, there are just a few things of which you need to be aware, and that is where this chapter comes in.

Understanding What Happens When You Buy Audio or Video from the iTunes Store

When you download content from the iTunes Store, whether you use 1-Click or the Shopping Cart, that content is added to your Library (see Figure 28.1). From there, you can listen to it, watch it, add it to playlists, burn it to disc, move it to an iPod, share it, and so on. In other words, it becomes mostly like content you have added to your Library from other sources.

The most important difference between content you purchase from the iTunes Store and other items in your Library is that a computer must be authorized to play content from the iTunes Store. You'll learn about this concept later in this chapter.

FIGURE 28.1
This music came from the iTunes Store; it doesn't look any different from other music in the Library and acts only a bit differently.

Using the Purchased Playlist

Immediately after your first purchase from the iTunes Store, the Purchased source will become available in the Store section on your Source List (see Figure 28.2). This source is actually a special smart playlist that captures all the audio and video you purchase from the iTunes Store. You can always return to your purchased content by using the Purchased source.

One thing you can't do with the Purchased smart playlist that you can do with others is to edit its criteria. The Purchased playlist is what it is; you can't change it (not that you'd ever want to anyway).

You can use the Purchased playlist like other playlists. To see its contents, select **Purchased** on the Source List. The first time you select it, you will see a dialog box explaining the function of the playlist. Read the information and click **OK** to move to the Purchased playlist.

You can then browse the Purchased playlist, search in it, play it, and so on. Of course, you can also configure view options for it, sort it, and do the other playlist tasks with which you should be familiar by now.

FIGURE 28.2
The Purchased source is actually a special playlist that always contains all the music, audiobooks, and video that you have purchased from the iTunes Store.

Understanding Authorization

The content you purchase from the iTunes Store is protected in the sense that it has certain limitations on what you can do with it. Fortunately, these limitations are not very limiting!

One of these limits is that you can play iTunes Store content (audio or video) on only up to five computers at the same time. To implement this limit, the computer on which you play purchased iTunes Store content must be *authorized*. When you authorize a computer, iTunes will connect to the Internet and register that computer with the iTunes Store so that you can use it to play the content purchased under the user account you used to buy it.

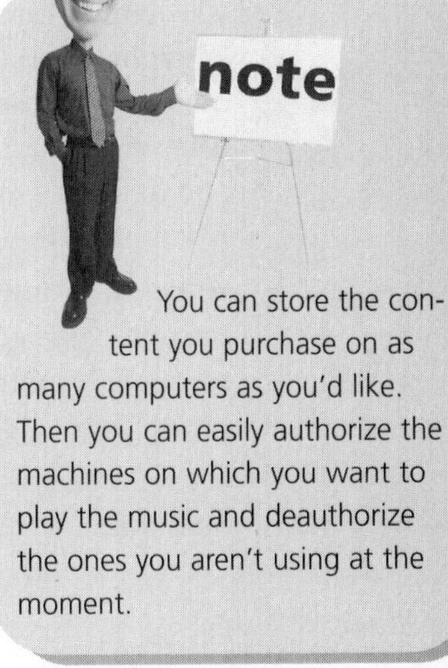

You can store the content you purchase on as many computers as you'd like. Then you can easily authorize the machines on which you want to play the music and deauthorize the ones you aren't using at the moment.

You can use iTunes Store content from the same iTunes Store account on as many iPods as you'd like, and you can include content from up to five different iTunes Store on one iPod.

To state this another way, you actually authorize the content for a specific iTunes user account on up to five computers at a time. When you authorize a computer, you authorize all the songs you have purchased under an iTunes Store account; you can't authorize some of the songs you buy under one account on one machine and a different set under that same account on another computer. When a computer is authorized, it can play all the music that has been purchased under an iTunes Store account. If it isn't authorized, you won't be able to play any of the music you purchased.

Fortunately, it is easy to authorize or deauthorize a computer, as you will see in the next sections.

Authorizing a Computer

The first time you purchase content on a computer, you must authorize that computer before you can play the music you purchase. Fortunately, when you purchase content under an account, the machine on which you purchase it is authorized to play it automatically. The first time you try to play the content on a different computer, you'll need to authorize it. After that, the computer remains authorized until you deauthorize it.

To authorize a computer to play purchased music, try to play the content you have purchased from the iTunes Store. If the current computer has been authorized, the content will begin to play. If it hasn't been authorized, you will see the Authorize Computer dialog box. Enter the username and password that were used to purchase the content and click **Authorize**. iTunes will connect to the Internet and authorize the computer. When that process is complete, the content will play.

> **tip**
>
> You can also authorize a computer by choosing **Store**, **Authorize Computer** and then entering the account information for which you want to authorize it.

You need to authorize a computer to play all the purchased content for a specific iTunes user account only one time. After you do so, you'll be able to play any content purchased under that account.

If you attempt to authorize more than five computers under the same user account, you will see a warning prompt explaining that you can have only five computers authorized at the same time. You must deauthorize one of the computers to be able to authorize the current one.

Deauthorizing a Computer

To deauthorize a computer, select **Store**, **Deauthorize Computer**. You will see the Deauthorize Computer dialog box (see Figure 28.3). Enter the username (Apple ID or AOL screen name) and password for the account you want to deauthorize on the machine and click **OK**. iTunes will connect to the Internet and deauthorize the computer. When the process is complete, you will see a dialog box telling you so. Click **OK**. The computer will no longer count against the five-computer limit for the user account. (You won't be able to play content purchased under that iTunes Store account on that computer, either.)

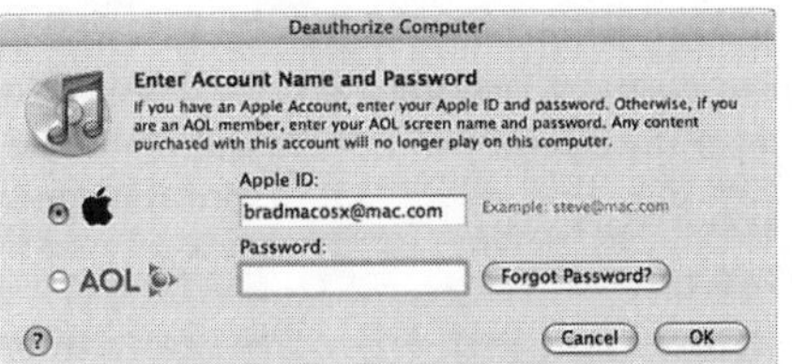

FIGURE 28.3
You use this dialog box to deauthorize a computer.

You can authorize a computer again by attempting to play purchased content and providing the user account and password for which you want to authorize the machine. As you can see, authorizing and deauthorizing computers is simple.

> **tip**
>
> You can share content you have purchased with other computers on your network. Just as with purchased content you play on your computer, for other machines to be able to play your purchased content, they must be authorized to do so and therefore count against the five-computer limit. Fortunately, as you have seen, it is simple to authorize and deauthorize computers, so you can keep up to five authorized quite easily.

Moving Purchased Content to Other Computers

You can move any iTunes content between computers, but often it is just as easy to import music from audio CDs to each computer on which you want to create a Library. However, if you have more than one computer, you might want to move content you've purchased from the iTunes Store to the other computers so you can play it from there.

Understanding the Ways You Can Move Your Content

First, you need to move the content files from the computer on which they are stored (for example, the machine from which you purchased the content) onto the machine on which you want to be able to play that content.

To move files to another computer, you need to know where those files are located. From Part II, "iTunes," you know that iTunes keeps all the files in the Library organized in the iTunes Music folder (assuming you followed my recommendations and set the preferences to allow this). You can move to this folder to find the files you want to move.

> **tip**
>
> If the computers can communicate with each other over a local network, there's less reason to store content on each computer. If you only want to play the content, it's much easier to use iTunes sharing. If you want to be able to create playlists and such on each computer, you'll need to place the content on each machine.

You can also find the location of content files by selecting a song, video, or other item in the Content pane and selecting **File, Show in Windows Explorer** or pressing **Ctrl+R** on a Windows computer, and **File, Show in Finder** or pressing **⌘+R** (Mac). iTunes will open a desktop folder window showing the location of the file for the item you have selected (see Figure 28.4).

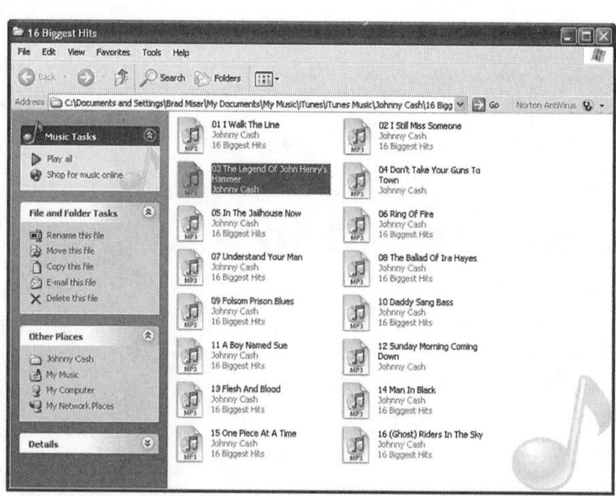

FIGURE 28.4
When you use the Show command, iTunes opens a window to show you where the content's file is located on your computer.

After you have located the files you want to move to another computer, you can move them in many ways, including the following:

- **Create a data CD or DVD containing the content you want to move**—You can do this from within iTunes by changing the Burning preferences to use the Data CD or Data DVD format and then burning a disc. This process is easy to do and works regardless of there being a network connection between the computers. The primary limitations are the size of the discs you use and the time it takes to burn the discs.

- **Back up your iTunes Library and restore it on a different computer**—As you learned in Chapter 24, "Maintaining iTunes and Solving Problems," you can use iTunes to create a backup of all your content. You can then use the backup discs you create to restore the content on a computer that is different from the one on which the backup was originally made.
- **Use a network to share files with the computer to which you want to move those files**—This method is simple and doesn't place a limit on the sizes of the files you move. You also don't need to spend time or money to burn discs. The downside is that you have to have the computers connected via a network and understand how to configure sharing appropriately.
- **Create an audio CD of music and import that into the other computer's iTunes Library**—This is also an easy process, but you are limited to the amount of music that can fit onto an audio CD.
- **Move the song files onto a networked drive, such as a server**—For example, if you use a hard drive that is accessible over a network, you can move the files onto that drive and then use the second computer to copy them from the network drive onto the computer's drive. This has the same pros and cons as moving files directly across a network.

tip

In Part I, "The iPod," you learned how to use an iPod as a portable drive. So, you can use an iPod to move content files among computers.

If you placed the files on a disc, you can import those files into the Library just like content on other discs, such as an audio CD. You insert the disc into the computer, select it on the Source list, and use the Import command to add its contents to the iTunes Library.

On Windows PCs, you can select the **Add to Folder** command, which enables you to select a folder to add. This works in the same way as adding files.

- **Copy the files onto a portable hard drive, such as a FireWire or USB drive**—This is faster than and doesn't have the same space limitations as using a CD or DVD. It's also easier than using a network because you don't have to configure the network or file sharing. Of course, the disadvantage is that you have to have such a drive available.

After you have copied content files from one computer to another, you need to import those files into the iTunes Library. On a Windows computer, choose **File**, **Add File to Library** or **File**, **Add Folder to Library**. On a Macintosh, choose **File**, **Add to Library**. Use the resulting dialog box to move to and select the content you want to add. After that process is complete, the content will be available in that computer's iTunes Library.

Moving Purchased Files over a Network

The following steps provide an example of how to move files that are shared over a network and add them to the iTunes Library:

tip

The keyboard shortcut for the Add to Library command is Ctrl+O (Windows) or ⌘+O (Mac).

1. Share the files on the original machine with the network.
2. From within iTunes on the computer to which you want to move the songs, select **File**, **Add to Library**. You will see the Add To Library dialog box.
3. Move to and select the files or the folder containing the files you want to add to the Library (see Figure 28.5).

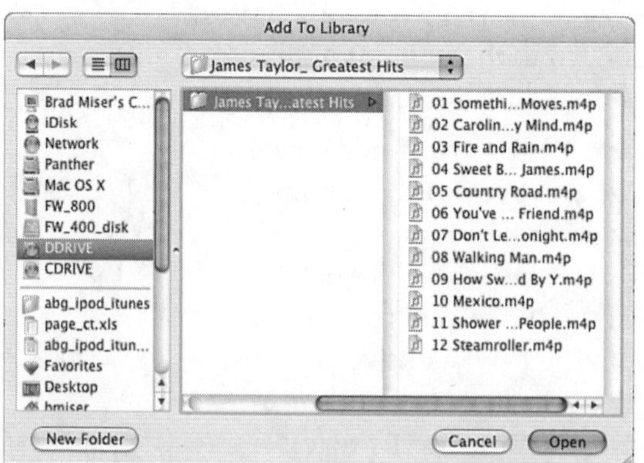

FIGURE 28.5
Here, I am accessing song files that are stored on a computer on the network. (In this case, the files are stored on a Windows computer, and I'm adding them to iTunes on a Mac.)

4. Click **Open** (Windows) or **Choose** (Mac). The songs you selected will be copied into your Library (see Figure 28.6). If the music you moved into the Library was purchased on a different computer, you need to authorize the current computer to play that music. (Try to play the songs and enter the iTunes Store account information under which they were purchased.)

tip

Purchased content that you move to a different computer won't be added to the Purchased playlist automatically. You can drag that content onto that playlist from the Library if you want to put it there.

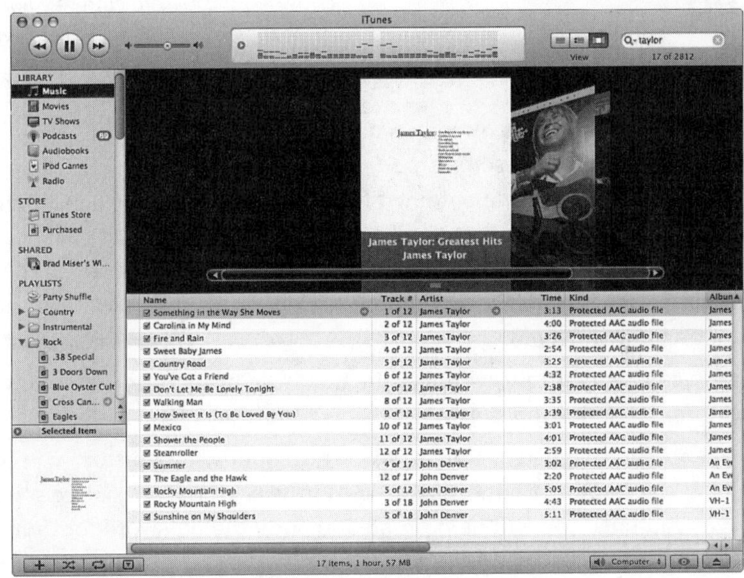

FIGURE 28.6
You can see that the files I selected in the previous figure are now in the Library.

You can create an audio CD from music you purchase from the iTunes Store and then import that music into a Library on another computer. Because the music is converted into the Audio CD format when you do this, it doesn't count against the five-computer limit for music you purchase from the iTunes Store. However, if you use this technique to play music you have purchased on more than five computers at the same time, you will violate the spirit and letter of the license agreement you accept when you purchase music from the store. I recommend that you use this method only if this won't result in more than five computers playing this music at the same time. This can be particularly useful if one of the machines on which you will be playing music can't connect to the Internet, which is required for authorization to take place.

tip

On the Apple Account Information screen, you will see the Computer Authorizations section that shows how many computers are currently authorized to play music from the account under which you are logged in. Unfortunately, this doesn't identify which computers are currently authorized. However, you can deauthorize all computers for this account, which you might need to do if you lose control over a computer that was previously authorized or if you have other authorization problems. (You'll learn how this works in Chapter 29, "Solving iTunes Store Problems.")

Viewing the Content You Have Purchased

You have a couple ways to see the content you have purchased.

The first way you have already read about. Select the **Purchased** source, and you will see all the content you have obtained from the iTunes Store. (This assumes you haven't removed any content from this playlist, of course; and because there isn't really any reason to do this, you probably haven't.)

The second way is to view the entire purchase history for a user account. To do so, perform the following steps:

1. 7While signed in under the user account whose history you want to see, click the **Account** button. (You need to select the iTunes Store source to see this button.) You will be prompted to enter the password for that account.
2. Enter the account's password and click **View Account**. The Content pane will be filled with the Apple Account Information window, which provides, amazingly enough, information about the user account.
3. Click the **Purchase History** button. The data will be retrieved, and the Content pane will show the content purchased during each shopping session (see Figure 27.7). At the top will be details for the most recent session. In the Previous Purchases section, you'll see a list of each purchase group.
4. To view the detail for a shopping batch, click its **Detail** button. The screen will be refreshed, and you will see a detailed list of all the content purchased during that session (see Figure 28.8).

FIGURE 28.7
Your purchase history will be organized by shopping sessions.

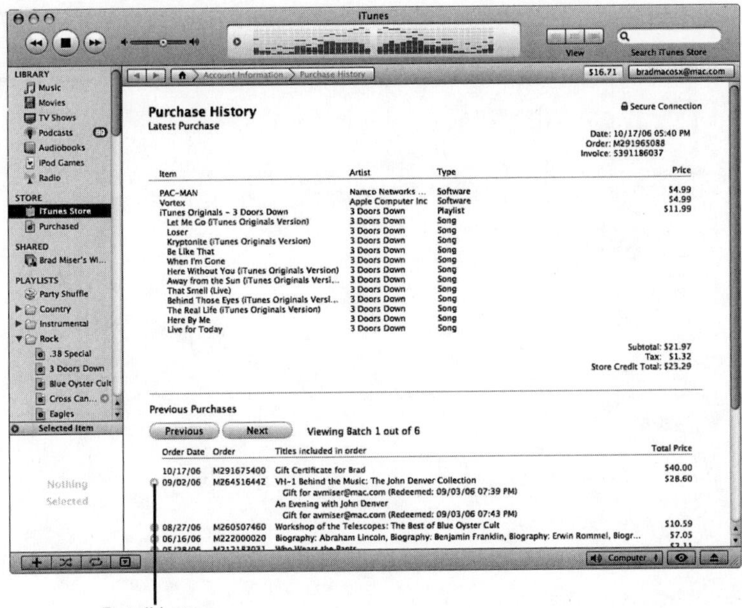

5. When you are finished viewing the details for the selected batch, click the **Done** button.
6. To see another batch of shopping sessions, click the **Next** button, or to move back to a previous batch of sessions, click **Previous**.
7. When you're finished viewing your purchase history, click **Done**. You'll move back to the Apple Account Information screen.
8. Click **Done** on the Apple Account Information screen. You'll move back to the iTunes Store.

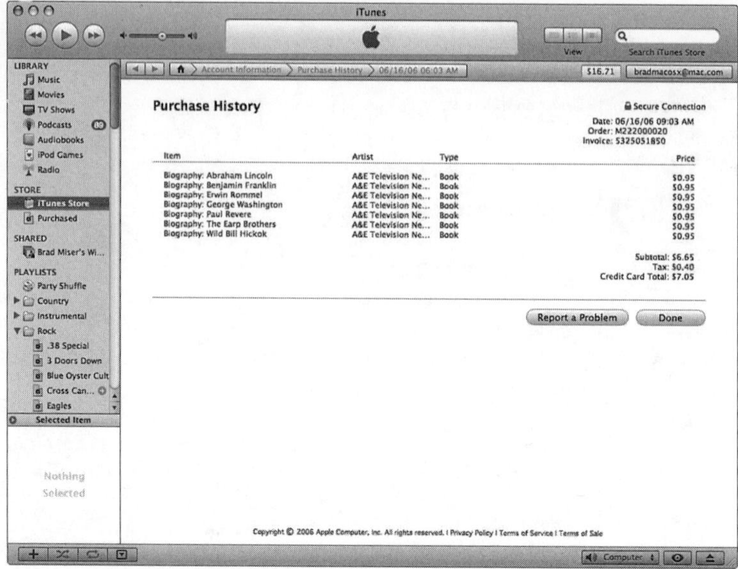

FIGURE 28.8
You can also view the detail for any shopping session.

Backing Up Purchased Content

Because you don't have content that you purchase from the iTunes Store backed up on a disc (as you do for the music you have on audio CD or video you've purchased on a DVD), you should make sure you back up the content you buy. The easiest way to do this is to use iTunes Back Up feature, which is described in detail in Chapter 24. When you create an iTunes backup, you can choose to back up only purchased content or to back up your entire Library. Of course, if you have purchased more than can fit on a single CD or DVD, you will need to use multiple discs to back up the entire collection.

The Absolute Minimum

The iTunes Store is well designed and makes finding and buying content—from individual songs from your favorite one-hit wonder to complete collections of classic artists or TV series to movies—easy. As you work with the goodies you buy, remember the following gems of wisdom:

- When you purchase content from the iTunes Store, it is downloaded into your Library.
- By default, all the content you purchase from the iTunes Store is stored in the Purchased playlist.
- To play purchased content on a computer, that computer must be authorized. You can have up to five computers authorized at the same time. You can deauthorize a computer by using the Deauthorize Computer command, located on the Store menu.
- To play purchased content on a computer that is different from the one on which you purchased it, you can share the content over a network or move the purchased content to another computer. There are several ways to do this.
- There are a couple of ways to see the content you have purchased. One is to use the Purchased playlist. You can also use the Purchase History information for your iTunes account to see a list of all the content you have purchased from the iTunes Store.
- You should back up the content you purchase from the iTunes Store. The easiest way to do this is using the iTunes Back Up feature.

In This Chapter

- Recover purchased content that wasn't successfully downloaded.
- Solve the dreaded (not really) "Not Authorized to Play" problem.
- Fix problems with your iTunes Store account.
- Get help with the store.
- Ask for more.

29

Solving iTunes Store Problems

You will see that this is a short chapter. The reason is simple: You just aren't likely to encounter that many problems when working with the iTunes Store. The store, like iTunes and the iPod, is well designed and works flawlessly most of the time. If you do encounter a problem, this chapter will help you find the solution.

Recovering Purchased Content That Wasn't Downloaded Successfully

If the download process for content you purchased wasn't completed for some reason (for example, you lost your Internet connection in the middle of the process), you can restart the download process to recover content you bought but weren't able to download successfully.

To do this, select **Store**, **Check for Purchases** (see Figure 29.1). You will be prompted to enter the user account and password for the account under which the content was purchased. Do so and then click **Check**.

The content you have purchased will be checked against the content that has been successfully downloaded. If content is found that hasn't been downloaded successfully, you will be able to download it again. If you have successfully downloaded all the content you have purchased, you will see a message stating so (see Figure 29.2).

FIGURE 29.1 Use the Check for Purchases command to recover audio or video you've purchased but weren't able to download for some reason.

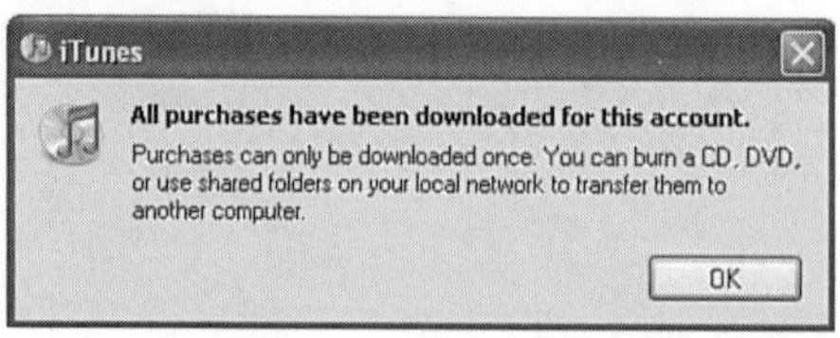

FIGURE 29.2 When you see this message, you have successfully downloaded all the audio and video you have purchased.

Solving the "Not Authorized to Play" Problem

As you learned in the previous chapter, you can play content you have purchased on up to five computers at the same time. If you try to play purchased audio or video and see the `This Computer Is Not Authorized to Play This Music` message, you need to authorize the computer before you can play the purchased content. If you have four or fewer computers authorized, this isn't a problem, and you can quickly authorize the current computer by entering the user account and password under which the content was purchased. If you already have five computers authorized, you need to deauthorize at least one before you can authorize another. (If you need help doing these tasks, refer to Chapter 28, "Working with Purchased Content.")

Also remember that computers with which you are sharing music also count against the five-computer limit. If you are unable to play music because of authorization, make sure computers on the network aren't the cause of your being over your authorization limit.

The challenge can sometimes be remembering how many and which computers you have authorized. The "how many" part is easy. Just access the Apple Account Information screen for your account. The Computer Authorizations section will display the number of computers currently authorized to play content for the account. (To learn how to access this screen, refer to "Viewing the Content You Have Purchased" on page **468**).

The "which ones" part is a bit more difficult. The easiest way to tell is to try playing purchased music from each computer you might have authorized. If it plays, the computer is authorized. If you are prompted to authorize the computer, you will know that it isn't currently authorized.

You need to be able to use a computer to be able to authorize it. That might seem obvious, but it can present a minor dilemma. Suppose a computer that is authorized to play your purchased content crashes hard and no longer works at all. You won't be able to use it to deauthorize it because it doesn't

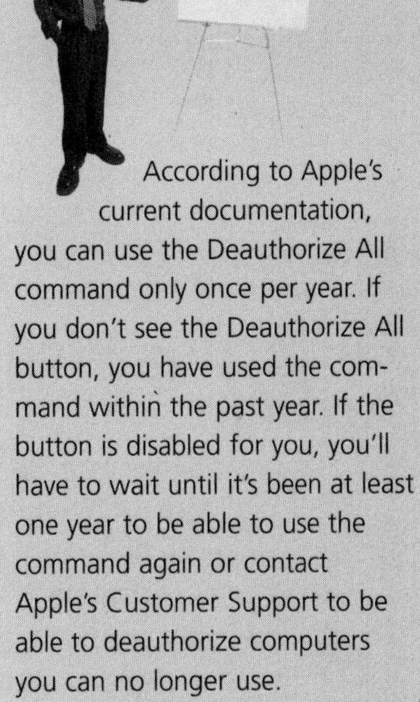

According to Apple's current documentation, you can use the Deauthorize All command only once per year. If you don't see the Deauthorize All button, you have used the command within the past year. If the button is disabled for you, you'll have to wait until it's been at least one year to be able to use the command again or contact Apple's Customer Support to be able to deauthorize computers you can no longer use.

work. So, it will continue to count against the five-computer limit even though it can't play the content anymore. (This becomes a major problem if the content is stored on only that computer and you haven't backed it up. In that case, you can kiss the money you spent to buy the content goodbye.)

Another problem might be that you simply can't figure out which computers make up the five you currently have authorized.

The solution to both of these issues is pretty simple, actually.

View the Apple Account Information screen for the account under which you have purchased content; you can do this from any computer that has iTunes installed on it as long as it also has Internet access. In the Computer Authorizations section, click **Deauthorize All**. You'll see the Deauthorize computers prompt. Click **Deauthorize all computers**. All the computers associated with the user account will be deauthorized and will no longer be able to play purchased content. You'll see the complete message when the deed is done (see Figure 29.3). Click **OK** to close the message.

The next time you try to play purchased content, you'll need to authorize each computer you use to play it. As you recall, this isn't hard. Just enter the account name and password when prompted to do so.

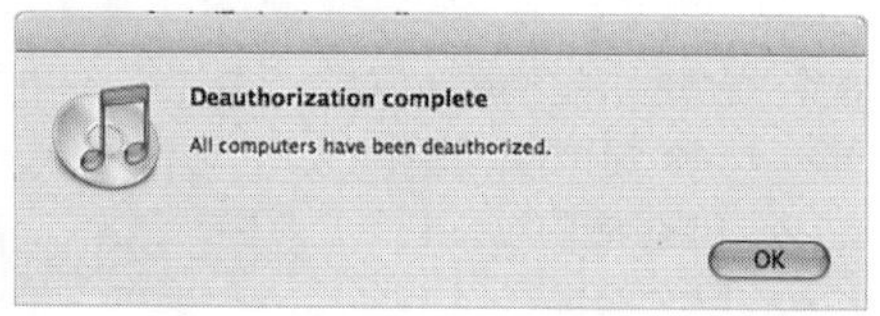
Deauthorization complete
All computers have been deauthorized.
OK

FIGURE 29.3
When you deauthorize all the computers for an iTunes Store account, you won't be able to play purchased content until you reauthorize each computer to play that content.

Correcting Problems with Your iTunes Store Account

You can change information for your iTunes Store account by accessing the Apple Account Information page and using its tools to make changes to your account, such as changing the credit card you use to purchase music. (For help using this page, refer to "Changing and Viewing Your iTunes Store Account" on page **425**).

If something has changed from the iTunes Store's side of the equation, you will be prompted to change your account information. The dialog box that appears will also enable you to access your Account Information page to make the required changes.

Getting Help with iTunes Store Problems

You probably will never have problems with the iTunes Store, but if you do, the information in this chapter should help you solve them. If not, don't despair, because help is just a few clicks away.

To access the iTunes Customer Service page, select **Help**, **iTunes and Music Store Service and Support**. Your default web browser will open, and you will move to the iTunes Support page (see Figure 29.4). Use the links and information on this page to get help.

FIGURE 29.4 The iTunes Service and Support page enables you to get help with any store issues you can't solve on your own.

Reporting Content You Can't Find in the Store

Although the iTunes Store is great, it isn't perfect. Its major flaw, which is a perfectly understandable one, is that it doesn't contain every song, audiobook, TV show, or movie ever produced (as if that were even possible). The good news is that Apple is continually adding content to the store, especially as producers companies see what a great way it is for them to distribute their products.

If you can't find the content you want to buy in the store, you can let Apple know about it. (Who knows—your contact might be the one that causes some specific music or audio to be added to the store!)

To request content, perform the following steps:

1. Use a web browser to move to www.apple.com/feedback/itunes.html. You'll see the Request Music form (which is somewhat misnamed because you use the form to request all kinds of content).
2. Complete the onscreen form by entering your name, email address, operating system, age, version of iTunes, type of request (such as a song or a TV show), and the specific request you are making in the **Comments** box.
3. Use the drop-down lists and check boxes to supply the additional information that is requested.
4. Click **Send Feedback**. Your request will be submitted, and you will see a confirmation screen that explains that you won't get a personal response to your request. At some point, with a little luck and some effort by Apple, the content you requested will be added to the store.

The Absolute Minimum

The iTunes Store is a great tool to search for and add content to your iTunes Library. In fact, you might never purchase a CD or DVD again. (Okay, that's a bit dramatic, but you get the idea.) Fortunately, the iTunes Store works very well, and you aren't likely to have problems using it, which is a good thing.

Just in case, in this chapter, you learned how to do the following tasks:

- Recover purchased content that didn't download successfully.
- Solve the "Not Authorized to Play" issue.
- Fix problems with your iTunes Store account.
- Get help from Apple.
- Request content you can't find in the store.

If you have problems that you can't solve with the information in this chapter, visit my website at web.mac.com/bradmacosx/. Click the **Books I've Written** button, and then click the image of the cover of this book. From the resulting webpage, you can move to a list of common iTunes questions and answers, including those about the Music Store. You can also ask me questions via email by clicking the **Email me** button.

Index

Symbols

A

C

D

How can we make this index more useful? Email us at indexes@quepublishing.com

E

F

How can we make this index more useful? Email us at indexes@quepublishing.com

K–L

M

N

Q–R

S

T

U

V

W–Z

How can we make this index more useful? Email us at indexes@quepublishing.com

Safari
BOOKS ONLINE
ENABLED